Arnulfo L. Oliveira Memorial Library

FRONTIERSMAN

SOUTHERN BIOGRAPHY SERIES

Bertram Wyatt-Brown, Series Editor

FRONTIERSMAN

★ DANIEL BOONE AND THE MAKING OF AMERICA ★

MEREDITH MASON BROWN

LOUISIANA STATE UNIVERSITY PRESS

BATON ROUGE

PUBLISHED BY LOUISIANA STATE UNIVERSITY PRESS
Copyright © 2008 by Louisiana State University Press
All rights reserved
Manufactured in the United States of America
First printing

Designer: Michelle A. Neustrom
Typefaces: Minion Pro, Egyptienne D
Printer and binder: Thomson-Shore, Inc.

Frontispiece: Chester Harding, *Daniel Boone,* oil sketch portrait, 1820. Painted a few months before Boone's death. The only known painting of Boone done from life. Courtesy of Massachusetts Historical Society. Gift of George T. Bigelow.

LIBRARY OF CONGRESS CATALOGING-IN-PUBLICATION DATA

Brown, Meredith Mason, 1940–
    Frontiersman : Daniel Boone and the making of America / Meredith Mason Brown.
        p. cm. — (Southern biography series)
    Includes bibliographical references and index.
    ISBN 978-0-8071-3356-9 (cloth : alk. paper) 1. Boone, Daniel, 1734–1820. 2. Boone, Daniel, 1734–1820—Influence. 3. Boone, Daniel, 1734–1820—Relations with Indians. 4. Pioneers—Kentucky—Biography. 5. Explorers—Kentucky—Biography. 6. Frontier and pioneer life—Kentucky. 7. Kentucky—Discovery and exploration. 8. Missouri—Discovery and exploration. 9. Frontier and pioneer life—United States. 10. United States—Territorial expansion. I. Title.
    F454.B66B77 2009
    976.9'02092—dc22
    [B]
                                                                              2008018153

The paper in this book meets the guidelines for permanence and durability of the Committee on Production Guidelines for Book Longevity of the Council on Library Resources. ♾

To Sylvia, Mason, Karen, Alison, and all the John Mason Browns

Contents

PREFACE   xiii

CHRONOLOGY   xvii

1   Old Boone   1

2   Quakers in Pennsylvania, Settlers in Backcountry North
     Carolina   3

3   Braddock's Defeat: How Not to Fight Indians   12

4   A Good Wife   21

5   Long Hunts   28

6   Boone's First Hunts in Kentucky   39

7   Boone Begins to Open the Wilderness: The First
     Attempt to Settle Kentucky   54

8   Transylvania, the Wilderness Road, and the Building of
     Boonesborough   68

9   Dark and Bloody Ground: An Introduction to Kentucky
     during the Revolutionary War   91

10   The Capture and Rescue of the Girls   104

11   The Shawnees Capture Boone   115

12   Boone among the Shawnees   130

13   The Siege of Boonesborough   145

14   Indian Raids and the Battle of the Blue Licks   170

15   Whites and Indians   185

16   Trading and Land Speculation: Master of All He
        Surveyed?   200

17   Living Legend, Shrinking Fortune   216

18   Out to Missouri   226

19   Boone in Missouri   238

20   Last Days   252

21   Life after Death   260

22   Coda   274

ACKNOWLEDGMENTS   285

NOTES   287

BIBLIOGRAPHICAL NOTE   343

INDEX   357

Illustrations

frontispiece: Chester Harding, *Daniel Boone,* oil sketch
portrait, 1820

PHOTOGRAPHS

following page 90

Birthplace of Daniel Boone, photograph c. 1860
Engraving of the Cumberland Gap by H. Fenn
Sketch purporting to be of John Floyd
Earliest known document written and signed by Boone
Sketch of Boonesborough
Portrait of Lt. Gov. Henry Hamilton
Henry Hamilton's line drawing of Pacanné, a Miami chief
Karl Bodmer, *Capture of the Daughters of D. Boone and
Callaway by the Indians,* 1852
James B. Longacre, line-and-stipple engraving of Simon
Kenton
Charles Bird King, *Payta-kootha, a Shawanoe Warrior*
Charles Bird King, *Kish-Kal-Wa, a Shawanoe Chief*

following page 184

Matthew Harris Jouett, *George Rogers Clark*
Eighteenth-century surveying instruments

John Filson's purported self-portrait

Title page of John Filson's *The Discovery, Settlement and Present State of Kentucke* (1784)

Saint-Mémin, *Le Soldat du Chêne, an Osage Chief*

"Col. Daniel Boon," stipple engraving by J. O. Lewis

Home of Nathan Boone in St. Charles County, Mo., in which Boone died in 1820

Thomas Cole, *Daniel Boone at His Cabin at Great Osage Lake*, c. 1826

George Caleb Bingham, *Daniel Boone Escorting Settlers through the Cumberland Gap*, 1851–52

Daniel Boone Protects His Family, color lithograph by H. Schile, 1874

Daguerreotype of Lyman C. Draper, c. 1858

Monument at Boone's tomb in Frankfort

MAPS

Boone's America and Its Transformation, 1740–1820   *xxiv*

The Backcountry: Northwestern North Carolina and the Cumberland Gap   9

Boone's Kentucky and Its Neighbors   45

Transylvania Purchase, 1775; Fincastle County Surveys, 1774   72

Boonesborough at the Time of the Siege in 1778   154

The Battle of the Blue Licks   180

Shingled Land Claims in Madison County, Ky.   207

Boone Country in Missouri   241

Preface

MANY OF US THINK WE KNOW SOMETHING ABOUT DANIEL BOONE. We grew up hearing about him or seeing someone in a movie or on TV acting the part of Boone—a cheerful, illiterate American patriot wearing a coonskin cap, who discovered Kentucky, built the first settlement there, and killed innumerable Indians. But little of what we think we know about Boone is true. Boone despised coonskin caps and did not wear them. He did not kill many Indians. He killed a few, but only when he had to. He was an adopted son of a Shawnee chief and had many friends among the Shawnees—even though Indians killed Boone's brother and two of Boone's sons. Boone was not illiterate; indeed, he wrote better than most on the frontier. His spelling was often phonetic and idiosyncratic, but so was that of Lewis and Clark and many of Boone's contemporaries. Boone was neither the first white to cross the Cumberland Gap into Kentucky nor the builder of the first settlement in Kentucky. While often thought of as an American patriot, during and after the Revolution Boone was not uniquely American in his ties: his first commission as a militia officer was signed by Virginia's last British colonial governor; he was Shawnee by adoption; and he became a civil servant in Spain's administration in Missouri, before the Louisiana Territory was acquired by the United States.

If the untruths about Boone are remarkable, the truths about Boone's life and achievements are much more so. During Boone's long lifetime—he lived from 1734 to 1820—America was born as a country and completely transformed. What had been disparate settlements of fewer than a million British colonists huddled near the Atlantic Coast became an independent nation reaching well beyond the Mississippi and numbering close to ten million.[1] Daniel Boone helped to bring about the making and transformation of America.

xiii

Boone was unexcelled as a woodsman and explorer of the American frontier. Born in Pennsylvania, he traveled through Virginia, Maryland, North Carolina, South Carolina, Georgia, Florida, Tennessee, Kentucky, Ohio, and Michigan, out to Missouri, and at least as far west as Kansas. This was at a time when one traveled by foot, on horseback, or by boat. Although he was not the first white to cross the Cumberland Gap, Boone and a party of axemen under him blazed what became the Wilderness Road from the Cumberland Gap to the Kentucky River. Hundreds of thousands of settlers entered Kentucky on that road. Boone was a founder of Boonesborough, led many immigrants into Kentucky, and by his example induced many others to follow. Between 1775 and 1800 the number of settlers in Kentucky grew from fewer than 200 to 221,000, and in 1792 Kentucky became a state. By 1820, when Boone died, Kentucky's population had reached 564,000.[2] Boone's leadership of the successful 1778 defense of Boonesborough against a sustained Indian attack was instrumental in keeping white settlers in Kentucky during the bloody years of the Revolution.

In 1799 Boone and his family moved to Missouri, then a Spanish territory with a non-Indian population of perhaps four thousand. Boone explored and hunted up the Missouri River at least as far as Kansas. His example helped to encourage an influx of settlers into Missouri. By 1820, when Boone died, sixty-seven thousand people lived in Missouri, which was then on the verge of statehood.[3]

Boone's achievements made it harder for him to do what he most loved to do. Boone excelled in hunting, opening up the wilderness, and guiding settlers into frontier territory. But by doing these things, Boone and other frontiersmen changed the land forever, so that he could not stay where he was and keep on hunting, trapping, and scouting. He was forced to move, with the advancing frontier, farther and farther west. That process of change and movement was key to the transformations in America in Boone's lifetime.

I have sought to give a full picture of Boone, stripping away the layers of myth that have encrusted Boone since the first book about him appeared in 1784.[4] There have been many biographies of Boone written since then, several of which are described in the bibliographical note at the end of this book— but none has focused to the same extent as this book on Boone as an example of and contributor to America's transformation, or on how Boone illustrates the conflicts in loyalties and the fluidity on the frontier until the new nation was formed, the Louisiana Territory was purchased, Indian power declined, and the British finally withdrew from their garrisons on American land. Boone fought Indians, but he was the adopted son of a Shawnee chief, and he remained friends with Shawnees for over forty years. During the Revolution he defended the frail young American settlements in Kentucky, yet like many on the frontier, his loyalties were not limited to the new nation that had yet to take shape. Boone fought the British not because he was a dyed-in-the-wool American—a national identity that was still being created—but because he was defending settlements against Indians armed and sometimes supported by the British. When Boonesborough was besieged, Boone was willing to discuss dispassionately the pros and cons of surrendering the fort and pledging allegiance to the British Crown. In 1799 Boone and his family moved to Missouri when it was still Spanish territory, and Boone became a civil servant in the Spanish administration of Missouri, although he probably expected at the time that Missouri would become part of the United States.

Quite apart from the conflicting loyalties Boone confronted, his own character was complex. He was a loner who loved being by himself in the wilderness, but at the same time a leader whom others trusted with their lives in the face of deadly dangers. He was a wanderer who was away from his family sometimes for years at a time, but he was also devoted to his family. He was a nurturer who cared for the young, the lost, the wounded, but also was a risk-taker who brought two of his sons and one of his brothers into perils that led to their violent deaths. Boone was not a regular church-goer, but his faith was strong and simple, as was his belief in the importance of treating others fairly.

Daniel Boone, though long dead, has been a part of my life since I was a child. My father was born and grew up in Kentucky. His family had lived there since Boone's time, and ancestors of mine knew Boone well. One of my relatives, Col. John Floyd, a founder of Louisville, helped Boone rescue his teenage daughter Jemima when she was captured by Indians in 1776. John Floyd married a relative, and his son married a daughter, of my ancestor William Preston, who in 1774, as colonel of the militia in western Virginia, made Boone a captain by inserting his name in a blank commission that had been signed by the British governor of the colony. Another ancestor, John Brown, congressman and senator from Kentucky, was one of Boone's lawyers in the litigation that soured Boone on Kentucky.

America is not an old country. You do not have to go back many generations to meet Daniel Boone. In 1845, twenty-five years after his death,

Kentuckians brought Boone's remains back from Missouri to Kentucky. My father's great-grandfather, Mason Brown, a judge in Kentucky, led the effort to reinter Boone in Frankfort, Kentucky's capital. When local dignitaries looked at the bones before the reinterment, Mason Brown put Boone's skull in the hands of his young son, John Mason Brown, so he could say that he had held it. Col. William Preston had lived only three generations before the boy who held Daniel Boone's skull.

My father, also named John Mason Brown (our family is not imaginative in naming children; my grandson is another John Mason Brown), had on the walls of his study, inherited from his uncle, the long and heavy rifle that Col. John Floyd was carrying in 1783 when Indians killed him not far from Louisville. That rifle now hangs on my brother's living room wall. I grew up steeped in stories my father told me about Daniel Boone and the settling of Kentucky. My father used to say that Daniel Boone had paid for part of my education. That was because in 1952 my father wrote a book on Boone for young readers, which kept on selling vigorously throughout my adolescence. That book, reprinted in 2007, continues to reward new young readers today, as it excited me when my father read it to me paragraph by paragraph while writing it years ago. I owe to my father the kindling of my abiding interest in Daniel Boone and in the opening of trans-Appalachian America. The acknowledgments and the bibliographical note show my indebtedness to others for their studies of Boone and his period.

I invite you to meet Daniel Boone, for the large role he played in America's birth and transformation, for the complexity of his character, and for the strength of the principles that underlay his achievements.

Chronology

1734   Oct. 22 (old style); Nov. 2 (new style): Daniel Boone (DB) is born to Squire Boone and Sarah Boone in Oley Township (near what is now Reading), Pa.

1742   Squire Boone's first rebuke from the Friends of Exeter Meeting, because his daughter Sarah had married a non-Quaker and was with child at the time of her marriage.

1747   DB gets first "rifle-gun" and starts hunting.
DB's older brother Israel marries a non-Quaker, prompting a second reprimand of Squire Boone by the Exeter Society of Friends.

1748   Squire Boone is "disowned" by the Exeter Society of Friends.

1750   DB's first long hunt.
Dr. Thomas Walker leads a group of Virginians through the Cumberland Gap into what is now Kentucky, looking for land on behalf of the Loyal Company.

1751   Squire Boone and his family settle on the forks of the Yadkin River in northwestern North Carolina. DB becomes a market hunter.

1752   John Findley establishes a trading post with the Shawnees at Eskippakithiki (in what is now Clark County, Ky.).
Treaty of Logstown—Six Nations, Shawnees, Delawares, and Wyandots confirm Iroquois cession of claims to Ohio land.

1753   Two 640-acre grants to Squire Boone of land near what would become Mocksville, N.C.

1754   The French erect Fort Duquesne at the site of what is now Pittsburgh.
The French force George Washington and his Virginia militia to surrender Fort Necessity in western Pennsylvania. Start of the French and Indian War (becomes in Europe the Seven Years' War).

1755   Shawnees kill Col. James Patton and others at Draper's Meadow in western Virginia. Crushing defeat near Fort Duquesne of General Braddock and his army of British regulars and American militia. DB is a wagoner with Braddock's army. DB meets John Findley, who tells him about Kentucky.

1756   May: Britain declares war on France.
Aug. 14: DB marries Rebecca Bryan.

1757   DB and Rebecca's first child, James, born May 3.

1758   Cherokee wars.
Oct.: Treaty of Easton. To induce the Indians to stop backing the French, Pennsylvania relinquishes to Six Nations its claims to land west of the Alleghenies.
Nov.: the French burn and abandon Fort Duquesne in the face of the advancing British army and the lack of Indian support. British start to build Fort Pitt on the site.

1759   DB's son Israel Boone born Jan. 25.

1760   DB's daughter Susannah Boone born Nov. 2.
During winter hunt DB first crosses Blue Ridge.

1762   Jemima born Oct. 4, DB and Rebecca's fourth child.

1763   Feb.: Treaty of Paris ends Seven Years' War. France cedes Canada and America east of the Mississippi to England and cedes Louisiana to Spain.

1765   Squire Boone dies Jan. 2.
DB and others explore Georgia's Altamaha River and Florida.

1767   DB hunts in eastern Tennessee and Kentucky

1768   John Findley and DB meet again in western North Carolina.
Nov.: Treaty of Fort Stanwix. Iroquois cede to the British their claims on land between the Ohio and the Tennessee rivers.

1769   John Findley leads DB through the Cumberland Gap into Kentucky. DB's long hunt lasts two years.
Dec.: Shawnees take the hunters' pelts and warn DB that if he comes back into Kentucky, he will feel the stings of the wasps and the yellow jackets. DB escapes from Shawnees.

1772   Virginia creates Fincastle County (most of what is now Kentucky) as a new county.

1773   DB leads families from the Yadkin Valley in North Carolina into Kentucky.

Oct. 9: Indians attack the immigrants. Five settlers are killed, including DB's oldest child, his son James, who is killed after being tortured. Settlers turn back.

1774   John Floyd leads party of Fincastle County surveyors into Kentucky.

Apr. 30: whites murder family of Mingo chief Logan.

Lord Dunmore's War. DB defends settlements on the Clinch River. DB goes to Kentucky with Michael Stoner—traveling eight hundred miles in sixty-two days—to warn Fincastle surveying crews of impending Indian attacks.

James Harrod establishes Harrodsburg in Kentucky.

Oct. 10: Battle of Point Pleasant, where the Kanawha flows into the Ohio. After the subsequent destruction of Shawnee towns north of the Ohio River, some Shawnee chiefs, at the Treaty of Camp Charlotte, agree to cede Shawnee claims to Kentucky.

1775   DB, representing Richard Henderson and his Transylvania Company, assembles Cherokees to meet with company representatives on the Watauga River.

Mar. 10: Treaty of Sycamore Shoals. Cherokees, in exchange for trade goods, cede to the Transylvania Company much of what is now Kentucky and a portion of northern Tennessee.

Mar.: DB and crew of axemen, working for the Transylvania Company, blaze what is later known as the Wilderness Road. Indians attack some of the axemen, kill Capt. Twitty.

May: start of building of Boonesborough in Kentucky.

Sept.: The Transylvania Company votes DB a present of two thousand acres for the "signal services he has rendered."

1776   July 14: Indians capture Jemima Boone and Fanny and Betsy Callaway near Boonesborough.

July 16: DB, John Floyd, and others rescue the girls.

Aug.: a copy of the Declaration of Independence reaches Boonesborough.

1777   Apr. 24: Indians attack Boonesborough. DB is shot in the ankle and nearly killed; Simon Kenton saves his life.

Nov.: Americans kill Shawnee chief Cornstalk, his son, and two other Shawnees in a cell in Fort Randolph, near Point Pleasant.

1778   Feb.: DB and a party of salt-boilers from Boonesborough are captured by Indians at Lower Blue Licks. DB and other captives run the gauntlet. The captives are taken to Shawnee towns north of the Ohio.

1779   Feb. 25: Col. George Rogers Clark captures the British fort at Vincennes as well as Lt. Gov. Henry Hamilton, the commandant of the British garrison at Detroit.

May: Blackfish is wounded in a fight with American militia. He later dies of gangrene.

Sept.–Oct.: DB leads a new wave of emigrants from North Carolina to Kentucky.

Dec.: DB establishes Boone's Station, not far from Boonesborough.

1780   Mar.: DB is robbed in Virginia of funds entrusted to him to buy land warrants or to register land claimed under warrants.

Oct.: Indians kill DB's brother Edward, thinking they are killing DB.

Nov.: Kentucky county is split into three new counties, Jefferson, Lincoln, and Fayette. DB is promoted to lieutenant colonel in the Fayette County militia.

1781   Mar. 3: birth of Nathan Boone, tenth and last child of DB and Rebecca.

May: Indians attack Squire Boone's Station.

June: DB is captured in Charlottesville, Va., by Tarleton's rangers but is soon released.

Oct.: General Cornwallis surrenders at Yorktown.

1782   Aug. 19: Battle of the Blue Licks. Indians defeat Kentucky militia. DB's son Israel is killed.

Nov.: Gen. George Rogers Clark and Kentucky militia (including DB) undertake retaliatory strike against Shawnees in Ohio.

1783   DB moves to Limestone (renamed Maysville in 1787), Kentucky. DB opens a tavern; surveys land.

DB is interviewed by John Filson, schoolteacher and land speculator.

1784   Oct. 22, DB's fiftieth birthday: publication of John Filson's book *The Discovery, Settlement and Present State of Kentucke, to which is added an Appendix Containing the Adventures of Col. Daniel Boon.*

1786   Suits relating to DB's land claims. DB loses most of his claimed land.

Oct.: DB participates in Col. Benjamin Logan's Ohio campaign against the Shawnees. Simon Kenton kills Big Jim, the Indian who had killed Boone's son James in 1773. Hugh McGary kills the peaceful chief Moluntha.

1787   DB mediates a prisoner exchange with Shawnees.

1788   DB transports a large load of ginseng to Hagerstown, Md.

1789   DB establishes a trading post at the mouth of the Kanawha River, at Point Pleasant (now in W.Va.).

1790   Oct.: Wabash and Miami Indians defeat over three hundred regular
         American troops and over one thousand Kentucky and Pennsylvania
         militiamen under Gen. Josiah Harmar in western Ohio.

1791   Nov.: Indians led by Little Turtle, a Miami war chief, crush an American
         army led by Gen. Arthur St. Clair, near what is now Fort Recovery, Ohio.

1792   Feb. 15: Kentucky is admitted as a state.

1793   Apr.: raid by Shawnees and Cherokees on Morgan's Station—last Indian
         raid in Kentucky.

1794   More land troubles for DB.
         Aug. 20: Americans under Gen. "Mad" Anthony Wayne defeat Indian
         confederacy under Blue Jacket (a Shawnee) and Michikinikwa
         (a Miami) at the Battle of Fallen Timbers.

1795   Treaty of Greenville opens up Northwest Territory to white settlement.
         Indians cede all but northwestern corner of Ohio.
         Boone moves to Brushy Creek, Ky.

1797   DB's son Daniel Morgan Boone hunts in Upper Louisiana (in what
         is now Missouri). The Spanish lieutenant governor, Don Zenon
         Trudeau, invites the Boones to settle there and promises them land.

1798   DB moves to the mouth of the Little Sandy River, in what is now
         Greenup County, Ky.
         Kentucky assembly names a county after Boone.
         Mason County, Ky., issues a warrant for DB's arrest for debt.

1799   Oct.: DB arrives in Missouri, then part of Spanish territory. He moves
         to Femme Osage, in what is now St. Charles County. DB receives
         a grant of one thousand arpents (c. 850 acres). Builds a cabin near
         what is now Matson, Mo.

1800   DB is appointed syndic and commandant of the Femme Osage District.
         Oct.: Treaty of San Ildefonso—Spain cedes Louisiana back to France.

1802   DB is captured by Osage warriors.

1803   Louisiana Purchase—United States buys Louisiana from France.
         DB is injured in a hunting accident.

1809   Indications are that U.S. land commission will reject DB's claim to land
         in Missouri. DB dictates an autobiographical narrative to his grand-
         son John Boone Callaway to help in the drafting of a petition to Con-
         gress for a land grant to DB.

1812   DB is said to have volunteered to serve in war with the British and to
         have been turned down because of his age (78).

1813   Daniel Bryan, perhaps a cousin of Rebecca Boone, publishes a 250-page
        epic poem about Boone, *The Mountain Muse: Comprising the Adven-
        tures of Daniel Boone and the Powers of Virtuous and Refined Beauty*.
        Mar. 18: Rebecca Boone dies.

1814   DB's autobiography, dictated to John Boone Callaway, and other papers
        are lost when a canoe capsizes in the Missouri River.
        Congress, acting on DB's petition, confirms DB's original grant of one
        thousand arpents of land in Missouri.

1815   DB starts to sell off most of his Missouri land to pay off debts.
        DB explores and hunts the upper Missouri.

1816   DB explores at least as far west as Fort Osage in western Missouri.

1817   DB falls sick during his last long hunt.

1820   June: Chester Harding paints DB's portrait while at the home of Flanders
        and Jemima (Boone) Callaway.
        Sept. 26: DB dies, a month before his eighty-sixth birthday.

1821   Aug. 10: Missouri is admitted as a state.

1823   Publication of canto 8 of Lord Byron's *Don Juan*, containing stanzas
        about DB, "back-woodsman of Kentucky."

1829   Jemima Boone Callaway dies.

1833   Timothy Flint's *Biographical Memoir of Daniel Boone, the First Settler of
        Kentucky* is published, with fourteen editions by 1868.

1845   Kentuckians demand that Missouri exhume DB's remains. Remains are
        reinterred on Sept. 13 in Frankfort, Ky.

1847   Publication of John Mason Peck's *Life of Daniel Boone, the Pioneer of
        Kentucky*.

1851   Lyman C. Draper, compiler of historical materials about the pioneers and
        would-be biographer of DB, interviews Nathan Boone and his wife,
        Olive Van Bibber Boone.

1856   Draper stops work on his life of DB.

1891   Aug. 27: Draper dies.

FRONTIERSMAN

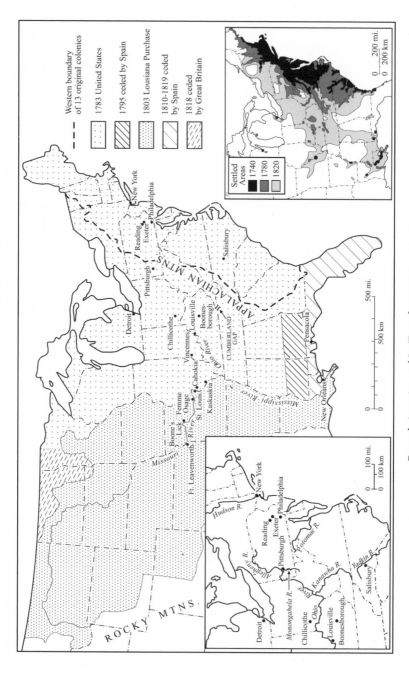

Boone's America and Its Transformation, 1740–1820

Map by Mary Lee Eggart

Western boundary
of 13 original colonies
1783 United States
1795 ceded by Spain
1803 Lousiana Purchase
1810–1819 ceded
by Spain
1818 ceded
by Great Britain

Settled
Areas
1740
1780
1820

200 mi.
200 km

New York
Reading
Exeter Philadelphia
Salisbury
Pittsburgh
APPALACHIAN MTNS.
Detroit
Chillicothe
Vincennes Louisville
Boones-
borough
Ohio River
CUMBERLAND
GAP
Pensacola
Cahokia
St. Louis
Kaskaskia
Osage
Femme
Boone's
Lick
Missouri River
Ft. Leavenworth
Mississippi River
New Orleans

ROCKY MTNS.

500 mi.
500 km

Hudson R.
New York
Reading
Exeter Philadelphia
Allegheny R.
Pittsburgh
Potomac R.
Monongahela R.
Kanawha R.
Yadkin R.
Detroit
Chillicothe
Ohio
River
Louisville
Boonesborough
Salisbury

100 mi.
100 km

1

OLD BOONE

WHEN DANIEL BOONE WAS WELL INTO HIS SIXTIES, HE MOVED WITH his family from Kentucky to Missouri. The story goes that he said there were "too many people!" in Kentucky (which at the time had been a state for less than a decade and which had about 200,000 people in it).[1] When Boone was in his eighties, after his wife, Rebecca, died in 1813, he lived mostly with his daughter Jemima and her husband, Flanders Callaway, in their house on the Missouri River, perhaps sixty miles upstream from St. Louis.

Because of Boone's immense reputation, many people came to visit him. Some were old friends, but others wanted to build their own reputations by being able to say they had seen the great Boone. In June 1820 Chester Harding, a young painter out to make a name for himself, traveled up the Missouri River to paint Boone's portrait. Harding was only twenty-seven; Boone was eighty-five. When Harding walked into the Callaways' cabin, Boone was "lying in his bunk, near the fire, and had a long strip of venison wound around his ramrod, and was busy turning it before a brisk blaze."[2] By this time Boone could no longer move well and could barely see—he was to die two months later. But residual strength pours out of Harding's picture of the man.

What did Boone do as an old man in Missouri? For a long time he still hunted. In 1816–17, already in his eighties, he and others went for a long hunt up the Missouri, reaching at least as far as Fort Osage near the western border of Missouri. Some say he made it as far as the mouth of the Yellowstone River, in what is now North Dakota. Boone and his companions came back with boatloads of pelts. That was Boone's last long trip. The next year uncontrollable shivering made him cut short a hunt with a grandson after three days. It was Boone's final hunt, though he kept hoping for more.

In his last three or four years, Boone stayed close to home and talked about things that had happened years earlier. He continued to hunt and trap near home, sometimes with Shawnees he had known and fought almost forty years earlier in Kentucky and who, like Boone, had moved to Missouri. His old Shawnee friends liked to reminisce, too. They reminded Boone that they had captured him in Kentucky—that was back in 1778—and their chief Blackfish had adopted him as his son, and Boone had said he would induce the settlers at Boonesborough to surrender the fort to Blackfish, but instead Boone escaped and led the settlers' successful defense of the fort against the Shawnees' attack.[3]

When the pilgrims came to see the great man, Boone generally tried to get out the back door if he saw them coming.[4] If he was not able to escape in time, he would talk to them. A lot of what he said was to debunk the exaggerated things that had been written about him. He told one pilgrim: "Many heroic actions and chivalrous adventures are related of me which exist only in the regions of fancy. With me the world has taken great liberties, and yet I have been but a common man." On why he had crossed the mountains into Kentucky and led others into the wilderness, Boone had a ready answer: he liked to hunt, and he was "naturally romantic."[5] Others asked him about all the Indians he had killed, citing an epic poem that Daniel Bryan had written under the ripe name *The Mountain Muse: Comprising the Adventures of Daniel Boone and the Powers of Virtuous and Refined Beauty.* What did Boone think of that poem? Boone said of it that Bryan had called him "a wonderful man who had killed a host of Indians"; yet, he said, "I never killed but three that I claimed"—though he added, "but many was the fair fire I have had at them."[6] Boone told another interviewer that he was sorry that he had killed any Indians, "for they have always been kinder to me than the whites."[7]

His children and his grandchildren remembered Boone's sayings, the wisdom of a long and hard life. "Better mend a fault than find a fault," he had told them. And "If we can't say good, we should say no harm."[8] In his last years Boone got ready for his long life to end. He had a coffin built, and he lay in it from time to time, to make sure it fit. He scared his grandchildren by saying that he slept in it sometimes. Maybe he did, or maybe he was funning them, the way he did by telling them, as if they were true, stories about the Yahoos, out of Swift's *Gulliver's Travels*—next to the Bible, Boone's favorite book. But he did check out his coffin from time to time. And he read his Bible.

2

QUAKERS IN PENNSYLVANIA, SETTLERS IN BACKCOUNTRY NORTH CAROLINA

DANIEL BOONE WAS BORN IN 1734 INTO A QUAKER FAMILY IN PENN-sylvania. Although Boone's father was expelled from his Quaker meeting when Boone was fourteen, and Daniel as an adult never went regularly to any religious services, Quaker principles surely shaped his values. Daniel's father, Squire Boone—"Squire" was his first name, not a title—was a weaver by trade, whose family came from near Exeter, in Devonshire, in southwestern England. They were Friends, or Quakers, members of a Protestant group often persecuted in England. Quakers refused to pay tithes to the established Church of England. Consistent with their belief that all men had an inner light—had within their souls an element of the divine goodness—Quakers would not doff their hats to others and addressed all men with the familiar second person singular *thee* and *thou*, not the more formal second person *you*. This practice irritated people who thought themselves socially superior. Nor would Quakers take oaths, including the required oath renouncing Catholicism. For all of these reasons Quakers in England often ended up in prison.[1]

In 1681 William Penn, a rich Quaker, was granted Pennsylvania as a colony by King Charles II, partly to pay off a debt the king owed to Penn's father. Penn, who had been imprisoned in England for his beliefs, set up Pennsylvania to be a haven for Quakers and other persecuted Protestant sects, a colony in which people could live together in "love and brotherly kindness." In that spirit Penn named the colony's principal city "Philadelphia"—"brotherly love"—and proclaimed that "liberty of conscience is every man's natural right."[2] Penn also set up the colony in the hopes (shared by many who came to America or who moved west as the American frontier shifted west) of substantial income from selling land to settlers. Between 1681 and 1685 alone, Penn sold over 700,000 acres of land in Pennsylvania.[3]

Quaker settlers by the beginning of the eighteenth century made up at least half of Pennsylvania's population. In 1713 Squire Boone became part of the Quaker emigration from England to Penn's colony. Seven years later he married Sarah Morgan, before a Quaker meeting in Gwynedd, some twenty miles northwest of Philadelphia. Daniel Boone was born on November 2, 1734, the sixth of eleven children of Squire and Sarah Boone.[4] Boone's family was then living in a log house in Oley Township, about fifty miles northwest of Philadelphia, near what is now Reading. The Oley Valley had rich farmland and a diverse group of settlers—English, French, Germans, Irish, Swedish, Swiss, and Welsh. Squire Boone owned a dairy herd as well as several looms and a smith's forge. The area where the Boones lived, named Exeter in 1741 after the town in England from which the family had come, was close to the western end of British settlement in Pennsylvania. At the time Britain's settlements in America on average were not more than a hundred miles from the Atlantic coast.[5] Indians lived not far to the west of the Boones—Delawares mostly, but also Shawnees, Tuscaroras, and others.

Penn and his agents sought to treat the Indians fairly. They paid for land, rather than killing for it.[6] There had been some Indian-white friction and fighting near where the Boones lived. In 1728, a few years before Daniel Boone was born, a Shawnee and two settlers had been killed, and Boone's grandfather George Boone, a local magistrate, had rescued two Indian girls from some angry settlers.[7] Until the French and Indian War started in the 1750s, however, Indian killings of whites (and vice versa) were far less common in Pennsylvania than they were to be in Kentucky in the 1770s and 1780s and less common than they were in Virginia and the Carolinas during the first half of the eighteenth century. The relative absence of violence between Indians and whites in Pennsylvania during this period (known as the Long Peace) resulted in part from the Quaker policy of treating the Indians fairly—coupled with the less aggressive penetration of western lands by Pennsylvanians at that time and the Pennsylvania proprietors' frugal reluctance to incur the heavy expense of warfare against the Indians.[8]

Boone would have seen Indians passing near his family's house. In 1736, for example, the Delaware chief Sassanoon and a party of twenty-five Indians stopped at George Boone's house on their way to Philadelphia, a visit showing both George Boone's status as a local official and his reputation among the Delawares.[9] The Boones would not have viewed all Indians with fear and hatred. Boone's family, and the Quaker meeting in Exeter to which the family belonged, would have taught Boone to think of Indians not as devils incarnate but, rather, as children of God. That attitude went back to George Fox, a founder of the Quaker movement. When Fox in the 1670s visited North Carolina, he met a doctor who disputed the Quaker claim that every man bore within him an inner spirit of God. The doctor said that no such spirit was in the Indians. "Whereupon I called an Indian to us," Fox wrote, "and asked him whether when he lied or did wrong to anyone there was not something in him that reproved him for it. He said there was such a thing in him, that did so reprove him, and he was ashamed when he had done wrong, or spoken wrong."[10]

William Penn's views of Indians accorded with those of Fox. The preamble to Pennsylvania's 1681 royal charter refers to Penn's desire not only to enlarge the English empire but also "to reduce the savage natives, by gentle and just manners, to the love of civil society and Christian religion."[11] In his first letter to the leaders of the Delawares, Penn wrote that the one great God had written his law in human hearts, that men should do good and not harm to one another. Penn told the Indians that he desired to "winn and gain their love and friendship by a kind, just and peaceable life," and if any Pennsylvania settlers were to offend the Indians, the Indians were to have full satisfaction by a jury made up of equal numbers of their people and settlers.[12] Penn also learned enough Delaware to be able to talk to the Delawares without an interpreter.[13]

Despite the Quaker rejection of war, relations between European settlers and Indians in Pennsylvania began to be strained by the 1750s, when Boone was in his teens. France by this time was inciting and backing the Indians as part of its growing effort to gain control of trade in the Ohio Valley, and Penn's descendants had irritated the Indians by sharp practices such as the "Walking Purchase" of 1737 of land as far as a man could walk in a day and a half, which the Penn agents measured by having an extremely fit man run sixty-five miles in that time period.[14] Indeed, the Penn family's desire for revenues from selling land to settlers had from the birth of Pennsylvania conflicted with Penn's stated kindly intentions toward the Indians.[15]

If Exeter in Boone's youth was not wild and bloody, it was nevertheless close to the frontier. The Boone family had a frontiersman's informal approach to the constraints of religious orthodoxy—an approach that led to Squire Boone's expulsion from his Quaker meeting. The Friends of Exeter Meeting first rebuked Squire Boone in 1742 because his daughter Sarah "hath contrary to the good order used amongst Friends joined herself in marriage to one that is not joined to our Society." Quakers at the time condemned "mongrel marriages" with "unbelievers."[16] Three Quaker men confronted Squire Boone about Sarah's marriage, and Squire Boone confessed "himself at fault in keeping [Sarah and the young man] in his House after he knew of their keeping company (but he was in a great streight not knowing what to do, seeing he was somewhat Sensible that they had been too Conversant before), & hopeth to be more careful in the future." Minutes of a later meeting of the Exeter Friends help us to decipher this entry about the couple having already been "too Conversant": a committee of Quaker women reported that Sarah "was with child before she was married." Sarah had to read a written confession before the Exeter meeting.

The incident indicates an openness on the part of the Boones toward sexual relations as part of life. That same openness was to be seen also in the adult Daniel Boone, in his wife Sarah, and in his daughter Susannah. Sex before marriage was common on the American southern and mid-Atlantic frontier. An Anglican priest in the Carolina backcountry in 1767 calculated that 94 percent of the brides at the weddings over which he officiated were pregnant on their wedding day, many them indeed "very big" with child.[17] This casual attitude toward premarital sex arose partly from the relative scarcity of women: many more men than women emigrated to America from England and Scotland, and the farther west the settlements were and the more frontier-like the conditions, the greater the ratio of men to women was likely to become.[18] To Quakers, however, sex before marriage, being fornication, could lead to being cast out of the Quaker meeting.[19]

As a boy, Boone had the job of following the family cattle in the woods and bringing them back each evening to the cow pens, where Boone's mother milked them. Boone became fond of life in the woods. Even as a boy of ten, he liked to hunt, killing birds and small game by throwing a knobbed club at them when he was meant to be tending his father's cattle. In 1747, when Boone was thirteen, his father gave him a "short rifle-gun," which enabled him to shoot deer. The boy became a good marksman. Boone's son Nathan said that his father "often neglected his herding duties to hunt, but this experience gave him his love of woods and hunting."[20]

Boone never went to school for any length of time—indeed, his son Nathan believed Boone never attended school.[21] According to one family tale, which sounds more like folklore than fact, while in Pennsylvania Boone briefly went to a school taught by an Irish teacher who used to go off into the woods to take a pull from a jug he had hidden in a tree. Boone found the jug, put an herbal emetic in the liquor, and laughed when the teacher began to suffer in class. When the teacher tried to cane the boy, Boone knocked him down and ran home, never to return to school.[22] Another family story had Boone's bachelor uncle John, who ran a school, trying to teach young Boone, who would not learn despite liberal encouragement with a rod. Squire Boone reportedly said, "It's all right, John; let the girls do the spelling and Dan will do the shooting, and between you and me that is what we most need."[23] Boone was not illiterate, however. The wife of his older brother Samuel taught him to read and write when he was in Pennsylvania. Boone later learned more reading and writing, and some arithmetic, from his daughter Susannah's husband, Will Hays.[24] Boone's spelling was often phonetic, but that was common on the frontier. It is at least possible to discern the meaning of what Boone wrote, which is more than can be done with the writings of some of his contemporaries, such as the great western military campaigner George Rogers Clark.[25]

In 1747 Boone's older brother Israel married a non-Quaker, causing the Friends of Exeter to issue a second reprimand to Squire Boone. It may well be that Squire Boone was perplexed by the idea that marriage was permissible only within one denomination and that he had had enough of being forced to acknowledge guilt and transgression in open meetings for things he did not think were wrong. He also may have felt less pressure to conform with Quaker requests following the death in 1744 of his observant Quaker father. Whatever the reason, when the Quaker brethren came around to remonstrate about Israel's marriage, Squire Boone was recalcitrant. According to the minutes of the Exeter meeting, "The Friends which were appointed to speak to Squire Boone report that they spoke with him and that he could not see that he had transgressed, and therefore was not willing to condemn it until he saw it to be a transgression." Instead of being "willing to give any satisfaction to the Meeting," Squire Boone argued back "even against his Friends who sought his everlasting Peace and Welfare, and against the Order and Discipline of Friends in general." The upshot was that in May 1748 the Exeter Society of Friends "disowned" Squire Boone; in other words, the group expelled him from their Quaker meeting, giving "publick testimony against him as not being a member amongst us, until such time as we may be sensible of his coming to a Godly sorrow in himself."[26] At the time of the expulsion, the Boone family was thinking about moving to northwestern North Carolina, having heard that large tracts of land were being sold there for little money. By 1750 Squire Boone had filed a claim for land along the forks of the Yadkin River in northwestern North Carolina, and the family was settled there the next year.

Boone left the Society of Friends when his family left Pennsylvania. After 1750, when Boone was sixteen, there is no record of Boone's regular attendance at Quaker meeting—or, for that matter, of his becoming a member of any church. This is not to suggest that the Boone family became irreligious. Boone's mother remained a Quaker in good standing, having requested and received in April 1750 from the Women's Meeting at Exeter her certificate as a traveling minister.[27] Boone's father, after the move to North Carolina, helped to found a nondenominational meetinghouse and often led services in it. Daniel Boone read the Bible regularly, especially in his later years, and liked listening to sermons "whenever preaching was in the neighborhood."[28] But Boone had little taste for the fine points of religious doctrine. "I never knew any good to come of religious disputes," he told his friend and hunting companion Peter Houston, a Presbyterian, after the two had had a heated discussion on the relative merits of Quakerism and Presbyterianism. At Boone's prompting the men agreed never again to have a dispute on the subject of religion.[29]

For all of Boone's lack of ongoing participation in Quaker meetings, if we look at what he did and how he did it after leaving Pennsylvania, it is hard not to see a consonance between many of Boone's principles and those of the Friends—in particular, about the inner light to be found in all humans, the virtues of simplicity and lack of ostentation, and the importance of fair dealing with other people (Indians as well as whites).[30]

In April 1750 Squire and Sarah Boone sold their Exeter property and started off for western North Carolina, part of a flood of settlers drawn to that region by low land prices. Between 1750 and 1770 the population of North Carolina more than doubled, from around 70,000 to between 175,000 and 185,000.[31] It took months for the Boone family to get from Exeter to the forks of the Yadkin River, an area that was still frontier.[32] Many Boones, relatives, and friends also made the trek, among them Squire Boone and Sarah's eight unmarried children, their three married children and spouses, and Squire Boone's apprentice, Henry Miller (Daniel's closest friend). In big Conestoga wagons they lumbered westward over the Allegheny Trail to the

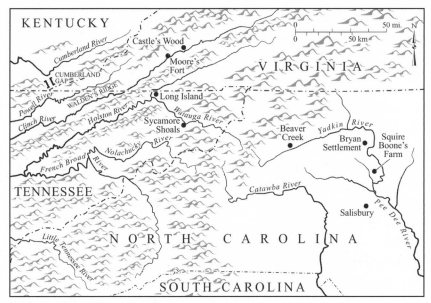

The Backcountry: Northwestern North Carolina and the Cumberland Gap
Map by Mary Lee Eggart

Susquehanna at what became Harrisburg, then followed along the Appalachians southwest to the Potomac and down the Shenandoah. They may have stayed in western Virginia near Squire Boone's sister and brother-in-law on the South Fork of the Shenandoah before pushing on into North Carolina.[33]

In the summer and fall of 1750 Boone, then fifteen years old, went on his first long hunt, with his friend Henry Miller. The two young men went east through the Blue Ridge and south to the high piedmont near the Virginia–North Carolina border. They killed and skinned many deer and brought the hides north to Philadelphia to sell them. Years later Miller remembered that he and Boone, with the proceeds from the sale, had gone "on a general jamboree or frolick" that went on for three weeks "until the money was all spent." The profligacy disgusted Miller, who decided to settle down, make money, and keep it. He grew up to become a substantial landowner in Augusta County, Virginia, where he set up an ironworks and also owned a paper mill, a sawmill, and a gristmill.[34] Judging by Boone's subsequent career, Boone must have drawn differing conclusions from his first long hunt: he liked hunting; he was good at it; he could make a living at it; and he may have enjoyed the occasional "frolick."

9

Land was cheap on the Yadkin. A square mile cost three shillings—this for land with clear streams and fine meadows. In 1753 Squire Boone bought two parcels, each of 640 acres, near what was to become Mocksville, North Carolina. There was enough land to set up each of the Boone children as they married. Squire Boone became a substantial citizen. When his neighborhood was organized as Rowan County in 1753, he became a justice of the peace and a member of the county court. The next year he was licensed to operate a "Publick House." There was plenty of clearing and farming and herding of the dairy cattle to be done on the Boone lands, but according to a nephew, Daniel Boone "never took any delight in farming or stock Raising."[35] Even in the summer, when his help was needed to build fences and work the fields, Boone would pray for rain so he could take to the woods with his rifle. He would stay out until evening even if the rain stopped in an hour because he was "so fond of gunning." As a teenager, Boone worked part-time as a teamster, or wagoner, for his father, taking produce and peltry to sell at the nearest market town, Salisbury, North Carolina. When fall came and the harvest was in, Boone would go off for hunts, lasting most of the fall and winter. By his later teens Boone was hunting "for profit and as a business of life."[36]

Game was abundant on the upper Yadkin. There were countless wild turkey in the bushes and beaver, otter, and muskrat in the streams and ponds.[37] Bear were common, too. According to one local story, Bear Creek, near the Yadkin forks, took its name when Boone killed ninety-nine bear on the creek in a single season. Deer were even more numerous. Boone and another hunter reportedly killed thirty deer in a single day near the head of the Yadkin.[38] Deerskin was a major part of the local economy and had been for years. In 1753 over thirty thousand deerskins were exported from North Carolina. As early as 1700, an average of fifty-four thousand deerskins were being exported each year to England from southern Carolina.[39] There was so much trade in deerskin that a "buck"—a dressed skin weighing about two and a half pounds, worth about forty cents a pound—became the synonym for a dollar in the American colonies.[40]

When young Boone had accumulated a wagonload of deerskins, he would take them to the county seat at Salisbury and trade them for supplies and money. He also entered the local shooting contests and generally won, sometimes with trick shots such as holding a long heavy Pennsylvania rifle in one arm and nevertheless firing it with winning accuracy. One day at a shooting match in Salisbury, Boone outshot a Catawba Indian known to the whites as Saucy Jack—could it have been for his propensity for rum? The Indian, at a local tavern, swore that he would kill Boone. Squire Boone, who was in Salisbury that day, heard of the threat, picked up a tomahawk, and said, "Well, if it had come to this, I'll kill first." The elder Boone's Quaker principles seem to have given way to defending the family. Saucy Jack, having been told what Squire Boone had said, prudently left town.[41]

3

BRADDOCK'S DEFEAT
How Not to Fight Indians

IN JULY 1755, WHEN BOONE WAS TWENTY, HE SAW HIS FIRST LARGE-scale military combat—not as a soldier but as a teamster. Boone drove wagons for the army of British regulars and American militia under the British general Edward Braddock that ended up being cut to pieces by French soldiers and their Indian allies at the Battle on the Monongahela—more commonly and less nobly known as Braddock's Defeat. In this minor supporting role Boone, for the first time, was engaged in the fight for control of North America. Braddock's Defeat was one of a series of British setbacks that marked the start of the French and Indian War—the North American aspect of the worldwide war between France and Britain, officially declared in 1756, that became known as the Seven Years' War. Despite its bloody beginning for the British, the war was to result in France ceding to Britain its control of Canada and its claims to America east of the Mississippi.

At the start of the 1750s three powerful groups had their eyes on the rich lands of the Ohio Valley—the British and the British colonists in America, the French and the French colonists in Canada, and the Indians living in the Ohio Valley. The British claimed them as part of their Atlantic colonies. The western boundary of Virginia, under its royal charter of 1609, extended at least as far as the Wabash River and, under an expansive reading, as far as the Pacific. Pennsylvania's western boundary was ill defined, and in the late 1740s and early 1750s Pennsylvanians were extending the reach of their fur and skins trade with the Indians as far west as the Wabash River.[1] The British interests in the Ohio Valley were not unitary: Virginia and Pennsylvania had conflicting claims to land there; traders from each colony wanted as much of the fur trade as possible; and Britain itself claimed ownership, in light of its purported paternal relationship with the Iroquois, whose claim was based on their earlier conquests of other Indian tribes in the area.[2]

The French, who had been jockeying with the British for control of North America since the seventeenth century, laid claim to the Ohio Valley, based on the explorations of René-Robert Cavelier, sieur de La Salle, in the late seventeenth century and those of later explorers such as Pierre-Joseph Céloron de Blainville, who asserted France's claim to the valley in a series of metal plates that he left in his travels up and down the river in 1749.[3] The French wanted the fur trade in the Ohio Valley and feared that British westward expansion could sever trade between French Canada and French Louisiana.

The Indians in the Ohio Valley—including the Shawnees, Mingos, Miamis, Delawares, and Cherokees—believed they should continue to be able to farm and hunt there. In particular, the Shawnees and the Delawares, having been driven within the past few decades by the pressure of British settlement first into western Pennsylvania and then into Ohio, were deeply wary of British intentions to occupy their land in the Ohio Valley.[4] In western Pennsylvania the Shawnees and the Delawares had seen the flood of British settlers—"where one of those People settled, like pigeons, a thousand more would Settle"—and, after moving to the Ohio Valley, had seen the British give land there "to a parcel of Covetous Gentlemen of Virginia called the Ohio Company" who "offered to Build Forts among us, no doubt, to make themselves Master of our Lands and make Slaves of us."[5] Delaware leaders, talking to the British, pointedly "desired to know where the Indians' Land lay, for that the French claimed all the Land on one Side the River Ohio and the English the other Side."[6] Other Ohio Valley Indians expressed the fear that "ye Virginians and ye French Intend to Divide the Land of Ohio between them."[7]

The clashing claims moved from theoretical to actual confrontation in the 1750s, as the French and the British vied for control of the lucrative fur trade with the Indians of the Ohio Valley and as British colonists kept moving west, driven by the desire for cheap land (as the Boone family had been in its move to western North Carolina). Between 1745 and 1754 the Council of Virginia issued land grants to more than two million acres in the Ohio Valley.[8] The Ohio Company, a group of British investors including George Washington's half-brother Lawrence Washington and Virginia governor Robert Dinwiddie, in 1749 received a British royal grant of a half-million acres of land west of the Alleghenies. The company argued that the settlement would provide a buffer and protection against French claims and would also be "the means of gaining a vast Addition and encrease to Your Majestys Subjects of that rich Branch of the Peltry and Furr Trade which Your Petitioners Propose by means of Settlement."[9] In 1750–51 the company sent Christopher Gist down the Ohio River to explore ways through the mountains, and by the early 1750s traders and settlers from the company began moving into what is now western Pennsylvania, arousing not only anxiety on the part of the different Indian groups in the Ohio Valley but also resentment on the part of the traders from Pennsylvania who had controlled trade with the Indians in much of the valley before the French expanded their presence there and the Ohio Company sent in settlers.[10]

To strengthen their own claims to the Ohio Valley and its fur trade, the French stirred up western Indians to attack Ohio Valley Indians who began to trade with British traders instead of French traders. In June 1752, for example, Ojibwas, Ottawas, and Potawatomis, at the urging of the French, attacked the Miami village of Pickawillany in what is now western Ohio, killed one English trader and ate his heart and also killed, dismembered, and ate the village chief, who had broken away from an alliance with the French and was trading with the British. The Miamis in the village sensibly decided to resume trading with the French.[11] As early as 1750, the French began talking to the Indians about building a fort on the Allegheny River. By 1753 the French were building a series of forts west of the Alleghenies, including Fort Presque Isle at what is now Erie, Pennsylvania, and Fort Le Boeuf, at what is now Waterford, inland from Erie. Alarmed by the increased French military presence in the Ohio Valley, the Iroquois and other tribes that liked to trade with the British asked Pennsylvania and Virginia to protect them and to build a fort where the Allegheny and Monongahela rivers join to form the Ohio River—the strategic location that was to become the site of Pittsburgh. When the British colonies dragged their feet, the Ohio Company in 1753 began on its own to build a fortified trading post there. Not until early 1754 did Virginia send a few dozen militiamen to help to build the fort.[12]

In 1753 George Washington, then twenty-two years old and already a colonel in the Virginia militia, was sent by Virginia's governor Dinwiddie to the French forts in western Pennsylvania to assert the British claims to the Ohio Valley and to request that the French leave. The French received George Washington courteously but made their views unmistakably clear.

As Washington noted in his journal, the French army officers, after they had "dosed themselves pretty plentifully with wine," which "gave a License to their Tongues to reveal their Sentiments more freely," told Washington: "It was their absolute Design to take possession of the Ohio, & by G—— they would do it."[13] In April 1754 the French seized the Ohio Company's fledgling fort and renamed it Fort Duquesne, after the governor-general of New France.[14] In July the French forced George Washington to surrender Fort Necessity, the small fort he had built not far east of Fort Duquesne. The Indians who had supported the British up to this point were shaken by the British lack of strength and by Washington's failure to build a strong fort. Washington, the Iroquois chief Tanacharison said, "was a good-natured man but had no Experience" and "would by no means take Advise from the Indians."[15]

The Indians in the Ohio Valley had seen their numbers plummet from the ravages of European diseases such as smallpox and measles, which caused Indian populations to drop drastically—estimates range from 25 to 95 percent—in the century following their exposure to the new viruses.[16] The Ohio Valley Indians had also lost most of their lands to the east through treaties and through wars with the Iroquois and with the whites, and they looked at both the French and the British as invaders seeking to dispossess them from their traditional lands. As the secretary to the Indians for the government of New York put it, the Iroquois and their allies, or "at least the Politicians amongst them, look upon the present disputes betwn the English and French . . . as a point of selfish Ambition in us both and are apprehensive that which ever Nation gains their Point will become their Masters not their Deliverers—They dread the success of either and their ablest Politicians would very probably rather wish us to continue destroying each other than that either could be absolute conquerors."[17] One Indian leader, having had something to drink, put it bluntly to a Pennsylvanian emissary who was trying to win the Indians to the British side and against the French: "D——n you, why do not you and the *French* fight on the sea! You come only to cheat the poor *Indians,* and take their land from them."[18]

Most of the Indians in the Ohio Valley saw the British as a greater threat than the French. The French tended to trap and trade for furs, but the British settlers, who were starting to survey land in what is now Tennessee and Kentucky, looked like incipient farmers, not just fur traders. Farming meant permanent and exclusive possession of the land and the ending of hunting and trapping by the Indians. Moreover, there were far more British than French in North America—around 1.6 million British and perhaps 75,000 French.[19] One Delaware explained the Indians' decision to join with the French against the British by saying that the Indians needed French aid to defeat the British who coveted their land because the British were "such a numerous People," but "we can drive away the French when we please."[20]

The Indians began to kill British settlers. The Shawnees started with a prominent target, Col. James Patton, an immigrant from northern Ireland who had become the leading land speculator in western Virginia. In 1743 Patton became the first British colonist to explore the Kanawha River, in what is now West Virginia, as well as two rivers to the west.[21] Two years later Patton and his associates were granted 100,000 acres in western Virginia, on the condition that they settle one family on each 1,000-acre tract.[22] Patton was one of the commissioners who negotiated the Treaty of Logstown with the Iroquois, Delawares, Shawnees, and Wyandots in 1752, in which Virginia asserted claims to lands south of the Ohio River. By 1755 Patton owned 17,007 acres in his own name as well as being a colonel in the militia, a leading negotiator with the Indians, and the lieutenant of Augusta County.[23] On July 8, 1755, at Draper's Meadow (now Blacksburg), Virginia, on the day before Braddock's Defeat near Fort Duquesne, Shawnees killed Colonel Patton and killed or captured several other settlers.

In light of Patton's prominence in exploring and developing western land, killing Patton was a good way for the Shawnees to stop the westward push of British settlers into the Ohio Valley. Patton may have also distinguished himself to the Indians by the inept way in which he had spoken in the preliminaries to the Logstown treaty meeting; his request for a council was taken as a threat, and the Indians were "generally affronted."[24] In the Draper's Meadow attack the Shawnees just missed killing Patton's nephew, William Preston, then twenty-four years old, who was to succeed Patton as a leading official and land speculator in western Virginia and who was to issue to Daniel Boone a commission as a captain in the Virginia militia. Early in the day of the Indian attack Patton had sent Preston to a neighbor to get help in harvesting. When Preston returned, he found the maimed bodies of Patton and other settlers. Near Patton's body were two Indians Patton had killed with his broadsword before he was shot to death.[25] In February 1756 Preston, as a militia captain, sought revenge for his uncle's killing by commanding a company of rangers in an expedition that marched in bitter weather from the settlements in southwestern Virginia, intending to attack the Shawnees in their own villages north of the Ohio River. The Virginians made it as far as the mouth of the Big Sandy River on the Ohio (what is now the northeast corner of Kentucky) but were so debilitated by cold and hunger that they had to go back without striking a blow.[26]

The British, determined to drive the French from the Ohio Valley, in February 1755 sent two regiments of regulars to America under Maj. Gen. Edward Braddock, with the mission of capturing a series of French forts: Duquesne, Niagara, and then Frontenac in Canada. Braddock had the benefit—and the detriment—of thirty-five years of fighting in Europe. Benjamin Franklin, helping to provide wagons and other supplies for Braddock's army on its march westward in Pennsylvania, warned Braddock that the army, in its long line of march, was in danger of "ambuscades of Indians, who, by constant practice, are dexterous in laying and executing them." According to Franklin, Braddock "smil'd at my Ignorance, and reply'd, 'These savages may, indeed, be a formidable Enemy to your raw American Militia; but, upon the King's regular and disciplin'd Troops, Sir, it is impossible they should make any Impression.'"[27]

Braddock declined the assistance of Indian scouts. The Delaware chief Shingas and representatives of the Shawnees and Mingos offered to help Braddock if he would assure them that if the British won, the friendly Indians would at least "be Permitted to Live and Trade Among the English and have Hunting Ground sufficient To Support themselves and Familys." Braddock said bluntly, "No Savage Shoud Inherit the Land." The Delawares left, and Braddock called after them "that he did not need their Help and had no doubt of driving the French and Indians away." Shingas and other Delawares ending up joining the Shawnees in attacking white settlements in the western frontier country, and Braddock's army ended up with only eight Indian scouts.[28] According to one Delaware chief, "A great many of our warriors left him & would not be under his Command" because "he looked upon us as dogs and would never hear any thing what was said to him, We often endeavoured to advise him, and to tell him of the dangers he was in with his Soldiers, but he never appeared pleased with us."[29]

Braddock's army started off from Frederick, Maryland, toward western Pennsylvania in mid-May 1755. The pace was ponderously slow. George Washington, serving as a captain in the colonial militia that accompanied the British regulars, wrote to his brother that the army was "halting to level every Mole Hill, & to erect Bridges over every brook."[30] Indians often scalped stragglers and outliers from the army, which made abundantly clear that the Indians and the French knew exactly where Braddock's men were. The Indians pinned the scalps to trees and left the mutilated bodies where they would be seen by Braddock's troops, in a form of psychological warfare.[31] A Delaware Indian working with the French told a young American captive that the Indians spied on Braddock's army every day and intended to surround it, take shelter behind trees, and "shoot um down all one pigeon."[32] The British, by contrast, had very few scouts ranging in front and alongside of their army.

On July 9, 1755, one day after the Shawnee raid on Draper's Meadow, several hundred French and Indians—many more Indians than French—encountered, in a clearing not far from Fort Duquesne, Braddock's advance party, which had just crossed the Monongahela. The French and Indians spread out in the woods around the clearing, flanking Braddock's troops, and started firing from behind the trees. The American militia made for the nearest trees, for frontier-style fighting—firing individually, behind the shelter of tree trunks. The British regulars stayed put for a while in the clearing, under withering cross-fire. The American militiamen were shot both by the British regulars firing from the clearing and by the French and Indians firing from the woods. Braddock himself, riding up to the clearing, was shot through the arm and in the chest.[33]

The British, confronted with "a manner of fighting they were quite unacquainted with," broke and ran back to the Monongahela, through the supply wagons in the army's rear.[34] Many of the troops "threw away their arms and Ammunition, and even their Cloaths, to escape the faster."[35] The wagoners in turn came under heavy fire from the French and Indians in the woods. Soon the wagoners who were still standing—Boone among them—cut horses loose from the wagons and rode off.[36] More of the American wagoners would have been killed if the Indians had not paused to loot the supplies from the wagons and to scalp the wounded. The fleeing British soldiers and American colonists could hear behind them the screams of the wounded being scalped. Twelve men taken captive by the Indians were led back to Fort Duquesne, had their faces painted black, were tied naked to stakes on the banks of the Allegheny near the fort, and were slowly tortured to death with red-hot irons and lighted pine splinters stuck in their bodies, while the Indians danced around them.[37] A young Pennsylvanian roadcutter who had been taken captive by Indian allies of the French a few weeks earlier stood on the wall of Fort Duquesne and saw the Indians begin to burn a prisoner: "They had him tied to a stake and kept touching him with firebrands, red-hot irons, etc. He screamed in a most pitiful manner, the Indians in the meantime yelling like devils." The Pennsylvanian stopped looking because, as he put it, "this scene was too shocking for me to behold."[38]

Of the thirteen hundred British and American men with Braddock, more than 900 were killed or wounded. The French and Indians reported twenty-three killed and sixteen wounded. Braddock died of his wounds three days after the battle. Washington buried him in the middle of the road and ran wagons over the site to hide the grave so that Indians would not scalp and maim Braddock's body.[39] Twenty years later a British visitor to the site of the battle reported in his journal: "Found great numbers of bones, both men and horses. . . . We could not find one whole skull, all of them broke to pieces in the upper part, some of them had holes broken in them about an inch diameter, suppose it to be done with a Pipe Tomahawk."[40]

For all the ghastliness of Braddock's Defeat, some good came out of it. The British committed additional resources to drive the French out of the Ohio Valley. George Washington, only twenty-three years old, learned how not to fight Indians. Boone, too, learned from the defeat. He never forgot what had happened because Braddock "neglected to keep out spies and flank guards"[41]—that is, to send out scouts and skirmishers to find out where the enemy was and in what strength.

Boone learned something else from Braddock's expedition. Around the army campfires Boone first heard of Kentucky, the rich land beyond the mountains and down the Ohio River. His source of information was John Findley (the name is also sometimes spelled "Finley" or "Findlay"—spelling on the frontier tended to be phonetic), also serving as a teamster on the expedition. Findley, as a trader with the Indians, had gone down the Ohio to the mouth of the Kentucky River and then up that river to a Shawnee town called Eskippakithiki (probably meaning "Town of the Blue Lick" in Shawnee), in what was to become Clark County, Kentucky. There he had traded profitably before the Indians allied with French efforts to gain control of the Ohio Valley fur trade robbed him of his goods and drove him off.[42] Findley told Boone that "Kentucke," as the Indians called it, was a country of clover, with land enough to provide for sons and grandsons as well as a "great speck" (that is, a speculation or investment opportunity) and with unimaginable wild game—deer and buffalo for the taking. Years later Boone was to say that Findley had painted "so charming a description of Kentucky, the

Falls of the Ohio, and wild game, that at once fired his imagination, and so completely promised to fulfill his romantic desires, that he resolved to visit the country."[43]

Yet Boone had to wait years to fulfill that goal. His immediate desire after escaping from the carnage of Braddock's Defeat was to get back to his own people. He went first on foot to eastern Pennsylvania to see relatives in Exeter. According to a story told over a century later, which smacks more of myth than of fact, Boone had to cross a high bridge over a gorge on the Juniata River. The bridge was blocked by a large, half-drunk Indian who drew a knife and told Boone "he had killed many a Long Knife [a white man, so called because some whites carried swords], and would kill some more on his way home." Boone was unarmed, and there was no way around the Indian. When the man lurched forward, Boone charged into him, giving him a shove that knocked him off the bridge to plunge forty feet to the rocks and water below.[44]

4

A GOOD WIFE

BACK ON THE YADKIN, BOONE ONCE AGAIN MADE HIS LIVING AS A hunter. As an old man, Boone would say that a man needed only three things to be "perfectly happy: a good gun, a good horse, and a good wife."[1] Judging by his success in hunting and in the shooting competitions at Salisbury, by the time Boone turned twenty he had already acquired a good gun. Based on the full loads of deerskins he was bringing in from his hunts, he already had at least one good horse. What Boone lacked was a good wife. He must have seen the need for one. To be over twenty years old was to be a fully grown man by frontier standards. British colonists in America married young, often by the age of sixteen. Boone would long since have figured out how pleasurable women's company could be. He certainly had plenty of opportunities—on his 1750 three-week "general jamboree or frolick" with his friend Henry Miller in Philadelphia, spending the proceeds of their long hunt; on his frequent trips to Salisbury when he cashed in the skins and furs from his hunts and visited the local taverns; and at the carryings-on that attended weddings in the backcountry.

And there were weddings aplenty in the Yadkin Valley neighborhood, cementing relationships between families, starting up new families to work the land. Boone's older brother Jonathan married a Carter, the daughter of a prosperous immigrant from Virginia who was on the county court with Squire Boone. In 1753 Boone's younger sister Mary, who was then sixteen, married William Bryan, one of a large Welsh family of Quakers that had lived in western Pennsylvania and the Virginia valley before coming to the Yadkin Valley in 1749. William Bryan's father, Morgan Bryan, the patriarch of the family in America, was the biggest landowner in the county, owning some five thousand acres, much of it about twenty miles north of where

Squire Boone had settled. Squire Boone's nephew John Boone then married a daughter of Morgan Bryan.[2] Soon Daniel Boone was the oldest of Squire Boone's children living at home. If Boone's parents were like most parents, Boone was getting strong and repeated suggestions that it was time to get married.

At one of the many Boone-Bryan weddings—probably the one in 1753 between Mary Boone and William Bryan—Daniel Boone took notice of Rebecca Bryan, Morgan Bryan's granddaughter, and she took notice of him.[3] They were both striking-looking young people. Rebecca was barely fifteen years old. Her hair was jet black, her eyes dark.[4] One descendant described her as "one of the handsomest persons she ever saw."[5] Rebecca was buxom and lively and very close to Boone's height—tall for a woman of the times. She was tidy in housekeeping, strong, and strong-willed.

Daniel was eighteen or nineteen when they met. He was not a tall man by present standards—about five foot eight, most say, though some say as tall as five foot ten—but that was average height for a man in Boone's day, and he was compact and muscular. As his son Nathan put it, Daniel Boone "had broad shoulders and chest and tapered down." Someone described him as "a sort of pony-built man"—not tall but built like a horse and similarly strong.[6] Boone's hunting friend Peter Houston said that at the end of a hand spike Boone "could lift more than any man I ever saw."[7] He weighed about 175 pounds when he met Rebecca. His eyes were blue, his skin fair and ruddy, his hair reddish sandy. He kept his hair plaited and clubbed—that is, the long hair was braided into a queue that was folded under itself and tied to keep it secured. His forehead was high, his brow heavy, his cheekbones prominent, his mouth tight and wide, his nose long and slender.[8]

Rebecca Bryan's family was richer, and her clothes more civilized, than Boone's. Boone looked like, and was, a backwoodsman. Like other hunters on the frontier, he wore deerskin moccasins reaching up his calves and a long hunting shirt of linsey or of deerskin reaching down to his knees. Often, instead of pants, he would wear a breechclout and deerskin leggings attached to a belt. His clothes looked a lot like an Indian's—because they were a lot like an Indian's. They were clothes well designed for moving through the woods and for camouflage. He wore a hat, often one made of beaver fur. According to his son Nathan, Boone "always despised the raccoon fur caps and did not wear one himself."[9]

Boone's daughter-in-law, Nathan's wife, said that the second time Daniel

and Rebecca met was at a place "where several young people met to eat cher-
ries. They sat upon a ridge of green turf among the cherry trees, and Daniel
Boone was beside Rebecca Bryan and doubtless turning over in his mind
whether she would make him a good companion. At that time he took out
his knife and, taking up one corner of her white apron, began to cut and
stab holes through it, to which she said nothing nor offered any resistance.
Daniel Boone afterward said that he did it to try her temper, thinking if it
was fiery she would fly into a passion."[10] Clothes were hard to come by on
the frontier. Rebecca must have liked Daniel a lot to put up quietly with him
playing ruinous mumblety-peg on her apron. Or could it have been that,
advertently or not, Boone was suggesting something to her by thrusting his
knife through her apron and she, by not protesting, was suggesting her willing compliance?

One day, to impress Rebecca with his food-providing abilities, Boone
brought to the Bryans' house a deer he had killed, and dressed the carcass
outside. He came in for the meal with his hunting shirt still bloody and
greasy from the butchering. Rebecca and her sisters laughed at his shirt,
while Boone drank milk from a wooden bowl. Boone held up the none-too-
clean bowl, stared at it, and said: "You are like my hunting shirt—you have
missed many a good washing."[11]

On August 14, 1756, Daniel Boone and Rebecca Bryan were married. By
this time he was twenty-one, she seventeen. The event was to cause Boone's
nineteenth-century biographer Lyman Draper to gush: "Boone led to the
Hymeneal altar the object of his affections, . . . whose brow had been fanned
by the breezes of seventeen summers."[12] Squire Boone, as justice of the peace,
performed the ceremony. Two other couples were married at the same time.
Presumably, the families had a party, with Black Betty, the liquor jug, being
passed from thirsty lips to thirsty lips and bawdy songs being sung below the
nuptial chamber.[13] The first child of Daniel and Rebecca, James, was born on
May 3, 1757—eleven days shy of nine months after the wedding date.

James was the first of 10 children Boone and Rebecca were to have between 1757 and 1781—on average, one child every 2.4 years. Rebecca was
eighteen when the first child was born and forty-two when the tenth child
arrived. The number of children they had was consistent with the record of
Daniel's and Rebecca's parents, both having had 11 children, and also with
Boone's own children. In all, the 7 children of Daniel and Rebecca who lived
long enough to marry had 68 children, an average of 9.7 apiece. Boone's last-

born child, his son Nathan, had 14 children by the same wife. Frontier people tended to have large families. Children helped in settling and working the land, but many of them died young. Among Rebecca and Daniel's children, one son died in infancy, and two others were killed by Indians before they were married. In any case, people living along the frontier at that time married young, contraception was minimal, and there were few forms of entertainment to compete with sex.

The marriage of Daniel Boone and Rebecca Bryan proved remarkably resilient, despite severe challenges, including the perils of Indian attacks, the squalor of frontier settlements, frequent and large financial reverses, repeated moves over thousands of miles, the killings of two sons by Indians, and Boone's recurrent and prolonged absences on long hunts and military campaigns. Among the first challenges for Daniel and Rebecca was the danger of Indian raids. In the late 1750s and early 1760s Indian attacks became common near the Yadkin settlements, starting after some settlers had taken the scalps of peaceful Cherokees in order to collect scalp bounties and Virginia militia had killed Cherokees without any cause.[14] Cherokees attacked British settlements in return, killing at least a dozen settlers along the Yadkin.[15] Because of the raids, Boone's family, like most of the Yadkin settlers, moved back east. The Boones moved to Culpeper County in the Shenandoah Valley of Virginia.

The Cherokee raids on the Yadkin settlements mirrored Indian raids, inspired by Braddock's Defeat and aided and encouraged by the French, on the western settlements in other British colonies. France's governor in Canada saw that a good way to stop the British advance into Canada was "to carry the war into their country . . . sending parties of Indians into the English Colonies."[16] In Pennsylvania in 1755 and 1756 Shawnees and Delawares killed or captured three thousand colonists and pushed settlers out of the western half of the colony. The bloody turmoil led pacifist Quaker deputies to resign from the Pennsylvania legislature because "the present situation of public affairs calls upon us for service in a military way"—which was not the Quaker way. Indian raids came within miles of where the Boones had lived near Reading.[17] Indians in 1756 similarly drove settlers out of most of western Virginia and Maryland.[18] The French commander at Fort Duquesne reported to his superiors, "I have succeeded in ruining the three adjacent provinces, Pennsylvania, Maryland, and Virginia, driving off the inhabitants, and totally destroying the settlements over a tract of country thirty leagues wide."[19]

George Washington reported in November 1756 "the ruinous state of the frontiers, and the vast extent of land we have lost since this time twelve-month, must appear incredible to those who are not eye-witnesses of the desolation."[20] The Indian onslaught did not begin to subside until the Pennsylvania government, in the Treaty of Easton in October 1758, by relinquishing the colony's claims to lands west of the Allegheny Mountains, induced the Indians to stop backing the French, who in November 1758, no longer having Indian support, burned and abandoned Fort Duquesne to a superior approaching British force.[21] The British built Fort Pitt on the site.

After traveling to Virginia, Boone went back out west by himself in the fall of 1759, away from Rebecca and their growing family—Israel had arrived in 1759, Susannah in 1760. In October 1759 he acquired 640 acres in Rowan County from his father, though there appears to be no evidence that he farmed the property.[22] Part of the time Boone hunted. Boone may have also fought with the militia against the Cherokees, a war carried on with numbing atrocities on both sides.[23] The successful defender of a fort in South Carolina, for example, wrote to the governor of the colony, "We have now the pleasure, Sir, to fatten our dogs with their carcasses and to display their scalps neatly ornamented on the top of the bastions."[24] After the Cherokees were beaten and had signed a peace treaty in November 1760, Boone went on another hunt, this time through eastern Tennessee and western Virginia, and looked for the first time west from the highest mountains in Virginia to the western slopes of the Appalachians. Boone went on to explore and hunt along the Holston River into eastern Tennessee.[25] After the hunt Boone went back to his farm on the Yadkin to plant a crop. Only after harvesting the crop did Boone rejoin Rebecca and the family in Virginia sometime in 1762, having spent some two years away from his young wife. On his return, according to several stories gathered many decades later (and denied or questioned by several Boone descendants and biographers), Boone encountered what his nineteenth-century biographer Lyman Draper referred to in his notes as "Boone's surprise": during her husband's prolonged absence Rebecca had conceived and given birth to another child, Jemima, born on October 4, 1762.

Rebecca reportedly burst into tears when she saw Boone and told him he had been gone so long that everyone thought he was dead. Boone asked who the baby's father was and was told it was a Boone—according to some stories, Boone's younger brother Edward, known as Neddy, who, Rebecca said, "looked so much like Daniel, she couldn't help it."[26] Boone took the news in stride. "It will be a Boone any how," he reportedly said in another telling of the story, "and besides I have been obliged to be married in Indian fashion a couple of times. Pho' pho! Dry up your tears and welcome me home." The teller of the story, who was seventy-six years old and who apologized for having "only a faint recollection of a mass of incidents without date or form," reported that Boone's wife was there when Boone told it to him, and she "made her knitting needles fly very fast" as the story was told.[27] Another account has Rebecca telling the returning Daniel as he sees the new child, "You had better have staid at home & got it yourself."[28]

Like much Boone lore, the stories about Boone's surprise were based on reminiscences of old frontiersmen and women (or their descendants) long after the time in question. The stories also are mutually inconsistent in key aspects, such as the date of the event and the identity of the child and of the father, and other puzzling aspects. When, before Jemima's birth, would Boone have taken an Indian wife? Boone did not live in a Shawnee village until he was taken captive by the Indians in 1778—sixteen years after Jemima was born. But that does not mean that he would not have had opportunities, traveling in Indian country, for encounters with Indian women.[29] Moreover, at least one other story suggests some openness in Boone's marriage. His daughter Susannah was known both for her good looks and for "frolicking" with the boys. When William Hays told Boone that he wanted to marry Susannah, Boone cautioned him about her, but Hays married her anyway. The young man later protested to Boone when Susannah turned out to be less than completely faithful as a wife. "Didn't I tell you she would —— you?" Boone said. "Trot father, trot mother, how could you expect a pacing colt?" That story was collected in the 1840s by a Boone biographer who was a Presbyterian minister and who found it hard to believe that Boone would ever have said such a thing. His informant told him to bear in mind that "Boone was raised in the backwoods of Carolina": "Those times were very different from these, and such things then were not what they now would be."[30]

The marriage of Daniel and Rebecca was not free from strain. How could it have been, given Boone's long absences from home on long hunts, Indian campaigns and Indian captivity, the squalor and terror of life on the frontier, the number of times they moved, and the loneliness exemplified by the stories of Boone's surprise? In 1771 George Soelle, a Moravian missionary, stopped by the family's cabin in the wilderness of the upper Yadkin in northwestern North Carolina and talked to Rebecca. That was after Boone, once again, had been away hunting for close to two years. The minister wrote in his diary that Rebecca "is by nature a quiet soul, and of few words. She told me of her trouble, and the frequent distress and fear in her heart."[31]

If Rebecca was lonely and feared for her life in northwestern North Carolina in 1771, her life cannot have been better in 1775, when she joined Daniel in Kentucky in the rough new settlement of Boonesborough, with its half-dozen unfinished cabins and its incomplete palisades in the midst of Indian country, or in the following year or two, when there were only about two hundred whites in all of Kentucky and only six women in Boonesborough.[32] In 1778, as we will see, Boone and more than twenty other Boonesborough settlers were taken captive by Indians and led across the Ohio to the Shawnee towns. Rebecca, despairing of ever seeing him again, took her family back to her father's house in North Carolina. Boone did not see her again for months, until he went to North Carolina and was able (with substantial difficulty) to persuade her to come back with him to Kentucky. In Filson's telling of Boone's life Boone says cryptically, "The history of my going home, and returning with my family, forms a series of difficulties, an account of which would swell a volume, and being foreign to my purpose, I shall purposely omit them."[33] One suspects that the unrecounted "difficulties" included some full and frank discussions between Daniel and Rebecca about their relationship and where their lives were going. But Rebecca did return to Kentucky. Their lives were bound together inseparably, as Boone's fortunes rose and fell and as Boone moved to Missouri.

Rebecca Bryan Boone was a spirited woman and a brave one. She played an important role, as we will see, in the defense of the settlers on the Clinch River against Indian attack in 1774. In later years, when Boone's rheumatism made it hard for him to carry his long rifle on hunts, Rebecca would carry it for him.[34] How important was Rebecca to Boone? When she died in 1813, Boone went into a depression that lasted for weeks. He never was the same after her death, which one granddaughter described as "the Saddest affliction of his life."[35]

5

LONG HUNTS

BOONE WENT ON LONG HUNTS FOR MORE THAN SIXTY YEARS—FROM
1750, when at the age of fifteen he went on his first long hunt, until 1817,
the year he turned eighty-three. He kept on hunting even as he grew older
and rheumatic and his vision had deteriorated, although the hunts became
shorter then, and Boone spent more time trapping and less time hunting. He
tried other ways of making a living—surveying, trading, ginseng gathering,
tavern keeping, among others—but he kept coming back to hunting. He was
good at it, and he must have loved it—being out in the woods or the cane-
brake, looking for sign (animal or Indian), waiting, knowing when to shoot,
shooting, preparing the skins, always taking care to reduce the risk that Indians would rob him of his pelts and his guns.

Boone was far from the only long hunter of his time. As long as game was
abundant, a good but dangerous living could be made by hunting outside of
the settlements and selling the peltry. But the more the hunting, the scarcer
the game became, and the farther the hunters had to range away from the
settlement. Starting in the 1760s, numbers of hunters from the British colonies went into Kentucky to hunt in the fall and winter months—among them
Anthony and Isaac Bledsoe, Benjamin Cutbirth, Simon Kent, Caspar Mansker, James Smith, Uriah Stone, and Michael Stoner.[1] Some of the long hunters were part of large groups sent out by substantial eastern trading firms.[2]
Like Boone, many of them were robbed of their pelts by Shawnees or Cherokees, who did not like whites coming into their hunting grounds and who
doubtless saw stealing the results of a season's work as an easy way to gain a
lot of peltry.[3]

Many of the long hunters liked to hunt in groups, working from a common hunting station. Boone preferred to hunt by himself or with one or two

others. Hunting in a group gave some protection from Indians, but as Boone discovered in his first long hunt into the bluegrass country of Kentucky, it also tended to leave far more sign for Indians who were looking for white hunters to rob.

The hunters' guns were single-shot muzzle-loading flintlocks. Deer hunting called for range and accuracy. Boone carried a long rifle, of the sort known as Pennsylvania or Kentucky rifles. These rifles, which evolved from German hunting guns, were big and heavy; the octagonal barrel by itself was over forty inches long.[4] The length of the barrel and the rifling made for greater accuracy than that of smoothbore muskets, but the rifles were not easy to carry. The rifle carried by Boone's friend Col. John Floyd when he was killed by Indians in Kentucky in 1783 was five feet long and weighed nine pounds.[5] Because Daniel Boone was five foot eight, his rifle would have stood nearly as tall as he did. Boone also would have carried a powder horn (a hollowed cow horn or buffalo horn) to hold his gunpowder, a shot bag to hold hand-cast lead balls (at the time typically from .50 to .60 caliber), and a pouch. Tucked in the belt around his hunting shirt would have been a tomahawk and a sheathed hunting knife.[6] Boone rode a horse on most of his hunts and on long hunts brought packhorses along to carry gear and pelts.

The need to reload between shots put a premium on accuracy. If you missed the first time, it would take you something like a half-minute to re-load, even if you were an experienced shooter, because of the number of steps involved in reloading. The shooter pulled out the plug from the spout of his powder horn and poured loose gunpowder into a hollowed-out antler tine that measured the charge. The charge was poured down the muzzle. A lead ball, nestled in a tallow-greased patch, was put in the muzzle and rammed home. The shooter pushed the ramrod back in place under the forestock, cradled the rifle, opened the frizzen—the L-shaped piece of steel over the pan—and sprinkled some gunpowder from the powder horn into the pan for priming. The shooter next snapped the frizzen shut and replaced the plug in the narrow end of the powder horn, and only then was he ready to shoot.[7] By this time, if you had missed on the first try, the deer you were shooting at would have long since run away. There was also the chance, when you pulled the trigger, that the flint wouldn't strike a spark against the frizzen or that the spark wouldn't fall into the pan or the powder in the pan wouldn't ignite or the flame from the pan wouldn't find its way through the touchhole to ig-nite the powder in the barrel—and you would have only a flash in the pan.

To hunt successfully and to survive in Indian country, you had to know where and when to find the game, how to prepare it, how to get it to market, how to tell whether Indians were nearby, and how to avoid them. Boone hunted many kinds of game, among them deer, bear, buffalo, beaver, otters, panther, and turkey. For Boone, and for white and Indian hunters overall, deer were the most important. There was nothing paltry about peltry commerce in Boone's day. In 1767, for example, the commissary at Fort Pitt, at the site of what is now Pittsburgh, recorded receipt of 282,629 deerskins—178,613 "fall Skins" and 104,016 "Summer Skins." That volume was comparable to the volume of deerskins passing through Charleston and New Orleans. White and Indian hunters at that time must have been killing far more than a million deer a year in the watershed of the Mississippi River.[8] Deerskins were important not only for sale in the colonies but also for export. In 1770 the British continental colonies in North America shipped out deerskins weighing 799,807 pounds and worth £57,750 sterling. That aggregate value was not large relative to America's dominant exports at the time, such as tobacco (£906,638), bread and flour (£505,553), dried fish (£375,394), and rice (£340,693), but deerskins accounted for close to 2 percent of all American exports.[9]

Animals need salt, so a good place to hunt was at salt licks, where the soil was impregnated with salt seeping up from underground deposits left over from dried-up prehistoric inland seas. Animals would lick the ground for its salt content, sometimes wearing it down more than six feet deep for several acres around.[10] Boone learned where the licks were and hunted there, but he also hunted deer in the woods and meadows.[11] He knew what time of year was best for hunting deer for their skins—in summer and fall, not in winter. In the depth of winter deer hair was longer for warmth, and the roots of the hair nearly penetrated the pelt and so reduced its value.[12] The fall and early winter were also the time of the rut, when bucks were busy following doe musk trails and so were less alert to danger from hunters.[13] Boone also knew the best time of day to find deer. While he often hunted all day, he generally would start early in the morning, when the dew-moistened leaves caused no noise when a hunter walked on them and the deer were more visible, being up on their feet feeding.[14]

To dress a deer skin, Boone would scrape off the hair and the grain. When the hide was dry, he would rub it across a staking board until it became somewhat soft. The skin then was said to be half-dressed and was fit for compact packing.[15] Half-dressed skins would be pressed and covered over with buffalo or bear hides.[16] According to Boone's son Nathan, a heavily packed horse could carry about a hundred half-dressed deerskins, each weighing 2 pounds.[17] The most a horse should carry was between 200 and 250 pounds of pelts. Hunters such as Boone were most vulnerable to being robbed by Indians when the dressed skins were bundled together to be brought to market because by that time much of the hard work of hunting had been done, and the product of that work was transportable and marketable. Indians, like white hunters, sold large quantities of skins to white traders. For Indians to relieve long hunters of a season's pelts was to gain in a single stroke valuable commodities that could be traded for guns, knives, tomahawks, ammunition, beads, blankets, liquor, and other trade goods.

Clothing being hard to come by on the frontier, Boone and other hunters often made their own clothes out of deerskin. They first tanned the deer hides—heating them in kettles with water laced with salt, alum, and ashes. As the hides dried, they were pulled and stretched to make them pliable and then were made into trousers, jackets, or moccasins.[18]

The long hunters found that bearskins were too heavy to carry to Carolina, but bears made good eating.[19] Bear grease helped to keep off bugs, and bears' dark fatty meat could be rendered into a superior cooking oil that lacked hog lard's strong biting taste and that was less likely than hog lard to turn rancid.[20] The bear fat could be preserved pure and sweet if slippery elm bark was added to the fat during its rendering.[21] Away from the settlements bear were so common that some hunters were able to put up over two thousand pounds of bear bacon in a season.

Buffalo, which we think of as animals of the western Plains, had spread into the eastern states before the whites came to America. By the time Boone began hunting in the 1750s, the buffalo were gone from the coastal colonies. He did not see and kill a buffalo until he entered Kentucky in 1767, but there he saw astounding numbers of them. He told his first biographer, John Filson: "The buffaloes were more frequent than I have seen cattle in the settlements, browsing on the leaves of the cane, or cropping the herbage on those extensive plains, fearless, because ignorant, of the violence of man. Sometimes we saw hundreds in a drove, and the numbers about the salt springs were amazing."[22] The cane that Boone mentioned is a woody reed, *Arudinaria,*

Kentucky's only bamboo. When Boone first came to Kentucky, cane was so prevalent along the banks of many rivers and creeks as to make them almost impassable. Within fifty years it became "scarce and a curiosity."[23]

Like bearskins, buffalo hides were heavy and bulky and so not of much commercial value to Boone. The transportation system—the steamboats, roads, and eventually railroads—that enabled trade in buffalo robes and hides to become a big business did not exist until the nineteenth century.[24] But buffalo were wonderfully useful in other ways. The meat was tasty, especially the meat from the hump. One young English traveler to Kentucky in 1775 claimed that buffalo hump "makes the finest steaks in the world."[25] Roast buffalo tongue was also viewed as a delicacy by white hunters and Indians alike.[26] Buffalo bone marrow, dug out of shanks heated on the coals of a fire and split open with a stone or the poll end of a hatchet, was another treat. Buffalo meat could be cooked slowly on a stick grid several feet above a smoky low fire to make buffalo jerk, which would last a long time without going bad. Boone must have carried buffalo jerk and parched corn or johnnycake (bread made from baking cornmeal mush) as lightweight foods on his travels.[27]

A killed buffalo could provide much more than meat. The wool could be shorn, washed, carded, and spun. The hide could make a robe or a blanket, or it could be tanned and made into tough, long-lasting shoe leather or else cut and twisted into tugs. Buffalo horns made fine powder horns or spoons or buttons, once the smelly cores were boiled out of the horns.[28] All in all, as a traveler in 1780 noted, "this Animal is of the greatest service" to the Americans in Kentucky: "They made fiddle strings of the Sinues of the spine of the buffalo and sewed their mockasins with them being very strong and when dried very easily divided into Small fibers . . . of the horns they make Combs etc. the flesh is their common food, the Skins tanned makes a good leather but a little spongier than some Cattle, the hair on the skin in May, June and July is short smooth and fine, in the winter the coat thickens turns wooly and Feby is at the best these they spin into yarn and work it into coarse clothes like wool."[29]

There really was not any downside to buffalo, but their size and toughness presented challenges. As Daniel Bryan put it, "Two men couldn't turn a big bull buffalo, if he had fallen on his side."[30] The temptation was just to take the hump and the tongue and leave the rest of the dead beast for scavengers, but the carcass could be gutted, split, and draped over a horse to be carried to camp for butchering. Buffalo were also hard to kill, if you didn't know where to shoot them. Shooting at their massive foreheads had little effect. One hunter in the Kentucky bluegrass in 1779 fired at a buffalo from ten steps away and hit it just above the eyes and between the horns. The ball bounced off, flat as a halfpenny. The hunter retrieved the flattened ball, chewed the lead into a round shape, loaded it back into his rifle, fired again, hit the buffalo frontally, and had to run away when the buffalo charged him.[31] In 1775 some travelers on the Ohio River seized a swimming buffalo by the tail and were towed by it for a half-hour. They "shot him eight times, let him get ashore and he ran away."[32] In the famously hard winter of 1779–80, Daniel Trabue, a Harrodsburg settler, shot and felled a buffalo bull not far from the settlement. Realizing he had shot the buffalo too high, Trabue told the men who were with him to shoot it again. A young Irishman said he would kill the animal with his tomahawk and began striking it on the forehead. Trabue described what happened next:

> I told him it would not Do, he could not hurt him, the wool and mud and skin and skull was all so thick it would not Do. But he kept up his licks, a nocking a way.
>
> The buffelo Jumped up. The man run, the buffelo after him. It was opin woods, no bushes, and the way this young Irishman ran was rather Descending ground and every Jump he cried out, "O lard! O lard! O lard! O lard!"
>
> The buffelo was close to his heels. The man Jum[p]ed behind a beech tree. The bufflo fell Down, his head against the tree, the tuck-eyho boys [the eastern Virginians traveling with Trabue] laughing, "Ha! Ha! Ha!"
>
> One of them went up and shot the buffelo again and killed him. The Irishmain exclaimed against them, saying this was no laughing Matter but that these boys . . . was such fools they would laugh at it if the buffelo had killed him.
>
> The young men kept mimicking him: "O lard! O lard!" The Irishman said "he would go no further with such fools," and split off from the group in a huff, taking with him a load of meat from the (finally) dead buffalo.[33]

Beaver and otter were valued for their furs, which became fuller, oilier, and more precious in the winter months, when deerskins were less valuable.

Boone trapped both animals, in Kentucky and, in later life, in Missouri. Beaver traps were set in streams within six feet of the shore, in only a few inches of water but at a place where the bank dropped off sharply. The trap was on a chain fastened to a stake in the ground. The preferred bait was beaver musk, or castor, extracted from the scent glands of a dead beaver and rubbed on the upper end of a pole stuck into the ground at the water's edge, in front of the trap. A swimming beaver that smelled the musk would swim toward it and put its forepaws down, and the trap would spring and close on a forepaw. The beaver would swim toward the deeper water, and the weight of the trap would usually pull the beaver under, drowning it. Sometimes the beaver would go back to shore and rub its caught forepaw against the trap or else gnaw on it until the skin and flesh could be severed and the beaver could escape. In the absence of musk, hunters sometimes would scent the stake with sassafras or spicebush root.[34] Otter traps would be set—either unbaited or baited with a fish or mussel on a stick in front of the trap—where an otter slide led into a stream. Otter were rarer than beaver and less likely to wring their feet off in a trap.[35] Beaver skins were stretched and dried on hoops, often made of grapevine. Otter skins were dried on a bow or drying board worked into the skin. A dried beaver skin might weigh a pound and a quarter, an otter skin a pound. A horse could pack close to two hundred beaver or otter skins, which were worth more than deerskins. A beaver skin was worth about $2.50, two and a half times the value of a deerskin. Otter skins were worth from $3 to $5 each.[36]

Boone hunted turkeys as food, not to sell, and he also occasionally killed panthers and wolves.[37] Panther skin was not readily marketable but had ceremonial value. When Boone and other Boonesborough leaders parlayed with their Indian besiegers during the siege of Boonesborough in 1778, the Indians spread a panther skin on a log for the negotiators to sit on.[38] Nor was there a ready market for wolf skins, though Boone killed several wolves. Once when Boone was hunting alone, a wolf snatched up his hat and ran off with it. Boone shot the wolf and retrieved his hat.[39] In 1775, after the Indians attacked Boone and his axemen as they blazed the road to lead settlers into Kentucky, a rabid wolf three times came into Boone's camp at night seeking to bite one particular member of the group, a man named James Nall. On the third try the wolf bit Nall on the forehead, and the others there killed the wolf. The forehead wound soon healed, but that autumn Nall had a hydrophobic fit and was tied up so he could not bite others. He died during his next fit.[40]

Once Boone or other hunters killed game and prepared their pelts, the pelts had to be taken to market. That was no easy task, before the Louisiana Purchase, if the hunting had been done west of the Appalachians. Most roads were rough paths or buffalo traces. The Ohio ran the wrong way to take goods easily by water to the east. Rowing or hauling boats upstream was hard and slow work, though some freight was carried upstream, and many pelts were traded at Fort Pitt.[41] A hunter could instead take the long trip downstream down the Ohio and, outside of the British colonies, down the Mississippi to St. Louis and New Orleans, in Spanish (later French) Louisiana. But would a hunter from the British colonies be welcome there? Access by trans-Allegheny traders to New Orleans, which became a critical question after the Revolution and before the Louisiana Purchase, was already a central issue for the long hunters in Kentucky. Even if a Kentucky hunter were permitted to trade in New Orleans, getting back to the British settlements was a challenge, as Boone knew from his own family's experience. Benjamin Cutbirth, who married one of Boone's nieces, joined other long hunters in Tennessee around 1767, then took his pelts down to New Orleans; on the way back to Carolina, traveling by foot, he was robbed by Choctaws.[42] Going back by water, up the Mississippi, against the current, before there were steamboats, was arduous and dangerous.[43] For all these reasons, until Boone moved out to Missouri, he typically took his pelts on horseback down through the Cumberland Gap and back to the settlements in North Carolina or Virginia for sale or else sold them to traders going to the settlements aboard pack trains or upstream by boat.

The long hunter's life in Boone's Kentucky was inherently transient. There was an inexorable dynamic to market hunting and the fur trade—one that pushed the hunters ever farther westward and that ultimately destroyed hunting as a significant factor in the American economy. The simple fact was that Boone and the other market hunters killed far more game animals each year than were born in the wild, and fewer and fewer of these animals would be born each year as the number of adults shrank and as encroaching settlements destroyed the animals' habitat. The yield from hunting was not sustainable.

Boone was able to put game on the table when he started hunting in Pennsylvania. When his family moved south and west to North Carolina's Yadkin Valley, there were plenty of deer and bears to shoot, though no buffalo. When Boone went on his first long hunt in 1750, he went farther afield to find quantities of deer—up to the high piedmont near the Virginia–North Carolina border. Boone was able to kill hundreds of deer when he entered Kentucky starting in 1769—and bears and buffalo too. But he and other long hunters had to move steadily farther and farther into the wilderness to find large amounts of game. One hunter in Kentucky moved his family thirty-four times in thirty-two years so that he could "follow the gaim to keep in the best hunting ground."[44] Boone moved just as often.

Boone saw herds of hundreds of buffalo when he arrived in Kentucky as well as buffalo traces—paths trod by buffalo—as big as a public road. The great buffalo trace between the Lower Blue Licks and Crab Orchard was "worn down often a foot or more by travel of the buffalos," and the buffalo road at the Blue Licks was reported to be "40 yards wide, and that for a good distance."[45] By the time Boone left for Missouri in 1799, buffalo were already scarce in Kentucky. By 1800 none, or only scattered survivors, were to be found in the state or, for that matter, anywhere in the United States east of the Mississippi.[46]

In Missouri there was enough game for eating near where Boone lived. One relative said that Boone "could sit in the door of his cabin, and lay in a winter's supply of meat for his family without hunting."[47] But Boone told a visitor in 1805: "Here are turkies and deer, but whare is the elk and buffalows? Oh, they have left for the west."[48] By the end of the nineteenth century the mighty herds of buffalo of the Plains had been reduced to near-extinction. In a single century, between 1800 and 1900, the North American bison population plummeted from an estimated thirty million to less than a thousand.[49]

This destruction of game was not brought about solely by profligacy on the part of the white hunters, destroying what would have been sustainable under ecologically sound Indian harvesting of game. Rifle-bearing whites undoubtedly engaged in prodigious waste. Even in Boone's day, huge buffalo were sometimes killed just for their tongues, or whole herds were killed just for the sport of it. As one Kentucky settler put it: "They did destroy and waste them then—at a mighty rate. If one wasn't young and fat, it was left, and they went on and killed another."[50] According to another settler: "Many a buffalo was killed by the whites, and only a little of the hump taken out, or a thigh bone for the marrow, . . . Many a man killed a buffalo, just for the sake of saying so." In contrast, "Indians never shot them but when they wanted them."[51] But Indians contributed to the unsustainable slaughter of the game, in large part because peltry gave them a commodity with which to buy from the whites trade goods, on which they were becoming increasingly dependent.

Wars were fought among tribes, and tribes were driven out of their traditional hunting grounds by other tribes, for control of beaver grounds. In that manner the Iroquois Confederacy in the mid-seventeenth century drove Shawnees and other Algonquian tribes out of Kentucky and in the Carolinas fought and pushed back Catawbas, Cherokees, and Creeks, in what were known as the "Beaver Wars."[52] Indians wiped out beaver populations in order to get skins to trade with the whites for guns and other trade goods. As one Indian told a Jesuit priest, "The Beaver does everything perfectly well, it makes kettles, hatchets, swords, knives, bread; in short, it makes everything." Of necessity, as beaver in the East were killed off, beaver trapping and trading moved progressively farther westward.[53]

Indians also killed and skinned deer in quantities that rivaled what white hunters did. The Moravian missionary David Zeisberger, who worked with the Delawares of western Pennsylvania and eastern Ohio, who had become "praying Indians," estimated that a single Delaware might shoot 150 deer a year, a rate at which "it can easily be appreciated that game must decrease," and also noted that "Delawares use no other than rifle-barreled guns."[54] Indians had been trading deerskins to the whites for trade goods, particularly in the South and Southeast, since the trade began in earnest in Spanish Florida in the sixteenth century. Trade expanded as more and more Indians acquired guns.[55] Market hunting by Indians in the eighteenth century, coupled with hunting by whites, caused deer populations to plunge and Indian groups to poach on each other's hunting grounds to find deer to skin.[56] By 1765 a Creek chief would argue that the British should lower the prices for their trade goods because the Creek hunters had to go much farther than they once did to get deerskins and even then could not supply their wants in trade.[57] In 1807 an Ottawa visionary named Le Maigauis, or the Trout, conveyed a message from the Great Spirit to the Indians around Michilimackinac: "You complain that the animals of the Forest are few and scattered. How should it be otherwise? You destroy them yourselves for their Skins only and leave their bodies to rot or give the best pieces to the Whites. I am displeased when I see this, and take them back to the Earth that they may not come to you again. You must kill no more animals than are necessary to feed and cloathe you." At about the same time, the Shawnee Tenkswatawa, known as The Prophet, was preaching a similar vision, condemning the killing of game for skins.[58]

Were the Indians less profligate in hunting buffalo than they were in hunting deer? When Boone and others in 1776 were pursuing Indians who had seized Boone's daughter and two other teenage girls near Boonesborough, they found a buffalo killed by the Indians, with only the hump cut out for eating.[59] That may have been an isolated instance, caused by the Indians' need to act quickly in light of the likelihood that they were being pursued by the whites. Out on the Plains, where whole tribes had become dependent on buffalo, Indians were taught not to kill more of the animals than they could skin and pack, but there was evidence during Boone's lifetime that Indians "when hunting take but the fattest and cut part of an animal," leaving the rest to rot, or cut out only the buffalo tongues, although often all of the meat was cut off to dry into jerky.[60] But even if the Indians generally used more of a killed buffalo than did the white hunters, once they adopted the horse and the rifle, they were already, in Boone's time, becoming able to kill large numbers of buffalo.[61]

Indians thus helped to bring about the crash in the population of commercially valuable wild animals, after they had access to more efficient ways of killing than using bows and arrows and moving on foot, and had commercial reasons to hunt more than they needed for food, clothing, and shelter.[62] The spread of farming and fencing and the increase in human population also transformed the environment in ways that helped to cause the population of game animals to plummet. Other contributing factors, in the case of buffalo, were competition with domestic cattle for pasture, domestic cattle diseases such as anthrax and brucellosis, and droughts and blizzards. But the sheer killing ability of market hunters such as Boone, left unchecked, by itself was enough to decimate animal populations to an extent that would drive the hunters farther and farther west in search of game.

The hunting that Boone and the other long hunters did so well, and that Boone clearly relished, could not be sustained. The long hunters' skill and firepower carried with them the seeds of the destruction of the hunters' way of life.

6

BOONE'S FIRST HUNTS IN KENTUCKY

BOONE DID NOT GO TO HUNT IN KENTUCKY TO FULFILL A LIFELONG objective of opening up new territory for white settlement. Although his hunting and trail blazing doubtless played a key role in opening up Kentucky to white settlement, it would be after-the-fact and ideological history to think that he went into Kentucky for that purpose. Boone wanted to go to Kentucky because he had heard from John Findley and others that the land was rich and the wild game plentiful. He enjoyed hunting, he made his living hunting, and like most American settlers, he was interested in getting good land cheap.

Game abounded in Kentucky. Boone may have heard about the amount of game killed by Dr. Thomas Walker and his group, who in 1750 were the first British colonists to go up through the Cumberland Gap into Kentucky from the south. A few earlier colonists had been taken across the gap as captives of the Shawnees or the Cherokees before Walker's trip, but they did not write about what they saw.[1] Walker did. Walker was a physician, merchant, surveyor, and landowner in Albemarle County, Virginia. In 1748 he had explored the Holston River in northeastern Tennessee with Col. James Patton, the first British settler to apply to Virginia for grants of trans-Appalachian land—the Patton who was to be killed by the Indians at Draper's Meadow seven years later. In 1749 Walker was engaged by the Loyal Company, to which the Virginia Council had awarded 800,000 acres west of the Appalachians, to "go to the Westward to discover a proper place for a Settlement."[2] The company set off on March 6, 1750, from Dr. Walker's home in Virginia, went west and south on the Holston River into northern North Carolina, crossed the Clinch and the Powell rivers, and then turned north up through a majestic gap that Dr. Walker called the "Cumberland Gap," in honor of the duke of Cumberland, who had defeated Bonnie Prince Charlie and the rebellious Scots at the Battle of Culloden in 1746. Walker and his men continued into the center of what is now eastern Kentucky. Instead of following an Indian trail northward, which would have led to the rich bluegrass country, Walker followed the Cumberland River toward the west and was discouraged by the thickness of the canebrake and the laurel thickets and by the lack of fodder for the horses. His party turned back, returning to Walker's home in Virginia on July 13. Walker noted in his journal for that day: "We killed in the Journey 13 Buffaloes, 6 Elks, 53 Bears, 20 Deer, 4 Wild Geese, about 150 Turkeys, besides small Game. We might have killed three times as much meat, if we had wanted it."[3] A bag of that size in four months—for men whose objective was to explore, not to hunt—would have sounded temptingly plentiful to a hunter like Boone.

Boone did not go to Kentucky directly after he rejoined Rebecca in 1762. He moved with her and his children back to the Yadkin, to a farm on Sugartree Creek that probably was part of the land owned by Rebecca's father. With the end of the French and Indian War in 1763 and the Indian attacks in 1763–64, settlers who had fled east came back to the Yadkin, and new settlers arrived. By 1765 there were four times as many people on the forks of the Yadkin as there had been when the Boones moved there in 1750.[4] As a result, it was harder for Boone to find much game around his place, and he ranged farther, frequently hunting in the Great Smoky Mountains of western North Carolina. On some of Boone's hunts up into the mountains, he took with him his young son James, his first child, who had been born in 1757, to teach him the business of hunting. Boone remembered hunting with James on snowy winter nights and "hugging him up to him" to try to keep him warm.[5]

Boone's debts mounted as he bought hunting provisions and as the game dwindled. A lawyer remembered him as having had "more suits entered against him for debt than any other man of his day, chiefly small debts of five pounds and under, contracted for powder and shot."[6] In 1764 the Rowan County Court entered a judgment against Boone for the considerable amount of fifty pounds on account of the claims of one of his creditors.[7] In the same year Boone and Rebecca sold their property on Bear Creek feeding into the Yadkin. Rebecca made her mark with an X on the bill of sale.[8] The Bryans were richer than the Boones, but Rebecca Bryan Boone was substantially less literate than Daniel Boone.

If the flood of settlers that followed the end of the French and Indian

War made hunting harder for Boone, the peace also brought a new opportunity in Florida that Boone was quick to explore. In the war the British had ultimately defeated the French in North America—Canada was taken, and the French had abandoned Fort Duquesne. In the Treaty of Paris in 1763 the French acknowledged that the British had won North America east of the Mississippi, other than New Orleans. In addition, Spain also ceded the Floridas to Britain, getting back Havana in exchange, and France ceded Louisiana west of the Mississippi to Spain. In all, in the words of Francis Parkman, "half a continent . . . changed hands at the scratch of a pen."[9] Britain divided the Floridas into two new provinces: East Florida, consisting of most of what is now the state of Florida except the western panhandle, governed from St. Augustine; and West Florida, consisting of most of Florida's western panhandle, the southern half of what is now Alabama, Mississippi, and Louisiana east of the Mississippi River, governed from Pensacola. West Florida's governor, anxious to make the new province a British settlement, issued a proclamation offering one hundred acres for free to any Protestant who would settle the land.[10]

This must have sounded like an attractive land opportunity to Boone, particularly because the British government had recently limited westward expansion by its Proclamation of October 1763, which barred warrants of survey or the issuance of land patents beyond the Appalachians. The ban was intended to give the British government a rest from the high cost of fighting Indians, which had contributed to a huge jump in Britain's national debt during the Seven Years' War.[11] That cost continued to mount after the Treaty of Paris well into 1764, as the Ohio Valley Indians and the Indians around Detroit, dismayed by France's cession of eastern America to Britain and inspired by the Ottawa leader Pontiac, attacked Detroit, Fort Pitt, and other British forts as well as settlements in western Pennsylvania and Virginia, until British troops advanced into the Ohio Valley and both sides reached an exhausted peace based in part on recognition of the Ohio River as a boundary beyond which British settlement would not extend.[12] The ban on settlement in the Proclamation of 1763 paralleled Pennsylvania's 1758 renunciation, in the Treaty of Easton, of its claims on lands west of the mountains, a move made to induce the Indians to stop backing the French.

The West Florida proclamation must have seemed to Boone a tempting exception to the ban on western settlement. Boone and his younger brother Squire—named for their father, who died in January 1765—heard about the proclamation from friends from Virginia who stopped by Boone's farm that fall on their way to look at the free land being offered in Florida. The price sounded right, and the land was little settled, which offered hope both of game and of appreciating land value. Another draw to trans-Allegheny backwoodsmen like Boone, having had no ready access to coastal markets, must have been Pensacola's location on the Gulf Coast.[13] Boone and his brother Squire, along with Boone's brother-in-law John Stewart, joined their Virginian friends on their trip to Florida in the autumn of 1765.[14] It was a trip of many hundreds of miles, but Boone promised Rebecca that he would return in time for her dinner on Christmas Day.

The Boones and their friends set off to backcountry South Carolina, then to Savannah and St. Augustine, and west across Florida to Pensacola. Not much is known about the trip. Boone's son Nathan said that the party paid most of their expenses in the settlements from deerskins and from the gambling winnings of a Virginian in their party named Slaughter, who "was fond of gambling and won money going and coming back from Florida."[15] One wonders whether Slaughter was an honest gambler. Boone himself was less lucky. In the earliest surviving manuscript in Boone's hand, an accounting of expenses that exemplified Boone's lifelong phonetic approach to spelling, he recorded a debit of three pounds "to one watsh plade away at dise."[16]

While the taverns and the gambling along the way may have been diverting, Boone and his traveling companions were unimpressed by what they found in Florida. The land was sandy and barren, the flies intense, and the only game they saw was deer and a few birds. The swamps were dismaying. Boone and the others came close to starving before they stumbled on a group of Seminole Indians who fed them venison and honey after Squire Boone gave a small shaving mirror to a young Seminole girl.[17]

Despite the disheartening conditions he found in Florida, Boone, according to Nathan, purchased a house lot in Pensacola and wanted to move there.[18] Why? Pensacola at that time cannot have been a prepossessing place. The settlement was small, the fort dilapidated. Not long after Boone was in Pensacola, an English captain described to the British commander-in-chief in America the "poor Huts" in the fort and the poor condition of the men in them: "Their Barracks are covered with Bark on the Sides and Roof, which naturely Shrivels in a short time in the heat of the Sun. . . . The Firmament appeared thro' the Top and on all sides, The Men walking About like Ghosts on a damp Sandy Floor, that is near a Foot under the Level." Nothing kept out the vicious mosquitoes.[19] But for all its flaws Pensacola had much to offer to Boone. Being on the Gulf Coast, it was accessible to European markets for exporting pelts and importing supplies. The Creeks, Choctaws, and Chickasaws traded there. The backcountry was open for hunting and settlement. Florida was far from Boone's creditors in North Carolina. Moreover, Boone never stayed in one place for very long.

Boone made it back to the Yadkin by Christmas 1765. He deliberately delayed a bit at the end so he could walk into his cabin at noon on Christmas and take his place at the dinner table on that day, as he had promised Rebecca.[20] Boone told Rebecca that he had bought a lot in Pensacola and wanted to move there. She had already moved many times in the nine years since they were married, and her family and friends were in North Carolina and Virginia. Rebecca declined the proposed new move to a place more than seven hundred miles away, and Boone abandoned the lot in Florida and went back to hunting in North Carolina.[21] Although Boone did not move to Florida, he did move his family three times in the next two years, each time farther up the Yadkin, farther away from the settlements and from creditors and closer to where Boone liked to hunt, high in the Blue Ridge. Moving upriver with him were members of his family and of Rebecca's family, including Boone's brother Ned (who had married Rebecca's sister Martha), Boone's brother Squire, and Boone's youngest sister, Hannah, and her husband, John Stewart.[22]

Boone evidently kept thinking about Kentucky and the rich hunting that was said to be there. In the fall of 1767 Boone and William Hill, who had been with him on the trip to Florida, went west in search of Kentucky, crossing the mountains with the intention of reaching the Ohio River. They reached the headwaters of the Big Sandy River in what is now the easternmost part of Kentucky and continued northward toward the Ohio River about a hundred miles but then, according to Nathan Boone, "ware Ketched in a Snow Storm and had to Remain the Winter." The country was hilly, scrubby, and uninviting, so the two went back to the Yadkin in the spring, not greatly impressed by what they had seen of Kentucky. It was not all bad, however. Boone and Hill had come across a lick near the present town of Prestonburg and had seen buffalo and other game lured to the lick by its saltiness. Boone was able to kill his first buffalo and to dine on its tasty hump.[23]

Late in 1768 John Findley, who had told Boone about the wonders of Kentucky when both of them were with Braddock's army in 1755, showed up unexpectedly on Boone's doorstep on the upper Yadkin. Perhaps Findley had been looking for Boone, who was already becoming known as a talented backwoodsman; perhaps Findley, by now an itinerant peddler working the backcountry, simply chanced on Boone as he traded from cabin to cabin. In any event Findley and Boone once again fell to talking about Kentucky, and Findley again described the richness of the game and the endless skins that had been brought to the trading station he had run at the Shawnee settlement Eskippakithiki not far from the Kentucky River, which ran north into the Ohio River. The settlement with the long Shawnee name may have given Kentucky its name, indirectly: the Iroquois called the town "Kanta-ke," an Iroquois word for "fields" or "meadowland," because the settlement was surrounded by hundreds of acres of cornfields.[24] But no one is quite sure where the word *Kentucky* comes from. Boone's biographers Filson and Draper thought it was a Shawnee word meaning something like "dark and bloody ground." Col. John Johnston, a longtime Indian agent among the Shawnees, thought it was Shawnee for "at the head of a river."[25]

As an Indian trader before the French and Indian War, Findley had traveled to Eskippakithiki by water, coming down the Ohio River and up the Kentucky River, and had never gone by land between North Carolina and Kentucky. Nevertheless, when Boone described the difficulties he and Hill had encountered crossing the mountains and heading north into the headwaters of the Big Sandy, Findley said that there had to be a better way across the mountains, probably to the west of where Boone and Hill had been, because the Cherokees regularly came north to make war against the northern Indians.[26] While Findley could not show Boone where the trail crossed the mountains south of Kentucky, not having been there, once they were in central Kentucky, he would be able to show Boone where to find salt licks, grazing grounds, and the Red and Kentucky rivers leading up to the Ohio.

The time was right for Boone to try again to find Kentucky's hunting grounds. Game was getting scarcer on the Yadkin, and Boone's creditors were pressing him. It was also more likely that Boone would be able to lay claim to land in Kentucky. It was true that the Proclamation of 1763 barred surveying and settling land west of the Appalachians, but the colonists were hopeful that the Proclamation was a temporary moratorium, not a permanent bar, and the British, their finances strained by the cost of the war with France, had done little to police the ban on trans-mountain settlement. Moreover, in November 1768, under the Treaty of Fort Stanwix, the Iroquois

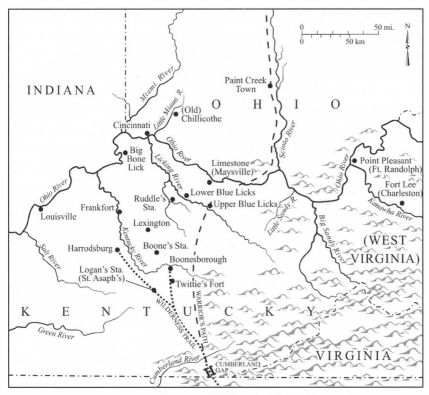

Boone's Kentucky and Its Neighbors
Map by Mary Lee Eggart

ceded to the British their claims to lands between the Ohio River and the Tennessee River. Few Iroquois lived in these lands, but the Iroquois claimed them by right of conquest and signed the treaty not only as the confederate nations of the Iroquois but also on behalf of their "Dependent Tribes," the Shawnees, Delawares, and Mingos of Ohio.[27] Among Indian tribes that left only the Cherokees, living to the south of Kentucky, with some claims to much of Kentucky.

The Shawnees had been largely driven out of the area by the Iroquois. The Shawnees no doubt still viewed Kentucky as theirs, and there were still many Shawnees, perhaps three thousand of them, despite the devastating effect of European diseases and of wars with the Iroquois and the Cherokees. Although the Iroquois claimed the land was theirs to cede by right of their earlier defeat of the Shawnees, the Shawnees, as the British general Thomas Gage recognized, "were exasperated to a great Degree" because the Iroquois "have Sold the Lands as Lords of the Soil, kept all the Presents and Money arising from the Sale, to their own use, and . . . the White People are expected in Consequence of it, to Settle on their [the Shawnees'] hunting Grounds."[28] After the British recaptured Fort Duquesne in 1758, many Shawnees moved their villages north of the Ohio River in what is now Ohio, but some still maintained at least winter hunting camps south of the river in Kentucky.[29] The Shawnees, after the Treaty of Fort Stanwix, became the spearhead of Indian resistance to white expansion into the Ohio Valley.[30]

The 1763 proclamation and the Shawnees were thus both substantial problems for whites who wanted to settle in Kentucky. Land speculators, however, tend to be optimistic about possible opportunities. Kentucky in 1768 must have looked to Boone to be comparatively devoid of claimants. Squatters might be able to get a leg up on claiming land in the Kentucky part of Virginia under that colony's law permitting a Virginian to settle up to five hundred acres of uninhabited land for himself.[31] As the British Board of Trade reported to the Privy Council in 1771, the colonies had always given preference to actual settlement and improvement, whether legal or not, when it came to granting land titles.[32]

Boone and Findley decided to look for the warrior's trail across the Cumberland Mountains and up into Kentucky.[33] They waited until early May 1769, after Boone and the other Yadkin men who went with them had finished the spring planting on their farms. The group consisted of Boone, Findley, Boone's brother Squire, Boone's brother-in-law John Stewart, and three neighbors from the Upper Yadkin—Joseph Holder, James Mooney, and William Cooley—who were to act as camp keepers, preparing and packing the skins. Among them they probably had some ten or fifteen horses to carry their gear—shot, powder, flints, kettles, traps, blankets, and the like—as well as the packed skins.[34]

Fighting miserable weather, the party headed west in northern North Carolina, crossing the Holston, Clinch, and Powell rivers, and came to the Cumberland Gap, which led at an elevation of some sixteen hundred feet through towering cliffs. Boone, seeing signs that many had traveled on the path through the pass, realized he was on the Warrior's Path. Going north through the gap, Boone and his group left North Carolina and entered what is now Kentucky. They crossed the Cumberland and Rockcastle rivers. Boone climbed the ridge to the north of the Rockcastle Valley and looked northward into the Kentucky River watershed. His party went on toward the northeast, to a creek that flows into the Kentucky River at what is now Irvine, set up a station camp (the creek to this day is called Station Camp Creek), and began going off in small groups to hunt and to bring the kill back to camp.

Findley went farther north to see if he could find what was left of Eskippakithiki, where his trading station had been. That was not hard because the Warrior's Path went close by their station camp and led past Eskippakithiki before continuing on northward to the Ohio River. Findley found the town burned, but the remnants of the stockade and gateposts were still recognizable. Findley showed them to Boone and Stewart. This evidence backed up what Findley had been telling Boone about Kentucky. It was also heartening that Findley now was where he had been before and so could orient Boone. While the rest of the men hunted, prepared skins, and kept camp, Boone and Findley explored farther north along the Kentucky River and the Elkhorn.

The country was already rich in bluegrass, even though that grass was probably not native to America but may have come into the region when Findley and other traders brought in trade goods packed in English hay.[35] Boone and some of his companions climbed a hill to look at the rich country to the north, and they liked what they saw. In his early biography John Filson has Boone say, "On the seventh day of June, we . . . from the top of an eminence, saw with pleasure the beautiful level of Kentucke."[36] Kentuckians to this day celebrate June 7, the date of this viewing, as Boone Day.

For six months Boone's group, as Boone put it, "practiced hunting with great success."[37] They prepared and packed hundreds of dollars' worth of deerskins. Boone may also have been scouting out the most desirable lands for possible future settlement, either for himself or for Col. Richard Henderson, the ambitious and grandiloquent North Carolinian who was later to organize a company to lay claim to almost all of Kentucky. It looked as if Boone and his companions would make good money on the long hunt into Kentucky, but that prospect was destroyed on December 22, 1769. On that day, as Boone put it in Filson's account: "John Stewart and I had a pleasing ramble, but fortune changed the scene in the close of it. . . . In the decline of the day, near Kentucke river, as we ascended the brow of a small hill, a number of Indians rushed out of a thick cane-brake, and made us prisoners. The time of our sorrow was now arrived."[38]

The Indians were Shawnees, led by a war chief known to the whites as Will Emery, or Captain Will. Having been on a fall hunt, the Shawnees were on their way back to their homes north of the Ohio River. They had recently taken some two thousand skins from a hunters' base camp on the Green River farther south and west in Kentucky. With raised tomahawks the Shawnees demanded to be taken to Boone's main camp. Boone led them first to small caches, making as much noise as possible in an attempt to alert his fellow hunters so they could hide most of their pelts. Unfortunately, when Boone finally led the Indians to the main camp, all of the skins were still there, and the other members of Boone's party were nowhere to be seen. The Indians took Boone and Stewart's long rifles and loaded the pelts—the fruits of some eight months of hunting—onto the white hunters' horses, which the Indians also took.[39]

Captain Will treated Boone and his companions with remarkable restraint, if we bear in mind that Boone's party was poaching on Indian land. "In the most friendly manner," as Boone later recalled it, the Shawnees provided Boone and Stewart with two pairs of moccasins apiece, a trade gun, and some powder and lead so that they could kill enough meat to survive on the journey back east across the mountains.[40] Captain Will also gave Boone and Stewart some firm parting advice: "Now, brothers, go home and stay there. Don't come here any more, for this is the Indians' hunting ground, and all the animals, skins, and furs are ours; and if you are so foolish as to venture here again, you may be sure the wasps and yellow jackets will sting you severely."[41]

After the Indians left, Findley and the three campkeepers returned to the station camp and decided, in light of the Indians' seizure of their goods and strong warning, to go back to the settlements. Boone asked them to stay a couple of days, to see if he and Stewart could retrieve some of the horses the Indians had taken. Boone and Stewart went after the Indians, overtook them in two days, and were able in the dark of night to make off with four or five horses and head back south toward their camp. The morning of the second day, however, Captain Will and a dozen mounted Shawnees caught up with Boone and Stewart and took them captive again. The Indians laughed with pleasure at their recapture of the horses and the two white men. They took a bell from a horse, tied it around Boone's neck, and made him prance around jingling it. "Steal horse, ha?" they said in English. Then they once again headed north toward the Ohio and their towns, taking Boone and Stewart with them. On the evening of the seventh day, only a day's journey from the big river, Boone and Stewart each grabbed a gun and ran into the thick cane while the Indians were making camp. The Indians could not find them before nightfall, did not go after them in the dark, and set off north for the Ohio in the morning.

Boone and Stewart, finding their station camp abandoned, headed south, meeting up with Findley and the campkeepers on the Rockcastle River. Boone and Stewart were pleased to find that the party had been joined by Squire Boone and another hunter, Alexander Neeley, who had come out from North Carolina with new supplies, traps, and ammunition.[42] Despite the Shawnees' warning about the stinging of the wasps and the yellowjackets, the two Boones, Stewart, and Neeley went northwest to continue their hunting. The campkeepers went back to North Carolina and never came back to Indian country. Findley went back to Pennsylvania, resumed trading, was robbed again by Indians, went west again in 1772, and disappeared without a trace.[43]

Boone, Stewart, Neeley, and Squire Boone were alone in Indian country. But the winter hunting was good. This time they had made their base camp at a place well away from the Warrior's Path, which had led Captain Will and his braves close to them before. The location of the new base camp, on the north bank of the Kentucky River not far from the mouth of the Red River, was rich in beaver and otter.[44] There was even an element of frontier literary culture in their hunting. The hunters went off by themselves or in twos— generally Boone with Stewart, Squire with Neeley—and came back to their base camp. Boone had a copy of *Gulliver's Travels*, which he read aloud to the others. One day, after Boone had been reading about Brobdingnab, the land of giants, and its capital, called Lorbrulgrud, or Pride of the Universe, Neeley came in and announced that "he had been that Day to Lulbegrud and had killed two Brobdernags in their Capital." Only with some effort were his companions able to figure out that Neeley had been hunting at a salt lick by a creek and had killed two buffalo. The men called the creek "Lulbegrud"—the name the creek still bears—which may have been as close as Neeley could come to pronouncing "Lorbrulgrud."[45]

Early in 1770 Stewart went to the south side of the Kentucky River to trap and hunt, while Boone worked the north side. They agreed to meet back at the base camp in a specified number of days, but Stewart did not show up. Boone crossed the river, found what was left of a recent fire, and saw Stewart's initials on the bark of a tree—but no Stewart. Had Stewart quit and run back to the settlements? Or had he decided to run away from his wife, Boone's youngest sister, Hannah? Boone thought it unlikely. Stewart had four children and was devoted to his wife. Boone once said "he never had a brother he thought more of than he did of John Stewart."[46] Five years later, when Boone and a team of axemen were blazing the Wilderness Road up through the Cumberland Gap to the Kentucky River, close to where Boonesborough was built, the axemen found human bones in a hollow tree, together with a powder horn that Boone would have recognized as Stewart's even if Stewart had not carved his name on it. Boone thought he could recognize Stewart's features from the skull. One of the arms had been broken, and discoloration from a lead ball was still visible on the bone. They saw no other sign of injury and did not find Stewart's rifle. Boone guessed that Stewart had been shot by Indians and had dropped his rifle as he sought to escape, perhaps because of his wounded arm.[47] Unable to hunt, he may have crawled into the hollow tree for some protection from the winter cold and froze or bled to death there.

Stewart's disappearance in 1770 was too much for Neeley, who went back to the settlements by himself. The next year Neeley, who had been hunting with another group of long hunters, became separated from his party and lost his gun. Half-crazed and starving, his only food was a stray Indian dog that he had managed to stab to death. Neeley was still carrying what was left of that dog, "alive with maggots," on his back when Boone and Squire, who were on the way back to North Carolina at the end of their long hunt, happened to find him in the woods. They fed Neeley and helped him back to the settlements. Later he moved with his family close to the Cumberland Gap and was killed by Indians near his house in the mid-1790s.[48]

Boone's group in Kentucky was getting smaller and smaller. In May 1770 Squire Boone left for North Carolina, carrying a full load of winter pelts to sell in the settlements. Until Squire's return with supplies in July 1770, Boone was completely by himself. So far as he knew, he was the only white man in Kentucky. Was he miserable? Evidently not. Boone could have gone back to the settlements with Squire but chose to stay in Kentucky, alone and with limited ammunition. He hunted and explored and moved his camp frequently, often sleeping in the canebrakes "to avoid the savages." In Filson's account Boone says: "I was happy in the midst of dangers and inconveniences. No populous city, with all the varieties of commerce and stately structures, could afford so much pleasure to my mind, as the beauties of nature I found here."[49] The florid language and the echoes of Rousseau certainly came from Filson, but there was other evidence that Boone loved being by himself in the woods. Sometime around 1770 a group of long hunters led by Caspar Mansker heard a strange sound in the wilderness of Kentucky. Mansker had his companions take cover, while he crept forward toward the noise. He found Daniel Boone, alone in the middle of a clearing, lying flat on his back on a deerskin and "singing at the top of his voice."[50]

Boone spent much of this time alone exploring the country. Filson's Boone was to say that "the diversity and beauties of nature I met with in this charming season, expelled every gloomy and vexatious thought."[51] Boone may well have been susceptible to the beauty of Kentucky. As a hunter, he must have loved the abundance of game. He may even have been taken by the beauty of living things that were not edible. Filson records among the birds of Kentucky, for example, "the ivory-bill woodcock, of a whitish colour with a white plume, [which] flies screaming exceeding sharp. It is asserted, that the bill of this bird is pure ivory, a circumstance very singular in the plumy tribe."[52] Boone may have told Filson about the ivory-billed wood-pecker. The birds were in Kentucky in Boone's day. A 1780 journal gave a vivid description of one shot not far from where Boonesborough was to be built, and a few decades later, John James Audubon, the celebrated painter of *The Birds of America*, painted his picture of two ivory-billed woodpeckers in Henderson, Kentucky, and wrote that people killed the ivory-billed wood-pecker "because it is a beautiful bird, and its rich scalp attached to the upper mandible forms an ornament for the war-dress of most of our Indians, or for the shot-pouch of our squatters and hunters, by all of whom the bird is killed merely for that purpose."[53]

Quite apart from aesthetic considerations, however, Boone through his solitary explorations was getting to know his way around Kentucky far better than any other white man. That knowledge was to prove valuable to him as a hunter and trapper, guide to settlers, scout, militia officer, surveyor, and land speculator—in all of the ways Boone, by leading settlers to Kentucky directly and by example, was to play a key part in the westward flood of settlement that transformed America. According to Boone's son Nathan, after Squire left, Boone discovered in his explorations several of Kentucky's principal salt licks by "following the well-beaten buffalo roads leading to them." He visited the Upper and Lower Blue Licks on the Licking River and saw thousands of buffalo at the licks. He went north to the Ohio River and followed its south-ern bank to the Falls of the Ohio, a place of obvious future commercial im-portance, because the falls were the only impediment to navigation on the

Ohio's long trip from Pittsburgh to the Mississippi. Unless and until a canal with locks was built on the site, freight would have to be handled and transshipped there. The south bank of the Falls was to become the site of the city of Louisville. Perhaps not surprisingly, Boone found near the lower end of the Falls of the Ohio, on the Kentucky side, the remnants of an old trading house.[54]

Boone turned back east, probably crossing the Kentucky River near what later became Frankfort. He tried to stay out of sight of Indians, but on the Kentucky River he came upon an Indian fishing, sitting on a fallen tree that was sticking out over the water. Boone later told his son Nathan, cryptically: "While I was looking at him he tumbled into the river and I saw no more of him." Nathan told Boone's biographer Draper, "It was understood from the way in which he spoke of it that he had shot and killed the Indian; yet he seemed not to care about alluding more particularly to it."[55] This is a strange story. Boone was not a random killer of Indians. If he was traveling by himself in Indian country, seeking to hide from the Indians, the noise of a shot could have given away his location. Other versions of the story, from other Boone relatives, suggest that Boone at the time had encountered Indian sign in other directions, and the fishing Indian had the bad fortune to be in the way of Boone's most promising escape route.[56]

Was Boone ever lost during his explorations? That was an obvious question and one he may have been asked often as his reputation grew. When Boone was eighty-five years old and living in Missouri, the young artist Chester Harding asked him one day, after Boone had described one of his long hunts, if he had ever gotten lost, having no compass. "No," he said, "I can't say as ever I was lost, but I was *bewildered* once for three days."[57]

After Squire rejoined Boone with new supplies in July 1770, the brothers went back to hunting. Not until March 1771 did they head back toward the settlements, their horses laden with pelts. They made it safely through the Cumberland Gap into Powell's Valley, when a group of six or eight Indians—accounts vary about whether they were Cherokees or northern Indians—showed up at the Boones' campfire. The Indians drank from Boone's flask, talked of hunting, and then proposed to swap their trade guns for the Boones' far better long rifles. When the Boones declined, the Indians, who outnumbered the Boones, took all of the Boones' furs and several of their horses. Once again, the Boones had lost the fruits of months of hunting and trapping.[58] Their only yield from a hunt of two long years was from the two loads of pelts Squire had been able to bring out of Kentucky before this second robbery.

Boone did not get back home to the upper Yadkin until May 1771. A story, perhaps apocryphal, captures just how long his hunt had been. When he got back to Beaver Creek, Boone found his family at a frolic at a neighbor's cabin. Boone's hair and beard were long and disheveled, and no one recognized him as he stood at the edge of the dancing. He went up to Rebecca on the dance floor and silently extended his hand for a dance. She declined. "You need not refuse," Boone cried, "for you have danced many a time with me." Recognizing his voice, Rebecca burst into tears and threw her arms around his neck. The neighbors, too, realized the hairy stranger was Boone; "the dancers now took a rest, while Boone related the story of his hardships and adventures in the romantic land of Kentucky, where he had encountered bears, Indians, and wild cats—and had seen a country wonderful in its beauty to behold."[59]

A dozen years later Boone told Filson—as recounted in Filson's florid words—that after his long trip to Kentucky he "returned home to my family with a determination to bring them as soon as possible to live in Kentucke, which I esteemed a second paradise, at the risk of my life and fortune."[60] Boone acted on this determination and would risk his life and ultimately make and lose a fortune in Kentucky.

7

BOONE BEGINS TO OPEN THE WILDERNESS
The First Attempt to Settle Kentucky

UPON HIS RETURN TO THE YADKIN, BOONE FOUND THAT MANY OF THE settlers from North Carolina and Virginia had moved farther west, into what is now Tennessee, along the upper reaches of rivers that ran into the upper Tennessee River—the Watauga, the Holston, and the Clinch. Boone and his family may have also moved to the Watauga River. In the fall and winter of 1771–72 Boone hunted bear along the Watauga. At one point he went as far west into Tennessee country as French Lick (which later became Nashville), where he met Frenchmen who were hunting buffalo at the licks.[1] In the winter of 1772–73 Boone was back in Kentucky, hunting along the Kentucky River with other North Carolinians, including not only his nephew-in-law and old hunting companion Benjamin Cutbirth but also Hugh McGary, a hotheaded young man whose rashness would contribute, ten years later, to the death of many Kentuckians—Boone's second son among them—at the Battle of the Blue Licks.

The hunting was good along the Kentucky River, but by the spring of 1773 Boone may have encountered signs of white surveyors—signs that portended more settlement, less game, and more fighting with Indians. The Iroquois in 1768, in the treaty of Fort Stanwix, had relinquished their rights to land between the Ohio and Tennessee Rivers, and by 1773 surveyors were beginning to come into Kentucky. In addition to the westward explorations on behalf of the Ohio Company, another company, in which Benjamin Franklin was a leading participant, was lobbying in London for the right to buy much of the lands ceded by the Iroquois, for a new province to be called Vandalia, and had sent surveyors into Kentucky.[2] Much of the surveying being done in Kentucky in 1773 was along the Ohio River, north of where Boone was hunting, but the McAfees from Virginia were looking for land along the Kentucky River, as was James Harrod of Pennsylvania, who was to found Harrodsburg in 1774, a year before the founding of Boonesborough.[3]

On the way back home in the spring of 1773, after the winter hunt in Kentucky, Boone went to Castle's Wood, Capt. William Russell's settlement at the head of the Clinch River in southwestern Virginia. Boone and Russell decided to organize a group of settlers to go into Kentucky, with Russell as the leader and Boone as the guide. It made sense that Russell be the leader, given Russell's greater position and social background. As grand a man as Lord Dunmore, the Scottish peer who in 1772 became the governor of Virginia, referred to Russell as "a gentleman of some distinction."[4] Russell, a prominent Virginian, had attended the College of William and Mary, married into a rich Tidewater family, served as a representative in the Virginia House of Burgesses, and was a substantial landowner. Boone, by contrast, had next to no formal education, moderate family connections, no political position, and at the time little, if any, land.

Boone went back to the upper Yadkin in April 1773 and started recruiting settlers for the Kentucky trip. Rebecca might not have been thrilled by the prospect of moving to Kentucky. For two years she had run the family farm in Boone's absence. Their eldest son, James, was now almost sixteen years old and was as tall as Boone. James and his brother Israel, fourteen, were big enough to do much of the heavy work around the farm. On May 23, 1773, Rebecca bore her eighth child, Jesse Bryan. Despite these reasons to want to stay on the Yadkin, Rebecca did not stop Daniel's planning of the trip. Unlike the proposed move to Florida, the move to Kentucky was not going to separate her from all of her family. Many of the Bryan men agreed to come along, traveling separately to meet Boone and Russell in Powell's Valley before going together up through the Cumberland Gap. Squire Boone and his family were also coming, as were Boone's niece and her husband, Benjamin Cutbirth, as well as several other neighboring families.

The Boones and the others from the upper Yadkin were at Castle's Wood by August 1773. Along the way they had been joined by others, including two of the best shots on the frontier, William Bush and Michael Stoner (the German immigrant George Michael Holsteiner). Perhaps forty in all, they set off for Kentucky on September 25.[5] The group did not travel quietly. There were no wagons. The trail into Kentucky was a narrow trace, wide enough only for horses riding single file. The horses were heavily laden. One Clinch River resident recalled: "They had prepared baskets made of fine hickory withe or splits of proper size and fastening two of them together with ropes they put a child in each basket and put [it] on a horse across a pack saddle. They had poultry with them which they carried in the same way." Cattle and hogs were driven. With the children crying, the cattle lowing, and the bells on the livestock clanging, "they made a terrible racket."[6]

The trip took longer than Boone had expected. Boone sent his son James, accompanied by two young brothers from North Carolina, John and Richard Mendinhall, back to Castle's Wood for more provisions. Russell had the extra supplies packed and reinforced the party with his seventeen-year-old son, Henry; two of his slaves, Charles and Adam; a hired man; and an experienced woodsman named Isaac Crabtree. The supply party headed back to the pack train, and Russell undertook to catch up as soon as possible.

On the night of October 9 the supply party camped on Wallen's Creek, in the southwestern corner of Virginia, on the eastern edge of the Powell Valley. They heard wolves howl, which scared the Mendinhall boys. Crabtree, a frontier veteran, told them that this was nothing: in Kentucky they would hear not only the howling of wolves but also buffalo bellowing from the treetops. The frontier humor calmed the party, and they went to sleep. They were being watched by a party of more than a dozen Delawares, two Cherokees, and two Shawnees. Perhaps the wolf calls the Mendinhall boys heard were made by Indians signaling to each other in the night. The Indians were apparently coming back from a trip south to discuss what to do about the whites spreading out west of the mountains. As Sir William Johnson, the British Indian superintendent, advised Lord Dartmouth, the secretary of state for the colonies, in the fall of 1773 the Shawnees were in a state of alarm over the large number of whites coming into the territory, "remote from the influence of Seats of Government" and many "with a general Prejudice against all Indians," particularly because "the young Indian Warriors or Hunters are too often inclined to retaliate."[7] An attack on the Russell/Boone supply party—like the 1755 attack on Colonel Patton at Draper's Meadow—must have seemed a good way to deter would-be settlers in Indian country.

At daybreak the Indians fired into the sleeping group. The Mendinhall brothers were killed in the first firing. Crabtree and Russell's hired man were wounded but were able to run away into the woods. Russell's slave Adam hid under some driftwood and saw what followed. Both James Boone and Henry Russell had been shot through the hips and could not move. While most of the Indians rounded up the horses, one or two Indians began slashing at the two wounded boys with their knives. Adam heard James Boone call to one of the Indians by name—Big Jim, a tall Indian who had often visited the Boone family and who was instantly recognizable by his high cheekbones, broad face, and distinctive chin. James Boone begged for his life, while Big Jim systematically tore the nails from the boy's fingers and toes. Soon Adam, watching from the driftwood, heard the boys beg to be killed. It was getting light, and the Indians by this time had packed the horses. The Indians tomahawked James Boone and Henry Russell to death and went off with the laden horses, driving the slave Charles with them. Not far from the camp the Indians caught and killed Russell's hired man. His bones were found twenty years later wedged between two rock ledges.[8] Charles was found some forty miles away, his skull split.

The killings were discovered the morning of the attack, soon after the Indians left, by a young man who had left Boone's camp before dawn to return to the settlements. Having been accused of pilfering, he had decided to quit the expedition, taking with him a stolen pack of deerskins. Coming on the bloody camp, he dropped the skins and hurried back to Boone's group with the news. Boone, expecting an attack, deployed most of his men behind trees and logs, but no Indians came. Squire Boone and a few others went to the supply party's camp, carrying two linen sheets Rebecca Boone had given them to wrap the dead. Captain Russell and others from Castle's Wood were already at the camp when Squire Boone's group arrived. They wrapped James Boone and Henry Russell in one sheet and the Mendinhall brothers in the other and buried them in a single large grave, piling logs on top to try to keep wolves from the bodies.

After Squire Boone and Captain Russell joined Daniel Boone at the advance party's camp, they and their men conferred on what to do next. Appalled by the killings and fearful of further Indian attacks, they overwhelmingly favored returning to the settlements. The group went back to Castle's Wood. Isaac Crabtree, though wounded by the Indians, managed to make it there, too, after a few days. Some days later Russell's slave Adam, who had been wandering in shock in the woods, came into Castle's Wood and described what he had seen and heard during the attack.

Boone and his family accepted an offer from Russell's associate Capt. David Gass to stay at a cabin on the Clinch over the winter. The other Carolinians went back to the settlements they had come from.[9] During the winter Boone hunted near the Clinch River. He also went by himself back to the ridge overlooking the Powell Valley to look at the boys' graves. Wolves had rolled the logs away and scratched down into the graves. Boone dug down with a handspike to get to the bodies of the boys and saw the blood still on their heads. He could readily distinguish his son James, who had fair hair, from Henry Russell, whose hair was black. Boone refilled the grave and built the logs back up, more securely than before, to keep out the wolves, but then a sudden violent storm came up. According to Boone's son Nathan, "The melancholy of [Boone's] feelings mingled with the howling of the storm and the gloominess of the place made him feel worse than ever in his life." Boone made a small fire a few hundred yards away and put his horse out on hobbles, but he could not sleep. Hearing Indians approaching in the night, he hid as the Indians came to the little fire. Boone retrieved his horse, stopped its bell from ringing, and got away in the darkness.[10]

The killings at Wallen's Creek attracted much attention, given Russell's prominence and Boone's growing reputation as a backwoodsman. The killings also spurred a cycle of violence begetting violence throughout the frontier, even though at the request of Virginia governor Lord Dunmore the Cherokees captured and killed the two Cherokees who had been involved in the attack.[11] In the spring of 1774 American settlers in the Watauga Valley organized a festival and horse race and invited Cherokees to attend. At the race Isaac Crabtree spotted some Cherokees, flew into a rage, and killed one, Cherokee Billy, who was related to a chief. Seeking to prevent a Cherokee uprising, Governor Dunmore and local magistrates announced rewards totaling £150 for Crabtree's capture. Dunmore was told that "it would be easier to find 200 Men to screen him from the Law, than ten to bring him to Justice."[12] Crabtree prudently moved to Kentucky, farther away from Virginia authorities.

In late April or early May 1774, about the same time as Crabtree's killing of Cherokee Billy, another act of baseless white violence against Indians took place—an act that Lord Dunmore, a man not known for his love of Indians, described as "marked with an extraordinary degree of Cruelty and Inhumanity."[13] A group of whites at Yellow Creek on the Ohio River fifty miles downstream from Pittsburgh, led by a man named Greathouse, plied a group of Mingos (Indians from different Iroquois tribes who had settled in the Ohio Valley) with liquor, induced the few Indians who remained sober to fire their rifles in a shooting match, and then, while the Indians' rifles were uncharged, killed and scalped all of them. The murdered Indians included the pregnant sister of the Mingo chief Tahgahjute, known to the whites as

Chief Logan. Greathouse's group tied the woman up by her wrists, slit open her belly with a tomahawk, and impaled her unborn child on a stake.[14] Hearing of these killings, Logan, who had previously urged friendship with the English, determined to seek revenge. Even before the Cherokee Billy and Yellow Creek killings, many white settlers, fearing imminent Indian attacks following up on the Wallen's Creek attack, had fled east with their families. One westerner wrote in March 1774 to Col. William Preston, the sheriff, surveyor, and militia colonel of Fincastle County (the westernmost county in Virginia, at that time including most of what became Kentucky), that families in the Clinch Valley were leaving "in such haste that they left all their stock, and the greatest part of their household furniture."[15]

Despite the Indian risk, in April 1774 Preston sent out a party of twenty-two men, led by John Floyd, to survey western lands on behalf of Fincastle County. The surveying trip itself increased the risk of Indian attack on whites living or hunting on the frontier. Hearing of the plans for the surveying expedition, the Shawnees, on March 8, 1774, complained to Alexander McKee, Sir William Johnson's deputy, that the king's orders forbade settlement west of the Great Kanawha River and that Shawnee hunting grounds were being overrun. They warned that young Shawnee warriors, if "they are disappointed in their hunting, and find the woods are covered with White People . . . are foolish enough to make reprisals."[16]

John Floyd was then only in his early twenties, but he was a brilliant and well-educated young man and an experienced surveyor. Born in the eastern Blue Ridge of Virginia, Floyd had taught school there before moving west to Botetourt County. When not yet twenty, he began teaching William Preston's children and acting as Preston's private secretary. Floyd was "upwards of six feet high, somewhat slender, straight as an Indian and almost as dark as one, . . . [with] brilliant black eyes and very straight black hair, presenting altogether a handsome appearance."[17] He may well have inherited his dark complexion from his mother's mother, whose father was said to have been a Catawba chief.[18] By 1772, thanks to Preston, Floyd was appointed deputy surveyor of Botetourt County. When Fincastle County was formed later that year, with Preston as its sheriff, Floyd became deputy sheriff of the county. In the fall of 1773 Preston sent Floyd out to survey lands in on the Holston River, not far from the Cumberland Gap, through which John Findley in 1769 had led Daniel Boone into the virgin hunting ground of Kentucky.

Young Floyd, in short, had several years of surveying experience by the spring of 1774, when Preston sent him out to Kentucky in charge of an expedition of Fincastle County surveyors. Early in that trip, Floyd's party, carrying out a promise Preston had made to George Washington, surveyed two thousand acres along the Kanawha River in what is now West Virginia, under land warrants that had been issued to Washington for his services as an officer in the French and Indian War.[19] Washington had decided to claim lands west of the mountains despite the bar in the 1763 proclamation, because, as he had put it in 1767 to another land speculator, "I can never look upon that proclamation in any other light (but this I say between ourselves) than as a temporary expedient to quiet the Minds of the Indians" that "must fall in a few years. . . . any Person therefore who neglects the present opportunity of hunting out good Lands & in some Measure Marking & distinguishing them for their own (in order to keep others from settling them) will never regain it."[20]

Floyd and his men continued farther west, in late May 1774 reaching the Falls of the Ohio. Near the Falls, at what was to become Louisville, they laid out thirty tracts for such leading Virginians as Preston, William Christian (colonel in the militia of Fincastle county, and brother-in-law of Patrick Henry), William Byrd (militia colonel and member of one of Virginia's first families), and Martha Washington's nephew Alexander Spottswood Dandridge.[21] Floyd also laid out two thousand-acre tracts for himself near the Beargrass Creek not far from the Falls.[22] In a period of ten days Floyd and his men surveyed over forty thousand acres, or more than sixty-two square miles, in and near the future Louisville.[23]

Floyd and his men began to hear rumors that war was likely. In late May they encountered on the Ohio River two Delaware Indians who had been sent down the river from Fort Pitt to warn Delawares who were hunting near Kentucky "to go home, as they expected a war between the white people & the Shawnese." The two Delawares on the river were so skittish they would not come near Floyd's group. One of Floyd's men noted in his journal: "This put our people into different opinions as to what to do. Some were for going down the river by way of the Mississippi[.] But Mr. Floyd and the rest of the surveyors were determined to do the business they came on, If not repulsed by a greater force than themselves."[24]

In June and July 1774 the Fincastle surveyors moved east to the bluegrass region of central Kentucky, surveying around what would become Frankfort and Lexington.[25] These surveys included one tract of a thousand acres for Floyd (close to a large spring) and one of the same size for Preston, both near what was to become Lexington, and tracts aggregating seven thousand acres for Patrick Henry.[26] The land was captivating. One of the surveyors entered in his journal for July 1: "All the land that we passed over today is like a Paradise it is so good & beautiful."[27]

As the Fincastle surveys progressed, it became more and more dangerous for whites to be in Kentucky, particularly after the killing of Logan's relatives at Yellow Creek and the ensuing Mingo raids on white settlers. In early June 1774 Preston received reports that "an Indian War is commenced, and the out Inhabitants are all Forting [or] fleeing in."[28] On June 10 Lord Dunmore started to mobilize British troops and American militia to defend the settlements and began to plan to invade the Shawnee lands north of the Ohio River and "destroy their Towns & magazines and distress them in every other way that is possible."[29] It may not be coincidental that Dunmore was personally interested in British title to lands in Kentucky, having an interest in a large tract of land there.[30] In early July, after Shawnees killed two whites from Harrodsburg, the settlers there abandoned the station and went back to the Clinch River settlements.[31] Pursuant to Lord Dunmore's instructions, Preston ordered rangers out and forts to be built.[32] Preston then sent out a circular letter to drum up recruits for the expedition to the Shawnee towns:

> We may Perhaps never have so fair an Opportunity of reducing our old Inveterate Enemies to Reason. . . . The House of Burgesses will without all Doubt enable his Lordship to reward every Vollunteer in a handsome manner, over and above his Pay; as the plunder of the County will be valuable, & it is said the Shawnese have a great Stock of Horses. . . . This useless People [the Shawnees] may now a[t] last be Oblidged to abandon their Count[r]y Theire Towns may be plundered & Burned, Their Cornfields Distroyed & they Distressed in such a manner as will prevent them from giving us any future Trouble.[33]

The imminence of what came to be known as Lord Dunmore's War put the Fincastle surveyors at great risk of their lives. Not knowing whether they were already aware of that risk, on June 20, 1774, Preston authorized Captain Russell to engage two "faithful woodmen" to find the Virginia surveyors in Kentucky and warn them. Russell chose Daniel Boone and his friend the German-American frontiersman Michael Stoner, who had been with Russell and Boone on the unsuccessful attempt to settle Kentucky the previous fall. Russell told Preston that Boone and Stoner were "two of the best Hands I could think of" and that "by the assiduity of these Men, if it is not too late, I hope the Gentlemen [the surveyors] will be apprised of the eminent Danger they are Daily in." In a later letter Russell wrote to Preston that if the surveyors were still alive, "it is indisputable but that Boone must find them."[34] Russell's letters testify to the esteem in which Boone was already held on the frontier—but they also suggest a class distinction: Russell was the militia captain, the leader of a frontier station, the college graduate; to Russell, Boone was an able "hand." It would be wrong to think that class distinctions did not exist on the frontier of colonial America.

The trip to find and warn the surveyors was dangerous. Stoner was to remember that whenever they stopped to eat or rest, he and Boone would sit back to back to avoid the possibility of Indians coming up from behind. They managed to avoid Indian attack, but Stoner at one point had to be nimble to avoid being gored by a buffalo he had startled at a lick.[35] Boone and Stoner went all the way to where the Kentucky River joins the Ohio and then followed the Ohio downstream to the Falls, only to find that Floyd's surveyors had already started back for the settlements. Boone and Stoner turned back themselves.[36] Floyd's group made it back safely to a station on the Clinch on August 9, 1774, after an exhausting trip, traveling twenty-five to thirty miles a day, not knowing the way, with only about fifteen rounds of powder among them and over mountains "so steep, that we were obliged to throw away all we had, except our Knit Leggins & Mockasons."[37] Another group of surveyors whom Preston had appointed were less fortunate. On July 27 Shawnees fired on them as they were paddling a dugout across the Kentucky River and killed two of them.

While Boone and Stoner were out in Kentucky looking for the Fincastle County surveyors, Shawnees had begun to raid settlers near Castle's Wood. The settlers along the Clinch gathered into the small forts they had built hurriedly and waited. Boone's family was at Moore's Fort, not far south of Castle's Wood. As at many of the little forts, discipline was lax. Rebecca Boone decided to do something to make it less so. One time when many of the men were outside of the fort playing ball and others who were not playing were lying around, all without their guns, Rebecca Boone and some other wives, along with Rebecca's oldest daughters, Susannah and Jemima, went out the other side of the fort with loaded rifles, fired a round of shots, and then ran back inside and locked both gates. The men sprinted back to the fort and ran around in terrified confusion when they discovered that the gates were bolted. Some men jumped into a pond. The women laughed at them, though the men did not think the joke was at all funny. Some of them threatened to have the women whipped, but that caused fistfights to break out among the men. Yet discipline did improve, especially after Boone came back and was placed in command of the fort.[38]

Boone and Stoner returned to the settlements on the Clinch River in late August 1774, having covered eight hundred miles in sixty-two days. Floyd appreciated the effort Boone had made to find him and his surveyors and warn them of the Indian danger. In a letter to Preston in August 1774 Floyd said he was thinking of appointing Boone to go with him on the expedition that Lord Dunmore was planning against the Shawnees, particularly because the local men were refusing to go and a local captain had told Floyd, "Boone has more interest [influence] than any man now disengaged." Floyd added: "& you know what Boone has done for me by your kind directions—for which reason I love the man."[39] Boone was recruited to lead a company joining the Virginia militia in Lord Dunmore's expedition but was recalled by orders from Captain Russell to organize the defense of the settlements along the Clinch against raids by Logan's Mingos and other Indians.[40] Floyd, in his capacity as a captain in the Fincastle militia, recruited troops and marched north and east to meet Col. William Christian, who was in charge of the Fincastle militia joining Dunmore's expedition.

It was not an easy time for the settlers or for Boone. Logan's warriors raided up and down the mountain ridges in western Pennsylvania, Virginia, North Carolina, and Tennessee, killing isolated settlers. Logan said of himself, "He knew that he had two souls, the one good and the other bad; when the good soul had the ascendant, he was kind and humane, and when the bad soul ruled, he was perfectly savage, and delighted in nothing but blood and carnage."[41] After the Yellow Creek killings of his family, Logan's blood and carnage soul was in the ascendancy. Logan and his band slaughtered the family of John Roberts in Tennessee not far from the Holston River and left as a calling card a war-club, to which was attached a note that Logan had made a white captive write in English in ink made out of gunpowder: "What did you kill my people on Yellow Creek for. [The white] People killed my kin at Conestoga a great while ago [this refers to the 1763 killing of Conestoga Indians by the Paxton mob in Pennsylvania], & I though[t nothing of that.] But you killed my kin again on Yellow Creek, and took m[y cousin prisoner] then I thought I must kill too; and I have been three time[s to war since but] the Indians is not Angry only myself."[42]

The settlers did not catch Logan's raiders, although Col. James Robertson told Preston "the men Seems Resolute for a Sculp or Two," and Robertson had offered "£5 for the first Indians hand that will be brought in to the fort."[43] Preston wrote on August 13, 1774, after describing the killing of several settlers in what is now Giles County in western Virginia: "Sundry other people have also been murdered along the frontier parts of the neighboring counties. The inhabitants of Fincastle, except those on Holston, are chiefly gathered into small forts, also great numbers in Botetourt; as Indians are frequently sighted, and their sign discovered in the interior parts of both counties. Such is the unhappy situation of the people, that they cannot attend their plantations, nor is it in the power of the scouts and parties on duty to investigate the inroads of the enemy, as they come in small parties, and travel among the mountains with so much caution."[44]

Soon after Boone's return from Kentucky, Mingos and Shawnees under Logan attacked settlements on the Clinch, including Boone's base at Moore's Fort. In late September a settler was shot a few hundred yards from the fort. Boone and others, running to help, saw a warrior rip off the settler's scalp before the Indians went off into the twilight. The Indians left a war club at the fort's spring as a calling card, as they had done at the site of the killing of the Roberts family.[45] A week later, at Blackmore's fort sixteen miles farther down the Clinch River, Indians shot and then tomahawked and scalped another settler, killing him within fifty-five steps of the fort.[46] Boone and others found tracks but did not catch up with the raiders. But thanks in part to Boone's work in the frontier settlements ("Mr. Boone is very diligent at Castle's woods, and keeps up good order," Maj. Arthur Campbell reported to Colonel Preston),[47] the killings were sporadic. The attacks were nevertheless unsettling. As Capt. Daniel Smith wrote to Preston, "The late invasions of Indians hath so much alarm'd the Inhabitants of this River that without more men come to their Assistance from other parts, some of the most timorous among us will remove to a place of Safety and when once the example is set I fear it will be followed by many."[48]

The settlers on the Clinch petitioned that Boone, who had been appointed a lieutenant and the commander of Moore's Fort, be made a captain and put in charge of all the defenses on the Clinch Valley, so he could act without awaiting orders from captains at the settlements along the Holston River, some distance away. The local officers endorsed the recommendation—though in ways that appeared to recognize Boone more for his backwoods talent than as traditional officer material. Once again, there is an element of class distinction, of Tidewater connections versus frontiersman, in the officers' letters. Capt. Daniel Smith told Colonel Preston that the petition to make Boone a captain "contains the sense of the majority of the inhabitants in this settlement. Boone is an excellent woodsman. If that only would qualify him for the Office, no man would be more proper. I do not know of any Objection that could be made to his character which would make you think him an improper person for that office."[49] Maj. Arthur Campbell, who had helped the British capture Detroit from the French in 1760 and who was not "popular with the mass of society," endorsed the idea of making Boone a captain, writing to Preston that the settlers believed that absentee officers "would not be so particularly interested in their safety, as he who lives among them." According to Major Campbell, "It is men, not particular Officers, that they [the settlers on the Clinch] are mowst in need of."[50] Major Campbell had earlier written to Preston, "I am well informed [Boone] is a very popular Officer where he is known."[51]

Col. William Preston was a powerful figure in western Virginia. A substantial landowner, he also had an accumulation of official positions and titles rivaling Pooh-Bah's. He was colonel of the county militia, sheriff of the county, and county surveyor. With all these positions, as Ohio Valley historians have noted, "practically all public business passed through his hands."[52] But for all his prominence at this point in his life, William Preston understood from his own early years how useful it could be to promote talented people of modest origin. Preston's father, a ship's carpenter, had eloped with the sister of the rich merchant James Patton who had shipping and trading interests with Virginia—the same Patton who acquired large landholdings in western Virginia before the Indians killed him at Draper's Meadow in 1755. Patton had brought Colonel Preston's father to America and helped him settle on some of the land Patton had been granted. Preston himself had very little formal education and had risen in the ranks of the Virginia militia and in other county offices in large part because of help from Patton, who had no son of his own.[53] These factors in his own background may have influenced Preston's decision to appoint Boone a captain in the Virginia militia, which he did by filling in Boone's name on a blank printed commission that Lord Dunmore had signed. Preston also gave Boone command of three forts on the Clinch.[54]

The Mingo raids on white settlers finally dwindled. Chief Logan, having killed many whites on the frontier mountain ridges, went back west and stopped killing. Speaking through an interpreter, he said that he had been the friend of the white man until whites, unprovoked, "murdered all the relatives of Logan, not sparing even my women and children. There runs not a drop of my blood in the veins of any living creature. This called on me for revenge. I have sought it. I have killed many. I have fully glutted my vengeance. ... Who is there to mourn for Logan? Not one."[55]

By the end of 1774 there was also a let-up in fighting between whites and Shawnees. On October 10, 1774, some eleven hundred white militia soldiers fought a battle with a somewhat smaller number of Shawnees and allied Indians at Point Pleasant, where the Kanawha runs into the Ohio River in what is now West Virginia. The Indians crossed the Ohio to attack the Virginians, who were assembling for a raid on the Shawnee villages in Ohio. The Fincastle County militia, led by Col. William Christian and Capt. John Floyd, arrived at Point Pleasant at midnight, after the battle was over. Given the difficulties the officers had experienced in recruiting and organizing the fractious backwoodsmen and in obtaining supplies, it is remarkable that the Fincastle militia made it to the scene at all.[56]

The Battle of Point Pleasant in itself was inconclusive. The Indians, led by the Shawnee chief Cornstalk, put up an impressive all-day fight. One of the Virginian commanders, Col. William Fleming, was shot twice in the arm and once in the chest. Fleming's lung protruded through his chest wound until an aide tucked it back in, guided by Fleming, who had been trained as a doctor. Fleming wrote after the battle, "Never did Indians stick closer to it, nor behave bolder."[57] While the whites claimed eighteen or twenty Indian scalps, the Indians also killed many whites, including the other Virginian commanding officer. Within days of the battle, however, the Virginian militia had pursued the Shawnees north of the Ohio River and to their towns on the Scioto River, until the Shawnees sued for peace. Under the Treaty of Camp Charlotte in October 1774, Cornstalk and some of the other Shawnee chiefs agreed to yield their hunting rights in Kentucky in exchange for Lord Dunmore's promise to keep the colonists south of the Ohio River.[58] Lord Dunmore's War was over. The local Fincastle County militia (including Boone) disbanded, with Boone signing certificates for service—some of the earliest writings that he signed. The spelling was sometimes phonetic ("James McCushin Sarved as a Solder 21 Days in ... the millitia of fincastle ... and was Ragelerly

Diescharged"), but the handwriting and the signature were large and clear.[59]

The Shawnee cession of rights in Kentucky had in it the makings of an opportunity for colonists like Boone who were determined to hunt in and bring settlers to Kentucky. The Proclamation of 1763 still remained in effect, with its prohibition against surveying and granting western lands (although the 1763 proclamation line had been adjusted westward as part of the Treaty of Fort Stanwix). Enforcing the prohibition was not easy, particularly after American protests to British actions such as the Stamp Act led the British to move their troops from forts in the Ohio Valley to the Atlantic colonies. For the distant British government to prevent the western settlers from trying their luck in the western lands was like King Canute ordering the tide not to rise. Lord Dunmore recognized as much, in a report he sent in December 1774, explaining to Lord Dartmouth, the British secretary of state for the colonies, why Dunmore had permitted some settlements west of the mountains as part of the colony of Virginia:

> I have had, My Lord, frequent opportunities to reflect upon the emigrating Spirit of the Americans, Since my Arrival to this Government. There are considerable bodies of Inhabitants Settled at greater or less distances from the regular frontiers of, I believe, all the Colonies. In this Colony Proclamations have been published from time to time to restrain them: But impressed from their earliest infancy with Sentiments and habits, very different from those acquired by persons of a Similar condition in England, they do not conceive that Government has any right to forbid their taking possession of a Vast tract of Country, either uninhabited, or which Serves only as a Shelter to a few Scattered Tribes of Indians. Nor can they be easily brought to entertain any belief of the permanent obligation of Treaties made with those People, whom they consider, as but little removed from the brute Creation. These notions, My Lord, I beg it may be understood, I by no means pretend to Justify. I only think it my duty to State matters as they really are.[60]

Lord Dunmore did not bother to disclose in the letter his own personal interest in lands west of the Alleghenies. Within weeks of Dunmore's report to Dartmouth, Boone, who was as little constrained by proclamations against western settlement as the colonists whom Dunmore described, was to take advantage of the opportunity afforded by the Treaty of Camp Charlotte.

8

TRANSYLVANIA, THE WILDERNESS ROAD, AND THE BUILDING OF BOONESBOROUGH

BY LATE 1774 THE CHEROKEES WERE THE ONLY INDIAN GROUP LEFT having colorable claims to Kentucky, though the Cherokees hunted mostly in the south of Kentucky and the Cherokee settlements were mostly in the western Carolinas and what was to become Tennessee. The Iroquois had given up their claims to lands south and east of the Ohio in the Treaty of Fort Stanwix in 1768. The Shawnees, or at least some of their chiefs, in October 1774 had given up their hunting rights in Kentucky after the Battle of Point Pleasant and the subsequent white incursions into Ohio.

Judge Richard Henderson of North Carolina saw this as a perfect chance to create a new proprietary colony—along the lines of the Vandalia province Benjamin Franklin and his colleagues were seeking to create in the Ohio Valley—by buying for himself and his associates the Cherokees' rights to most of Kentucky and much of northern Tennessee. According to Henderson's brother, Richard Henderson "was induced to attempt the purchase of Kentucky from the Cherokees, through the suggestions and advice of . . . Daniel Boone."[1]

One might think that Henderson would have been daunted by the prohibitions in the Proclamation of 1763 against any surveying or granting of land west of the Appalachians or by the fact that the royal charters of Virginia and North Carolina gave those colonies rights to the land in question. Moreover, this was late 1774. Americans outraged by the British tea monopoly had already dumped British tea into Boston Harbor in December 1773. The Continental Congress had opened in September 1774 "to consult upon the present unhappy State of the Colonies." In many of the colonies there was profound unhappiness about perceived overreaching by colonial lords proprietor. With all these clouds already lowering on the horizon, the time was less than ideal to propose a new proprietary colony in America. One North Carolina official wrote to another, on hearing of Henderson's plan, "Pray, is Dick Henderson out of his head?"[2] Richard Henderson, however, was not easily daunted.

Henderson was the kind of person who would have liked the idea of being a proprietor of a Crown colony. The son of the sheriff of Granville County, North Carolina, he had married the daughter of an English peer.[3] A tall, imposing man, Henderson, then thirty-nine, had lived in North Carolina for some thirty years and had served on North Carolina's superior court from 1767 until settlers calling themselves "Regulators," irritated by the "devilish devices" of lawyers and by taxes and fees charged by representatives of North Carolina's lord proprietor, shut down Henderson's court and torched his house and barn.[4] These acts did not enhance Henderson's liking for the populace, whom he tended to refer to as "the vulgar," "wretches," and "scoundrels." But Henderson's grandiloquence, optimism, and yen for land speculation remained undampened.

Henderson and other leading merchants and lawyers from western North Carolina decided to form a company, eventually called the Transylvania Company, to buy the Cherokee claims to the land north of the sources of the Cumberland River and south of the Ohio River and to promote and develop that huge tract.[5] To support his position that the Cherokees could convey the land without the need for action by the British government, Henderson may have looked to a British legal opinion issued in 1757 to the effect that land grants by east Indian princes were sufficient to convey rights in land without any action by the British Crown.[6] Henderson and his colleagues asked Boone to help arrange a meeting in March 1775 between Cherokees and company representatives at Sycamore Shoals on the Watauga River, in what is now eastern Tennessee, to enter a treaty to receive trade goods in exchange for ceding to the company their claims to the land.

On Christmas Day 1774, months before the treaty meeting with the Cherokees, "Richd Henderson & Co."—without any shred of claim to ownership of the land in question—published a proposal for the company's sale of lands "purchased from the Cherokee tribe of Indians." The proposal was not modest. Subject to quit-rent payments, a soldier would get five hundred acres for free; five thousand acres would be granted to the builder of an ironworks; a thousand acres to the builder of a "salt manufactory"; five hundred acres for erecting a sawmill or a gristmill. Settlers who stayed and raised corn could buy land at twenty shillings sterling per hundred acres.[7]

The Virginia and North Carolina authorities were outraged. Col. William Preston, the Fincastle County sheriff who had authorized Floyd's surveys in Kentucky and who already had large land claims of his own in Kentucky, warned George Washington (who hoped to perfect his own land claims in Kentucky) about Henderson's assertions that even officers claiming land surveyed in Kentucky under warrants for military service "must hold [their land] under him."[8] Similarly, Preston warned Virginia's governor Lord Dunmore that hundreds of people from Carolina and Virginia were preparing to settle Kentucky in the spring, "let the consequences be what they will," and said "the matter is now become Serious & demands the Attention of Government otherwise it is too likely that valuable & extensive Territory will be forever lost to Virginia." If Dunmore wished to have the land sold for the Crown, Preston offered to survey the land into lots and look to payment of his fees only out of the proceeds. Preston noted that Henderson's company had declared it would not suffer any land below the Kentucky to be surveyed by others, so that surveying for Virginia might not be possible unless "supported by an armed force."[9]

In February 1775 Josiah Martin, the royal governor of North Carolina, proclaimed that Henderson and his partners were violating the Proclamation of 1763 as well as North Carolina law forbidding whites from buying Indian land without prior permission of the governor and council. Martin condemned Henderson's "daring, unjust and unwarrantable Proceeding" as one "of a most alarming and dangerous Tendency to the Peace and Welfare of this and the neighboring Colony," because "Richard Henderson and his Confederates" have agreed to pay "a considerable quantity of Gunpowder" to the Indians for the land and because "a settlement may be formed that will become an Asylum to the most abandoned Fugitives from the several Colonies." Governor Martin sternly forbade "the said Richard Henderson and his Confederates, on pain of his Majesty's highest displeasure, and of suffering the most rigorous Penalties of the Law, to prosecute so unlawful an undertaking" and also enjoined "all his Majesty's liege subjects to use all lawful means in their Power to obstruct, hinder and prevent the Execution of his Design of settlement, so contrary to Law and Justice and so pregnant with ill consequences." The governor also warned that every treaty, bargain, and agreement contrary to the 1763 proclamation was "illegal, null and void."[10] In March 1775 Lord Dunmore issued a similar denunciation of "Richard Henderson, and other disorderly persons, his associates," who had claimed land within Virginia contrary to law, and strictly charged Virginia's colonial officers "to use their utmost endeavours to prevent the unwarrantable and illegal designs of the said Henderson and his abettors."[11]

None of these fulminations deterred Henderson and his "abettors." Their planned meeting with the Cherokees took place, with Boone's help, at Sycamore Shoals in March 1775. Henderson's company brought to the treaty site many wagonloads of trade goods, feasted the Cherokees, orated to them, and heard orations in return. One of the Indians who spoke in support of the treaty was an aged chief named Attakullakulla, known to the whites as the Little Carpenter, reportedly for his skill at putting together a consensus view. Attakullakulla, a leading Cherokee spokesman for decades, in 1730 had been to England and had dined with the king. He was a small, skinny, wizened man said by some to be ninety years old, marked with scars on each cheek, his earlobes cut and stretched down to his shoulders by silver ornaments.[12]

The trade goods were laid out so all the Indians could see what they were to get. The goods' value is open to question. Draper estimated their worth at ten thousand pounds, but the written treaty described the consideration as two thousand pounds, and a writer in 1784 said there were "only ten wagons loaded with cheap goods, such as coarse woolens, trinkets, and spirituous liquors."[13] One settler who was there estimated that about a thousand Cherokees had gathered at Sycamore Shoals, "counting big and little, and about half of them were men."

One of the men at the parley was Uskwaliguta—meaning "Dragging Stomach"—known to the whites as Hanging Maw, a headman from the Overhills Cherokee settlements, who opposed accommodation with the whites and who in 1776 was to be one of the Indians who took Jemima Boone captive.[14] Another Cherokee chief, Dragging Canoe, even though he was Attakullakulla's son, opposed the treaty because the Indians were being asked to give up too much hunting land for too little and predicted that this encroachment on Cherokee lands would be followed by successive other encroachments until the Cherokees were "compelled to seek a retreat in some far distant wilderness" and eventually driven to extinction. Dragging Canoe stormed out of the conference, taking several other younger warriors with him.[15] But most Cherokees at the meeting were swayed by Attakullakulla's

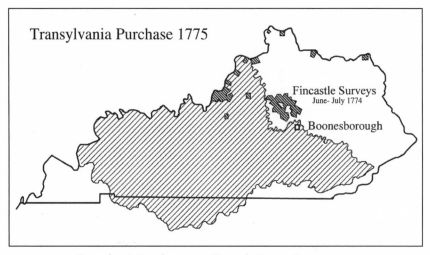

Transylvania Purchase, 1775; Fincastle County Surveys, 1774
Courtesy of Neal O. Hammon

words, the trade goods they were to receive, and perhaps by the fact that most Cherokees lived outside the land being sought by the Transylvania Company. On March 17, 1775, more than a month after Governor Martin's proclamation and days before Lord Dunmore's blast against Henderson and his "disorderly associates," the Treaty of Watauga was signed. Attakullakulla and two other Cherokee chiefs, Oconostota and the Raven, inked their marks on a deed granting to Henderson and his partners a vast area that included a triangle between the Kentucky River on the east, the Ohio River on the north and west, and, to the south, the sources of the Cumberland, reaching down into northern Tennessee—in all, more than seventeen million acres.[16] Once the deed was signed, Henderson ordered cattle to be killed and roasted and rum broken out for a feast.

When the transaction seemed certain to go forward, an old Cherokee chief, one of the three who signed the deed, took Boone by the hand and said to him: "Brother, we have given you a fine land, but I believe you will have much trouble settling it." Eight years later, after hundreds had died in fighting between Indians and whites—including one of Boone's brothers and one of his sons—Boone was to say that he had verified the saying of the old Indian.[17]

Boone had agreed with Henderson to lead a party of axemen to mark out the best route from the settlements to the Transylvania Company's intended settlement, where Otter Creek runs into the Kentucky River. By the time the treaty was actually signed, Boone had joined the axemen at Long Island on the Holston River, northwest of Sycamore Shoals. The well-armed group of about thirty set off to blaze and widen the trail, measuring some two hundred miles long, initially known as Boone's Trace and later to become known as the Wilderness Road.[18] Felix Walker, one of the axemen, later wrote a description of the trip. He had joined the group with a number of western North Carolinians, led by Capt. William Twitty. According to Walker, Twitty's group and the others "by general consent, put ourselves under the management and control of Col. Boon, who was to be our pilot and conductor through the wilderness." It was noteworthy that Boone was given command of the group, rather than Henderson's colleague Richard Callaway, who was on the trip, was ten years older than Boone, was the son of a substantial Shenandoah Valley landowner, and, having served as a colonel in the French and Indian War, outranked Boone. Callaway must have resented Boone's leadership of the road-blazing party. Callaway's friction with Boone was to grow over the years and to erupt in his leadership of Boone's court-martial in 1778 after the siege of Boonesborough.

Walker was only twenty-one years old when the trail was blazed. His memories of the trip, written decades later, still reflect a young man's excitement. As he described the setting off, "Every heart abounded with joy and excitement in anticipating the new things we would see, and the romantic scenes through which we must pass."[19]

The trip went smoothly for a couple of weeks, retracing the path Boone and Findley had taken through Powell's Valley and the Cumberland Gap. The axemen broadened the path to be wide enough not for wagons but for the packhorses Henderson and his settlers would be taking after the road had been blazed. Boone's party then followed a buffalo trace to the Rockcastle River. Leaving that river, they cut through miles of dead brush and then through cane and reed. As the cane ceased, Walker and the other axemen "began to discover the rapturous appearance of the plains of Kentucky. . . . So rich a soil we had never seen before; covered with clover in full bloom, the woods were abounding in wild game—turkeys so numerous that it might be said they appeared but one flock, universally scattered in the woods."[20]

The idyll ended two days later, on March 25, 1775, when the group was only about fifteen miles from its destination on the Kentucky River. An hour before dawn Indians fired on Boone's camp. Twitty was shot through both knees. His slave Sam, shot dead, fell face-first into the campfire. Felix Walker, badly wounded, managed to crawl into the bush. An Indian rushed up to scalp Twitty. Twitty's bulldog seized the Indian by the throat and threw him to the ground. Another Indian tomahawked the dog to death. The camp came awake. Whites took to the bush with their rifles. The Indians vanished without taking any scalps. It was still dark. The whites made their way back to the camp and took stock. The Indians had taken some horses, but the baggage was intact. Twitty was too badly wounded to be moved.[21] Walker was in little better shape.

To Boone the attack must have seemed dismayingly like the one less than two years earlier in which Indians, at the same time of day, killed Boone's son James and others at Wallen's Creek. Fear and uncertainty from that earlier attack had caused Boone and the rest of the first party of whites seeking to settle Kentucky to retreat to the settlements. This time, after the shootings, Boone and his men built a low log shelter to make it easier to care for Twitty and Walker. Twitty, who never regained consciousness, died a few days after the attack. About the time Twitty died, Boone discovered that Indians had also fired on a separate camp of men who had been hunting apart from the main group. Boone and Squire found the scalped bodies of two of those men.

The men's nerves were on edge. Soon after the attack on Boone's party, a female slave belonging to Colonel Callaway, while out gathering wood, saw a man peeping out from behind a tree. "Indians!" she cried out. Boone took up his rifle and ordered his men to take cover behind trees. The man behind the tree called out to identify himself. He was one of Boone's party who had hidden in the woods and had come quietly up to the camp because he wanted to be sure that the whites were in control of it before he made himself known.[22]

The Indian attacks were unlikely to have been random. Although no one was sure which Indian group attacked the axemen, one strong possibility is that Cherokees associated with Dragging Canoe, who had opposed the treaty with Henderson, believed that attacking Boone's advance party was a good way to deter further white settlement of the Cherokees' hunting ground in Kentucky—just as the 1755 killing of Col. James Patton at Draper's Meadow and the 1773 killing of James Boone and of Captain Russell's son appeared to be aimed at key leaders of settler efforts to expand into Indian territory.[23] In 1774, during Lord Dunmore's War, the Tennessee leader Capt. James Robertson had warned Col. William Preston to be on watch because, he said, the Indians have "white men amongst them they Undoubtedly know men of the Best Circumstance and that is What they Generaly Aim at."[24]

The attack on Boone's party had caused settlers to turn back in 1773. The anti-accommodationist Indians must have hoped that a similar attack on a Boone-led party would have the same result in 1775. The Cherokee chief Oconostota, one of the signers of the Henderson treaty, was to blame the attacks on two "ill disposed" Cherokees—presumably anti-accommodationists like Dragging Canoe and Hanging Maw.[25]

This time, however, the white settlers did not turn back. Boone's calm leadership in defense of his group held his nervous axemen together. Boone also tended to Walker, whose wounds, as Walker later remembered, were "pronounced by some to be mortal." As Walker put it, Boone "was my father, physician, and friend; he attended me as his child, cured my wounds by the use of medicines from the woods, nursed me with paternal affection until I recovered, without the expectation of reward."[26] Boone and his party decided not to go back to the settlements but to push on to the site of the proposed fort on the Kentucky River. As he set off, he sent a letter back to Judge Henderson as they set off to complete the trip:

April the first, 1775

Dear Colonel:

After my compliments to you I shall acquaint you with our misfortune. On March the 25th a party of Indians fired on my Company about a half an hour before day and killed Mr. Twetty and his Negro and wounded Mr. Walker very deeply, but I hope he will recover. On March the 28 as we were hunting for provisions we found Samuel Tate's son who gave us an account that the Indians fired on their camp on the 27 day. My brother and I went down and found two men killed and sculped, Thomas McDowell and Jeremiah McPheeters. I have sent a man down to all the lower companies in order to gather them all to the mouth of Otter Creek. My advise to you, sir, is to come or send as soon as possible. Your company is desired greatly, for the people are very uneasy, but are willing to stay and venture their lives with you, and now is the time to flusterate their intentions and keep the country, whilst we are in it. If we give way to them now, it will ever be the case. This day we start from the battle ground, for the mouth of Otter Creek, where we shall immediately erect a fort, which will be done before you come or send—then we can send ten men to meet you, if you send for them.

I am sir your most obedient
Daniel Boone

N.B. We stood on the ground and guarded our baggage till day, and lost nothing. We have about fifteen miles to Cantuck at Otter Creek.[27]

Walker was carried on a litter between two horses to the Kentucky River. On the south side of the river, not far from the mouth of Otter Creek, near a salt lick, Boone and his men began building a settlement, first called Fort Boone and later Boonesborough. Henderson, though shaken by news of the attacks and by seeing men streaming south out of Kentucky and back toward the settlements, set out for Kentucky on April 8 with the rest of his men. William Calk, who traveled into Kentucky with Henderson and his company, recorded in his journal for April 8: "We all pact up & Started Crost Cumberland Gap about one oclock this Day. We met a great maney people turning Back for fear of the Indians but our Company goes on Still with good Courage."[28]

On April 10 Henderson sent a volunteer up to let Boone know that the main group was coming. The group pressed on, despite mud, frost, Indian sign, a night visit by a wolf, and meeting more people returning to the settlements filled with dire news of Indian attacks. On April 18 four men from Boone's camp came to meet Henderson's group and guide it the rest of the way.[29] On April 20, his fortieth birthday, Henderson recorded in his journal: "Arrived at Fort Boone on the mouth of Otter Creek, Cantuckey River where we were saluted by a running fire of about 25 Guns, all that was then at Fort—The men appeared in high spirits and much rejoiced on our arrival."[30]

Boone's determination to stay in Kentucky was crucial to the new settlement. As Henderson wrote to his partners, "It was beyond a doubt, that our right, in effect, depended on Boone's maintaining his ground—at least until we should get to him." Boone's willingness to keep going led to Henderson's decision to continue, in the face of growing fears and rumors. "It was owing to Boone's confidence in us, and the people's in him, that a stand was ever attempted in order to wait for our coming," Henderson wrote. "The general panic that had seized the men we were continually meeting was contagious;

it ran like wild fire; and, notwithstanding every effort against its progress, it was presently discovered in our own camp; some hesitated and stole back, privately; others saw the necessity of returning to convince their friends that they were still alive, in too strong a light to be resisted."[31]

Felix Walker also bore witness to the importance of Boone's resolution to continue. Walker wrote, speaking of the effect of the March 25 Indian attack: "So fatal and tragical an event cast a deep gloom of melancholy over all our prospects. . . ; hope vanished from the most of us, and left us suspended in the tumult of uncertainty and conjecture. Boon, and a few others, appeared to possess firmness and fortitude. . . . Boone conducted the company under his care through the wilderness, with great propriety, intrepidity and courage; and was I to enter an exception to any part of his conduct, it would be on the ground that he appeared void of fear and of consequence—too little caution for the enterprise. But let me, with feeling recollection and lasting gratitude, ever remember the unremitting kindness, sympathy and attention paid to me by Col. Boone in my distress."[32]

Much was done after Henderson's arrival at the little settlement. Henderson decided to move the site of the fort a few hundred yards. Together with Boone and Callaway, he laid off lots for the settlers. A magazine was built for the fort's gunpowder, and the fort began to be built. It was not large. By the summer of 1775 Boonesborough consisted of twenty-six one-story log cabins, laid out in a hollow rectangle perhaps 260 by 180 feet. At each of the four corners was a blockhouse with a projecting second story, from which to fire down on attackers. There were gaps between the blockhouses and the nearest cabins—gaps intended to be stockaded, but the settlers kept deferring this important work. Rigid discipline was never the strong suit of frontiersmen. Henderson told the other proprietors how hard it was to get the men to stand watch: "There is a mistaken notion amongst the vulgar . . . [that standing watch] . . . has the appearance of cowardice, and that it is beneath a soldier to be afraid of anything, especially when a little fatigued."[33] Like many of the frontier forts, Boonesborough initially had no well inside the fort. That would create an obvious weakness in case of siege, but Indian attacks had tended to be short, small raids rather than prolonged sieges.[34]

Building a fort addressed only one of Henderson's problems. He also needed to persuade his group that the Transylvania Company had the legal ability to grant good title to land in Kentucky, and he needed to work together with the other small bands of whites who had recently settled nearby.

In March 1774 James Harrod had led Pennsylvanians from the Monongahela to a site about fifty miles west of Boonesborough, where he started the station known as Harrodsburg. Harrod's party had left Kentucky in July 1774 following Indian attacks, but Harrod and forty-two men had come back to Harrodsburg by mid-March 1775.[35] John Floyd, whom Col. William Preston had sent out to survey lots in Kentucky in 1774, had returned to Kentucky in April 1775 and established a camp of western Virginians on Dick's River, about twenty-five miles south of Harrodsburg, at a station called St. Asaph's, later known as Logan's Station. Harrodsburg and St. Asaph's probably had more than a hundred men between them—more than the fifty or eighty who were at Boonesborough. How to keep the different small groups of whites working together, at least against the common threat of Indian attack? How to prevent fights over land, with conflicting claims based on surveys of officers who had fought in the French and Indian War, the rights the Transylvania Company claimed to have acquired from the Cherokees, and settlers' preemption claims?

Dick Henderson's approach to these problems combined representative government, seigneurial showmanship, and targeted largesse. On the political front he proposed to have the different small settlements in the neighborhood form a single legislature to adopt laws for the common good. He also sought to impress the settlers with a bit of pomp and ceremony, and to give financial inducements to leaders of other settlements to support the Transylvania Company.

Soon after Henderson arrived, leaders from the St. Asaph's and the Harrodsburg stations came by to see what was going on at Boonesborough. On May 3 John Floyd arrived, saying, according to Henderson's diary, that he had been sent by the men at his station on Dick's River "to know on what terms they might settle our lands.—That if terms were reasonable they would pitch on some place to make corn, or otherwise go on the north side of the River." Henderson wrote in his journal: "Was much at a loss on account of his [Floyd's] message as he was Surveyor of Fincastle under Col. Preston who had exerted himself against us. We thought it most advisable to secure them to our interest if possible. Accordingly though the season was too far advanced to make much corn, yet promised them land." A reasonable allotment of land to an influential competitor must have seemed a sensible way to seek support rather than enmity. The Transylvania Company in December 1775 was to follow up this land allotment with a further inducement to Floyd, by selecting him, on the recommendation of the company's representatives, as Transylvania's principal surveyor—though Floyd may well have merited that appointment solely on his skill and experience as a surveyor.[36]

Henderson told Floyd of the plan to elect representatives to make laws for the neighboring settlements, with a convention to be held in late May and representatives to be chosen from St. Asaph's and Harrodsburg as well as from Boonesborough. Floyd said he liked that idea.[37] It is hard to believe that Floyd was not also acting as the eyes and ears of his patron Colonel Preston, to keep track of Henderson and to figure out how to ensure that Henderson's activities did not jeopardize the claims of Preston, Floyd, and the others to lands surveyed by the Fincastle County surveyors. But a leading Virginian, Col. William Christian, had told Floyd that Patrick Henry believed that the Transylvania purchase "would stand good" and had advised Floyd to deal with Henderson.[38]

On May 7 Captain Harrod and Col. Thomas Slaughter arrived at Boonesborough from Harrodsburg. They, too, were told about the proposal for the settlements to elect representatives to make legislation, and they said they liked the idea. The convention was scheduled for May 23.[39] Each settlement elected representatives. Boone and his brother Squire were two of Boonesborough's six representatives. The other stations elected a total of twelve representatives. The legislative convention met at Boonesborough from May 23 to May 27, outdoors under a huge spreading elm, with enough shade for a hundred people—in Henderson's characteristically unrestrained words, "the most beautiful tree that imagination can suggest."[40]

Furthering the pomp and ceremony part of his approach, Henderson had the proceedings start off with "divine service" performed by the Rev. John Lythe, an Anglican minister from Virginia who was a representative from Harrodsburg. Henderson had confided to his journal that he hoped at the convention "to perform divine service for the first time—in a public manner and that to a set of scoundrels who scarcely believe in God or fear a devil if we were to judge from most of their looks, words and actions."[41] After the minister's invocation of divine assistance, Henderson, as leader of the proprietors, delivered an address. The first, interminable, sentence of his address conveys the speech's tone:

> You are called and assembled at this time for a noble and an honorable purpose—a purpose, however ridiculous or idle it may appear at first view, to superficial minds, yet is of the most solid consequence;

and if prudence, firmness and wisdom are suffered to influence your councils and direct your conduct, the peace and harmony of thousands may be expected to result from your deliberations; in short, you are about a work of the utmost importance to the well-being of this country in general, in which the interest of each and every individual is inseparably connected, for that state is truly sickly, politically speaking, whose laws or edicts are not careful equally of the different members, and most distant branches, which constitute the one united whole.

He went on in a similar vein:

You, perhaps, are fixing the palladium, or placing the first cornerstone, of an edifice, the height and magnificence of whose superstructure is now in the womb of futurity, and can only become great in proportion to the excellence of its foundation. These considerations, gentlemen, will, no doubt, animate and inspire you with sentiments worthy the grandeur of the subject.

Having set forth the "grandeur of the subject," Henderson pointed to the "one common danger"—the threat of Indian attack—that must secure a "union of interests . . . so essential to the forming good, wise and wholesome laws." Invoking representative government principles worthy of John Locke, Henderson noted that the laws adopted by the elected representatives of the people would be effective because "all power is originally in the people." He went on to suggest to the representatives what they might wish to address in their legislation: establishing courts; creating a mechanism for collecting debts and resolving disputes; setting up a militia for mutual defense; and regulating the "wanton destruction of our game."

The delegates' formal answer began in a manner that suggested acknowledgment of Henderson's proprietary rights: "We received your speech with minds truly thankful for the care and attention you express towards the good people of this infant country, whom we represent." While that opening smacked of forelock-tugging obsequiousness, the representatives also noted their "absolute right . . . to frame rules for the government of our little society." The convention docilely went on to address the topics for legislation that Henderson had suggested—bills to establish courts, to regulate the militia, and to preserve game.

Daniel Boone moved the bill to preserve game. Henderson had noted in his journal two weeks before the convention started how hard it was "to stop great waste in killing meat": "Some would kill three, four, five or ½ a dozen buffaloes and not take half a horse load from them all. For want of a little obligatory law our game as soon as we got here, if not before, was driven off very much. Fifteen or 20 miles was as short a distance as good hunters thought of getting meat, nay sometimes they were obliged to go thirty, though by chance once or twice a week buffaloe was killed within 5 or six miles."[42] This was a sharp change from what the wounded Felix Walker had seen when he first came to Boonesborough a few weeks earlier, a sight he had never seen before: "A number of buffaloes, of all sizes, supposed to be between two and three hundred, made off from the lick in every direction; some walking, others loping slowly and carelessly, with young calves playing, skipping and bounding through the plain."[43] Henderson, Boone, and their colleagues were becoming vividly aware of the inexorable dynamic of large-scale hunting in new territories, which was one of the transformations Boone was helping to bring about: the number of game animals had plummeted, and the remaining game had moved away. The week before the convention Henderson had complained in his journal that he "almost starved" for lack of meat, particularly because there was no bread and the settlement's little plantings were just beginning to yield something edible.[44]

Boone also brought in a bill "for improving the breed of horses" and a bill "to preserve the range." The titles of Boone's bills give us an idea of the political concerns that were closest to his heart. Other delegates were appointed to a committee "to draw up a compact between the proprietors and the people of this colony," and the Rev. Mr. Lythe moved to bring in a bill "to prevent profane swearing and Sabbath breaking." Henderson seems to have held a disparate group together for a time by giving each of several leaders a chance to introduce a bill on a topic dear to him. All of these bills on May 27 were passed and signed by Henderson and by the chairman of the convention on behalf of the delegates.

Also on May 27, Henderson sought to buttress the validity of the land claims of the Transylvania Company by more ceremony. Henderson came to the convention with John Farrow, whom the Cherokee chiefs in the Watauga deed had appointed as one of their attorneys-in-fact. Farrow "in presence of the convention, made livery and seisin of all the lands, in a deed of feofment then produced"—the Watauga treaty deed. "Livery of seisin" was a bit of feudal land conveyancing that was already obsolete, though it was described in Blackstone's *Commentaries*, which Henderson had probably read when studying for admission to the North Carolina bar. On behalf of the Cherokees, Farrow symbolically "enfeoffed" the proprietors—that is, conveyed fee title—in the lands in question. To do this Farrow presumably handed to Henderson a piece of turf cut from the soil beneath them and, while they both held it under the giant spreading elm, declared his delivery to the Transylvania Company of seisin and possession of the land, according to the terms of the title deed.[45]

After the livery of seisin, the proprietors and the representatives on May 27 signed a formal compact. The principles in the compact included some that foreshadowed the Constitution of the United States—for example:

4. That there be perfect religious freedom and general toleration; Provided, that the propagators of any doctrine or tenets, evidently tending to the subversion of our laws, shall, for such conduct, be amenable to, and punished by, the civil courts.

12. That the legislative authority, after the strength and maturity of the colony will permit, consist of three branches, to wit: the delegates or representatives chosen by the people; a council, not exceeding twelve men, possessed of landed estate, who reside in this colony, and the proprietors.

Other principles in the compact, less high-minded, reflected the strong interest of proprietors and settlers alike in land claims and development. For example:

6. That the quit-rents never exceed two shillings sterling per hundred acres.

14. That the land office be always open.[46]

The fourteenth principle addressed a basic objective shared by every white in Kentucky: getting rich through laying valid claim to frontier land. The convention was adjourned on Saturday, May 27—"Everybody pleas'd," Henderson noted in his journal.

Was "everybody pleas'd"? What could the delegates sitting on the ground under the spreading elm have thought of Henderson and the proprietors? The need for a militia and for common defense against Indians was clear enough. The leaders of the different settlements did agree to work together for mutual defense. Henderson wrote to the proprietors in North Carolina that Harrod (the leader of Harrodsburg), Floyd (the leader of the St. Asaph's settlement), and he "are under solemn engagements to communicate, with the utmost dispatch, every piece of intelligence respecting danger or sign of Indians, to each other. In case of invasion of Indians, both the other parties are instantly to march and relieve the distressed, if possible."[47] But what did the frontiersmen think of the livery of seisin—the mumbo jumbo with the piece of turf? The proprietors' claim to own all the land the settlers on the other stations were living on? The liturgy of the Church of England, with its prayers for the king, performed before frontiersmen, many of whom were Presbyterians or other dissenters or who paid no heed to organized religion, and who backed the incipient revolution against the British Crown? Only two days after the close of the convention, the settlers at Boonesborough were to learn that on April 17, more than a month earlier, Americans at Lexington and Concord had fired on British troops.[48]

What about Henderson's airs and grandiose language? What did Boone and the other frontiersmen think of working on "an edifice, the height and magnificence of whose superstructure is now in the womb of futurity"? If Henderson in his journal and in his letters to the proprietors referred to the settlers at Boonesborough as "the vulgar" and "a set of scoundrels who scarcely believe in God or fear a devil," was he able to conceal those views from the representatives? Some at the convention liked Henderson's tone and oratory. Felix Walker, who was to fight hard against Tories and British soldiers during the Revolution, wrote that Colonel Henderson's address "was considered equal to any of like kind ever delivered to any deliberate body in that day and time."[49] Other settlers in Kentucky, however, resented "a Certain Set of men from North Carolina stiling 'emselves Proprietors."[50]

At the same time that Henderson was trying to make common cause with the other Kentucky settlements in ways that would further the Transylvania Company's claims, he and his fellow proprietors sought to protect the interests of the company both with the Virginia Convention and with the Crown—a balancing act of impossible delicacy, as America moved ever closer to outright revolution. On April 26, 1775, the proprietors wrote to Patrick Henry to thank him for "the eloquence and good sense with which you defended, and the liberal principles on which you supported our claim to the benefit of our engagement with the Indians," at the Virginia Convention.

The proprietors began their letter by noting that "the copartners in the purchase of lands . . . from the Indians, neither intending by their distant and hazardous enterprise, to revolt from their allegiance to their sovereign, nor yet to desert the grand and common cause of their American brethren and fellow subjects, in their . . . glorious struggle for the full enjoyment of the natural rights of mankind, and the inestimable liberties and priviledges of our happy constitution, were anxious to know the result of the wise and mature deliberation of the Convention." The proprietors' difficulty in trying to stay on the good side of the patriots while at the same time not offending the Crown fairly leaps from the page. The proprietors also noted that it "would have afforded us the most singular satisfaction to have had it in our power to give you a more substantial evidence of our gratitude," but conceived "the general disinterestedness of your principles and publick conduct to be such, that even our thanks may be more than you expected or wished for."[51]

Henderson and his fellow proprietors did the best they could to exploit their deed from the Cherokees. There was no dearth of interest in settling in Kentucky. Rev. John Brown, a Presbyterian minister in western Virginia, wrote to his brother-in-law Col. William Preston in May 1775: "What a Buzzel is amongst People about Kentuck! To hear them speak of it, one would think it was a new-found Paradise; & I doubt not if it is such a place as represented, but ministers will have their congregations."[52] As Henderson in June 1775 wrote his fellow proprietors who had stayed behind in North Carolina, the Kentucky country "surely will be settled immediately upon some principles or other: the grand affair, on our part, is to manage matters so as to have our rights acknowledged, and continue lords of the soil."[53] Henderson and the other proprietors worked hard at their "grand affair," but the cards were stacked against them becoming "lords of the soil." It was not easy to get settlers to come to Kentucky in the midst of Indian raids and title uncertainties, and the Transylvania Company's claim to most of Kentucky, fatally flawed from the outset, came under strong attack from other settlers, was inconsistent with the thrust of the Revolution, and was quickly dying.

Henderson continued to promote the wonders of Kentucky with a torrent of superlatives. In June 1775 he told his fellow proprietors in North Carolina that the country "far exceeds the idea which I had formed of it; and indeed it is not surprising, for it is not in the power of any person living to do justice to the fertility of the soil, beauty of the country, or excellence of its range."[54] The following month Henderson and fellow proprietor John Luttrell wrote to the proprietors who remained in North Carolina: "The country might invite a prince from his palace, merely for the pleasure of contemplating its beauty and excellence; but only add the rapturous idea of property, and what allurements can the world offer as an equivalent for the loss of so glorious a prospect?"[55]

In September 1775 the proprietors ran in the Williamsburg newspapers an advertisement calculated to cause prospective settlers to salivate:

> This country lies . . . in a temperate and healthy climate. It is in general well-watered with springs and rivulets, and has several rivers, up which vessels of considerable burden may come with ease. In different places of it are a number of salt springs, where the making of salt has been tried with great success. . . . The fertility of the soil and goodness of the range almost surpass belief; and it is at present well stored with buffalo, elk, deer, bear, beaver, and etc., and the rivers abound with fish of various kinds. Vast crowds of people are daily flocking to it, and many gentlemen of the first rank and character have bargained for lands in it, so that there is a great appearance of a rapid settlement, and that it soon will be a considerable Colony, and one of the most agreeable countries in America.[56]

It is hard to square the advertisement's claims with Henderson's descriptions in his journal and letters of actual conditions in Kentucky: lack of meat, lack of salt, diminishing game, frequent Indian attacks, and settlers leaving the country. On June 12 Henderson had told the proprietors in North Carolina that "our company has dwindled from about eighty in number to about fifty odd, and I believe in a few days will be considerably less," and that the number of settlers in the two neighboring settlements to the west had dropped from about one hundred to not more than sixty or seventy.[57] But promotion is promotion, and sellers of real estate have been known from time to time to overstate the virtues of what they seek to sell.

Boone and his brother Squire were able to bring more settlers in, to offset the departures. Boone had left Boonesborough on June 13, 1775, to go back to North Carolina so he could be with Rebecca in childbirth. Accompanying Boone were some men from Boonesborough out for salt, which was in short supply at the fort. On June 23 Indians attacked four settlers in Powell's Valley and wounded two of them. Henderson and Luttrell, after describing that attack to the proprietors in North Carolina, noted that the number of men at Harrodsburg and Boonesborough had dropped and that news of the Powell's Valley incident would likely keep settlers out of Kentucky for a time. Henderson and Luttrell reported that Boonesborough was out of salt and that Boone had not come back yet and that "until he [Boone] comes the devil himself can't drive the others [the men who had gone with Boone to look for salt] this way."[58] That was strong testimony to the confidence the frontier settlers placed in Boone.

Rebecca finally gave birth to her ninth child, William, after her most difficult pregnancy. The boy died soon after he was born. After waiting several weeks until Rebecca was well enough to travel, Boone set off for Kentucky in mid-August, leading a party of about fifty emigrants he had rounded up, including Rebecca and Jemima Boone. About half of the party went to Harrodsburg, with Boone and the others coming to Boonesborough in early September.[59] Later in September, Squire Boone arrived with his wife and several other settlers (some of them relatives of Rebecca) from the Yadkin, and Col. Richard Callaway arrived with his family and about forty other settlers, mostly from western Virginia.[60]

With Boone back to be in charge of Boonesborough and the number of settlers in the fort rebounding, Henderson went to North Carolina to see what could be done to buttress his company's faltering land claims. According to the minutes of the May convention at Boonesborough, the next meeting was to be held there in September—but the representatives who had been elected in May never again met together as a house of representatives in Boonesborough. By September Henderson and two of the other proprietors who had been at the May convention had moved back to North Carolina, and the disparate land claims and interests of the different neighboring settlements in Kentucky already made it impossible for their representatives to continue as a legislative body of the Transylvania Company.

Instead of meeting in Boonesborough with elected Kentucky representatives, Henderson and the other proprietors met by themselves in North Carolina on September 25, 1775. The minutes evince concerns over threats to the company's title claims. The proprietors, having elected Henderson as their president, appointed another proprietor, James Hogg, to represent their would-be colony in the Continental Congress sitting at Philadelphia and to submit a memorial to "that august body."[61] As with the proprietors' earlier letter to Patrick Henry, the memorial sought, awkwardly, to balance allegiance to King George with concern for American liberties—but by this time the proprietors appeared to recognize that the winds of change were blowing in the direction of united action by the American colonies. After reciting that the "Proprietors of Transylvania," having purchased their land from the Aborigines "in fair and open treaty and without the violation of any British or American law whatever," are "determined to give it up only with their lives," the memorialists said they "by no means forget their allegiance to their Sovereign, whose constitutional rights and pre-eminences they will support at the risk of their lives. . . . At the same time, having their hearts warmed with the same noble spirit that animates the United Colonies, and moved with indignation at the late Ministerial and Parliamentary usurpa- tion, it is the earnest wish of the Proprietors of Transylvania to be considered by the Parliaments as brethren, engaged in the same great cause of liberty and of mankind." The memorial asked the United Colonies to "take the in- fant Colony of Transylvania into their protection," to add Transylvania to the United Colonies, and to admit James Hogg to a seat in the Continental Congress.[62]

The proprietors also addressed the ongoing operations of the company. They appointed Col. John Williams to be the company's agent in Boones- borough, with power to appoint one or more surveyors. With evident hope of finding hidden mineral treasure, they directed the company's agent, in granting deeds, to reserve to the proprietors one-half of all gold, silver, cop- per, lead, and sulphur mines on the deeded lands. They increased the price of land per one hundred acres from twenty to fifty shillings. Seeking to reward Daniel Boone, the proprietors resolved "that a present of two thousand acres of land be made to Col. Daniel Boone, with the thanks of the Proprietors, for the signal services he has rendered to the Company." Boone never became the owner of any of the promised two thousand acres, however, because the claims of the Transylvania Company to its seventeen million acres of land were soon to be rejected.[63]

James Hogg in January 1776 described to his fellow proprietors his lack of progress with the Continental Congress. Samuel and John Adams told him that for the Continental Congress to take under its protection people who had acted in defiance of the king's proclamations (evidently referring to the Proclamation of 1763) would be inconsistent with the congress's con- tinuing efforts to reach an accommodation with the royal government. The Adamses also told Hogg that he must sound out the views of the Virgin- ians because the land was within Virginia's charter. Thomas Jefferson told

Hogg that the congress would do nothing without the Virginia Convention's approval. Although Hogg did not know it, Jefferson was also fundamentally opposed to all efforts by large land companies such as the Transylvania Company to develop the western lands at the expense of independent small farmers.[64] Silas Deane of Connecticut and others warned Hogg that "quitrents is a mark of vassalage" and threatened opposition if the Transylvania Company did not "act upon liberal principles."[65]

Opposition to the Transylvania Company's claims continued to build at the other settlements in Kentucky, particularly after the company increased the selling price of land. In May 1776 the Virginia Convention received a petition signed by eighty-eight settlers, led by James Harrod of Harrodsburg, complaining of the price increase and questioning the company's title because the lands the company claimed had apparently been ceded to the Crown by the Iroquois in the Treaty of Fort Stanwix. The petitioners humbly implored "to be taken under the protection of the honorable Convention of the Colony of Virginia."[66] The following month "the Committee of West Fincastle of the Colony of Virginia"—a group that included George Rogers Clark, Isaac Hite (one of the Harrodsburg representatives at the May convention at Boonesborough), and Hugh McGary—sent from Harrodsburg a petition to the Virginia Convention implying that the Transylvania proprietors were opposed to the Revolution. The petitioners said they desired "to support the cause of American freedom" and noted "how impolitical it would be to Suffer such a Respectable Body of Prime Rifle Men to remain in a state of Neutrality, when at the same time a Certain Set of men from North Carolina stiling 'emselves Proprietors and claiming an Absolute Right to these very Lands taking upon 'emselves the Legislative Authority, Appointing Offices both Civil and Military, having also opened a Land Office Surveyors General & Deputys appointed & act, conveyances made, and Land sold at an Exorbitant Price." They went on to say that if "these pretended Proprietors have leave to continue to act in their arbitrary manner out of the controul of this Colony [Virginia] the end must be evident to every well wisher to American Liberty."[67] On June 24, 1776, the Virginia Convention resolved that settlers on the western frontiers should hold their lands without paying anything to private persons until the validity of title under the purported purchase from the Cherokees was determined by the Virginia legislature. The convention also forbade any purchase of lands in Virginia from Indian nations without the approval of the Virginia legislature.[68]

John Williams and other colleagues of Henderson sought to address the settlers' complaints. In response to their unhappiness that all of the most desirable lands near the Falls of the Ohio had been claimed by the proprietors and a few of their cronies, Williams resolved to "stop all clamors of that kind" by granting no more than a thousand acres of land to anyone near the Falls and by permitting no existing grantee to keep more than a thousand acres.[69] The proprietors also decided not to complete the sale of entered or surveyed tracts until the proprietors' title to the lands was resolved.[70] As John Floyd put it in a letter to William Preston, the proprietors decided they "would not ask any money for lands already sold till September next, in order to give them time to enquire into the validity of their title, but in the mean time should go on with surveying in order that the bounds of each person's claim might be ascertained, to give those who want to settle an opportunity of knowing where the vacant land lay."[71]

All these measures were palliatives, not cures. They did not and could not address the basic flaws that the proprietors' claims contravened the Proclamation of 1763, the charters of North Carolina and Virginia, and the competing claims of other settlers and land speculators and that the establishment of a new proprietary colony was inconsistent with the idea of an independent American republic. Floyd also told Preston that as soon as Henderson left Kentucky to lobby the Virginia Convention and the Congress, "most of the men about Harrodsburg have re-assumed their former resolution of not complying with any of the office rules whatever. . . . All of the people out of that neighborhood go on with entering and surveying as usual."[72]

In December 1776 Virginia drove a stake into the heart of the Transylvania Company's pretensions by carving out of Fincastle County a new county, Kentucky County, including most of the land that the company had claimed.[73] Colonel Henderson's opposition only delayed Kentucky from officially becoming part of Virginia.[74] Patrick Henry, by this time Virginia's governor, led the efforts to invalidate the Transylvania Company's claims. Henderson and his colleagues shifted their efforts from claiming outright ownership of most of Kentucky and a chunk of Tennessee to seeking a grant of far less acreage in payment for their expenses and the benefits that had resulted from their settlements in the wilderness. This rearguard action, waged over the following several years, ultimately resulted in Virginia and North Carolina each awarding 200,000 acres to the proprietors.[75] In the late 1790s, after lingering Indian claims had been resolved by Congress, the 400,000 acres were surveyed and allotted among the proprietors—who did not see fit to share any part of the awarded land to Daniel Boone for his "signal services" to them.[76]

In a single year, 1775, Daniel Boone had led the blazing of the road over which hundreds of thousands were to enter Kentucky within the next twenty years. He had held the Transylvania settlers together in the face of a murderous Indian attack much like the one that had caused settlers to turn back in 1773. He had played a key role in the building of Boonesborough, one of the earliest settlements in Kentucky. He and his brother Squire had led substantial numbers of settlers into Kentucky after the first trip in March and April. Together these were substantial steps toward a transforming westward expansion of America.

Despite all these accomplishments, at the end of 1775 the white settlements in Kentucky were small and frail. Indian attacks continued. In late December 1775 Col. Arthur Campbell and two young men were fired on as they were locating land across the Kentucky River from Boonesborough. Campbell escaped. Boone and others ran to look for the young men but found only moccasin tracks. Four days later one of the young men was found lying "killed and sculped in a corn field" about three miles north of Boonesborough. John Williams, on behalf of the Transylvania proprietors, sent out rangers to look for the raiders, for two shillings a day and "five pounds for every scalp they should produce," but the raiders were not found.[77]

The Indians, Boone later told Filson, "seemed determined to persecute us for erecting this fortification" at Boonesborough.[78] In light of the fighting that had already broken out between British troops and American colonists, whites in Kentucky correctly feared that the British would stir up Indian attacks upon the western settlers, as the French had done in the French and Indian War. All of these uncertainties caused settlers to leave Kentucky in large numbers, until only about two hundred remained in Kentucky's settlements as 1775 came to an end.[79]

Birthplace of Daniel Boone. Largely rebuilt in 1750s after the Boone family left for North Carolina. Photograph c. 1860.

Courtesy of Wisconsin Historical Society (WHi 4531)

Engraving of the Cumberland Gap by H. Fenn (D. Appleton & Co., 1872)

From an engraving in the possession of the author

Artist unknown, sketch purporting to be of John Floyd
Filson Historical Society, Louisville

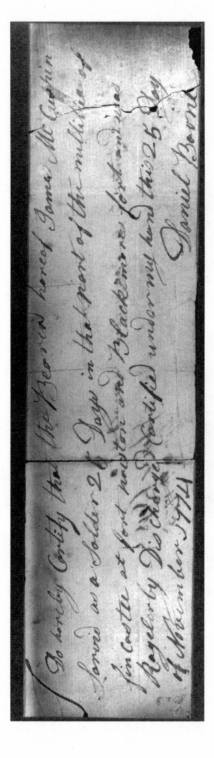

Certificate, signed by Boone, of military service in and discharge from Fincastle County Militia, for James McCushin [*sic*], Nov. 25, 1774. Earliest known document written and signed by Boone.

Filson Historical Society, Louisville

Sketch of Boonesborough

Filson Historical Society, Louisville

Portrait of Lt. Gov. Henry Hamilton. Hamilton, the British commandant at Detroit, instigated and supplied the Indian attacks on Boonesborough and other frontier settlements during the Revolution.

Hamilton Papers (pfMS Eng 509.2,), courtesy of the Houghton Library, Harvard University

Henry Hamilton's line drawing of Pacanné, or Pecan, a Miami chief who accompanied Hamilton's expedition from Detroit to Vincennes

Hamilton Papers (pfMS Eng 509.2), courtesy of the Houghton Library, Harvard University

Karl Bodmer, *Capture of the Daughters of D. Boone and Callaway by the Indians*, 1852. Lithograph, 17 ⅛" x 22 ⅛" . *Mildred Lane Kemper Art Museum, Washington University in St. Louis. Transfer from Special Collections, Olin Library, Washington University, 1988.*

Engraved by R.W. Dodson from a Portrait by J.W. Morgan Painted for the National Portrait Gallery and in possession of James B. Longacre.

SIMON KENTON.

Simon Kenton

James B. Longacre, line-and-stipple engraving of Simon Kenton, from
National Portrait Gallery of Distinguished Americans (1835)
Photograph courtesy of Richard Taylor

Charles Bird King (1785–1862), *Payta-kootha, a Shawanoe Warrior*, from McKenney and Hall, *History of the Indian Tribes of North America* (Philadelphia: Frederick W. Greenough, 1838–44). Paytakootha, or Flying Clouds, representing the Shawnees, signed several treaties ceding Shawnee lands, including the 1795 Treaty of Greenville. The Shawnees proposed to cut Boone's ears in similar fashion when Boone was a Shawnee captive.

Courtesy of University of Cincinnati Digital Press

KISH-KAL-WA

A SHAWANOE CHIEF.

Charles Bird King (1785–1862), *Kish-Kal-Wa, a Shawanoe Chief,* from McKenney and Hall, *History of the Indian Tribes of North America* (Philadelphia: Frederick W. Greenough, 1838–44). Kish-Kal-Wa's ears have been cut like those of Paytakootha. *Courtesy of University of Cincinnati Digital Press*

9

DARK AND BLOODY GROUND

An Introduction to Kentucky during the Revolutionary War

THE REVOLUTIONARY WAR WAS A LONG ONE. THE FIGHTING WITH the British began in April 1775, more than a year before the Declaration of Independence. The peace treaty was not signed until September 1783, though fighting in the coastal colonies substantially ended with the defeat of Gen. Charles Cornwallis at Yorktown in October 1781. The fighting in distant Kentucky lasted even longer, however, and, in proportion to the population of settlers, was far bloodier. Between 1775 and 1782 some 860 Kentuckians in the central bluegrass region alone died war-related deaths.[1] Relative to the population during those years, that loss was seven times as great as the comparable number of war-related deaths in the thirteen coastal colonies. George Rogers Clark, an American military leader on the frontier, estimated that "upward of two thousand souls have perished on our side, in a moderate calculation," during the Indian wars in Kentucky.[2]

The Kentuckians kept close track of the progress of the Revolution unfolding in the east and honored revolutionary turning points in the names they gave to Kentucky towns (Lexington, for the early clash in Massachusetts; Washington and Georgetown, for the commander of the rebel army; Louisville, Paris, and Versailles, for America's French ally) and counties (Bourbon and Fayette, again for the alliance with France).[3] The fighting and the issues in Kentucky, however, were largely different from the fighting in the coastal colonies. Knowing about those differences helps in understanding the engagements in which Boone was involved, including the attacks on Boonesborough in 1776, the capture and rescue in 1776 of Boone's daughter and the Callaway daughters, the Indians' capture of Boone and the salt-boilers from Boonesborough in 1778, the siege of Boonesborough in 1778, the Indians' crushing defeat of the Kentucky militia at the Battle of the Blue Licks in 1782, the subsequent American retaliation against the Shawnees north of the Ohio River, and the campaigns against the western tribes that led to the opening up of the Northwest Territories to American settlement.

The fighting in Kentucky during the Revolutionary War, unlike that in the coastal colonies, was not, for the most part, directly with the British, but with Indians funded and armed and incited by the British and sometimes accompanied by British or Canadian soldiers. Kentucky's struggling was frontier warfare, marked more by raids and hand-to-hand combat—and by destruction of crops and homes—than by pitched battles or prolonged sieges. There was much less fighting in Kentucky between American settlers (pro-independence Whigs vs. pro-British Tories) than there was in the Carolinas, although there were white renegades who led Indian attacks on the settlers, and there were also acute tensions between settlers in Kentucky (Harrodsburg vs. the Transylvania proprietors, for example; squatters vs. claimants under officers' warrants; Virginians vs. settlers from North Carolina vs. Pennsylvanians). The killing in Kentucky also lasted much longer. Indeed, it went on more than ten years after Cornwallis's surrender at Yorktown in 1781.

Just as the battling in the Ohio Valley during the French and Indian War had been three-cornered—French and French colonists versus British and British colonists, with each assisted by Indians seeking to preserve their lands—so the fighting in the Ohio Valley during the Revolution involved three forces: Americans, Indians, and British. None of the three was a monolith; rather, each was a congeries of disparate groups, often with conflicting aims.[4]

Several of the American colonies (notably Virginia, Pennsylvania, New York, and North Carolina but also Connecticut) had conflicting claims to land in the Ohio Valley. Americans from different colonies, in the years since 1763, had staked claims to lands in Kentucky and elsewhere in the Ohio Valley (including lands north of the Ohio River that the British Parliament in October 1774, in the Quebec Act, had proclaimed were part of Quebec).[5] These settlers and absentee claimants alike sought to preserve their land interests during the Revolution. Americans of widely different backgrounds—former officers in the French and Indian War such as George Washington; grantees of the Transylvania Company; settlers with claims under Virginia land law based on preemption or improvements—had claims that involved much of the best land in Kentucky. They shared a strong common interest in keeping the land they had claimed. With few exceptions victory by the British in the Revolutionary War would have hurt that interest.[6]

In the case of officers and claimants under officers' warrants, the British had officially interpreted the 1763 proclamation to permit trans-Appalachian land grants only to British regular officers, not to colonial militia officers such as Washington. Land claimants under Virginia officers' warrants had to be concerned about whether the Crown would honor warrants that had been issued in contravention of the 1763 proclamation and by a colony that had rebelled against Britain. Similar issues threatened the land claims of settlers such as those at Harrodsburg who based their land claims on preemption or on improvements to claimed lands, under provisions of Virginia's land acts.

Virginia's governor Lord Dunmore had not won the hearts of Kentucky settlers by issuing a proclamation in March 1775, under directions from the British Ministry of Trade, that all land in Kentucky was to be auctioned off to the highest bidder, rather than being sold at set low prices. As John Floyd wrote to William Preston in April 1775: "The people in general seem not to approve the Governor's instructions with regard to settling the lands" because the settlers had little money and did not want to pay top dollar but preferred to exercise settlement rights and preemption privileges and to pay a fixed low price intended to encourage settlement. After hearing from Lord Dunmore of the 1775 proclamation, Preston, knowing how unpopular it was, sought guidance from the increasingly anti-British Virginia Convention, which advised the surveyors "to pay no regard to the Proclamation."[7] Through Boone, Preston directed Floyd and the other Fincastle surveyors not to stretch a chain to survey any land under Dunmore's proclamation.[8]

Even the Transylvania Company, for all its ambivalence about the Revolution (coupling professed loyalty to the British sovereign with praise of the patriots' pursuit of liberty), came to have economic reasons to back the rebels. By the end of 1776 the company's proprietors had seen their grand hopes of becoming "lords of the soil" ended by Virginia's formation of Kentucky as a county of Virginia. Thereafter, the proprietors' only hope was to gain substantial compensatory acreage from Virginia and North Carolina. That hope was more likely to be realized if the Revolution succeeded.

The Ohio Valley Indians were fighting a last-ditch effort to keep their lands. Boone recognized this fact dispassionately and without demonizing the Indians. Boone told his first biographer, John Filson, that in 1778 "the Indians ... were greatly alarmed with our increase in number and fortifications.

. . . They evidently saw the approaching hour when the Long Knife would dispossess them of their desirable habitations; and anxiously concerned for futurity, determined utterly to extirpate the whites out of Kentucke."[9] And while Lord Dunmore's War had ended with some Shawnee chiefs agreeing to yield rights to lands east and south of the Ohio River, that agreement recognized the Indians' rights to lands on the other side of the Ohio. The Shawnees and other Ohio Valley Indians wanted to preserve those rights and remembered that in 1764, after two years of bitter fighting in Pontiac's War, the British had agreed to respect the Ohio as the boundary between British settlers and the Indians.[10] Many Ohio Valley Indians may have thought that once again they could fight the whites to a standstill—though much had changed between 1764 and 1775, including tremendous growth in the number of white settlers west of the Alleghenies. Perhaps, with British support, the Indians could also drive American settlers out of Kentucky.

Not all of the Indians favored war with the whites. Even before the beginning of the Revolution, some of the Indians of the Ohio Valley saw the futility of opposing white expansion. One of the leading Shawnees, Cornstalk, the principal chief of the Maquachake division of the Shawnees, who had been one of the signers of the Camp Charlotte agreement, generally urged accommodation with the whites—although when the Americans in 1776 sought a promise of neutrality from Ohio Valley Indians, Cornstalk pointed out that the whites' taking of Shawnee lands south of the Ohio "sits heavy upon our Hearts" and "is the cause of our discontent."[11] Cornstalk, whose division of the Shawnees was the most inclined to seek peace with the Americans, was killed in 1777 by whites while he was being held hostage in an American fort. Although his murder enraged all Shawnees and united most of the Ohio Indians against the Americans, many Shawnees, as the fighting with the whites continued and as whites destroyed Shawnee villages north of the Ohio River, moved away from the Ohio Valley to get farther away from the Americans. Many went to Missouri.[12] Most of the Shawnees who remained in Ohio, however, were determined to fight against any further encroachments by American settlers and allied themselves with other tribes in that struggle.[13]

The British, in supporting Indian attacks on Americans in Kentucky and elsewhere in the Ohio Valley during the Revolution, sought to further three objectives: to reassert control over the Ohio Valley; to hold onto Canada; and to divert American military forces from the coastal colonies. While

Britain after the French and Indian War had taken control of the string of forts the French had built between Detroit and the forks of the Ohio, by 1773 Britain had abandoned several of the forts, ordered Fort Pitt to be razed, and maintained garrisons only at Detroit, Kaskaskia, and Michilimackinac. In effect, the British pullback from the Ohio Valley had left most of the valley to the Indians and the American frontiersmen crossing the Alleghenies, despite the proclamation's ban against western settlement.[14] The American capture of Montreal in November 1775 and the American attack on Quebec the following month showed how serious was the risk that Britain might lose Canada. Although most of the British military strength in Canada was near Montreal, well to the east of Kentucky, the British undertook, from headquarters in their fort at Detroit, to recruit and support Indian allies to attack the American settlements in the Ohio Valley.

Detroit in the mid-1770s may have had as many as two thousand residents—French, Indians, and a few British—making it far larger than any of the settlements in Kentucky.[15] Lieutenant Governor Henry Hamilton, who had taken command of the Detroit garrison in November 1775, in June 1777 was directed by London to employ Indians "in making a Diversion and exciting an alarm upon the frontiers of Virginia and Pennsylvania."[16] Hamilton carried this out by arranging Indian attacks in Kentucky and campaigns against Wheeling on the Ohio River that kept American forces at Fort Pitt on the defensive. Not infrequently, British or Canadian officers accompanied the Indian attackers—according to Hamilton, with "the strictest injunctions to discourage and restrain them from their usual barbarities."[17] British or French-Canadian soldiers accompanied Indians at several of the most important engagements in Kentucky during the Revolution, including the siege of Boonesborough and the Battle of the Blue Licks. Much of the fighting in Kentucky, however, particularly the smaller-scale raids, was between American settlers and Indians, without any British or Canadian participation.

The British enlisted help from the Indians in part by diplomacy, assisted by whites who lived with Indians, dressed like Indians, were fluent in Indian languages, and could orate Indian style—such men as Simon Girty and his brothers, who went over from the American side to the British side in 1778. The British also furnished the Indians with guns, tomahawks, ammunition, and other war necessities, including (this being Indian warfare) war paint. In September 1778, for example, the month the Indians besieged Boonesborough, Governor Hamilton included in a report listing goods on hand in the fort at Detroit for the Indian department "eighty pounds of rose pink and five hundred pounds of vermilion."[18]

The British paid Indians for American militia captives. Reputedly—certainly the Americans believed it to be so—Governor Hamilton also offered Indian five pounds for each American scalp. That was the same price that the Transylvania Company had agreed in 1776 to pay its rangers for each Indian scalp they brought in.[19] A Virginian woman in Detroit, married to one of Hamilton's interpreters, told an American trader in 1778 "that Governor Hamilton did all in his Power to induce all Nations of Indians to massacre the Frontier Inhabitants of Pennsylvania and Virginia and paid very high prices in Goods for the Scalps the Indians brought in."[20] This scalp-buying allegation, which Hamilton always denied, prompted George Rogers Clark and many other Americans to refer to the governor as "Hair-Buyer" Hamilton. The name had a catchy alliterative ring to it, and the charge made the settlers in the Kentucky forts more immune than they might otherwise have been to Hamilton's attempts to win them over to the British side by promising them free land. The evidence is inconclusive about specific payments having been made for American scalps, but Hamilton undoubtedly received American scalps from Indian raiding parties that had been armed and equipped by the British at Detroit. In September 1778, for example, Hamilton reported to his presiding general, Sir Frederick Haldimand, "Since last May the Indians in this district have taken thirty-four prisoners, seventeen of which they delivered up and eighty-one scalps, several prisoners taken and adopted not reckoned in this number."[21]

Hamilton was a well-born Anglo-Irishman—grandson of a viscount, son of a member of the Irish Parliament who served as collector for the ports of Dublin and Cork. He himself wrote well and drew skillful portraits of Indians.[22] Yet for all his breeding and culture, as governor at Detroit Hamilton was, as his letter to General Haldimand demonstrates, at the very least willing to accept large numbers of American scalps from his Indian allies. He also used American scalps to encourage the Indians to help the British. In his notes on a council with Indians at Detroit on June 2, 1778, he wrote, "Some Delawares are this day arrived who are desirous of showing their intention of joining their brethren & have presented me two pieces of dryed meat (scalps) one of which I have given to the Chippoweys, another to the Miamis, that they may show in their villages the disposition of the Delawares."[23] The reference to American scalps as "dryed meat" is unpleasantly flip.

In drafting the Declaration of Independence, Thomas Jefferson listed among the "repeated Injuries" that King George had inflicted upon the Americans the king's endeavors "to bring upon the Inhabitants of our Frontiers, the merciless Indian Savages, whose known Rule of Warfare, is an undistinguished Destruction, of all Ages, Sexes and Conditions." Jefferson doubtless had in mind the efforts of British leaders such as Henry Hamilton. Indeed, he was to use very similar words to justify the Americans' "strict confinement" of Hamilton after he was taken prisoner.[24]

The frontier warfare in Kentucky was much smaller in scale than the fighting in the coastal colonies. On the American side there were only about two hundred American settlers in Kentucky at the beginning of the war, not all of them capable of soldiering with a heavy rifle. The Shawnees had many more warriors in their villages north of the Ohio, but their traditional style of fighting was in small raids, like the dawn attacks in which James Boone and Captain Twitty had been killed. The Shawnees and other Ohio Valley Indians, however, were rapidly learning how to fight in larger-scale operations—in large part by having warriors of different tribes act together. The shared threat of increasing American settlement in the Ohio Valley, coupled with British supplies to different Indian groups, led to combined operations against the Americans.[25] At the Battle of Point Pleasant in October 1774 between five hundred and one thousand Shawnees and allies fought a sustained battle against the Virginia militia. Perhaps four hundred Indians and forty Canadians besieged Boonesborough in September 1778.

As the fighting went on, there were more large-scale engagements, with Indian tribes acting jointly and the number of American settlers in Kentucky and elsewhere in the Ohio Valley continuing to rise. In June 1782 the Indians in Ohio were strong enough to beat a force of some 500 Virginia and Pennsylvania militiamen on the Sandusky River in Ohio. That same year several hundred Indians from Great Lakes tribes, along with Shawnees, crossed the Ohio into Kentucky for raids and the decisive defeat of perhaps 180 members of the Kentucky militia at the Battle of the Blue Licks. Even greater numbers were involved in some of the battles between Americans and Indians in the 1790s, leading up to the Battle of Fallen Timbers in 1794.

Most of the combat in Kentucky during the Revolution, however, involved smaller numbers of participants. It was also a far more personal kind of fighting than the battles in the coastal colonies. Artillery, which played a key role in many of the eastern battles, was not a factor in any of the fights in Kentucky that Boone was involved in, though the presence of two small British field guns led to the surrender of two forts there in 1780—the only forts that were surrendered by the Americans in Kentucky during the Revolution. There were rumors that the British at Detroit were sending swivel guns to their Indian allies for the attack on Boonesborough in 1778. Even light artillery would have destroyed that fort's flimsy palisades. But the guns never appeared there, probably because of the difficulty of hauling them from Michigan. The weapon with the longest range in Boone's fights during the Revolution was the Kentucky rifle, capable of killing at little over a hundred yards.

Much of the fighting was at much closer range. The time needed to reload the single-shot rifle was often sufficient for a combatant, after an enemy had fired, to run up close enough to throw a tomahawk at the shooter or to strike him with a tomahawk, knife, clubbed rifle, or club. How personal was the fighting? Very, as Boone would discover outside of Boonesborough in April 1777, when he was shot and nearly tomahawked by Shawnees. And on September 11, 1777, while Squire Boone and other white settlers were shelling corn near Harrodsburg, Indians attacked. Squire Boone took a shot at the Indians and squatted behind a tree to reload. An Indian shot dead another white, who fell next to Squire Boone. The Indian ran up with his tomahawk to scalp the fallen man, just as Squire Boone was drawing a short three-edged sword. A glancing blow from the Indian's tomahawk cut a three-inch gash in Squire Boone's forehead, while he stabbed the Indian in the belly with one hand. With his other hand, Squire Boone grabbed the Indian's sash and pulled him closer as he pushed his sword in, until the sword stuck out a foot behind the Indian's back. The Indian reached for the hunting knife that hung from Squire Boone's shot pouch, but the blood from Boone's forehead and from the Indian's wound made the knife handle so slippery that the Indian could not draw the knife. Squire Boone pushed the Indian back over a low wall. The fall pushed the sword up inside the Indian and broke off its point, and the Indian died. Squire Boone would later say it was "the best little Indian fight he was ever in."[26]

The Indian attacks in Kentucky and the retaliatory white expeditions into Indian country in Ohio also differed from fighting in the coastal states in terms of the amount of food that was destroyed. Shawnees attacking Boonesborough and other Kentucky forts, for example, frequently burned all of the settlers' corn and killed all their livestock.[27] The whites, in their many expeditions into Ohio between 1779 and 1794, regularly torched Indian villages, cornfields, and stored corn. The warfare was total warfare. Destroying food was a key component of the Americans' eventual defeat of the Ohio Valley Indians.[28]

In the Carolinas much of the bloodiest fighting during the Revolution was between Tories, those who favored the British, and Whigs, as American Revolutionaries were called. Part of it was class warfare. The hostility between the haves and the have-nots, manifest in the 1768 storming of Richard Henderson's courthouse in North Carolina and in the burning of his house and barn, burst out during the Revolution into all-out warfare—although in topsy-turvy fashion, with the highland Scots and other western North Carolinians often fighting for the Crown against the richer lowlanders, whom they hated for actual and perceived land sales abuses. The richer lowlanders in North Carolina tended to favor the Revolutionary cause, no doubt in part because of their interest in western lands.

In Kentucky there were no major fights between Tory and Whig settlers, though there were British sympathizers, including many of Rebecca Boone's family, the Bryans. Some who settled in Kentucky during the Revolution, particularly emigrants from North Carolina, were clearly British sympathizers— "all grand tories, pretty nigh," who "Had been treated so bad [in Carolina], they had to run off."[29] Others came to Kentucky not just because of the lure of cheap land but also to avoid having to choose between fighting for the British side or the rebel side. There were also whites, including the notorious Simon Girty, who joined the British cause and fought with the Indians against the Americans in Kentucky. Boone himself had British ties. In addition to the Tory sympathies of his Bryan in-laws, Boone's captain's commission had been signed by Lord Dunmore. If Boone fought the British, it was not so much from ideological commitment to American independence as it was part of his efforts to defend the settlements in Kentucky against Indian attacks (and the British who aided them).

There were also social strains among the Kentucky settlers, linked both to class differences and to land claims. We have seen how settlers at Harrodsburg wrote to the Virginia Convention describing Henderson and the other Transylvania proprietors as "men from North Carolina stiling 'emselves Proprietors" and saying—ominously, if vaguely—that if the self-styled proprietors "have leave to continue to act in their arbitrary manner out of the controul of this Colony [Virginia] the end must be evident to every well wisher to American Liberty."[30] In addition, there was tension between settlers from different colonies— Virginia, Pennsylvania, and North Carolina. The Continental Congress was brand new and the concept of an American national government was still nascent. Different groups of settlers based their right to land in Kentucky on conflicting claims of different colonies under their royal charters. Many settlers from Pennsylvania and North Carolina, seeing little chance that Virginia would recognize their land claims, petitioned to have Kentucky governed by Congress, not by Virginia—on the theory that Kentucky had been part of the royal domain that had fallen to Congress when the colonies declared their independence.[31]

There were other economic bases for disagreements between settlers from different colonies. Virginia, Pennsylvania, and North Carolina had long vied with each other for control of the Ohio Valley fur trade. In the French and Indian War, for example, George Washington, who had his own interest in land claims in the Ohio Valley through his membership in the Ohio Company, had urged Virginia's lieutenant governor "immediately" to open a new road from Virginia to the Ohio so that Virginia could stake claims to land and trade ahead of "a set of rascally Fellows divested of all faith and honor"—that is, traders from Pennsylvania.[32] In December 1774 Virginia's governor Lord Dunmore wrote to Lord Dartmouth, the secretary of state for the colonies: "The trade carried on with the Ohio Indians has been almost engrossed by the Province of Pennsylvania, which they have draw[n] to themselves, artfully enough, but with what degree of propriety or right I must leave to your Lordships Judgment, by repeated treaties held of their own Authority, and at such times and for such purposes as they think fit. . . . [The Pennsylvania traders] have made it their constant business to discredit the Virginians (who lye much more convenient for carrying on a Trade with these Indians than the Pennsylvanians) and make the Indians consider them in the most odious light."[33]

Other differences between the settlers in Kentucky were based on competing land claims—not just those of the Transylvania Company versus those based on grants by Virginia, but also claims of squatters and improvers versus claims based on officers' warrants and those made at different times. One fruitful cause of discord was the 1779 ruling of the Virginia legislature that land would be given to settlers who came to Kentucky before 1778—that is, before the great bulk of the settlers had come to Kentucky.[34] That ruling gave the more recent settlers an economic incentive to back the Crown: if the Revolutionary Virginia government had already decreed that they were not entitled to free land, the Crown could hardly do worse to them. One anonymous discontented settler wrote that the land mess in Kentucky was "entirely oweing to a Set of Nabobs in Virginia, taking all the land there by Officer Warrants and Pre-emption Rights." He predicted that if the English were to go to Kentucky and offer the settlers "protection from the Indians, the greatest Part will join" the British side.[35] In May 1776 John Floyd wrote to William Preston that there was "the D—l to pay here about land—pray try to get something done by the Convention with regard to selling those lands, or there'll be bloodshed soon. . . . Hundreds of wretches come down the Ohio & build pens or cabins, return & sell them; the people come down & settle on the land they purchase; these same places are claimed by some one else, & then quarrels ensue. In short they now begin to pay no kind of regard to the officers land more than any other. Many have come down here & not stayed more than 3 weeks, & have returned home with 20 cabins a piece, & so on. They make very free with my character, swearing I am engrossing the country [with surveys] & have no warrants for the land, & if I have, they will drive me & the officers, too, to hell."[36]

Conflicting claims to land in Kentucky gave rise to fifty years of litigation. Neither those conflicting claims nor the other tensions among settlers in Kentucky, however, gave rise to outright fighting between different groups of settlers in Kentucky during the Revolutionary War—unlike the bitter warfare between Whigs and Tories in the Carolinas. The settlers in Kentucky were few in number, and their immediate need was not to kill each other but to act together in mutual defense against Indian attack.

A final distinguishing characteristic of the bloodshed in Kentucky in the Revolutionary period was its length. Well before gunshots were exchanged between British soldiers and American minutemen at Lexington and Concord in April 1775, Indians and whites were killing each other in Kentucky—in the Indian attacks on Boone's parties in October 1773 and in March 1775, for example, and in the Battle of Point Pleasant in 1774. Combat in Kentucky continued well after the surrender by General Cornwallis at Yorktown in October 1781, which substantially ended fighting in the coastal colonies. The biggest clash in Kentucky during the Revolution, the Battle of the Blue Licks, took place in August 1782, almost a year after the Yorktown surrender, and raids in Kentucky continued well after the British and the Americans signed their peace treaty in February 1783.

The post-treaty fighting in Kentucky was primarily between Americans and Indians, but with strong British encouragement of the Indians, who were unified as never before by the westward flood of American settlement and by the American government's relentless pressure for Indian land cessions.[37] The Indians at first were remarkably successful in this fighting, even against large American forces. In October 1790 Wabash and Miami Indians defeated over three hundred regular American troops and over a thousand Kentucky and Pennsylvania militiamen under Gen. Josiah Harmar in western Ohio. In November 1791 over six hundred Americans were killed near what is now Fort Recovery, Ohio, when Indians led by the Miami war chief Little Turtle crushed an American army led by Gen. Arthur St. Clair.[38] St. Clair's defeat—the worst ever inflicted on Americans by Indians—breathed new life in the Indian resistance to the whites because, as an American general put it, "the Indians began to believe Themselves invincible, and they truly had great cause of triumph."[39] The Indians in the Ohio Valley were not finally beaten until troops under Gen. "Mad Anthony" Wayne defeated an Indian confederation at the Battle of Fallen Timbers, fought in August 1794 just south of what is now Toledo, Ohio, and then methodically destroyed the Indians' villages and cornfields.

Much of the larger post-Yorktown encounters in the Ohio Valley took place in Ohio, but Indian raids continued in Kentucky until 1793—fully ten years after the treaty that purported to end the War of Independence. In the last Indian attack in Kentucky, at Morgan's Station, east of Lexington in what is now Montgomery County, a band of Cherokees and Shawnees killed two, took over twenty hostages, and tomahawked twelve captives to death on their retreat to the north.[40]

The British did not themselves fight the Americans in the Ohio Valley after the Revolution, though seventy Canadians fought alongside the Indian confederacy against General Wayne's troops at the Battle of Fallen Timbers. Yet the British encouraged the Indians' resistance to the Americans by Britain's continued occupation of Detroit and six other posts on American territory, by Canadian trade with the Indians from those posts, and by supplying ammunition and provisions. The 1783 peace treaty required all British garrisons on American soil to be withdrawn "with all convenient speed," but Britain's home minister instructed the governor of Canada not to evacuate the forts—presumably to enable Canadians and British to continue to benefit from the fur trade in the hunting grounds between the Great Lakes and the Ohio River. The British justified their delay, however, by claiming that America was in breach of its treaty obligations to assist in British collection of prewar debts and in Loyalists' reclamation of confiscated properties. The British even suggested the creation of a neutral Indian state between the Great Lakes and the Ohio River, which would have allowed indefinite Canadian control of the fur trade in the region.

Yet the Battle of Fallen Timbers and its aftermath made bitterly clear to the Indians that they could expect no further significant help from the British. When Indians retreating after the battle sought refuge at the nearby British post Fort Miami, the British shut the fort's gates in their faces. The British garrison did nothing to prevent Wayne's men from destroying Indian houses and cornfields (Wayne said he had never seen "such immense fields of corn," which he described as "the grand emporium of the hostile Indians of the West") on the Maumee, in the Auglaize Valley, and, in Wayne's words, "for about fifty miles on each side of the Miami."[41] Within months Britain, by signing Jay's Treaty in November 1794, confirmed America's rights to the lands between the Great Lakes and the Ohio and agreed to evacuate its garrisons there. Even though the British did not finally evacuate Detroit and the garrisons south of the Great Lakes until 1796, Wayne was able to point to Jay's treaty and Britain's promise to abandon the garrisons when he negotiated with the Indians the Treaty of Greenville in 1795, by which all but the northwestern corner of Ohio was ceded to the Americans and the balance of the Northwest Territory was opened up to American settlement and the Indians acknowledged the United States "to be our father" and that they "must call them brothers no more."[42]

For all of the ways in which fighting in Kentucky during the Revolution differed from the war fought in the colonies to the east, there was one basic similarity. In Kentucky, as in the coastal colonies, the American settlers and the British (in the case of Kentucky, acting primarily through their Indian allies) were contending for control of land. Through prolonged and determined efforts the American settlers won the struggle in both arenas. Boone played a key role in the fighting in Kentucky and thereby in the Americans' lasting hold on that valuable land.

10

THE CAPTURE AND RESCUE OF THE GIRLS

AT THE BEGINNING OF 1776 THE FEW SETTLERS IN KENTUCKY FACED a dire situation. Indians raiding near Boonesborough in December 1775 had killed and scalped one settler. Further raids were highly likely. Ammunition was growing "scant."[1] The British, from their fort in Detroit, were believed to be stirring up the Miamis and other Indian tribes to attack the barely two hundred settlers still in Kentucky.

The threat of large-scale Indian attacks, and the fact of Indian raids, kept the settlers "forted up"—confined to or near their crude forts at Boonesborough, Harrodsburg, and St. Asaph's, greatly restricted in what they could plant or harvest, unable to hunt far from the forts, unable to obtain new clothes, and without enough salt to preserve the meat they had. The cabins were small and dark, glass not being used in early Kentucky settlements. At least in Boonesborough's case, cabin floors may have been bare dirt.[2] Beds were covered with skins of buffalo, bear, and elk.[3] Picture, as settlers remembering those days described it, long confinement in "a row or two of Smoky cabins, among dirty women and men with greasy hunting shirts." Picture people "dirty, lousy, ragged and half starved."[4] Add stink and ghastly hygiene to the picture. Col. William Fleming, a physician by training, visiting Harrodsburg in the bitter winter of 1779–80, noted that the fort's one spring was situated in the lowest corner of the fort: "The whole dirt and filth of the Fort, putrified flesh, dead dogs, horse, cow, hog excrements and human odour [ordure?] all washed into it. Furthermore, the situation could hardly have been improved by the Ashes and sweepings of filthy Cabbins, the dirtiness of the people, steeping skins to dress and washing every sort of dirty rags and cloths in the spring makes the most filthy nauseous potation of the water imaginable and will certainly contribute to render the inhabitants of this place sickly."[5]

The stations housed few men and far fewer women. A member of a party surveying land around the Falls of the Ohio for the Transylvania Company in January 1776 said Boonesborough had only six women—the wives of Daniel Boone and of Squire Boone, Daniel Boone's daughter Susannah (married to William Hays), and three others.[6] The hollow square in which Boonesborough cabins were arranged was still incomplete.[7] Harrodsburg was not much bigger, having, according to a May 1777 census, only eighty-five men and twenty-four adult women.[8] Harrodsburg grew both by the arrival of new settlers, including some who moved from Boonesborough, and by births. Early in 1776 a woman named Mrs. Hugh Wilson gave birth to the first non-Indian child born in Kentucky. According to Boone's nineteenth-century biographer Lyman Draper, the child "was named Harrod Wilson and grew up to be a worthless man."[9]

It would have made sense, as George Rogers Clark recognized, under the threat of Indian attack, to consolidate the settlements' scattered feeble forces into one larger fortification, but the settlers' "dependence upon hunting for the greatest portion of [their] provisions forbade this": "No people could be in a more alarming position. Detached at least two hundred miles from the nearest settlement of the states, we were surrounded by numerous Indian nations, each one far superior to ourselves in numbers and spurred on by the British Government to destroy us."[10] The settlers' confinement in their forts hindered their ability to plant or harvest crops and increased their dependence on hunting. An analysis of bone fragments from a hearth at Boonesborough—probably dating back to forting-up times, judging by the presence of buffalo bones—gives some indication of what the settlers ate: some beef and pig but also deer, black bear, buffalo, turkey, elk, and channel catfish.[11] The settlers' reliance on hunting increased the killing of game and decreased the game population in Kentucky. The cycle that threatened Boone's favorite way of life was accelerating.

Despite the Indian threat, beginning in the spring of 1776, more settlers came into Kentucky, both up though the Cumberland Gap and down the Ohio River. Each succeeding spring saw more settlers arrive, even though the Indian threat kept growing. In March 1776 an Indian trader named Louis Lorimier came from Montreal to the British garrison at Detroit to help to incite the Indians against the American settlers. Lorimier was not physically imposing—by some accounts he was less than five feet tall and skinny—but he was an experienced trader who spoke several Indian languages, and he had earned the Indians' respect through his honest trading.[12] In April 1776 Mingos, after killing one settler not far from what is now Frankfort, captured other young settlers nearby.[13] To the south of Kentucky anti-accommodationist Cherokees, led by Dragging Canoe, attacked American settlements and ambushed immigrants passing through the Cumberland Gap.[14] The Cherokees had been incited to attack the Americans by Indians from the north. In April 1776 a delegation of Shawnees, Ottawas, Mohawks, and other northern Indians, their faces blackened, had arrived in the Cherokee Overhill towns to urge joint Indian action against the Americans who were taking the Indians' lands. After the Mohawk and the Ottawa deputies had spoken, the leading Shawnee delegate produced "a War Belt about 9 feet long and six inches wide of purple Whampum strewed over with vermilion," recounted the encroachments by Americans, and said it is "better to die like men than to diminish away by inches." Dragging Canoe accepted the war belt, and the warriors joined in singing the war song.[15]

In mid-July 1776 the Indian threat became a concrete reality to Boone and the other Boonesborough settlers, when Indians seized Boone's thirteen-year-old daughter, Jemima, along with two other girls from Boonesborough, the daughters of Col. Richard Callaway—Fanny Callaway, aged fourteen, and her sixteen-year-old sister Betsy, who was engaged to marry Col. Richard Henderson's nephew Samuel Henderson. The capture and subsequent rescue of the girls seized Americans' imaginations and contributed to Boone's growing reputation but also tell us much about the conditions in which Boone and his colleagues were living.

The afternoon of Sunday, July 14, 1776, was a quiet one at Boonesborough. The men and the few women at the settlement were wearing their Sunday best. Most of the men wore pantaloons rather than their usual weekday breechclouts and leggings. Boone was resting in bed. Betsy Callaway's fiancé, Samuel Henderson, Richard Henderson's nephew, was halfway through his weekly shave. Jemima Boone, who had hurt her foot stepping on a broken cane stalk, wanted to cool the injured foot in the water of the Kentucky River. She was also tired of being confined in the squalid little station.[16] Jemima and the Callaway girls decided to take a canoe out into the river.

The Kentucky River now has been turned into a series of lakes by a string of dams. In Boone's day there were no dams, just pools and rippling shoals, with trickier currents than in today's dam-tamed river.[17] Boone had warned

Jemima to keep the canoe close to Boonesborough's cabins, but the current took the girls downriver and toward the north bank, where a war party of two Cherokees and three Shawnees was waiting for them. When the canoe got close to the bank, one Indian dove in and grabbed the buffalo tug at the boat's bow. One of the girls thought she recognized the Indian at the bow as an Indian who had stayed at Boonesborough from time to time. "Law, Simon! How you scared me!" she called out. Then she realized that he was not the man she knew and began to hit him on the head with her canoe paddle.[18] The Indians pulled the canoe to shore. The girls screamed until an Indian grabbed Betsy Callaway by the hair and made a scalping gesture to make plain what would happen if they did not shut up. The Indians then dragged the girls into the woods.

One of the Indians was Hanging Maw, a Cherokee whom Jemima had encountered before, probably around the Watauga River in North Carolina.[19] He spoke English. When Jemima told him she was Boone's daughter, he asked if the other girls were her sisters. Jemima said yes, thinking they would be better treated if Hanging Maw thought all of the girls were daughters of his old acquaintance Boone. "We have done pretty well for old Boone this time," Hanging Maw said.[20]

Some Boonesborough settlers heard the girls' cries across the river. A Callaway boy ran up to John Floyd and his friend Nathan Reid, screaming, "The savages have the girls!" Boone jumped up from his bed, pulled on his pants, and ran barefoot to the riverbank. Samuel Henderson ran there too, his face half-shaved and half-covered with shaving soap. So did Floyd and Reid. The sisters' father, Col. Richard Callaway, mounted up with his nephew Flanders Callaway, who had his eye on young Jemima and soon was to marry her. With John Holder and a few other Boonesborough settlers, the Callaway men galloped to a ford about a mile away.

The Kentucky River was not wide behind Boonesborough. The settlers who had run to the riverbank could see on the far side the capsized canoe. John Gass, only twelve years old, stripped, swam across the river, and brought back the canoe. In it Boone, Floyd, Reid, Boone, Samuel Henderson, and others crossed to the north shore. Once there, the settlers split to search for and follow the Indians' trail in what little daylight was left, before making camp for the night. Boone sent young Gass back to the fort in the dark for ammunition, food, moccasins, and breechclouts. Boone was barefoot, and, as Nathan Reid put it, pantaloons "impeded our movement."[21] Frontiersmen such as Boone found they could move more quickly in the woods dressed like Indians in breechclouts and leggings than in European pants.

The girls had been dressed up for Sunday. After cutting off their dresses at the knees so the girls could move more quickly, the Indians led the girls off at a fast pace north toward the Ohio River and the Shawnee towns across it. By the afternoon of the second day the Indians and their captives were twenty-five miles from Boonesborough. The girls kept breaking branches and dropping bits of cloth as signs for the settlers to follow. Betsy Callaway ripped her white handkerchief into pieces—one conveniently embroidered "E. Callaway"—and dropped them along the way. She also took care to press her wooden-heeled shoes into any moist ground along the way (and there were plenty of buffalo wallows, soft and bare of grass), until an Indian, seeing what she was doing, knocked the heels off her shoes. Jemima used her sore foot as an excuse to scream out loudly whenever she stumbled or fell. No rescuers, however, were within earshot. An Indian found an old horse in the woods and piled the girls on it, one or more at a time. To slow the trip down and give more time for the rescue party they hoped was behind them, the girls encouraged the horse to caper and repeatedly fell off it, as if they had no clue how to ride. The Indians eventually turned the horse loose, and the group went forward on foot.[22]

Led by Boone, the settlers pursued. On the second day Boone became concerned that they were not gaining on the Indians because the captors' trail was hard to follow. There was also the risk that if the settlers followed in the Indians' footsteps, the Indians would hear them coming and have time to tomahawk the girls before the settlers could get to them. The tracks told Boone that the Indians intended to cross the Licking River at the Upper Blue Licks. Boone decided not to follow the tracks but to head directly to where he thought the Indians were likely to cross. As Reid remembered it, "Paying no further attention to the trail, [Boone] now took a strait course through the woods, with increased speed, followed by the men in perfect silence."[23] Later in the day the settlers once again came upon the tracks of the Indians, which renewed their confidence in Boone's woodcraft. Mid-morning on the third day Boone and his men came upon a creek. Boone paused, Reid said, "and remarked that from the course [the Indians] had traveled, he was confident they had crossed the stream a short distance below." The men went downstream "and strange to say, we had not gone down more than 200 yards before we struck the trail again."[24]

The Indians' trail followed a buffalo trace parallel to the Warrior's Path. Boone started jogging, and the other men followed. The pace was dauntingly fast, and they had already covered over thirty miles. Some of the men were quite young—Samuel Henderson was thirty, John Floyd around twenty-six, Nathan Reid twenty-three—but Boone, who was setting the pace, was forty-one. There was more frequent sign now—a wounded and dying snake, the carcass of a recently killed buffalo calf, blood still trickling down from its back, where part of its hump had been cut off. Boone was sure the Indians would stop to cook the buffalo meat at the first water they reached.[25]

A few miles from the Licking River the Indians paused to kindle a fire to cook the piece of buffalo hump. One of the Indians playfully pulled at Betsy Callaway's hair while she was near the fire. She scooped up some hot coals on a piece of bark and poured them on the Indian's moccasins, causing him to "hop around lively." The other Indians thought this was pretty funny and called her "a fine young squaw."[26]

Hanging Maw admired Jemima's looks, especially the long black hair that fell nearly to her knees. On that morning he asked Jemima to dress his hair and "look over his head"—that is, check for lice, as the girls regularly did for each other. Jemima did so. (Many years later Jemima's niece, hearing Rebecca tell the story, said, "I wouldn't have done it, look at a lousy Indian's head, not I." "Oh yes, you would," Jemima told her. "Every such thing tended to delay their progress, and that was what we studied every art to effect, for we felt sure father and friends would exert every nerve for our rescue.")[27]

Betsy Callaway sat on a log not far from the fire. After Jemima had finished with Hanging Maw's hair, Jemima and Fanny Callaway knelt near Betsy Callaway, the oldest of the three girls. Betsy began "opening their hair, lousing their heads, and shedding a torrent of tears."[28] Jemima heard a sound in the woods, looked up, and saw her father a hundred yards away, "creeping upon his breast like a snake."[29] She kept still. Fanny Callaway, who was looking at an Indian standing by the campfire, saw blood spurt from the Indian's chest before she heard the gun that shot him.[30] "That's Daddy," Jemima cried out.[31]

Floyd fired too, at the same time as Boone, and was certain he had shot his target through the body.[32] Jemima and Fanny dropped to the ground. Betsy stood up. An Indian hurled his war club at her. She later told her children that she felt the club "touch her head as it passed."[33] Boone, Floyd, and the others raised the war whoop and charged the camp. The Indians fled, as

Floyd put it, "almost naked, some without their mockisons, and not one of them with so much as a knife or tomahawk."[34] Betsy Callaway ran toward the rescuers, disheveled, her dress cut short, her dark hair loose. One of the rescuers, thinking she was an Indian, raised his just-fired rifle to club her. Boone yelled out, "For God's sake, don't kill her when we've traveled so far to save her!"[35] Boone's cry stopped the man just before he brained her.

The girls' clothes were torn to shreds; their legs were bleeding. Boone covered them with blankets. "Thank Almighty Providence," he said, "for we have the girls safe. Let's all sit down by them now and have a hearty cry." Jemima remembered that "there was not a dry eye in the company."[36]

The rescuers and the girls made their way back to Boonesborough. They found the wandering old horse the girls had ridden before, and the girls took turns riding it—now without the difficulty they had feigned before. They teased Samuel Henderson about the aesthetics of his half-shaved face. They were joined by Colonel Callaway and the others who had ridden ahead to the Lower Blue Licks and had found the tracks of the Indians going north to Ohio. It was a tired and deeply relieved group that made its way back to Boonesborough. The fort was intact, though Indians had burned the outlying cabin, crops, and orchard of one settler, Nathaniel Hart.

Three weeks later Samuel Henderson and Betsy Callaway were married at Boonesborough. There being no minister at the fort, Daniel Boone presided, as an official of Transylvania. Perhaps reflecting his doubts about the legitimacy of the Transylvania government, and his concern about the absence of an officiant from Virginia's established Anglican Church, Betsy's father, Colonel Callaway, consented to the marriage on the condition that Samuel Henderson undertake to have the union solemnized again at the earliest possible opportunity by a less doubtful authority. The groom did so. Within a year or so, in a double wedding, Jemima Boone was to marry Colonel Callaway's nephew Flanders Callaway and Fanny Callaway was to marry John Holder, who, with Flanders Callaway, had been among the mounted rescuers with Colonel Callaway.

The story of the capture and rescue of the girls spread quickly through the Kentucky settlements and into North Carolina and Virginia. The event had obvious human interest, but it also brought home how vulnerable the tiny settlements in Kentucky were. The human interest came in part from the recurring fear that women and girls, seized by Indians, might be raped by them. That fear was a theme in many of the narratives of whites taken captive by Indians that became a popular genre in the eighteenth and nineteenth centuries. The possibility of rape was never far from the minds of the many nineteenth-century artists who depicted the girls' capture, including Karl Bodmer and Jean-François Millet in 1852 and Carl Wimar in 1853. One art expert went so far as to say of Wimar's picture that "the triangular form of the brown drapery falling across her arms hints at the shape of female genitalia, while the brilliant red drapery at her knees hints at the bloody prospect of sexual violation."[37] The theme of possible sexual violation, apart from its prurient interest, served a political goal as a justification for white seizure of Indian lands—if the Indians were so brutal as to rape helpless captives, then perhaps the morally superior whites were justified in taking their lands.[38]

Col. Callaway worried, as any father would, about whether the Indians had raped the girls.[39] Boone's descendants were unanimous in saying that it never happened. As one put it, "No attempt was made on the part of the Indians to make love to the girls."[40] Jemima Boone told her niece, "The Indians were real kind to us, as much so as they could well have been, or their circumstances permitted," and she stressed their "honorable conduct to her and her fellow captives."[41] In fact, a review of the accounts of settlers taken captive by Indians in the eastern part of America shows that the Indian captors did not rape their women prisoners, for several likely reasons. Indians believed that having sex while on the warpath could weaken the Indians' war medicine. They also believed that the body of an unmarried woman belonged to herself alone and that sleeping with another man's wife was wrong. In addition, female captives were likely to be adopted into Indian families, and rape of a prospective relative was incestuous and not to be contemplated.[42]

The reports of the girls' capture make clear that Jemima Boone, like Daniel Boone, did not hate Indians. Jemima's own account also makes clear that Hanging Maw liked her. He praised her as a "pretty squaw," while he patted her head.[43] In some stories he asks her permission to take out the combs in her hair. When it hung loose, Jemima's long black hair fell nearly to her knees.

The capture and rescue bound Jemima much closer to Boone. She had sworn to herself, while a captive, that if she ever saw her father again, she would never disobey him. Back at Boonesborough, "so glad she was to be under his Care and Counsel she would not let him leave her one minute."[44] As we will see, Jemima stayed at Boonesborough in 1778 after the Indians took Boone himself captive and after Rebecca, despairing of ever seeing her husband again, went back to her family in North Carolina. Jemima was to help in the defense of the besieged Boonesborough and to be shot in so doing. Boone spent most of his last years in Missouri with Jemima and her husband, Flanders Callaway.

The human interest inherent in the girls' story led to many tellings, which also served as the prototype for James Fenimore Cooper's account of the capture and rescue of the Munro sisters in *The Last of the Mohicans*, published in 1826, fifty years after the Boonesborough girls' capture. In Cooper's story, after Cora and Alice Munro are taken captive by the Hurons, Cora bends twigs and drops her glove as signs to guide the rescuers she hopes are following. Magua, the ferocious Huron leader, offers to spare the girls' lives if Cora agrees to live in his wigwam, draw his water, hoe his corn, and cook his venison (and presumably perform other unnamed and unnamable services). Should she do it? Her admirer the young Major Heyward bursts out: "Name not the horrid alternative again; the thought itself is worse than a thousand deaths." Many pages later, the Boone-like scout Natty Bumppo (a/k/a Hawkeye, a/k/a La Longue Carabine) cries out to Cora, "Courage, lady; we come—we come," and with his trusty rifle brings down the evil Magua, who once again has given Cora the choice: "The wigwam or the knife!" But Bumppo is too late; another Huron has slain Cora during the rescue attempt.[45] The historical Boone was more successful as a rescuer than his fictional counterpart Bumppo; Boone's daughter and her friends were saved intact before their captors could kill them.

Quite apart from its human interest, the Boonesborough girls' capture underscored just how risky the white settlements in Kentucky were. The seizing of the girls was alarming, and so was the raid on Nathaniel Hart's homestead, only a half-mile from Boonesborough. More disturbing still was the evidence that Shawnees and Cherokees, traditional enemies, had worked together in the capture of the girls and in the trip toward the Shawnee towns north of the Ohio River. That alliance betokened more Indian attacks, of greater size.

Reports of the capture, the attack on the Hart homestead, and the joint action by Shawnees and Cherokees caused even more settlers to leave Kentucky. Station after station broke up. In some cases the settlers moved to more strongly fortified settlements in Kentucky. Others left Kentucky altogether. John Floyd, in a letter to William Preston describing the girls' capture and rescue, said that Hinkston's Station had been abandoned and that all the settlers who had been at the station were at Boonesborough on their way to

Virginia and Pennsylvania. Floyd said the settlers "all seem deaf to anything we can say to dissuade them":

> Ten, at least, of our own people are going to join them, which will leave us with less than 30 men in this fort. I think more than 300 men have left the country since I came out, and not one has arrived, except a few cabiners [that is, settlers who put up cabins as a basis for a land claim] down the Ohio.
>
> I want as much to return [away from the frontier] as any person can do, but if I leave the country now, there is scarcely one single man hereabouts but that will follow the example. When I think of the deplorable conditions a few helpless families are likely to be in, I conclude to sell my life as dear as I can, in their defense, rather than to make an ignominious escape.
>
> I am afraid it is in vain to sue for any relief from Virginia, yet the [Virginia] convention encouraged the settlement of this country; and why should not the extreme parts of Fincastle be as justly entitled to protection as any other part of the colony?

Floyd urged Preston to support an armed expedition against the Indians, pointing out that such a move might relieve those in Kentucky by drawing the Indians off to defend their towns. He closed:

> I do, at the request and in behalf of all the distressed women & children and other inhabitants of this place implore the aid of every leading man who may have it in their power to give them any relief.
>
> I cannot write. You can better guess at my ideas from what I have said than I can express them.
>
> I am, Sir, yours most affectionately to my last moments.[46]

The foreboding, the sense of peril, in Floyd's letter proved to be fully warranted, as borne out by the bloody fighting in Kentucky in the years ahead and by Floyd's own death from an Indian bullet in 1783.

A month after the girls' rescue and a few days after Betsy Callaway married Samuel Henderson, news reached Kentucky of the issuance of the Declaration of Independence by the Continental Congress early in July. A settler brought a copy of the document with him to Boonesborough in August 1776. The declaration was read aloud, and the Boonesborough residents that night lit a bonfire and had a celebration.

The principles of the Declaration of Independence and the strength of the words proclaiming them were causes for rejoicing. One wonders, however, if the settlers in Boonesborough that celebratory evening also thought of the danger to Kentucky that the declaration entailed. The fighting in the coastal colonies was bound to intensify because of it. The British would be fighting all-out war to keep the colonies in the British Empire. The coastal colonies that might have sent aid to the settlers in Kentucky—North Carolina, Pennsylvania, and above all Virginia—were bound to focus their soldiers and military supplies on fighting the British troops in the east. The declaration was likely to cause the British and Canadians at Detroit, Kaskaskia, Vincennes, and the other British forts in the west to stir up the Indians to attack the settlers in Kentucky and elsewhere in the Ohio Valley, so as to divert American resources from the east, to increase the chances of British victory in the coastal colonies, and to preserve British and Canadian control of the Ohio Valley fur trade. Many settlers thought the name *Kentucky* was an Indian word for "bloody ground." The dark clouds that came with the Declaration of Independence foretold that the territory was about to become just that.

11

THE SHAWNEES CAPTURE BOONE

FOR A TIME AFTER THE CAPTURE AND RESCUE OF THE GIRLS, WHITE settlers in Kentucky feared Indian attacks, but few occurred. Settlers were able to raise and harvest large crops of corn in 1776.[1] The Cherokee threat in the south receded, after combined militia forces from Virginia and both Carolinas in July and August crushed the Cherokees, burning many of their towns and cornfields.[2] Dragging Canoe's followers, calling themselves "Ani-Yuniwiya," or "the Real People," split off from the accommodationist Cherokees and moved to the Chickamauga Creek region in southeast Tennessee, near what is now Chattanooga, becoming known to the whites as Chicka-maugas.[3] The situation in Kentucky, however, deteriorated at year-end 1776 and grew steadily worse over the next two years.

The shortage of gunpowder and lead in Kentucky was acute. The settlers at Harrodsburg in June 1776 elected George Rogers Clark and John Gabriel Jones as delegates to the Virginia convention, directing them to petition to organize Kentucky as a new county of Virginia. Clark and Jones not only did this but also sought powder and shot for Kentucky. In August Clark convinced Virginia's Executive Council to grant Kentucky five hundred pounds of gunpowder. Jones was killed and Clark's cousin Joseph Rogers was captured by the Indians on Christmas Day 1776 as they attempted to get the powder into Kentucky.[4]

Virginia's organization of Kentucky as a county in December 1776, which effectively quashed the Transylvania Company's claims to most of Kentucky, also deprived John Floyd of what looked like a lucrative opportunity. The Transylvania Company proprietors in December 1775 had appointed Floyd as Transylvania's principal surveyor—but by late 1776 that position had become meaningless because Transylvania did not exist as a legitimate political entity with the authority to register land claims. Floyd came east to Williamsburg to look for an attractive position that would have the approval of the Virginia government. Not finding one, he tried a different way to improve his fortunes: he bought a privateer and went after British commerce in the Caribbean, before his ship was captured by a British man-of-war. Sent to prison in England, Floyd escaped, made his way to France, borrowed money from Benjamin Franklin in Paris, and sailed back to Virginia. Not until October 1779 did Floyd return to Kentucky and again become an important factor in Boone's life.

Virginia's organization of Kentucky as a county of Virginia also increased the threat of Shawnee attacks on Kentucky, because Shawnees disliked Virginians much more than Americans from other colonies. Virginia's governor Lord Dunmore in 1774 had launched the war against the Shawnees that bears his name. Settlers in Pennsylvania, anxious to preserve good fur-trading relations with the Shawnees, had been quick to tell them "that Pennsylvania had no part in the mischief already done, and that the Virginians were entirely at fault."[5] In truth, Virginians had launched Dunmore's War, had fought the Shawnees at Point Pleasant, and had waged the subsequent campaigns in Ohio that led Cornstalk and other Shawnee chiefs to give up Shawnee hunting rights in Kentucky. While the Shawnees doubtless viewed all American colonists with suspicion, they must have been particularly suspicious of the Virginians. As Detroit's commandant Henry Hamilton wrote in 1775 to Sir Guy Carleton, the governor of Canada, the Indians were "not likely to continue upon terms with the Virginians. . . . The Virginians are haughty Violent and bloody, the savages have a high opinion of them as Warriors, but are jealous of their encroachments. . . . In the inroads of the Virginians upon the savages, the former have plundered, burnt and murdered without mercy. Tis to be supposed from the Character of the Savages that opportunity only is wanting to retaliate, and that there can be but little cordiality between them."[6]

Hamilton was in his early forties when he arrived in Detroit as its governor late in 1775. Although classically educated, he served in the British army from 1755 until 1775. He thought like a soldier, and he knew how the Indians fought from his own experience as a British soldier in the French and Indian War. Taken captive by the French in 1760, he had seen, "not without a very unpleasant feeling, the Savages employed in scraping and dressing Englishmen's scalps."[7] From the moment he arrived in Detroit, Hamilton urged his superiors to play the Indian card—to stir up the western Indians and the

Ohio Valley Indians against the American frontier—in essence, the same tactic that the French had used with such effect in the French and Indian War. In September 1776 Hamilton received word of the American declaration of independence from Britain as well of a message from the Virginians borne by White Eyes, a pro-American Delaware chief, sending belts of wampum to the Shawnees and asking them to come to a council at Pittsburgh. This news provoked Hamilton, who was then presiding over a council at Detroit of Ottawas, Chippewas, Wyandots, Shawnees, Senecas, Delawares, Cherokees, and Potawatomis. Having first sounded out the Indians' feelings, Hamilton, before the assembled representatives of the different tribes, ostentatiously tore up the messages from the Virginians and cut up their belts of wampum.

Hamilton wrote to Lord Dartmouth, secretary of state for the colonies: "I have told the Savages assembled at the Council, to content themselves, with watchfully observing the Enemy's motions, that if the Virginians attacked them, I should give notice to the whole confederacy, and that an attack on one nation should infallibly be followed by the united force of them all to repel or as they term it strike the Virginians." That was probably all Hamilton was authorized to say by Governor Carleton. But he also told Lord Dartmouth, "As soon as the Council breaks up, I expect to hear several small parties falling upon the scattered settlers on the Ohio, and Rivers which fall into it—a deplorable sort of war, but which the arrogance, disloyalty and imprudence of the Virginians has justly drawn upon them."[8] One strongly suspects that Hamilton's expectation of such attacks was based on his encouragement of them. In his letter Hamilton also urged Lord Dartmouth to authorize Indian attacks on the Virginia and Pennsylvania frontiers.[9]

The Indian attacks in Kentucky began in earnest in March 1777. A few days before the attacks, commissions had arrived from Virginia for the officers of the new Kentucky County—George Rogers Clark (then only twenty-six years old) as major and Daniel Boone, James Harrod, Benjamin Logan, and John Todd as captains. On March 5 the militia mustered at Harrodsburg, Boonesborough, and Logan's Station (formerly known as St. Asaph's). The settlers' forces were not large. Harrodsburg was the biggest station—84 men fit for duty, 40 families. Logan's Station had only 15 men. Boonesborough was not much bigger: 22 men defending 10 to 15 families, including a dozen adult women, 30 children, and 10 or 15 slaves.[10] The muster showed that even in the early days of white settlement, slaves made up a significant percentage of the population—not surprisingly, given that the settlers following

Boone, Henderson, and the other leaders came in large part from Virginia and North Carolina.

As the militia mustered, Shawnees were coming to attack the settlements. Their war chief Cottawamago, known to the whites as Blackfish, led some two hundred Shawnees south across the Ohio and down the Warrior's Path. Blackfish, a fighter, not a compromiser, had opposed Cornstalk and urged retaliation for the white raids into Ohio after the Battle of Point Pleasant. On March 6 an estimated fifty Shawnees raided a group of Harrodsburg settlers who were boiling maple sap into sugar water. One white was captured. Another, young William Ray, stepson of the impetuous Hugh McGary, was killed and scalped. McGary and Captain Harrod found Ray's mutilated body that evening when they went out to look for the missing settlers.[11] The news caused McGary's wife, the young man's mother, to fall into a stupor from which she never recovered. She died over a year later. The next day, March 7, McGary and other Harrodsburg guards drove off Indians who were setting fire to cabins outside of the Harrodsburg stockade. McGary shot and killed a Shawnee. Seeing that the Indian was wearing his dead stepson's hunting shirt, McGary chopped the Indian's body into pieces and fed the pieces to his dogs.[12] The sight of his mangled stepson lingered in McGary's mind. Harrodsburg women said that when McGary went to see another woman (as they euphemistically put it) while his ailing wife was still alive, McGary's stepson would "appear to him as a spectre, wrapped up in sheets, and talk to him of it."[13]

Also on March 7, Indians shot and killed a slave working in a field in front of Boonesborough and wounded the slave's owner. The settlers, who had been preparing their fields for planting, came into the fort. Boone divided the men into two companies, one to farm while the other stood guard, and sent out scouts to range the country.[14] Indians remained near Harrodsburg for the rest of March 1777, killing and scalping several settlers, one by one. The settlers managed to bring into the fort the corn they had cribbed the previous fall, but hunting for meat—which involved going much farther away from the fort than the cornfields—was hard and dangerous.

On April 24 the Indians turned their attention to Boonesborough. It was a day that would prove the worth of Simon Kenton. Kenton was a rough backwoods giant, said to be six foot four, who could barely sign his own name. He had come to Kentucky in 1775 under an assumed name (Simon Butler) to escape prosecution, believing that he had beaten to death in

Virginia a man who was his rival for a woman's attentions. Not until 1779 did Kenton, learning that the man he had pummeled was still alive, resume the use of his real name.

On the morning of April 24, 1777, the cows that had been brought into the Boonesborough fort for safety overnight refused to go out the gate. That was not a good sign. Boone sent out two men to check and to drive in horses from a field a few hundred yards away. When the men were about seventy yards from the fort, Indians opened fire, and the men ran for the gate. One, Daniel Goodman, was hit and brought down. An Indian ran up and cut off Goodman's scalp. Simon Kenton, who had been standing near the gate about to go out hunting, went outside the fort and shot the Indian dead. Boone, Michael Stoner (the German with whom Boone in 1774 had ranged Kentucky seeking to warn Floyd's surveyors about the impending war with the Shawnees), William Bush (with Stoner, one of the men who had accompanied Boone on the failed attempt to enter Kentucky in 1773), and perhaps ten other men rushed out of the fort with their rifles. Kenton, spotting an Indian about to fire on Boone's group, fired first and killed the Indian. Indians sprang up out of a hollow between the fort and the white men, cutting off the settlers' line of retreat to the stockade. Kenton estimated there were forty or fifty Indian attackers. "Boys, we are gone!" Boone shouted. "Let's sell our lives as dear as we can!"

The whites fired at the Indians blocking their way, clubbed their fired rifles, and charged for the fort. One Indian was shot in the head. Boone was knocked to the ground by a ball that smashed his left ankle. An Indian, tomahawk raised, ran up to scalp Boone. Kenton brought the Indian down with a shot to the body. Another Indian ran up with a knife to take Boone's scalp. Kenton clubbed his discharged rifle, smashed the Indian down with it, picked up Boone, and ran with him to the stockade. Jemima Boone ran out of the fort and helped her father in.

As Stoner was aiming at one Indian, another one shot Stoner through the right wrist, causing him to drop his rifle. Bending to pick it up, he was shot in the hip, knocking him over. Two Indians running up to scalp him were shot dead. Billy Bush and others helped Stoner to his feet and to the fort. Bush slowed pursuing Indians by turning from time to time to point his unloaded rifle at them. At least six Indians were killed in the attack on the fort. Daniel Goodman was the only white killed. Several others besides Boone and Stoner were wounded. The bullet in Boone's ankle was extracted from the side opposite its entrance, "mashed as thin as a knife blade" by the bone it had fractured. Boone's leg was in a sling for weeks, and his ankle hurt for the rest of his life, whenever he was tired or the weather was changing.[15] While Boone was having his wound dressed, he sent for Kenton and was (for Boone) effusive in praising him. "Well, Simon," Boone said, "you have behaved like a man today; indeed, you are a fine fellow."[16]

Throughout the summer of 1777 the Indians made scattered attacks on the Kentucky settlements. Logan's Station was shot at for several days. A number of settlers were killed at Harrodsburg, to which James Harrod and others had returned after leaving in 1774 for the comparative safety of the Clinch River settlements. On May 23, 1777, close to two hundred Indians attacked Boonesborough a second time, wounding several and killing numerous cattle. Another attack on Boonesborough began on July 4, killing one man and wounding two more, while Boone hobbled around the fort on a crutch, directing the fort's defense. Although Boone claimed that the defenders killed seven Indians, the Shawnees, before they left, burned all of Boonesborough's cornfields.[17] When Blackfish took his forces back across the Ohio River in July, he had the satisfaction of knowing that the American settlers would face a hungry winter. By attacking the separate settlements in Kentucky at or close to the same time, the Shawnees had prevented the whites from combining their small forces and had been able to destroy much of the settlers' crops and cattle.

The coastal colonies, despite their need to husband military resources to fight the British in the east, responded to the news of the attacks in Kentucky by sending reinforcements. In August Col. John Bowman arrived at Boonesborough from Virginia with one hundred troops and took charge of the Kentucky militia. Close to fifty more militiamen came to Boonesborough in September, many—Bryans and Boones among them—from the Yadkin Valley in North Carolina. Other men came to bolster the garrisons at Logan's Station and Harrodsburg.

If the Americans were building up their frail defenses in Kentucky, however, the British, led by Hamilton in Detroit, were building up a confederacy of Indian allies and encouraging them to attack American settlements throughout the frontier. To the north and east Guy Johnson, nephew and successor as Indian superintendent of Sir William Johnson, the "Mohawk Baronet," had enlisted the support of the Six Nations of the Iroquois, Britain's traditional Indian allies, in the fight against the Americans in New York and Pennsylvania.[18] Late in May 1777 Canada's governor, Sir Guy Carleton, forwarded to Hamilton a letter from Lord George Germain, who had succeeded the earl of Dartmouth as secretary of state for the colonies, granting the authorization that Hamilton had requested to back Indian raids on the Virginia and Pennsylvania frontiers. Lord Germain had written to Carleton that "it is the King's Command that you should direct Lieut. Governor Hamilton to assemble as many of the Indians in his District as he conveniently can, and placing proper persons at their Head, to whom he is to make suitable allowances, to conduct their Parties, and restrain them from committing violence on the well affected and inoffensive Inhabitants, employ them in making a Diversion and exciting an alarm upon the frontiers of Virginia and Pennsylvania."

Lord Germain went on to authorize Hamilton to offer land to Americans who join the British forces for the duration of the rebellion, noting:

> These offers . . . may enable Lt. Gov. Hamilton to extend his operations, so as to divide the attention of the Rebels, and oblige them to collect a considerable Force to oppose him, which can not fail of weakening their main army & facilitating the operations directed to be carried on against them in other Quarters, and thus bring the War to a more speedy Issue and restore those deluded People to their former State of Happiness and prosperity, which are the favorite wishes of the Royal Breast and the great object of all His Majesty's measures.
>
> A supply of presents for the Indians & other necessaries will be wanted for this Service, and you will of course send Lieut. Govr. Hamilton what is proper and sufficient.[19]

In mid-June 1777 Governor Hamilton assembled at Detroit representatives of the Ottawas, Hurons, Chippewas, Potawatomis, Miamis, and Shawnees. Armed with Germain's letter, he declared to the assembled Indian leaders "that he was authorized to put the Hatchet into the Hands of the Indians, and expected an implicit obedience to the orders of His Majesty. He then informd the Indians of what he thought they should do upon the occasion, shewed them the Hatchet then sang the War Song—as did Mr Hay, Depu[t]y agent, the officers of the Garrison, all the Nations present, & some of the French & English. G[overnor] Hamilton then thanked them for their Zeal and Unanimity, & adjourned to the open Field, to a feast prepared for the Purpose."[20]

Hamilton knew how to behave at a gathering of Indian leaders. He used the traditional symbols of going on the warpath—the taking up of the hatchet, the singing of the war chant. He knew the importance of a first-rate feast. Hamilton may have been classically educated , but, according to an eyewitness, the Delaware chief John Montour, Hamilton on this occasion "was painted and dressed like an Indian, and presented a large black belt painted red [that is, the wampum belt signifying war] sent by the Six Nations."[21] On adjournment of the gathering "an ax was presented to each Nation." Hamilton told the Indians that "they should be furnish'd with ammunition & necessary for their Yg. Men," but (at least according to his journal) he also "recommended it to all the Nations to remember they were men, & were desired to make war against men, and not against women or Children, and to forbear to dip their hands in the blood of the two latter."[22] That recommendation, it may be noted, did not include a recommendation against scalping American men.

Pursuant to Germain's authorization, Hamilton also distributed to the Indian leaders copies of a proclamation, to be spread among the American frontier stations in an effort to win the settlers over to the Loyalist cause. The proclamation assured "all such as are inclined to withdraw themselves from the Tyranny and oppression of the rebel Committees, & take refuge in this Settlement, or any of the Posts commanded by his Majesty's Officers" that they "shall be humanely treated" and promised that Americans who "come off in arms & shall use them in defence of his Majesty against Rebels and Traytors, 'till the extinction of this rebellion, shall receive pay adequate to their former Stations in the rebel service, and all common men who shall serve during that period Shall receive his Majesty's bounty of two hundred acres of Land."[23]

The Indians who had been at the Detroit parley returned to their villages. By June 30 the different Indian groups had sent to Detroit "sticks" tallying the numbers of warriors ready to take to the field. Hamilton wrote in his journal, "In a Month I don't question one thousand Warriors going against the Frontiers."[24] Within weeks Americans on the frontier heard of the meeting at Detroit and knew of the tribes involved.[25] They also heard that of the four Shawnee clans, the two closest to the American settlements did not want to take up the hatchet against the Americans, but the two westernmost and closest to the British garrisons did.[26]

On July 26 David Zeisberger, Moravian missionary to the Delawares at

Cuchachunk (now Coshocton, Ohio), reported to Gen. Edward Hand, the American commander at Fort Pitt, that the Wyandot chief the Half King had recently arrived there and at a great council "drew out the War Belt with the Tomahawk, told the Delawares all the Nations . . . had join'd & taken hold of it, that the Delawares only had not," and delivered the belt to the Delawares. The Delawares, after consulting among themselves, returned the belt, saying that they had promised "they would never fight no more against the white people as long as the Sun shineth & the Rivers run" and that they would keep that promise.[27] Hearing of the attempts to sway the Delawares, American leaders wrote to them, declaring their friendship. Virginia's lieutenant governor, John Page, assured the Delawares "that the State of Virginia is determined to hold fast the chain of friendship and support you as she would her own children against all your Enemies as long the Sun or Moon shall shine and rivers flow."[28] General Hand pledged to the Delawares: "I say Brothers if any Nation strikes you on our Account, I will consider your Quarrels as our own."[29]

The American initiatives had no effect on the militant western Indians, who, supplied by the British from Detroit, began armed attacks on the American settlers in the Ohio Valley. On August 25, near Logan's Station, Indians attacked six soldiers who had been sent to the fort by Colonel Bowman as part of his effort to strengthen the settlers' defenses in Kentucky. One soldier was killed; two were wounded. By the body of the slain American the Indians left copies of Governor Hamilton's proclamation offering land (and for officers, equal rank and commensurate pay) to Americans who come over to the British side. Captain Logan prudently kept the proclamations out of sight, lest the beleaguered settlers be tempted by them.[30] On September 1 some two hundred Indians attacked Fort Henry, at what is now Wheeling, West Virginia. The American militia was ill organized, despite having been warned by General Hand of the likelihood of an attack. The Indians killed an American lieutenant and fourteen soldiers.[31] American militiamen found copies of Hamilton's proclamation and were sworn to secrecy not to divulge its contents. "As might be expected—this having of a secret, and being sworn to it, made a great rumpuss in the fort."[32]

Patrick Henry, the governor of Virginia, in July 1777 wrote to General Hand that "offensive operations can alone produce Defence agt. Indians."[33] That judgment jibed with Hand's own belief that the best way to prevent Indian killings on the frontier settlements was to attack the Indians in their own country. Hand, however, unable to line up the troops he needed to mount an effective expedition into Ohio, had to settle for consolidating and strengthening the Americans' existing defenses in the Ohio Valley. In September 1777, at Hand's order, Fort Kittanning on the Allegheny River was abandoned and torched by American troops.[34] On November 5 Hand countermanded his orders for an expedition into Indian country, "expressing his great mortification at finding he could not collect a sufficient body of men to march into the Indian country."[35] Hand, with fewer than 800 men under his command, wrote to Patrick Henry that he was "obliged to content myself with ordering 250 men to be stationed in each of the frontier counties to prevent as much as possible the inroads of the savages."[36]

Within days the situation of the settlers in Kentucky turned far worse as a result of the baseless killing by frontiersmen of the Shawnee chief Cornstalk, who had been a force for peace with the Americans ever since he signed the peace treaty that ended Lord Dunmore's War. Cornstalk had gone so far as to warn settlers of Shawnees who were going on raids against the whites and to encourage the settlers to "waylay and kill" fifteen Shawnees who were going to join the Cherokees "on some bad design."[37] In September and October 1775, when representatives from Virginia and the Continental Congress, alarmed by British incitement of the Indians against the Americans, met at Fort Pitt with Indian tribes to seek their neutrality in the war between the British and the Americans, Cornstalk spoke in favor of the American request. The Indians agreed to remain neutral, as Cornstalk urged, and in exchange the Americans agreed not to go north of the Ohio River.[38]

In October 1777 General Hand had written to a friend that the men in the Fort Pitt militia, though not much inclined to enter the Indian country, "are well disposed, savage like, to Murder a defenceless unsuspecting Indian."[39] Unfortunately, General Hand was prescient in this respect. Early in November Cornstalk, accompanied by a young Shawnee warrior named Redhawk and a one-eyed chief known to the whites as Old Yie, came to Fort Randolph, where the Great Kanawha River flows into the Ohio River at Point Pleasant. Cornstalk spoke to the commanding officer, Capt. Matthew Arbuckle, expressing his concerns about the mounting pressure on the Indians to fight the Americans. Cornstalk said that he was opposed to "joining the war on the side of the British, but that all the rest of the nation but himself and his wife were determined to engage in it," and he thought "he should have to run with the stream." Captain Arbuckle decided to detain Cornstalk and the others as hostages and so informed General Hand.

Arbuckle was not a friend to Indians. He referred to them as "Damnd. Savages" and had also expressed skepticism about a promise of lasting Shawnee-white peace that Cornstalk's brother had made to him, when Arbuckle believed Cornstalk was in Detroit talking to the English.[40] On November 9 Cornstalk's son Elinipisco came to the fort to see if his father was well and could be released. Even though Elinipisco in September 1775 had helped the Americans organize the Fort Pitt meeting seeking Indian neutrality in the British-American fighting, Arbuckle detained him too.

On November 10 some of the Fort Randolph militia went out hunting for deer. One of the hunters, a young ensign named Gilmore, was shot and scalped by Indians. The other white hunters brought Gilmore's bloody body back to the fort in a canoe. Capt. John Stuart, who was there, told what happened next:

> But the canoe was scarsely landed in the creek when the cry was raised let us kill the Indians in the fort and every man with his gun in his hand came up the bank pale as death with rage. Capt. Hall was at their head. Captain Arbuckle and myself met them endeavoring to dissuade them from so unjustifiable an action but they cocked their guns threatened us with instant death if we did not desist and rushed into the fort....
>
> ... [T]he Interpreter's wife ..., hearing the uproar and seeing the men coming to kill the Indians for whom she seemed to have an affection, run to their cabin informed them the people were cumming to kill them and that the[y] said the Indians that killed Gilmore came with [Cornstalk's son] the day before. he [Cornstalk's son] utterly denied it declared he knew nothing of them, and trembled exceedingly; his father encouraged him told him not to be afraid, for the great Spirit above had sent him there to be killed. the men advanced to the door, the Corn Stalk arose and met them, seven or eight bullets were fired into him, and his son was shot dead as he sat upon a stool. Redhawk made an attempt to go up the chimney but was shot down, the other Indian was shamefully mangled. I grieved to see him so long a dying.[41]

American officers up and down the frontier instantly realized how gravely Cornstalk's murder imperiled settlers throughout the Ohio Valley. Having heard about "killing the Cornstalk and some other Shawnesse Chiefs in cold Blood," Col. William Preston wrote, "I am apprehensive this Conduct will be followed by very bad consequences to the Frontiers, by engaging us in a war with that Revengeful & Warlike Nation and their Allies."[42] General Hand wrote to a close friend that in view of the murder of the Shawnees at Fort Randolph, "if we had anything to expect from that Nation it is now Vanished." Hand added, "I am so heartily tired of this place that I have petitioned Congress to be recal'd"—which he was, in May 1778.[43] Hand noted in a letter to Governor Patrick Henry, "It would be vain for me to bring the perpetrators of this horrid act to justice at that time."[44] Unfortunately, General Hand was prescient in this respect as well. Captain Hall, who had led the killers of Cornstalk, and three other militiamen were brought to trial, separately, for Cornstalk's murder. Each was acquitted because no witness appeared against any of them.[45]

As 1777 came to an end, the settlers in Kentucky prepared for a grim winter. The raids in Kentucky led by Blackfish through July had kept the settlers confined to the forts. During the year McClelland's Station was abandoned. Several other stations in Kentucky had been abandoned the previous year. Less than a handful of stations remained at the end of 1777. That December Col. John Bowman reported to General Hand that "the poor Kentucky people . . . have these twelve months past been confined to three forts, On which the Indians made several fruitless attempts. They have left us almost without horses sufficient to supply the stations, as we are obliged to get all our provisions out of the woods. . . . Our corn the Indians have burned all they could find the past summer, as it was in cribs at different plantations some distance from the garrisons, & no horses to bring it in. At this time we have not more than two months bread. . . . I find it difficult to keep the garrisons plenty in meat, & if we have no bread we must at any rate suffer."[46]

There was another pressing problem. Without any corn or other harvested crops, and with few domestic cattle, the settlers had to subsist on meat from hunting. The settlers needed salt to keep the meat unspoiled. In late November 1777 Boone and other settlers signed a petition for salt to the Virginia General Assembly, noting: "Your Petitioners are and have for some time past been almost destitute of the necessary Article Salt. That by reason of the Incursions of the different Nations of Indians this year past we have been prevented from making what Quantities would be necessary for ourselves and Families as we formerly did, for small parties would be in great danger of being cut off and larger ones could not be spared from the defence of the Families."[47]

Early in January 1778 Boone led a group of about thirty men to the Blue Licks, on the Licking River, to make salt for Kentucky's different garrisons.

They took with them horses carrying the big kettles needed to boil down the water to recover the salt. Some 840 gallons of water had to be boiled off to make a bushel of salt.[48] With the horses, the number of men, the cutting and gathering of firewood, the flame and smoke from the boiling kettles, and the rifle shots of hunters to feed the men, Boone's salt-boilers made a very visible and noisy group. Thirty men were enough to deter small parties of Indians, however, although at the cost of substantially weakening the frail defenses of Boonesborough and the other remaining Kentucky stations. Moreover, Indians generally did not go on raids in the dead of winter.

But this year was different. The British at Detroit were supplying and encouraging the Indians with arms and ammunition. The Shawnees were hungry for revenge against the whites who had killed Cornstalk and his companions. It is also likely that Blackfish—having vied with Cornstalk for influence among the Shawnees when Cornstalk was alive—was eager to mount a successful raid on American settlers in order to enhance his position as a leading Shawnee chief, now that Cornstalk was dead.

Fort Randolph, where Cornstalk had been killed, was too strongly defended for easy Indian attack. The Shawnees had learned that lesson painfully at the Battle of Point Pleasant, fought next to the site of Fort Randolph. But there were easier targets in Kentucky, which was part of Virginia—and Virginians were the people who had murdered Cornstalk and his son. The Shawnees must have known there were not many men in Harrodsburg and fewer still at Boonesborough. Early in 1778 Blackfish led over one hundred Shawnees south across the Ohio River to attack Boonesborough. Two Frenchmen who worked with the British garrison at Detroit accompanied the group, the wiry little Indian trader Louis Lorimier and Charles Beaubien, the British agent and interpreter among the Miamis.

While most of his party boiled water to retrieve salt, Boone and two other men—one of them Flanders Callaway, Jemima Boone's husband—generally ranged, scouting for Indian sign and hunting for game to feed the party. On Saturday, February 7, Boone went in one direction to hunt and to check his beaver traps, while the other scouts went in another. It was bitterly cold. By afternoon, as the sky darkened, snow started coming down. Boone killed a buffalo, butchered it with his knife, and tied the best cuts of meat to his horse with tugs of green buffalo hide. He headed back to camp on foot, leading his laden horse on a buffalo trail alongside the Licking River.

Boone's horse spooked as he led it over a fallen tree. Boone saw four

Indians who had been hiding behind the tree. He tried to undo the tugs holding the load of buffalo meat so he could mount and ride away but was unable to untie the frozen tugs. Nor was he able to draw his knife to cut the load loose. The knife had been bloody from butchering the buffalo when Boone sheathed it, and the blood had frozen solid around the knife. Unable to mount the horse, Boone ran. He ran as fast as he could for a half-mile, his trail easy to track in the new-fallen snow. One Indian, having cut the load off Boone's horse, rode after Boone. The other three ran after him on foot. The pursuers got close enough to shoot, the balls kicking up snow on either side of Boone. The Indians reloaded and came closer, firing again from about ten paces. One bullet severed the strap of Boone's powder horn. Exhausted, Boone saw he could not escape. He put himself behind a tree and leaned his rifle in front of the tree as a sign of his surrender.[49]

The Indians came up whooping and laughing, shook Boone's hand, took his weapons, and led him to their camp. Boone was startled by the size of the party—over a hundred Indians, the two French Canadians, and a black named Pompey, who, it turned out, had lived with the Shawnees for years and spoke their language well. "Howdydo, brother," the Indians said. By this time many Indians in Kentucky had enough English for at least the usual courtesies and the basic curse words. "Howdydo," Boone replied. He looked at one Indian more closely. The man was Capt. Will Emery, who in 1769 had taken Boone's furs and warned him about wasps and yellow jackets attacking him if he ever came back to Indian country. "Howdydo, Captain Will," Boone said. Captain Will looked puzzled, until Boone reminded him of the capture eight years earlier. Captain Will's face lit up. He started shaking Boone's hand again in earnest. Other Indians came up for more hand shaking and howdydos, which Boone took "with all grace and politeness, of which he was master."[50] The Indians took Boone to Blackfish, and Pompey interpreted. Blackfish asked about Boone's men at the Lower Blue Licks. What men? Boone asked. Blackfish said his scouts had seen the men at the licks and that his warriors were going to kill them before going on to take Boonesborough.

The Indians were well armed, and they outnumbered the salt-boilers more than four to one. There were twenty-seven salt-boilers at the licks, two or three having already returned to Boonesborough with salt. The Indians were likely to kill all the salt-boilers, who had no warning that Indians were in the area. Any men who managed to survive an initial attack would be easily tracked in the snow and later be caught or killed. Boone also knew that the Indians were likely then to take Boonesborough, given that its stockade was still unfinished and that many of its men were part of the salt-boiling party. If the women and children in the fort were led back to the Shawnee towns on foot in the bitter cold, many would die on the way.

Boone told Blackfish that the salt-boilers were numerous and skilled fighters and that the fort was strong, as Blackfish knew from his attacks on it. Even if the Indians were to succeed, they would suffer large losses, and many valuable white captives would die on the long trip to the Shawnee towns. Boone proposed instead something better for the Indians and for the whites: he would cause all the salt-boilers to surrender and go peacefully to the Shawnee towns, if Blackfish would agree that the men would be treated well and not have to run the gauntlet—referring to the Indian custom of making their captives run between two lines of Indians who hit the captives as they ran. Blackfish and his warriors could come back with Boone in the spring, with more men and more provisions, and with horses to carry the women and children, and Boone would work to cause the fort to surrender. By that time the settlers at Boonesborough would be happy to join the British cause, particularly after suffering through a full winter without any corn as a result of the Shawnees' having burned all of their crops the previous summer.

Blackfish and his warriors consulted. If Boone was telling the truth, the proposal sounded good. If Boone was lying and could not deliver the salt-boilers, the Shawnees were no worse off; if the salt-boilers resisted, the Shawnees would kill Boone and the salt-boilers, before going on to Boonesborough. Blackfish told Boone that his proposal was accepted but that he would be killed if there was any resistance by his men.

The next morning the Indians and Boone went to the salt-boilers' camp, getting there about noon. Although there was a half-foot of snow on the ground, the day was sunny, and, it being Sunday, the men were taking it easy, lounging on their blankets. Boone made straight for the camp. Some of the men, seeing the Indians, took up their rifles. "Don't fire!" Boone yelled. "If you do, all will be massacred!" Boone told the men that they were surrounded by Indians and that they would have to trust him and the Indians' promise of good conduct because they had no choice. Years later one of the salt-boilers wrote in a pension application: "We were ordered by Colonel Boone to stack our guns and surrender, and we did so."[51] As soon as the guns were stacked, the Indians encircled the unarmed men.

12

BOONE AMONG THE SHAWNEES

BOONE AND THE SALT-BOILERS WERE AT THE SHAWNEES' MERCY. According to one of the men with Boone, Joseph Jackson, the Shawnees came very close to killing all of their captives on the spot. Many of the Shawnees argued that only the blood of whites could avenge the killing of Cornstalk and the other hostages at Fort Randolph and that, despite Blackfish's promise to Boone, they should kill all the white captives and march quickly to attack Boonesborough. As Jackson remembered it years later, the warriors sat in a circle to debate the question. Blackfish invited Boone to sit in the circle, with Pompey beside him to interpret. One after another, the Indians stood to argue the matter. Finally, Blackfish allowed Boone to speak.

Boone spoke in English, pausing for Pompey to translate:

Brothers! What I have now promised you, I can much better fulfill in the spring than now. Then the weather will be warm, and the women and children can travel from Boonesborough to the Indian towns, and all live with you as one people. You have got all the young men; to kill them, as has been suggested, would displease the Great Spirit, and you could not then expect future success in hunting nor war. If you spare them, they will make you fine warriors, and excellent hunters to kill game for your squaws and children. These young men have done you no harm.... I consented to their capitulation on the express condition that they should be made prisoners of war and treated well. Spare them, and the Great Spirit will smile upon you.[1]

The warriors voted. The vote was 59 for death, 61 for life. The Shawnees loaded up, packing the kettles, salt, axes, and guns they had taken from the whites, and started north toward the Shawnee towns. When they stopped that night, the Indians cleared in the snow a path some hundred yards long, which Pompey told Boone was for running the gauntlet. Boone protested that Blackfish had promised not to make the men run the gauntlet. It was not for Boone's men, who had surrendered under a stipulation, Blackfish said; it was for Boone, who had been taken without any such stipulation. Boone stripped to his breechclout, leggings, and moccasins to run between two lines of Shawnee warriors armed with sticks and clubs.

A kick in Boone's rear was the signal for the start of his run through the lines. "I set out full speed," Boone later told one of his grandsons, "first running so near one line that they could not do me much damage, and when they give back, crossed over to the other side, and by that means was likely to pass through without any hurt." Several of the warriors went easy on him. Others staggered him with blows, opening a cut on the top of his head that bled into his eyes. Toward the end of the run one "fellow broke the lines for the purpose of giving me a home lick. The only way I had to avoid his intention was to run over him by springing at him with my head bent forward, taking him full in the breast, and prostrating him flat on his back, passing over him unhurt." The crowd cheered. Indians came up, Boone recounted, "giving me their hand saying 'velly good sojer'" and calling the fellow sprawled on the ground "one damn squaw."[2]

That same evening the Indians debated another issue: whether to slit the captives' ears, Indian fashion. Many Shawnee men, as a form of body adornment, slit the rims of their ears two or more inches and hung silver bobs or other ornaments in the opening when the wound healed.[3] A witness to one such ear slitting said the Indian performing the operation "laid his patient on his back, and placing a piece of wood under his ear, he cut, with his jack nife, which was rather dull, the rim of each ear, from top to bottom. . . . On the bow made of the rim, he fixed pieces of thin lead, to prevent adhesion and to stretch it."[4] An English traveler to Virginia in late 1774 described the effect, as he saw it in four Shawnee chiefs being sent to Williamsburg as hostages after Dunmore's War: "Their ears are cut from the tips two thirds of the way round and the piece extended with brass wire till it touches their shoulders, in this part they hang a thin silver plate, wrought in flourishes about three inches diameter."[5] The weight of the metal ornaments caused the ear lobes to be stretched downward.[6] According to Boone's son Nathan, the two French officers with Blackfish "argued this point [whether to slit their white captives' ears], one for and one against. They became so heated that they drew swords against each other. The Indians prevented the bloodshed." Pompey explained the debate to Boone, who must have been pleased that the ear-slitting proposal did not carry. One suspects little Lorimier, who dressed in Indian style, spoke Shawnee, and was to marry into the tribe, was the French Canadian who advocated ear slitting.

The next day the party resumed its trip north. It took ten days, in what Boone described as "very severe weather," to get to old Chillicothe.[7] There have been several towns in what is now Ohio that were called Chillicothe, each being wherever the headquarters of the Chlahgatha clan of the Shawnees was located at the time. The town that Boone called "old Chelicothe" was on the Little Miami River, near what is now Xenia, east of Dayton, Ohio, fully a hundred miles from the salt-boilers' camp.

The white captives were heavily laden. Some balked at the loads they were asked to carry. A warrior tried to make Col. Richard Callaway's nephew James Callaway carry a heavy kettle, but he refused. The Indian raised his tomahawk. James Callaway leaned forward, took off his hat, bent his neck, patted his head, and said: "Here, strike! I would as lief lie here as go along, and I won't tote your kettle." Scalps were worth less in Detroit than live prisoners. The Indian found someone else to carry the kettle.[8]

There was next to nothing to eat on the trip. Game could not be found in the bitter cold. The Indians killed and ate their dogs and offered some to the captives. Not all accepted the offer. Nathan Boone remembered Boone talking of eating slippery elm bark, which loosened the bowels, and then oak bark ooze, to counteract the effects of the slippery elm bark.[9]

The arrival of the warriors back at Old Chillicothe on February 18 involved a graver risk to the captives than hunger. Like many other eastern tribes, Shawnees from time to time tortured captives to death by burning them at the stake. If an Indian had been killed by enemies, the death could be "covered" by adopting an enemy—or by killing a member of the enemy group. In this case, as Boone and the other captives must have known, the Shawnee chief Cornstalk had recently been unjustly killed by the whites, and execution of the captives was a real possibility. Adult male captives were burned to death by Shawnees not infrequently. While the practice was discouraged starting in the 1790s by Shawnee leaders, including Tecumseh and his brother the Prophet, the Prophet remembered seeing two white men burned to death by Shawnees near Fort Wayne before Gen. Anthony Wayne's expedition in 1794, following the killing by whites of a Shawnee chief in Ohio.

The Prophet also described in detail the burning of a white man about a year after the Battle of Tippecanoe in 1811, to avenge the killing of a chief in that battle. Warriors painted the prisoner black before taking him to their village. Prisoners painted black were destined for death by torture unless they were met and claimed first by the female peace leader of the village. In the post-Tippecanoe burning the prisoner, after a night's confinement, was led to a site outside the village, where a large white oak sapling was stuck into the ground. A grapevine attached to the top of the sapling came down far enough to fasten to the prisoner's raised arms. After his arms were tied to the vine, the Indians yelled in unison four times, and torture began. Brands were seized from a nearby fire, and Indians one after another applied the burning end to the captive. When the pain forced him to jump, the elasticity of the pole would swing him back, where others stood waiting with torches. "Thus he was continued in the most excruciating pain, from sun rise until past noon, when he died. He was then skinned & quartered, and his limbs were boiled for a feast, and distributed among the spectators. A young man who is now here with the Prophet, says he was at that time quite a boy, but he recollects very well that he ate a piece of the body for venison, and thought it good."[10] A Shawnee in 1790 told a white captive that a fellow captive had been burned at the stake and then eaten and said the flesh "was sweeter than any bear's meat!—a food in the highest repute with the Indians."[11] Indians believed that eating the flesh of slain captives "inspired the warriors with courage in attack"; by ingesting an executed warrior, the Indians sought to gain the warrior's powers.[12]

Boone would have heard, at least as early as the aftermath of Braddock's Defeat in 1755, about Indians torturing white captives to death at the stake. Despite the Indians' promise of good treatment, the possibility of such a death must have been in Boone's mind as he and the other captives were brought to Old Chillicothe. But none of the salt-boiler captives was painted black and selected for torture—perhaps because of the captives' value as salable commodities in Detroit; perhaps because many were to be adopted; perhaps because Blackfish hoped, with Boone's help, to obtain the surrender of Boonesborough when warm weather returned. Boone told Filson (in Filson's words): "The generous usage the Indians had promised before in my capitulation was fully complied with," and he and his men "received as good treatment as prisoners could expect from savages."[13]

If the captives were not to be killed, the Shawnees needed to decide

133

which captives to ransom to the British and which to adopt. Adopting white captives was customary among Indians, in part as a way of replacing those who had died in warfare or to disease. Adoption meant full acceptance into the tribe, although adopted captives were watched closely, especially at first, to guard against any attempts by them to escape. The most intractable of the salt-boiler captives—people like James Callaway, who had refused to carry a kettle on the trip, or William Brooks, who had attempted to drown the Shawnee women who tried to wash him—were obvious candidates for sale to the British, rather than for adoption. Boone, however, had real value to the Shawnees, as a leader of the Boonesborough settlers and because of his promise to seek to cause Boonesborough to surrender.

Blackfish thought he might adopt Boone himself. Blackfish was only a few years older than Boone, but Boone plainly had warrior and leadership qualities, and Blackfish needed to replace a son who had been killed by the whites when Jemima and the Callaway girls were rescued. Had Boone killed Blackfish's son during the rescue? Soon after Boone's arrival at Old Chillicothe, a Shawnee who spoke some English asked him whether he had led the whites who killed Indians in the rescue. Boone said he had been there and that he had taken part in the shooting, but he did not know whose gun had done the killing. "Many things happen in war," Boone said, "that were best forgotten in peace." The Shawnee questioner thought about that for a moment, and Boone thought he might be killed on the spot. But the Shawnee instead smiled and clapped Boone on the shoulder. "Brave man! All right!" he said. "When we in war you kill me, I kill you. All right!"[14]

So Blackfish adopted Boone as his own son. From Peck's biography of Boone and from other accounts of Indian adoptions, we can reconstruct the ceremony. Boone's hair would have been plucked, leaving only a scalp-lock, which was decorated with ribbon and feathers. Boone would have been taken to the river, stripped, pushed under the surface of the water, and scrubbed by Indian women to remove the whiteness from him.[15] One captive adopted by the Shawnees said of his scouring, "I never was washed so clean before or since."[16] Given the standards of personal hygiene on the frontier at the time, that may not have been saying much. Boone was given the name Sheltowee, or Big Turtle. Maybe that was what Boone looked like—a compact, barrel-chested man, coming up dripping and naked out of the water of the river. But it was also an honorable name. Shawnees were organized into nonlineal name groups, each with a totemic animal name. A member of the

Turtle group had the honor of being one of the two keepers of the Shawnees' sacred fire.[17] In a Shawnee origin legend the Great Spirit sent the Shawnees to an island he had made for them, which rested on the back of a great turtle. He told the Shawnees: "You must call this Turtle your grandfather. He will hear all your complaints & will treat you as his Grand Children."[18]

On March 10 Blackfish, with his new son, Sheltowee, and some forty Shawnees, set off for Detroit, taking with them the ten or more salt-boilers whom they intended to sell to the British.[19] Henry Hamilton, the British commander at Detroit, described Boone's arrival in a letter to the governor of Canada:

> April the 5th. Mr. Charles Baubin who acts at the Miamis came in from a scout—not have been able to prevail on the Miamis to act with spirit. He with a young man named Lorimier engaged four score Shawanese from Tchelacasé and Pecori [Chillicothe and Piqua] to go toward the Fort on Kentuck River, east of the Ohio into which it discharges directly opposite the great Mineanomis or Rocky River. The Fort [Boonesborough] is about 30 miles from the mouth. The number of men in it is about 80. Here they had the good fortune to make prisoners Captain Daniel Boone, with 26 of his men, whom they brought off with their arms without killing or losing a man. The savages could not be prevailed on to attempt the Fort, which by means of their prisoners might have been easily done with success. These Shawanese delivered up four of their prisoners to me; but took Boone with them, expecting by his means to effect something.
>
> By Boone's account, the people on the frontiers have been so incessantly harassed by parties of Indians they have not been able to sow grain; and at Kentucke will not have a morsel of bread by the middle of June. Cloathing is not to be had, nor do they expect relief from the Congress—their dilemma will probably induce them to trust to the Savages, who have shewn so much humanity to their prisoners, & come to this place before winter.[20]

In Filson's account, written five years later, Boone tells a somewhat different version, saying that the Indians' "affection for me was so great, that they utterly refused to leave me there [at Detroit], although the Governor offered them one hundred pounds Sterling for me, on purpose to give me a parole to go home."[21] Rebecca's father, Joseph Bryan, said that "the true reason [Boone] was treated so well at Detroit" was that he displayed his captain's commission from Lord Dunmore.[22] According to Boone's son Nathan, when Hamilton found that the Indians would not give up Boone, the governor ordered his commissary to furnish Boone with a horse "and also with a quantity of Indian silver trinkets to use among the Indians as currency."[23]

The different accounts can be reconciled to reconstruct what happened at Boone's meeting with Hamilton. The best way for Boone to get back to Kentucky was to convince Blackfish and Hamilton that he could help to cause the Boonesborough settlers to come over to the British. To do that, he emphasized how desperate Boonesborough was likely to be by the end of winter and indicated that he had fought for the British before, having been commissioned as a captain in the militia by Virginia's last colonial governor. Boone presumably showed Hamilton the printed commission that bore Lord Dunmore's signature, without bothering to tell Hamilton that Boone's name had been filled in by William Preston, who now was working hard against the British as an officer in the American militia.

The following year Boone, accused in a court-martial of working with the British and against the Americans, was to say "he Did tell the Britesh officers he would be friendly to them and try to give up Boonesborough but that he was a trying to fool them."[24] It worked. The prisoners Hamilton bought from the Indians remained, for the most part, prisoners of the British for years—several of them until 1781.[25] At least one died in a British prison. But Boone left Detroit with Blackfish—in part because Blackfish liked him but largely because, as Hamilton noted, by taking Boone with them, the Shawnees were expecting "to effect something"—namely, the capture of Boonesborough.

Blackfish and Boone returned to Old Chillicothe on April 25. On the way they visited Mingo and Shawnee villages on the Scioto River, at which Blackfish spread the word that the Indians should assemble in the spring for an attack on the Kentucky settlements. For close to two months after his return, Boone lived in Old Chillicothe as Blackfish's adopted son. Through Filson, Boone described this important town, home to many hundreds of Shawnees:

> Their huts are generally built of small logs, and covered with bark, each one having a chimney, and a door, on which they place a padlock.
>
> Old Chelicothe is built in the form of a Kentucke station, that is, a . . . long square; and some of their houses are shingled. A long

Council-house extends the whole length of the town, where the King and Chiefs of the nation frequently meet, and consult of all matters of importance, whether of a civil or military nature.

Some huts are built by setting up a frame on forks, and placing bark against it; others of reed, and surrounded with clay. The fire is in the middle of the wigwam, and the smoke passes though a little hole. They join reeds together by cords run through them, which serve them for tables and beds. They mostly lie upon skins of wild beasts, and sit upon the ground. They have brass kettles and pots to boil their food; gourds or calabashes, cut asunder, serve them for pails, cups and dishes.[26]

Boone was closely watched by the Shawnees—the more so because during Blackfish's trip to Detroit, Andrew Johnson, a salt-boiler captive who had been adopted and had remained in the village, had managed to escape and make his way back to Kentucky. Johnson, given by the Shawnees the name Pe-cu-la, or Pequolly, meaning "Little Duck," was a small man who played the fool to gain greater latitude from his captors. Although he was a fine woodsman, Johnson pretended to be scared of guns and to be a terrible shot. Asked where Kentucky was, he would point the wrong way—to the Shawnees' amusement. Boone furthered the deception, by saying that Johnson "was mad, and of no sort of account anyhow." The result was that the Shawnees paid little attention to Johnson, who escaped one night when his adoptive father was at a dance in the village and headed back to Harrodsburg to warn the settlers of the Indians' planned attack on the Kentucky settlements.[27]

Boone got on well with the Shawnees. In Pennsylvania he probably had learned some Delaware, an Algonquian language close to Shawnee (the Shawnees referred to the Delawares as their grandfathers).[28] He presumably had picked up some Shawnee words during his years in Kentucky. As a captive in Old Chillicothe, Boone learned more Shawnee so that he could communicate with Blackfish, Blackfish's family, and the rest of the village. He told his biographer Filson:

At Chelicothe I spent my time as comfortably as I could expect; was adopted, according to their custom, into a family where I became a son, and had a great share in the affection of my new parents, brothers, sisters, and friends. I was exceedingly familiar and friendly with them, always appearing as cheerful and satisfied as possible, and they put great confidence in me. I often went a hunting with them, and frequently gained their applause for my activity at our shooting-matches. I was careful not to exceed many of them in shooting; for no people are more envious than they in this sport. . . . The Shawanese king [presumably Moluntha, who became the tribal chief after Cornstalk] took great notice of me, and treated me with profound respect, and entire friendship, often entrusting me to hunt at my liberty. I frequently returned with the spoils of the woods, and as often presented some of what I had taken to him, expressive of duty to my sovereign.[29]

Boone's friendship for his adoptive family may have been partly feigned, to put Blackfish off guard so as to make escape easier. Knowing he had been watched closely during his initial hunts to see if he would try to escape, Boone worked hard to cause the Shawnees to trust him. But it is also clear that Boone liked Blackfish, who called Boone "my son" and who sometimes, while sucking a lump of sugar, would show his affection for Boone by taking the sugar from his mouth and giving it to Boone as a treat. Boone also liked the younger of Blackfish's two small daughters. He gave both girls maple sugar that he bought with the silver trinkets Hamilton had given him in Detroit.[30] Decades later one of Boone's granddaughters met in Fort Leavenworth, Kansas, an old Indian woman who beamed when she heard that the white woman talking to her was Boone's granddaughter. It turned out that the old woman was one of Blackfish's daughters, who remembered how kind Boone had been to her back in Chillicothe.[31]

William Hancock, a salt-boiler captive adopted by Will Emery, "didn't see how [Boone] could be whistling and contented among a parcel of dirty Indians," while Hancock himself was so discontented with his captivity.[32] The fact was, however, that Boone liked the Indians and liked a lot about his life with the Shawnees. Once the Shawnees permitted Boone to hunt on his own, he was doing what he loved to do best. It is also likely that Boone found the Shawnees' ethical principles in line to a considerable extent with what he had learned as a child from the Quakers. At least within their own tribe—to which Boone now belonged by adoption—Shawnees advocated Golden Rule principles: "Do not kill or injure your neighbor, for it is not him that you injure, you injure yourself. But do good to him, therefore add to his days of happiness as you add to your own. Do not wrong or hate your neighbor, for it is not him that you wrong, you wrong yourself. But love him, for Moneto loves him also as He loves you."[33] Shawnees also espoused sharing. If two Shawnees hunted together, "the first game killed or trapped by either of them was graciously offered to the other, with the remark 'Gi tap-il-wa-ha-la' which signifies 'I enliven your spirit' or 'Gita il-ani cha-la' which means 'I enliven you as to a man.'"[34]

It is easy to conceive of Boone fitting in as a Shawnee. Nothing suggests, however, that he ever thought of living permanently as one. Stephen Aron, in his excellent study of changes in Kentucky between the times of Boone and of Henry Clay, expressed regret that most of the salt-boiler captives fled from the Shawnees when they had the chance to do so and suggested that they had lost a unique opportunity to join forces with the Indians and to preserve a frontier way of life combining the best of both cultures.[35] That view may be more romantic than realistic. The actions of Boone and most of the other salt-boilers bear out that they wanted to get back to their families. In addition, Boone, a leader among the white settlers would have been hard-pressed to gain a comparable position among the Shawnees, even if he learned to speak fluent Shawnee and proved his loyalty to the Shawnees by fighting American settlers. Boone's actions also indicate that he—like so many Kentucky settlers—wanted to improve his fortunes by owning and trading in land. Boone realized that the Indians were fighting the whites, and vice versa, over control of land. He must have seen that the whites, thanks to their greater weaponry and ever greater numbers, would ultimately prevail. It is hard to see why Boone would have bet on foreseeable losers in that struggle, though it is doubtless true that there was much in the Shawnees' way of living that Boone would have found congenial and attractive.

Boone may well have taken an Indian wife when he lived among the Shawnees. Over a hundred years later a Boone granddaughter wrote: "Grandfather Boone said he had a squaw that Claimed him as her Buck. He said she mended and dried his leggins [and] patched his mocksins." Boone said she was an "Old Squaw" who "made him help her do all her drudgery work," like making him stand in a tub of hot hominy corn, tramping the husks off the corn with his bare feet. When Boone hallooed and ran away to give the hot water time to cool down, "she would laugh, take a club & beat him back."[36] Perhaps the Shawnee woman was not actually an old squaw. Boone would have been unlikely to tell one of his granddaughters if the Shawnee woman in fact had been good-looking. The frank physicality of the tub scene

Boone described to his granddaughter sounds consistent with the account of an early-nineteenth-century Shawnee that if a Shawnee husband struck his wife, "frequently the wife retaliates, by pulling his hair, or his testicles, the latter of which they most generally resort to."[37] It may also be significant that Filson, after his account of Boone's career, describes Indian weddings: "Their form of marriage is short—the man, before witnesses, gives the bride a deer's foot, and she, in return, presents him with an ear of corn, as emblems of their several duties."[38] Could this information have come from Boone describing his own Indian wedding?

Even if Boone did not take an Indian wife in a traditional ceremony, it is likely he had offers of female companionship. Nicholas Cresswell, a young Englishman who traveled down the Ohio in 1775, records in his journal several such encounters with Delaware women and the sister of a Mohawk. Cresswell pretended to be sick in declining the first such offer but accepted the others. He also records how much he liked the Indian women and how helpful they were—gathering food, making camp, packing and unpacking horses, cooking, guiding, and interpreting, for example.[39] Similarly, the missionary David McClure noted that at Pittsburgh in 1772 "the greater part of the Indian traders [kept] a squaw as a temporary wife": "They allege the good policy of it, as necessary to a successful trade."[40] Moreover, deaths in wars had caused many Indian groups to have more women than men, and Indian widows not infrequently took white adopted men to replace their dead husbands.[41]

During Boone's captivity with the Shawnees conditions at Boonesborough worsened. The capture of Boone and the salt-boilers had stripped the small settlement of its best woodsman and the leader of its militia as well as of a third of its fighting men. The lack of salt remained an acute problem because there was still nothing but meat to eat and no salt to preserve the meat. A settler who arrived in Boonesborough on March 26, 1778, remembered "a poor, distressed, ½ naked, ½ starved people, daily surrounded by the savage, which made it so dangerous, the hunters were afraid to go out to get Buffaloe Meat."[42] Daniel Trabue, who came to Boonesborough about three weeks later, said: "The people in the fort was remarkable kind and hospetable to us with what they had. But I thought it was hard times—no bred, no salt, no vegetables, no fruit of any kind, no Ardent sperrets, indeed nothing but meet."[43]

Senior Virginian officials sought to undo the harm done by Cornstalk's murder by issuing formal proclamations of friendship to the Shawnees. Cols.

William Preston and William Fleming, for example, wrote on April 3, 1778, to the chiefs and warriors of the Shawnees:

> It is with the deepest Concern and sincerest Sorrow that we reflect on the Murder committed by some of Our rash young People, on the Corn Stalk and three Others of your Nation. Yet this Accident we hope will not lessen the Great Council Fire, before which your Father and Ours, and Yourselves and we, have sat and smoaked the Pipe of Peace. . . . we are Commanded to Assure you, that the Governor and all the Great Men of Virginia detest the crime and are much concerned that the Chain of Friendship which binds us together as Neighbours, Antient Allies & Friends, should contract any Rust. And to convince you of the sincerity of Our great Men, we are ordered to send you some of the Governors Proclamations, in which a reward is offered for Apprehending the Murderers, And every method taken to bring them to Justice. You may be Assured they will be punished by our Laws, when they are taken in the same manner, as if they had killed so many of our own People. We are Ordered to propose to you that Commissioners for Virginia, meet some of your Wise Old Men in treaty at Fort Randolph, in hopes that they can make such reparation as will satisfy Your Nation, and convince you of the Peaceable disposition of Virginia towards you. . . . We wish to be Friends with you. We covet nothing you have. All we desire is Peace with you. . . . In order to forward this happy work, . . . when you come to treat an equal number of white persons shall be sent over the Ohio, and put in your Peoples hands, for your sincerity and safe treatment. . . . we send you this String of White Wampum, And subscribe ourselves, Your Friends & Brothers.[44]

The Shawnees paid no heed to these proclamations. They knew that Cornstalk's killers had not been punished. Moreover, none of the Shawnee "Wise Old Men" wanted to go to negotiate with the whites at Fort Randolph, where Cornstalk and his son had been seized and killed. Instead, the Shawnees continued to prepare for an attack in strength on Boonesborough.

The Boonesborough settlers were demoralized not only by the squalor of their fort, the lack of food and salt, and the fear of renewed Indian attack but also by the news that Boone and the salt-boilers had been captured without a shot having been fired. Why would Boone have done such a thing? Rumors began to spread that Boone had gone over to the British. After all, many of his Bryan in-laws were Tories. Moreover, other leading frontiersmen were defecting to the British that spring. On March 28, 1778, for example, Alexander McKee and Simon Girty fled from Fort Pitt to go to Detroit to join the British cause. McKee, whose mother was a Shawnee, was a leading Indian agent. Girty and his brothers were whites who had been captured as boys by the Shawnees and Delawares. Simon Girty spoke Shawnee, Delaware, and Seneca and was to become infamous as a "white Indian" renegade, leading Indian attacks on American settlements.

Was Boone, too, a turncoat? Col. Richard Callaway certainly thought so. Callaway had disliked Boone at least since 1775, when Boone, not Callaway, had been chosen to lead the group that blazed the trail through the Cumberland Gap and on to the Kentucky River. Callaway cannot have been happy to see Boone's name, not his, given to the settlement on the Kentucky or to see the influence Boone had with the settlers, even though Boone was only a captain in the militia, while Callaway was a colonel. Callaway liked Boone even less now that two of Callaway's nephews, who had been part of Boone's salt-boiling party, had been captured by the Indians—one ending up as a British prisoner, the other adopted by the Shawnees.[45]

Rebecca Boone stayed in Boonesborough for three months after Boone's capture. It must have been a miserable time for her. She did not know whether Boone was still alive and, if so, whether he had gone over to the British.[46] It could not have been pleasant to hear other settlers question Boone's courage and his loyalty to the American cause. At the beginning of May Rebecca and her children joined a group of rangers who were leaving Kentucky and started back to the Yadkin to be back with the Bryans. Her daughter Susannah and Susannah's husband, William Hays, accompanied her. Of Boone's family only his daughter Jemima and her husband, Flanders Callaway, stayed at Boonesborough.

As the weather warmed in the spring and early summer of 1778, Boone thought more and more about escaping from the Shawnees.[47] But it had to be done right. An unsuccessful escape attempt could lead to death by torture, to discourage other captives from trying to escape.[48] Boone sought to allay the Indians' suspicions that he might try to get back to Kentucky. According to one story he told years later, one time when he was out hunting with Blackfish and other Indians, he woke up early one morning while the Shawnees were still asleep and, with a bullet screw, took the lead balls out of every loaded gun in camp. He then woke the Indians. "I'm going home," Boone said. "No, you ain't," Blackfish said; "if you attempt it, I'll shoot you." "Shoot then," Boone said, walking off. The Shawnees fired at him, noisily but without any effect. Boone came back to the surprised Indians, the lead balls nestling in his buckskin shirt, which he was holding up like an apron. "Here, take your bullets," he said. "Boone ain't going away."[49] Eventually, the Indians allowed him to hunt alone. Over time Boone managed to secrete some powder and shot from the meager amounts doled out to him for hunting.

At the beginning of June the Shawnees under Blackfish took Boone with them to the salt springs on the Scioto, where for ten days they made salt, and Boone "hunted some for them, and found the land, for a great extent about this river, to exceed the soil of Kentucke, if possible, and remarkably well watered."[50] In addition to salt making, Blackfish went to the Shawnee and Mingo villages on the Scioto to recruit warriors for the coming attack on Boonesborough. The Indians gave Boone guns to repair, and he was able to squirrel away an unstocked rifle barrel and a lock.

Returning to Old Chillicothe, Boone saw "four hundred and fifty Indians, of their choicest warriors, painted and armed in a fearful manner, ready to march against Boonesborough."[51] The Indians had been unsettled by a raid close to Old Chillicothe led by Andrew Johnson, the little woodsman who had pretended to be a fool in order to escape. Johnson and a handful of Kentuckians came into Shawnee country, killed two Shawnees in a nighttime attack, and took seven horses back with them to Kentucky.[52] Johnson's raid undercut what Boone had been telling the Shawnees about the Kentuckians' lack of spirit and their likely willingness to surrender and to go over peacefully to the British. Boone realized he could not delay his escape until he was able to take most of the salt-boiler captives with him. He had to get back to Boonesborough as soon as possible.

Boone took few words to tell the story of his escape to Filson in 1783: "On the sixteenth [of June 1778], . . . I departed in the most secret manner, and arrived at Boonesborough on the twentieth, after a journey of one hundred and sixty miles; during which, I had but one meal."[53] Stories told in later years add flesh to this skeletal sentence. According to Boone's son Nathan, when the warriors Boone was with were distracted shooting at a flock of turkeys, he took a horse, rode it south till it gave out, ran the rest of the way to the Ohio River, and swam across with the help of a makeshift raft. On the Kentucky side Boone made an oak bark poultice to treat his run-damaged feet and fashioned an improvised rifle out of a barrel he had brought from the Indian village and a stock he had carved. He kept on running to Boonesborough, stopping once for a meal from a deer he killed with his jerry-built weapon. He later told a friend: "You may depend upon it, I felt proud of my rifle."[54]

Boone arrived at Boonesborough late in the day on June 20, 1778. He called out to the settlers from some distance away to identify himself, to be sure they would not take him for an Indian and shoot him, dressed as he was and wearing his hair in a scalp-lock. The settlers were not effusive in their welcome. Apparently, they had heard from Harrodsburg the suspicions that Andrew Johnson had voiced about Boone's going over to the British. Where's Rebecca, Boone asked. He was told: "She put into the settlements a long time ago; she thought you was dead, Daniel, and packed up and was off to the old man's in Carolina."[55] Boone's cabin was empty and squalid. As he sat in it, the family cat, left behind by Rebecca, appeared and jumped into Boone's lap. A little later Jemima—the daughter Boone had saved from the Indians two years earlier—ran into the cabin and hugged him.

Boone was back in Boonesborough. There was still work to be done to secure the fort's defenses, and the loss of more than twenty salt-boilers to captivity had left a large gap in the fort's firepower. But if the settlers could manage to hold off an Indian attack on the fort, Boone's months among the Indians would strengthen the settlers' ability to take the fighting directly to the Indians. As Johnson's raid had already demonstrated, the Kentuckians now knew the exact location of the Shawnee villages on the Miami River. Boone, from his travels with Blackfish, also knew his way to many other Indian villages, including the Shawnee villages on the Scioto and the Little Miami and villages farther west and north on the way to Detroit. Boone's son Nathan told Lyman Draper: "The worst act the Indians ever did, Father used to say, was showing [the salt-boilers] the way to their towns and the geography of the Indian country."[56]

13

THE SIEGE OF BOONESBOROUGH

BOONE TOLD THE SETTLERS AT BOONESBOROUGH ABOUT THE INDIAN forces being readied to attack their little fort. He said that "he was now come home to help his own people fight and they must make what preperration they could but the indeans would certainly be there in a few days."[1] There was much to be done and little time to do it. Boone told Filson that he had "found our fortress in a bad state of defence."[2] William Bailey Smith, the major who had brought fifty reinforcements to Boonesborough in the fall of 1777, put Boone in charge of restoring the defenses. One of the palisade walls had fallen down almost completely and had to be rebuilt. The gates and posterns were strengthened. At the southeastern and southwestern corners new bastions, or blockhouses, were built, two stories high, with the second story projecting out over the first and with openings left in the floor to permit defenders to fire on attackers who came close to the walls. ("What is meant by a block house?" Daniel Trabue wrote, describing the ones at Logan's Station at this time, and then answered his own question: "The upper story to be much biger than the lower story and to Jut over so that you may be up on the upper floor and shoot Down if the indeans was to come up to the walls, and they cannot climb up the walls of these houses.")[3] Because the old well inside the fort did not give much water, work was started on digging another one. Women cast lead into bullets, smoothed the mold marks off the cast bullets, and prepared bandages. Brush around the fort was cut down.[4]

Boonesborough asked the neighboring settlements for reinforcements. Men were scarce. The small settlements had been further depleted by supplying men to George Rogers Clark on his bold expedition to take the fight west to the British by attacking the British stations at Kaskaskia and Cahokia in Illinois and Vincennes along the Wabash in Indiana. Clark had realized that "if the Indians destroyed Kentucky they'd attack our frontiers—obliging the states to keep large bodies of troops for their defense" and, as he knew that "the commandant [Henry Hamilton] of the different towns of the Illinois country and the Wabash was busily engaged in exciting the Indians against us, their reduction became [Clark's] first object."[5] Aided by Kentucky riflemen, Clark was able to capture Kaskaskia, Cahokia, and Vincennes in the summer of 1778 and, after the British retook Vincennes in December 1778, to take it again in February 1779.

Despite the depletion of their own ranks, however, Logan's Station sent about fifteen men, and Harrodsburg a few, to buttress Boonesborough.[6] To increase the firepower "arms and ammunition were given to the Negro men" in the fort, and any "well-grown boy became a fort soldier, and had his port-hole assigned him."[7] Still, there were not many rifle bearers in Boonesborough— perhaps sixty, as against the more than four hundred Indians who were about to attack them.

One more rifle bearer joined the Boonesborough settlers on July 17— William Hancock, one of the captive salt-boilers, who had been adopted by Captain Will, the Indian who had taken Daniel Boone captive when Boone was hunting in Kentucky in 1769. To prevent Hancock from escaping, Captain Will had Hancock sleep naked, while Captain Will slept with his head on the doorway to block the way out. Hancock waited until a night when Captain Will had drunk too much rum. That enabled the unclothed Hancock to flee his soddenly sleeping adoptive father. Carrying with him only three pints of raw corn, Hancock rode a stolen horse to the Ohio, swam across the river, and made it to Boonesborough nine days after he left Captain Will. He arrived at the fort, still naked, so weak that he had to be carried inside. Hancock reported that the Indians were coming four hundred strong and intended, if the settlers declined to come over to the British, to batter down the fort with four swivel guns that the British were providing to them from Detroit.[8] That was a scary prospect: the fort's frail palisade could not withstand pounding even from light artillery. The only good news in Hancock's report was that Boone's escape had caused the Indians to postpone their expedition into Kentucky for three weeks so they could send runners to Detroit for instructions and militia reinforcements.

Hearing Hancock's report, Boone wrote to Col. Arthur Campbell, commander of the Fincastle County militia, asking for reinforcements: "If men can be sent to us in five or six weeks, it would be of infinite service, as we shall lay up provisions for a siege."[9] Colonel Campbell, unwilling to act on his own, sought authorization from Virginia's Executive Council, which was thoroughly absorbed by the fighting with the British and the Tories in the east. Not until early September did relief start on its way from Virginia. The relievers showed up at Boonesborough long after the siege was over.[10]

The Indians, fortunately, were slow to act in launching their attack. Boonesborough's settlers had time in August to lay in most of the corn harvest. At the end of the month Boone took a step that has been a puzzle ever since: he took twenty or thirty men—close to half the fort's fighting strength—for a raid on a Shawnee village called Paint Creek, across the Ohio on the Scioto River. Boone said that "these indians was rich in good horses and beaver fur," so the Boonesborough party "could go and make a great speck and Git back in good time to oppose the big army of Indians." Col. Richard Callaway "apposed the plan with all his might but they went."[11]

Boone's men crossed the Ohio and headed for the Paint Creek village. Simon Kenton, scouting ahead of the group, stumbled into a party of Indians heading south toward Boonesborough. A firefight broke out. Kenton killed and scalped one Indian. Two Indians were wounded. There were no settler casualties. Kenton went on ahead and reported that the Indians had left Paint Creek, evidently as part of the large expedition against Boonesborough. Boone and the others turned back south and saw signs that hundreds of Indians had crossed the Ohio and were on the Warrior's Path, heading to Boonesborough. Only by leaving the trail and going through the woods were Boone and his raiders able to bypass the much larger Indian force and get back to Boonesborough before the Indians got there. Boone and his men arrived at the fort on the evening of Sunday, September 6, 1778, and told the settlers that the Indians were at hand and the siege would likely start the next morning.[12]

It is hard to justify Boone's Paint Creek raid. Was it to gain intelligence about the Indians' planned attack? Boone's information on these subjects was somewhat stale, dating back to his escape in late June. Hancock's information was only slightly more recent, because he had escaped in mid-July. Was it to bring home to the Indians their own vulnerability and so dissuade them from their planned attack on Boonesborough? But Boone's raid did little more than Andrew Johnson's raid had done to show the Indians that the whites now knew the way to the Shawnee villages. Moreover, a raid by twenty or thirty settlers was hardly likely to cause four hundred warriors to stop in their tracks. Was the raid intended to show the men at

Boonesborough that Boone was on their side and was willing to fight the Indians? There was some morale boost from the raid; a Williamsburg paper reported, "Captain Boone, the famous partisan, has lately crossed the Ohio with a small detachment of men, and nearing the Shawanese towns, repulsed a party of the enemy, and brought in one scalp, without any loss on his side."[13] Did Boone seek to renew the men's liking for him by enabling them to get plunder from a quick raid, including horses that the Boonesborough settlers needed badly? Perhaps. Boone knew how much the Boonesborough settlers liked a "good speck" and the chance for booty.

But all these possible benefits, even taken together, were small relative to the raid's risks. The Paint Creek raid took away manpower badly needed to strengthen Boonesborough's defenses. It also carried the risk that many who went on the raid would be killed or captured and so would not be able to shoulder rifles in the fort's defense. The word *rash* comes to mind as well as the one caveat about Boone noted by Felix Walker, the young axeman whom Boone had nursed back to health after the Indian attack on Boone's trailblazers in March 1775: Boone "appeared void of fear and of consequence—too little caution for the enterprise."[14] In the event, however, Boone and the raiding party had managed to make it back safely to the fort. The Boonesborough settlers had only one night before the Indians would be there. The settlers readied their guns, molded and trimmed more bullets, brought in vegetables from the fields, and fetched water.

The next morning the Indians appeared before the fort—hundreds of them. Squire Boone's boys, Moses and Isaiah, who had been out watering horses, started to ride out to meet them, thinking the arrivals were the longed-for reinforcements from Virginia. Boone yelled at his nephews to get back in the fort. Boone and the other scouts followed, and the fort gate was closed and barred.

The attackers rode in front of the fort, just out of range of the fort's rifles. They rode single file, which made them look even more numerous than they were, but there were plenty of them. Boone said there were 444 Indians. The Indians—mostly Shawnees but with some Cherokees, Wyandots, and others—were in full war paint. There was also a French-Canadian officer and eleven other French Canadians with him, the troop of militia that Hamilton had sent from Detroit. The parading riders bore British and French flags. The men inside Boonesborough—about 60 in all—were outnumbered more than 7 to 1.[15] To the defenders the only good to be seen in the attackers' show of strength was the absence of swivel guns, the light cannon William Hancock had heard would be sent from Detroit to enable the attackers to batter the fort.

Pompey—the black man living among the Shawnees who had acted as an interpreter when the Shawnees captured Boone in February 1778—came close enough to the fort to be able to call out Boone's name. Boone called back to him. Pompey cried out that Blackfish had come to accept the surrender of the fort—which Boone had promised. He told Boone that Blackfish was carrying letters from Governor Hamilton promising safe conduct for everyone. A voice called out from the Indians, farther away from the fort: "Sheltowee!" It was Blackfish, the war chief, Boone's adoptive father. Boone went outside the fort to a stump about sixty yards from the fort, within range of the defenders' rifles, to meet with Blackfish and Moluntha, Cornstalk's successor as the Shawnees' head chief.

"Howdy, my son," Blackfish said—reaching out his hand. "Howdy, my father," Boone replied, shaking Blackfish's hand. Boone had enough Shawnee and Blackfish enough English that they could communicate a bit without an interpreter. "What made you run away from me?" Blackfish asked. "I wanted to see my wife and my children." "If you had asked me," Blackfish said, "I'd have let you come."[16]

Moluntha broke in. "You killed my son the other day, across the Ohio River," he said. So the Indian that Simon Kenton had killed and scalped on the Paint Creek raid was Moluntha's son? That was not going to make things easier. Boone said he had not been there. That was not true, and Moluntha knew it. "It was you," Moluntha said. "I tracked you here."

Blackfish handed Boone the letters from Hamilton. The letters reminded Boone of his pledge to cause the fort to surrender. If the settlers surrendered, they would be given safe conduct to Detroit. Officers who came over to the British side would be kept at their present rank. If the settlers resisted, Hamilton said he could not be held responsible for the bloodshed that would result.[17] Blackfish also produced a wampum belt with red, white, and black rows of beads. The belt, Blackfish said, showed the path from Detroit to Boonesborough and the ways it could be traveled. Red was the path of war, the way they had come to Boonesborough. White was the path of peace, the path they would go back on together if Boone and the others surrendered peaceably. Black was death. Black was the death that would happen if they did not surrender.[18] Blackfish asked Boone what he thought about the letters and the belt—which, he wanted to know, would Boone choose?

Boone said there was much to consider, and he needed to consult with his colleagues, including the officers who had come to the fort since his capture. Blackfish said he understood. He let on that his warriors were hungry. Boone, knowing that the Indians could take whatever they wanted without his blessing, said, "You see plenty of cattle and corn; take what you need, but don't let any be wasted." Blackfish in turn presented Boone with "a gift for your women"—seven smoked buffalo tongues. The men smoked together, and Boone returned to the fort with Blackfish's present.

Inside the fort the leaders looked at the letters from Hamilton. To Colonel Callaway the letters, with their references to what Boone had said he would do to encourage the surrender of Boonesborough, were further proof that Boone had agreed to betray the fort. Boone said he had led Hamilton to believe that he would do so, but only as a way of being able to get back to defend Boonesborough. Boone told the Boonesborough settlers that he was prepared to fight, but he also said he thought "they could make a good peace with the Indians," and if people decided to surrender, he would be compelled to go along with the decision of the majority.[19]

There was plenty to think about. As Filson recorded Boone's thoughts a few years later, there was, in Filson's florid words, "a powerful army before our walls, whose appearance proclaimed inevitable death, fearfully painted, and marking their footsteps with desolation," and "if taken by storm we must inevitably be devoted to destruction."[20] This was not like any earlier attack on a station in Kentucky. Instead of a handful of Indians content to lurk near the fort and pick off hunters and stragglers, but without the strength to mount an all-out attack, this was a well-armed force of hundreds, accompanied by French-Canadian soldiers who presumably knew how to conduct a siege.

Young John Gass thought Boone laid out the choice carefully for the settlers so that Boone would be "free from blame should they hold on and the Indians overcome them."[21] It is also possible that Boone was simply being a realist and that he saw the call as a close one, given the extent to which the attackers outnumbered the defenders. Another settler who was a boy at the time remembered that there had been a great difference of opinion, "half of the men willing to surrender, and the other half ready to fight, and rather die" than surrender.[22]

After some back-and-forth Col. Richard Callaway, the fort's commanding officer, "swore he would kill the first man who proposed surrender."[23] That doubtless shortened the discussion. Maj. William Bailey Smith, second in command, chimed in that they should "refuse the offer and defend the fort."[24] Squire Boone said "he would never give up" but "would fight till he died." All the men favored resistance. "Well; well," Boone said, "I'll die with the rest."[25] So the decision was to fight—but it made sense to continue to stall as long as possible, in the hope that reinforcements would finally arrive from Virginia. Boone and Smith, who were appointed to talk further with Blackfish, agreed to meet with the Indian leaders late that afternoon.

Blackfish was accompanied by Moluntha and a few other Indians. Panther skins were spread out on logs for the speakers to sit on. Major Smith wore full military regalia, including a scarlet coat and a macaroni hat with an ostrich feather in it, perhaps to make an impression and to support what Boone had said about the need to consult with new officers at the fort.[26] After hand shaking, introductions, and pipe smoking, Blackfish asked Smith and Boone their views of the surrender offer. It was a kind offer, Smith said, but the trip would be hard for the women and children. "I have brought forty horses and mares for the old people and women and children to ride," Blackfish said. "I am come to take you away easy."[27] Boone said they needed more time to discuss it because there were many chiefs to consult. Blackfish agreed to one more day of talking, but Boone came away from the meeting convinced that they would not be able to stall any longer.

One heartening thing from the palaver was the Indians' belief, evidenced by the number of extra horses they said they had brought, that there were forty women and children in the fort—not a dozen or twenty. Given the usual ratio of men to women and children in the frontier forts, if the Indians thought there were forty women and children in Boonesborough, they must have thought there were least a hundred men there—not sixty. In fact, the Indians had overestimated the number of rifle-bearing men in the fort— partly because an American captive in Detroit had misled Hamilton into thinking that two hundred reinforcements from Virginia had already arrived at the Kentucky forts. The Boonesborough defenders worked to strengthen that misconception. While the men were visible on the stockade walls, the women put on men's hats and hunting shirts and marched back and forth inside the fort with the gate open so the Indians could see their numbers.[28]

As had been agreed with Blackfish, the women were also allowed to go out to the spring to get water. It was uneasy work, hauling water within easy rifle range of the Indians. The water bearers must have regretted the absence of a sufficient well inside the stockade. "Fine squaws," the Indians called as the women drew and hauled water.²⁹ At midday the Indians made an unusual request: the Indians had heard how pretty Boone's daughter was, and they asked that she please be brought to the gate so they could see her and the other squaws. Maybe the Indians had heard from Hanging Maw or others who took Jemima and the Callaway girls captive in 1776 about the girls' beauty. To buy more time, Boone agreed. Jemima and one or two other women came to the open gate, accompanied by riflemen, as Blackfish and several warriors looked on. The Indians made signs that the white women should let down their hair. They "took their Combs out," according to Jemima's daughter, "and let their hair flow over their shoulders."³⁰ The Indians nodded their approval and left.

Toward evening Pompey called out that it was time to talk again about the surrender. Pompey's officiousness as an interpreter was grating on the Boonesborough defenders, many of whom were slaveholders from Virginia and North Carolina. Boone, Smith, and others met with Blackfish and other Shawnee leaders and delivered the settlers' conclusion: "We were determined to defend our fort while a man was living."³¹

Blackfish seemed surprised by the reply. After a time Blackfish said the Indians' orders "from Governor Hamilton [were] to take us captives, and not destroy us, but if nine of us would come out, and treat with them, they would immediatly withdraw their forces from our walls, and return home peaceably. This sounded grateful in our ears; and we agreed to the proposal." Both sides agreed to get together again the following day. Blackfish said that "he had many chiefs from many different towns with him and that all would have to participate in the treaty." That apparently sounded a little fishy to Boone, who said "there were so many officers in the fort . . . and that they all would have to participate in the treaty."³²

On the morning of Wednesday, September 9, 1778, the women of Boonesborough laid out in front of the fort a big meal for the Indians—venison, buffalo tongue, cheese, milk, corn—in an effort to show the attackers that the defenders had plenty of food, more than enough to outlast a long siege. After the meal the Americans walked to the meeting ground, within sixty yards—that is, well within rifle range—of the fort. The Americans included Boone, Col. Richard Callaway, Maj. William Bailey Smith, Squire Boone, Flanders Callaway, Isaac Crabtree, and several other leading settlers. Riflemen were placed in the corner bastions of the fort, with orders to keep their guns trained on the Indians and to shoot at the first sign of trouble. Boone told the riflemen not to wait for fear of hitting him and the others but to "fire at the lump"; "fire among the crowd; as the Indians were most numerous, they were most likely be the sufferers."[33]

The Indians at the meeting ground far outnumbered the whites. Boone saw many strong young warriors at the meeting place, in addition to Black-fish and the elders. "These are not chiefs," Boone said. Blackfish sent the young men away, but the Indians still outnumbered the whites two to one and seated themselves with an Indian on either side of each settler. What Boone did not see was that, just as the settlers had riflemen poised in the bastions of the fort, Indian riflemen were covering the meeting from brush in a nearby hollow lined with sycamore trees. The discussions began in earnest after the peace pipe was passed around. Blackfish initially proposed that the Indians would agree to make peace if all whites agreed to pull out of Kentucky en-tirely in six weeks. The Americans said they could not agree to this. "Broth-ers," Blackfish said, "by what right did you settle in this country?" Boone said the country had been purchased from the Cherokees. Blackfish asked a Cherokee who was there if that was true. The Cherokee confirmed it.[34]

Blackfish then proposed that his army would go home if both sides would recognize the Ohio River as the boundary between their settlements, though each could hunt and trade on either side of the river. There appears to have been another important provision in Blackfish's proposal, one men-tioned by Boone late in his life, though understandably not told to Filson: the settlers had to pledge allegiance to the British Crown and submit to the authority of Lieutenant Governor Hamilton at Detroit.[35] The settlers' leaders agreed to these terms, and, as Boone told Filson, "the articles were agreed to and signed."[36]

Did this mean that the Boonesborough leaders—including Colonel Cal-laway, who had vowed to shoot the first settler who proposed surrender—actually agreed to go over to the British side, in the middle of the Ameri-can Revolution? And if they made such an agreement, did they intend to honor it? It is much more likely, given their previous and subsequent fighting against the British and their Indian allies, that the Boonesborough men were willing to misrepresent their intentions, as Boone had done to Hamilton at Detroit, in order to be able to fight another day and to buy time for the ar-rival of the promised reinforcements from Virginia.

The signed articles have not survived, and the oral agreement they pur-ported to reflect vanished within minutes. After Blackfish declaimed in

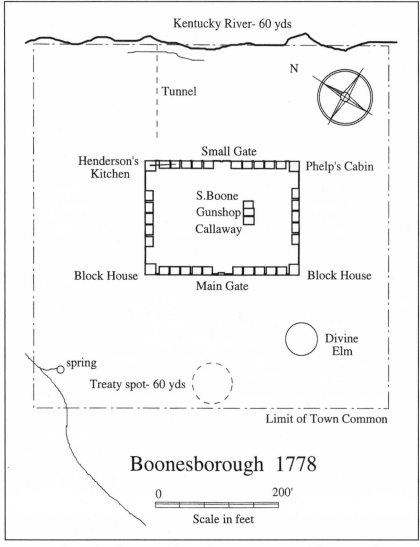

Kentucky River- 60 yds

N

Tunnel

Small Gate

Henderson's
Kitchen

Phelp's Cabin

S.Boone
Gunshop
Callaway

Block House

Block House

Main Gate

Divine
Elm

spring

Treaty spot- 60 yds

Limit of Town Common

Boonesborough 1778

0   200'

Scale in feet

Boonesborough at the Time of the Siege in 1778. After a sketch by Moses Boone.
Shows where the "treaty" was held, sixty yards in front of the main gate.
Courtesy of Neal O. Hammon

Shawnee to his warriors, who were some distance away from the meeting place, he turned back to the white representatives. Among us it is customary, he said, when concluding a treaty intended to be lasting, "to shake long hands," with two Shawnees shaking hands with each of the men with Boone—to bring their hearts close together. "We agreed to this also," Boone told Filson, "but were soon convinced their policy was to take us prisoners.—They grappled us; but, although surrounded by hundreds of savages, we extricated ourselves from them."[37] It may be that, as Daniel Trabue reported, Colonel Callaway "was the first that Jirked away from" the Indians, triggering shots from the bastions. It may be that Indians fired at the whites from the sycamore hollow. It may also be that some of the whites outside the fort, in thinking the Indians were trying to seize them, misunderstood what was in fact a customary Indian way of sealing an agreement by locking arms, and in doing so brought on a fight that could have been avoided. What is clear is that a melee broke out—a "dredful skuffil," in Trabue's words.[38] Boone threw his adoptive father Blackfish to the ground hard. The Indian who had passed around the pipe tomahawk before the discussions tried to hit Boone with it but managed only to gash the skin on the back of Boone's head with the handle. The wound, more than two inches long, left a scar over which hair never grew.[39]

The whites ran for the fort. Several Indians were hit in the first volley from the bastions. One rifleman posted in the southwest bastion of the fort had his rifle trained on an Indian sitting behind the treaty council, wearing brooches, half-moons, and other silver ornaments. "That's a fine mark," the rifleman thought—and pulled the trigger as soon as the shooting started, killing the Indian.[40] Squire Boone was shot, the ball grazing one shoulder and the backbone and lodging in the other shoulder. The shot knocked him down, but he got back up and made it into the fort.

The time for pipe smoking and treaty making was over. The attackers were pouring fire into the fort, and the defenders were firing back. Squire Boone picked up a rifle and fired at an Indian from his assigned post in the southwest bastion. In reloading, he found his shoulder hurt so much from his wound that he could not ram the ball home. His wife looked at the wound and pronounced it a slight one—but the pain in Squire Boone's shoulder grew worse. When the Indian fire slackened, Daniel Boone made a deep cut and dug out the ball, which had been lodged in his brother's shoulder bone. Squire Boone took to his bed, keeping beside him a light broadaxe that he said he would use if the Indians made it into the fort.[41]

The Indians rushed the fort that afternoon but were driven back by fire from the bastions. Inside the fort many of the women and children huddled in Colonel Callaway's cabin in the center of the yard. The noise was deafening—the gunfire, the whooping and screaming of attackers and defenders, the barking of the fort dogs, the panicked cattle and horses milling around the yard.[42] As Moses Boone, who was only ten years old at the time, remembered it, "The women cried and screamed, expecting the fort would be stormed."[43] Elizabeth Callaway, one of the girls who had been captured by the Indians in 1776, found one of the settlers under a bed in the cabin and drove him out with a broomstick. The man was a German named Matthias Prock. "I was never made for a fighter," Prock said. "I was made for a potter."[44] Boone and Callaway set him to work digging the new well deeper.

Jemima Boone loaded guns, carried ammunition, and ran from cabin to cabin with food and water. Coming into a doorway, she felt as if she had been slapped on her backside. She had been hit by a bullet in what Boone's daughter-in-law euphemistically described as "the fleshy part of her back." Fortunately, the bullet was spent and did not make it through her petticoat but instead drove the cloth into her flesh. When she tugged at her clothes, the bullet fell out.[45] The defenders realized that the attackers could look down and fire into the center of the fort from hills on either side, even though the hills on the far side of the river were more than two hundred yards away and the hills on the same side were over three hundred yards away—long shots but just barely feasible if rifles were heavily charged with powder.[46] The Boonesborough defenders opened holes in the walls of adjoining cabins so that the settlers could move from cabin to cabin in shelter, without being exposed to the attackers' fire.

For nine days and nights the attacks continued. The settlers had limited ammunition, and the women "used to gather the Spent Balls at night to mold up to fight the Enemy next day."[47] Beginning with the second night, the Indians, not being able to take the fort by rifle fire during the day, attempted to torch the fort at night—using tactics that had enabled Indians to capture forts during the Seven Years' War and Pontiac's War.[48] They set fire to flax drying alongside the stockade wall. John Holder, Colonel Callaway's son-in-law, ran out the fort's gate, doused the fire with water, put the fire out, and ran back inside, while bullets splattered around him. Holder was a swearing man.[49] As the Indians shot at Holder, he cursed them creatively. When Holder made it back inside the fort, glad to be still alive, his mother-in-law, Mrs. Callaway, suggested, "It would be more becoming to pray than to swear." "I don't have time to pray, goddammit," Holder thundered.[50] It was a phrase the defenders found pleasure in repeating.

The Indians kept coming at night, aiming to throw on the cabin roofs torches made of shellbark, hickory bark, splints, flax, and black powder, all tied around a stick for a handle. Many of the burning torches fell into the central yard of the fort, where they did no harm. Some torches fell on the roofs—but most of the roofs sloped inward toward the courtyards, and the women managed to pull off any burning shingles with long poles. Squire Boone also improvised water-filled squirt guns made out of old musket barrels with pistons in them. The squirt guns, squirting up to a quart of water, worked well against the rooftop fires. The torches did little harm to the fort but lit up their bearers on the way in, making the Indians who carried them prime targets for the fort's defenders. Many torch-bearing Indians were wounded or killed.

Squire Boone came up with another invention: a wooden cannon, made of two sections of black gum tree banded together with iron. The first firing of the jerry-built cannon, loaded with a swivel ball and some twenty leaden bullets, broke up a crowd of Indians perhaps two hundred yards from the fort. "O Lord, how I made the Indians fly," was how Squire Boone remembered it. The noise itself was formidable. On the second firing, however, the cannon burst, which the Indians found funny. "Fire your damned cannon again!" they called out.[51]

On Friday, September 11, the firing died down some. The defenders heard a new sound, a sound of chopping and digging, coming from the rear of the fort, the side that ran parallel to the Kentucky River. The riverbank was about sixty yards away from the fort. The defenders saw muddiness in the river water near where the sound was coming from. They suspected that the Indians were digging a tunnel to the fort—perhaps to blow it up, perhaps to give the attackers a safe passage into the fort. Boone and the other defenders started a countermine, or trench, under the rear wall of the fort, across the tunnel's likely course.[52]

For all the shooting only two Americans were killed during the siege, both on the night of Friday, September 11. One was a slave named London, a valued rifleman. London had dug out under a cabin to push away a fire that had been set in a fence adjoining the cabin. Spotting an armed Indian crouched behind a tree stump near the fort, London asked the men in the cabin for a loaded rifle. He aimed at the Indian and fired, but the striking flint lit only the powder in the pan of his rifle. The flash in the pan gave away his position. The Indian fired, hitting London in the neck and killing him.

The other defender who was killed was a German American named David Bundrin, who was looking out a stone-lined porthole in the southwest bastion when an incoming bullet hit a stone next to the porthole and split. Half of the bullet penetrated Bundrin's forehead. His brain ran out of the wound as he rocked back and forth, his elbow on his knee in a sitting posture, never saying a word, sometimes wiping the oozing brains with his hand. Bundrin's wife did not realize how badly he had been hurt. Until he died, she kept saying it was God's blessing he had not been hit in the eye.[53]

For the next six days and nights the fighting went on—the Indians firing into the fort, the defenders shooting back; the Indians' trying to torch the fort at night; the mining and countermining. During much of the siege the fighters yelled insults at each other. The Shawnees' trade English was up to the exchange. "What are you doing down there?" the defenders called out. "Digging a hole; blow you all to hell that night, may be so!" the Indians called. The defenders called back, "Dig on—we'll dig and meet you—we'll make a hole to bury five hundred of you yellow sons of bitches!"[54] One Indian delivered a nonverbal insult by climbing up a tree at what he believed to be a safe distance from the fort. On his perch he lifted his breechclout, "turned the insulting part of his body to the besieged and defiantly patted it." One of the recurring stories of the Boonesborough siege is that a defending rifleman took a large-bore rifle, loaded it with extra powder, fired, and brought down the distant Indian.[55]

As the defenders dug their countermine under the rear wall of the fort, John Holder and some of the other riflemen hurled unearthed stones over the stockade to roll down toward the tunneling Indians. "Come out and fight like men," the Indians called out, "don't try to kill us with stones, like children!" One of the older women in the fort, a woman named Mrs. South, told the defenders "not to throw stones at the Indians, for they might hurt them, make them mad, and then they would seek revenge."[56] That became a byword among the defenders—O, don't do that, you might hurt the Indians and make them mad, and then they might try to hurt us in revenge.

Pompey, the black interpreter, popped up repeatedly from the cover of the riverbank to fire both bullets and insults at the defenders. Eventually, he was shot and fell back out of sight behind the bank. He was not heard from again. "Where's Pompey?" the Americans yelled. At first the Indians called back, "Pompey ne-pan"—Pompey's sleeping—but eventually they called out, "Pompey ne-poo"—Pompey's dead.[57]

On the night of Thursday, September 17, the Indians launched their most massive attack. Firing on both sides was continuous. Between the flashing gunpowder, the torches carried and hurled by the Indians, and the fires on the cabin roofs started by the torches, Moses Boone remembered that "it was so light in the fort that any article could be plainly seen to be picked up, even to a pin."[58] Another witness to the attack, William Patton, was a Boonesborough resident who had come back after a long hunt only to find the fort besieged by hundreds of Indians. Watching the siege from a hiding place outside the fort, Patton saw that "the Indians made in the night a Dreadfull attack on the fort. They run up to the fort—a large number of them— with large fire brands or torches and made the dreadfullest screams and hollowing that could be imagind." Without waiting for more, Patton ran from the scene to Logan's Station, where he reported that the Indians had taken Boonesborough by storm and that he had "heard the woman and Children and men also screaming when the indeans was killing them."[59]

But Boonesborough had not been taken. There had indeed been many torches and fires carried by the attackers that night—but they lit up the Indians so that the Boonesborough men could shoot them. More Indians were killed that night than in the whole rest of the siege. The weather also helped. It poured rain, which helped put out the fires on the cabin roofs and caused the Indians' tunnel to collapse. When morning broke on Friday, September 18, no Indians were to be seen. Settlers cautiously went out to fetch cabbages to feed the cattle that had been penned up in the fort during the siege. The cattle "could scarcely low," they "were so nigh famished for want of water."[60] Other defenders gathered the lead that the Indians had shot into the logs of the bastions and walls of the fort, so it could be refashioned into bullets. At the riverbank the settlers found the entrance to the tunnel the Indians had been digging and followed it in from the river fully forty yards—two-thirds of the way to the fort, until they were blocked where the water-sodden roof had collapsed. A British official later told Simon Kenton, when Kenton was a British prisoner, that the tunnel collapse caused the Indians to quit.[61]

Boone later summarized to Filson the outcome: "During this dreadful siege, which threatened death in every form, we had two men killed, and four wounded, besides a number of cattle. We killed of the enemy thirty-seven, and wounded a great number. After they were gone, we picked up one hundred and twenty-seven pounds weight of bullets, besides what stuck in the logs of our fort; which is certainly a great proof of their industry."[62] Boone's next sentence elides the next twelve months, as if nothing worth mentioning happened in that time: "Soon after this, I went into the settlement, and nothing worthy of a place in this account passed in my affairs for some time." In fact, much happened during that year—including an event Boone must have found so humiliating that he wanted no record of it: his own court-martial.

Boone described the siege and its outcome in a letter he wrote to Rebecca, who was still back on the Yadkin with her Bryan kin. In addition to saying he looked forward to rejoining her and the children, Boone mentioned allegations that he was a Tory and had taken an oath of allegiance to the British at Detroit. As to the British, Boone wrote, "God damn them, they had set the Indians on us." The letter has not survived; Rebecca destroyed it, perhaps because of Boone's uncharacteristic use of profanity, perhaps because of the reference to the court-martial. But Rebecca showed the letter to Bryan relatives, who remembered both the mention of the impending court-martial and Boone's cursing of the British. Boone's nephew said, "Boone was very little addicted to profanity," and remembered that Rebecca had cut the oath out of the letter with some scissors.[63]

The only surviving record of Boone's court-martial is a short account written in 1827, almost fifty years after the siege, by Daniel Trabue, who was a young settler, eighteen years old, at Logan's Station during the trial. As Trabue remembered it, Colonel Callaway charged that Boone "was in favour of the britesh" and "ought to be broak of his commission." Callaway said that Boone had led the Indians to the salt-boilers and caused the captives to be taken to Detroit "against their consent" and at Detroit "did Bargan with the British Commander that he would give up all the people at Boonesborough, and that they should be protected at Detroyt and live under British Jurisdiction." Callaway also said that when Boone came back to Boonesborough, he encouraged men to go with him across the Ohio [the raid on Paint Creek], and they returned only hours before the Indian attackers arrived. Finally, Callaway claimed that Boone took all the Boonesborough officers to the Indian camp, out of sight of (and rifle protection from) the fort.

According to Trabue, Boone said he gave up the salt-boilers because he thought he had had to "use some stratigem" to prevent the Indians from going ahead with their plan to take Boonesborough, which was "in bad order" at the time, so Boone said the Indians would need to come back in the summer with more warriors. He said that "he Did tell the Britesh officers he would be friendly to them and try to give up Boonesborough but that he was a trying to fool them."[64]

The court-martial acquitted Boone. At the same time, Boone was promoted from captain to major in the militia. The settlers had seen Boone in action in defending Boonesborough. The court's decision showed that the men trusted Boone and his leadership and believed Boone when he said that his promises to help to cause Boonesborough to surrender had been made to save the lives of the salt-boilers and of the Boonesborough settlers. Most of the salt-boilers, when they came back to Kentucky, were to say that Boone, by agreeing to their capture, had saved their lives and the lives of those at Boonesborough.[65] On Boone's willingness to negotiate with the Indians be-sieging Boonesborough, Simon Kenton noted that the negotiation was an effort to gain time for relief to arrive and declared emphatically, "They may say what they please of Daniel Boone, he acted with wisdom in that matter."[66] But the very fact of the charges galled Boone. Soon after the decision, he left for North Carolina, taking with him Jemima, her husband, Flanders Calla-way, and his son-in-law William Hays.

Richard Callaway stayed at Boonesborough. Reportedly, he never spoke to Boone again. Callaway did not have long to live. He managed to get the Virginia Assembly to appoint him as one of two commissioners in charge of a major improvement in the Wilderness Road that Boone had blazed— an appointment that must have been satisfying to Callaway (who had re-sented Boone's leadership of the 1775 road-blazing expedition) and galling to Boone.[67] But Callaway was killed before he could start to work on the Wil-derness Road project. In October 1779 he had obtained a license to operate a toll ferry across the Kentucky River near Boonesborough. In March 1780, not far from Boonesborough, Callaway's body was found scalped, stripped na-ked and rolled in a mudhole near where he and another man (also killed and scalped) had been building a ferryboat. His head bones had been hacked into pieces no bigger than a man's hand. A man who saw Callaway's body said he was "the worst barbecued man he ever saw."[68] Days later Joseph Jack-son, one of the salt-boilers who had been adopted by the Shawnees, saw a scalp stretched and drying near a campfire in the Indian town where he was living and recognized the scalp as Callaway's "by the long black and grey mixed hair."[69] Callaway's dislike and distrust of Boone, though rejected by the court-martial, was passed on to at least one of his descendants, who years later—pointing to Boone's repeated meetings with the Indians during the siege—said that "if it hadn't been for Col. Callaway, the fort [Boones-borough] would have been surrendered" and that "Boone was willing, & wished, to surrender."[70]

Boone had gone back to the Yadkin by early November 1778. He did not start back to Kentucky until September 1779. Part of the intervening time was spent recruiting Bryans, Boones, and other Yadkin neighbors to make the trip, but part may also have been spent convincing Rebecca to come to Kentucky, despite the squalor and danger of the Kentucky stations, rather than stay in North Carolina. Boone was deliberately elliptical about this period in his life with Rebecca, saying only (in Filson's telling): "The history of my going home, and returning with my family, forms a series of difficulties, an account of which would swell a volume, and being foreign to my purpose, I shall purposely omit them."[71] It stands to reason, however, that Daniel would have had trouble convincing Rebecca to return to a land marked by a substantial risk of death or captivity at the hands of the Indians and by the certainty of hardship and privation.

Yet Rebecca did decide to come back to Kentucky in 1779. It must have helped that so many other Bryans and Boones were coming. Land was available for purchase at reasonable rates. Land claims based on grants from Virginia had become less chancy, with the repudiation of the Transylvania Company's claims, the recognition of Kentucky as a county of Virginia, and the American successes against the British in the Revolutionary War. Moreover, in May 1779 the Virginia legislature had passed a law for granting land in Kentucky, spelling out comprehensible ways of claiming "waste or unappropriated lands upon the western water" based on settlement or preemption, and a procedure for buying from Virginia (initially at a price of £40 per hundred acres) treasury warrants for the purchase of the unclaimed land.[72] Virginia also had appointed a commission to go to Kentucky to resolve conflicting land claims in that county. The commissioners worked hard and settled thousands of claims—and managed to award themselves some land in the process.[73] Within a year of the act's effective date Virginia had sold warrants redeemable for over 1.9 million acres—more than 7 percent of the total area of Kentucky.[74] Greater certainty of title helped to encourage settlement. It is also likely that some Yadkin settlers, including some of Rebecca's Bryan relatives, decided to come to Kentucky because they were Tories, who saw the imminence of bloody fighting between rebels and British sympathizers in North Carolina and felt they would be safer in Kentucky. One non-Tory settler said that all the settlers coming from Carolina were Tories who "had been treated so bad there, they had to run off, or do worse."[75]

Fully one hundred emigrants left the Yadkin with Boone in September

1779. They were joined by emigrants from Virginia, including Abraham Lincoln, the grandfather of the future president. It was one of the largest groups to come to Kentucky through the Cumberland Gap. At about the same time settlers were coming into Kentucky from Pennsylvania down the Ohio River. The river trip was still hazardous. Indians continued to attack boats on the river, in several cases first forcing white captives to call out for help from the riverbank, so as to lure boats within rifle range. But the risk of attack on the river was somewhat reduced by the protection of a fort that Col. George Rogers Clark had built near the Falls of the Ohio and later by an armed boat that he had patrolling the river, starting in 1782.[76]

Boone's group was a significant part of the increased flow of immigration into Kentucky that began in 1779. The successful defense of Boonesborough encouraged that immigration, as did Clark's astounding victories over the British to the north and west. When Clark, then only in his mid-twenties, with barely two hundred troops, recaptured Vincennes in February 1779, he also captured Lieutenant Governor Henry Hamilton himself.[77] Clark's ability to beat the British and to seize the "Hair-Buyer General" shook the western tribes' loyalty to the British cause, even though Clark was not able to muster the number of American troops he needed to take Detroit, which continued to arm Indians attacking the American frontier settlements.[78]

The expanding flow of settlers into Kentucky in 1779 was also encouraged by the success of an American raid on the Shawnee villages in retaliation for the siege of Boonesborough and by the movement of many Shawnees out of Ohio. In May 1779 Col. John Bowman led about three hundred Americans across the Ohio to attack Shawnee villages on the Little Miami, including a dawn assault on Old Chillicothe. In the opening volley of that attack an American bullet ripped open Blackfish's leg from knee to thigh. The Shawnee warriors took shelter in the town's central council house. The Americans failed in their attempts to storm the council house but looted the town, burned cabins, and destroyed the corn crop before withdrawing back south of the Ohio and selling off the loot. Blackfish's ragged wound became infected, leading some weeks later to his death from gangrene poisoning. Many Shawnees, seeing the likelihood of ever-increasing white incursions, left Ohio and moved farther west, away from the American settlements. In the spring of 1779, even before Bowman's attack, some four hundred Shawnee warriors moved with their families to Spanish-controlled Missouri, at the invitation of the Spanish authorities.[79]

For all these reasons, by the time the Boone party arrived in Boonesborough in October 1779, there was at last the prospect of being able to plant and to harvest crops in the following year, though the winter of 1779–80 promised to be short of food. There had been no massive Indian attacks on the Kentucky forts since the siege of Boonesborough in September 1778. This is not to suggest, however, that the Kentucky to which Boone and his family returned was peaceful. There were still small-scale Indian raids in Kentucky—witness the killing of Colonel Callaway in March 1780. Most of the Shawnees who remained in Ohio were militant opponents of American settlements in Kentucky. Rebecca had good reason to be concerned about the risks of living near Boonesborough. Between 1775 and 1779 forty-seven people were killed defending or while hunting from Boonesborough.[80]

Boonesborough by late 1779 may have been less prone to large-scale Indian attack, but it remained small, filthy, ill fed, and dangerously unhealthy. Col. William Fleming described it: "Boones burg has 30 houses in it, stands in a bottom that is surrounded by hills on every side that commands it, . . . from which hills, small Army can do execution in the Fort which is a dirty place in winter like every other Station, there is a lick close to the post . . . in which there is a spring which serves the people in common that smells and tastes strong of sulphur there is likewise a Salt Spring or two but water weak in it."[81] The squalor and confinement in Boonesborough and the other Kentucky stockaded stations were sickening. There was little besides meat to eat. In January 1780 John Floyd wrote to William Preston: "If anybody comes by water I wish we could get a little flour brought down if it was dear as gold dust. Since I wrote, corn has been sold at the Fall for $165 a bushel." In June of that year Floyd wrote to Preston: "People this year seem generally to have lost their health: but perhaps it is owing to the disagreeable way in which we are obliged to live, crowded in forts, where the air seems to have lost all its purity and sweetness. Our poor little boy has been exceedingly ill, & is reduced to a mere skeleton by a kind of flux which is common here, and of which numbers die. His mother is almost disconsolate, and I myself am much afraid we shall lose the child, and if we do I shall impute it to nothing but living in dirt and filth."[82]

The settlers' dependence on meat, and meat alone, had also harmed the settlers. Colonel Fleming, who had studied medicine at the University of Edinburgh, described how sick the settlers were in 1779 at the Falls of the Ohio: "Several people died whilst we were here the disorder they complained of was occasioned by a relaxation of the solids, from bilious Complaints which brings on such Corruption of the fluids with a Visidness of the Juices that it degenerates and breaks out in cancerous eating soars I have seen the Maxillary and the glands about the throat and tongue in Old and Young persons entirely destroyed some have Vomited corrupted bile as green as Verdigrease so that the whole of the disorders that at this time reign here is occasioned by bile."[83] Fleming himself soon suffered at Harrodsburg from ailments like those he had seen at the Falls of the Ohio. His journal entry for March 1780 describes his condition:

> Much indisposed. Got bled 12 Oz. . . . [T]he blood was solid like liver and black as tarr the symptoms returning with violence my head paining me greatly through the temples, above my eyebrows along the Sutures of my head and the hind part my eyes seemed so full and tense in the sockets that I could not turn them, I was bled the 22nd being determined to let the Vein breath till I found an abatement of the Symptoms . . . this did not happen till three pints . . . was in the basin and I was giddy . . . the blood would leave the extremities my fingers would turn pale and have all the Appearance of a Corps a noise like the rustling of waters was constantly in my ears and my memory failed me the blood now taken was covered all over with a seemingly putrid gelly. . . . I was no longer at a loss to account for the different disorders I had observed for cancerous like ulcers in the throat and glands and for the different symptoms in the fevers I had lived for a constancy on poor dried Buffalo bull beef cured in the smaok . . . without any addition but a piece of Indian hoe cake which made my breakfast and the same for dinner—it was owing to this coarse food that I had such a thick vicid and black blood.[84]

Colonel Fleming may have come close to killing himself by exsanguination, but he had the sharpness of mind to attribute his symptoms to diet. For months he, like the settlers at Boonesborough, had been eating only buffalo meat, with occasional bits of cornmeal cake. The throat and jaw sores that he described on himself and that he had observed in the settlers at the Falls of the Ohio sound like classic symptoms of scurvy, or vitamin C deficiency—including swollen, purple, friable, often bleeding gums.[85] When Fleming returned to the Falls of the Ohio in 1783, after the Indian threat had receded and the settlers had more varied food, he reported in his journal that the inhabitants near Louisville were much healthier than they had been in 1779 and were "not subjected to the Phagadencie [teeth-eating] Cancerous ulcers and malignant fever so general when I was there in 1779."[86]

Boone and his family did not linger at Boonesborough after their return there in 1779—whether that was because of the unhealthiness of the place or the unpleasantness of being in the same small station with Col. Richard Callaway, who had accused Boone of treason. Boone stayed in Boonesborough only long enough to confirm land claims before the Virginia Land Commission for himself (fourteen hundred acres on Stoner's Creek), his brother George, and his son Israel. In late December 1779 Boone and his family and some other settlers, many of them Boone relatives, moved to a site six miles northwest of Boonesborough, where he had built a cabin and put in a corn crop. The settlement, called Boone's Station, was near what is now Athens, in Fayette County. It was a simple and rough station that first winter—just half-faced camps put up in the snow that greeted them on their arrival.[87]

The winter of 1779–80 was so rough it became known as the "Hard Winter." Colonel Fleming said the weather was "as severely cold as ever I felt it in America," and in his journal he described the cane almost all killed by the cold, the hogs frozen to death in their beds, the deer, turkeys, and buffalo frozen or starved to death.[88] By the end of 1779 the Kentucky River was so solidly frozen it could bear the weight of horses. In December John Floyd wrote to William Preston, "The Day is so cold that . . . the Ink freezes every moment so that I cant make the letter."[89] In January 1780 the frost at Bryan's Station had penetrated the ground more than fourteen inches—as the settlers discovered when they tried to dig graves to bury two young men who had died of illness and cold. The next month Fleming reported the ice on the Kentucky River was nearly two feet thick.[90]

Daniel Trabue, camping that winter near the Green River, west of Boonesborough, said: "The snow was fully knee Deep. . . . The Turkeys had got poore. They would set on the treers all Day and not fly Down. . . . We could kill as many of them as we wanted but they weare too poore to eat." By the time the hard winter finally broke at the end of February, Trabue reported: "The turkeys was almost all dead. The buffeloes had got poore. People's cattle mostly Dead. No corn or but very little in the cuntry. The people was in great Distress. Many in the wilderness frostbit. Some Dead."[91] One family not far from Harrodsburg had camped in a rise in the ground near running water. The water rose in a winter storm and surrounded the rise, and a hard rain put out the family's campfire. The man, seeing fire at another camp across the stream, went into the cold water to seek fire from the neighboring camp to relight his family's fire. He was never seen again. His wife and children "perished in the Night with the extremity of the Weather."[92]

Boone's group survived the bitterness of the Hard Winter on scrawny buffalo, bear, deer, and turkeys and on the small amount of corn Boone had brought from North Carolina. In March, when the snow melted, the group put up cabins and stockades to guard against Indian attack.[93] Within a few years there were fifteen or twenty families in Boone's Station, many of them Boone kin, including three of Boone's brothers, his married daughters Jemima and Susannah, and cousins named Scholl. Boone himself, with his family, moved several years later a few miles to the southwest, to a cabin on another land claim of his on Marble Creek.[94] He and Rebecca lived there with their five children who were not yet married, six motherless children of Rebecca's uncle James Bryan, and the Boones' daughter Susannah and her husband, Will Hays, and their children. As if the cabin were not sufficiently filled with Boones, Rebecca became noticeably pregnant during the summer of 1780. It was her tenth pregnancy. Their last child, Nathan, was born on March 3, 1781, when Boone was forty-six and Rebecca was forty-two.[95]

At Boone's Station Boone hunted, as he did throughout his life. He had also become a substantial citizen. He headed a large family and a large group of families. His settlement not only bore his name but was led by him. On lands his family owned, worked in part by their slaves, the Boones were growing corn and tobacco and raising cattle and horses. As the need to fight Indians receded, Boone turned more and more of his attention to the core passion of most settlers in Kentucky: accumulating real estate and trying to become rich in the process. Boone was not yet a licensed surveyor, but he had walked or ridden over much of Kentucky. Using his knowledge of the country, starting in 1779 he began to locate claims for others, typically holders of Virginia land warrants good for a specified number of acres in Kentucky. In 1781, for example, he entered into a contract with Geddes Winston, a Virginian holding warrants for five thousand acres in Kentucky, "to Locate the Said Warrants, for which Consideration the said Geddes Winston doth agree to give to Said Boon Two thousand acres of the aforesaid Lands."[96] It is likely that Boone also acted as a jobber, or middleman, for others—in each case finding a tract he believed to be unclaimed, estimating its size, buying a warrant for the appropriate number of acres with funds from a prospective purchaser of the tract (or using a warrant already owned by the prospective purchaser), entering a description of the tract with the county surveyor to be surveyed, and then selling the tract.

Apart from his activities as a locator and jobber, because Boone often went to Virginia's land office in Williamsburg (moved to Richmond by the end of 1780), a number of Kentucky land buyers also entrusted Boone certificates showing their entitlement to a specified amount of land at a specified location, together with the funds needed to file their settlement and preemption claims.

In February 1780 Boone and several others set off for Williamsburg, carrying in their saddlebags more than $20,000 in Virginia currency, together with a number of land certificates. They spent the night at an inn in a small town not far from Williamsburg, locked the door to their room, and woke up the next morning to find the door open and the saddlebags and the money and certificates gone. The saddlebags were found empty at the foot of the stairs to their room, and a small fraction of the money was found stuffed in bottles in the cellar of the inn. Boone believed he had been drugged, "that the landlord was the chief plotter of the scheme, and that an old white woman was the instrument, and that she must have hidden in the room, either under the bed or elsewhere," to unfasten the locked door. Some of those who had given funds and certificates to Boone did not hold him responsible. Others demanded repayment of their money. It took Boone years to repay these sums. "It was a heavy loss to him," his son Nathan said.[97]

In 1778 Boone had been accused of seeking to betray Boonesborough to the British. Now some suspected he had made off with money others had entrusted to him. Nathaniel Hart, Boone's friend and neighbor for years at Boonesborough, who did not look to him to repay the large sum he had given Boone for the purchase of warrants, wrote to his brother, who was similarly situated: "I feel for the poor people who perhaps are to loose even their preemptions by it, but I must Say I feel more for poor Boone whose Character I am told Suffers by it. Much degenerated must the people of this Age be, when Amoungst them are to be found men to Censure and Blast the Character and Reputation of a person So Just and upright and in whose Breast is a Seat of Virtue too pure to admit of a thought So Base and dishonorable. I have known Boone in times of Old, when Poverty and distress had him fast by the hand, And in these Wretched Sircumstances I ever found him of a Noble and generous Soul despising every thing mean."[98]

Other settlers in Kentucky must have agreed with Hart's assessment of Boone and his character. In November 1780, when Virginia divided its westernmost county Kentucky into three counties (Jefferson to the west around Louisville; Fayette in the center, including most of the bluegrass country; and Lincoln to the south of Fayette), Boone was promoted to the rank of lieutenant colonel in the militia of Fayette County. Soon afterward he was elected to be the county's representative in the Virginia Assembly. In 1781 he was made the county's sheriff.[99]

Boone had saved the lives of the salt-boilers from Boonesborough, painful as captivity was for many of them. He had been a leader in the defense of Boonesborough against attackers who outnumbered the defenders seven to one. Kentucky was being transformed by a flood of immigration that resulted in substantial part from that successful defense and from immigrant groups led by Boone or encouraged by his example. Boone had risen in rank and political position as well as in land that he owned or claimed. His fighting with the Indians, however, was far from over, and his land troubles were just beginning.

14

INDIAN RAIDS AND THE BATTLE OF THE BLUE LICKS

LIEUTENANT GOVERNOR "HAIR BUYER" HAMILTON, AFTER BEING captured at Vincennes by Clark in February 1779, was led away a captive to Williamsburg, Virginia. He stayed close to his captors going through Kentucky because settlers threatened to kill him for the Indian raids he had encouraged. Hamilton noted that the people in the Kentucky forts were "in a wretched state, obliged to enclose their cattle every night with the fort, and carry their rifle to field when they go to plow or cut wood."[1] In Virginia he was put in irons—handcuffs at first, then eighteen-pound fetters—on his trip to jail, on the orders of Governor Thomas Jefferson, who had been incensed by reports that Hamilton had paid for American scalps. Hamilton languished in an airless dungeon in Williamsburg until 1781, when he was allowed to go to New York and, after being exchanged for an American held by the British, to go to London.[2]

The British continued to incite Indian attacks on the Kentucky settlements without Hamilton. Maj. Arent Schuyler De Peyster, a New Yorker by birth and a British Army regular since 1755, took Hamilton's place as commandant at Detroit and held that post until 1784. Soon after taking command, De Peyster ordered over £55,000 in "Indian goods,"[3] including:

1,956 lb. vermilion	£1,956
8,000 lb. powder	£2,000
14,975 ball, lead & shot	£1,123
476 dozen scalping knives	£428
188 tomahawks	£119

These were customary goods for Indian war parties, but the quantities were large—5,712 scalping knives is a lot of scalping knives. De Peyster also buttressed the traditional weaponry of Indian warfare with British artillery—not many guns, but enough to batter down Kentucky's forts. In April 1780 De Peyster sent Capt. Henry Bird of the British Regular Army from Detroit with a small field gun and a six-pounder, as well as a squad of British bombardiers, to lead attacks on stations in Kentucky. By June 1780 Bird, the artillery unit, and several hundred Indians appeared before Ruddle's Station on the Licking River. On June 24, after Bird's light field gun had fired twice, the larger six-pounder was hauled up and sighted at the fort. Seeing this, the defenders raised a white flag—the first time a fort in Kentucky had been surrendered.[4] A few days later a nearby fort, Martin's Station, surrendered. The presence, range, and power of the two artillery pieces were compelling, though it was also true that many of the settlers in the two stations were recent arrivals from North Carolina who were suspected of being Tory sympathizers. Despite Bird's efforts to restrain them, the Indians plundered both forts and stripped the clothes off their hundreds of prisoners. As Bird wrote in disgust, the Indians, disregarding the surrender terms, "rushed in, tore the poor children from their mothers' breasts, killed and wounded many."[5] The Indians also killed all the settlers' cattle, so there were no provisions to feed the Indian force on the way to the attack that the British had planned to make on the settlements at the Falls of the Ohio. A frustrated Bird led the Indians, their captives, and their plunder back to Canada.

George Rogers Clark organized a retaliatory raid on the Shawnee villages. He marched with his company of regular troops and the Jefferson County militia to the mouth of the Licking River, where they were joined by militia from Fayette County (presumably including Lt. Col. Daniel Boone) and from Lincoln County. Clark and this ragtag force of close to a thousand men crossed the Ohio on August 1, 1780, and marched into Shawnee country. The Indians fled north, abandoning Old Chillicothe. The village and its cornfields were torched. On August 7 the Shawnees, after first killing many of their American captives, made a stand at Piqua against the advancing Americans. The Indians held their ground in fierce fighting "till they were powder burnt," in the words of one of the American fighters, but eventually retreated to the north and west while Clark's men burned the town to the ground before withdrawing, heavily harassed by the Indians, back south across the Ohio into Kentucky.[6] The whites could take no plunder other than some Indian horses; not being able to carry off the Indians' skins and furs, they burned them up.[7] Clark reported that his men had torched eight hundred acres of cropland and taken forty Indian scalps.[8]

For a month or two after the Clark expedition, Indian-white fighting in Kentucky subsided. In October 1780 Boone and his younger brother Ned were hunting out by the Blue Licks. On their way back to Boone's Station, Ned stopped to gather walnuts. Boone shot and killed a bear. When he went to bring in the dead bear, he heard shots behind him. Turning, he saw Indians gathered around Ned's body. In one telling Boone was close enough to hear the Indians say they had killed Daniel Boone. Boone ran off into the canebrake. Boone told Filson, "[The Indians] pursued me, by the scent of their dog, three miles; but I killed the dog, and escaped." Boone ran back to Boone's Station, getting there after dark. The next morning he went back with a score of settlers from the station and found Ned's body, decapitated. The Shawnees may well have taken the head, rather than just the scalp, to be able to show their people that they had indeed killed Daniel Boone. In one account Boone remembers what Rebecca had told him after his long hunt years ago—she couldn't help sleeping with Ned because he looked so much like Boone. Boone and his kinsmen pursued Ned's killers, following their trail to the Ohio River, but the Indians had already crossed into Shawnee country, and the Boone's Station men were too few to go into the Indian villages by themselves.[9]

The Indian raids did not stop the inflow of settlers into Kentucky. In May 1780 John Floyd told William Preston that "near three hundred large boats have arrived at the Falls this spring with families," and there were by that time on Bear Grass Creek six stations with "no less than six hundred men."[10] While the area around Louisville was largely being settled by immigrants coming down the Ohio Valley, many thousands of others were coming into Kentucky through the Cumberland Gap on the road that Boone's axemen had blazed, unpleasant though that trip was. John May, who was to become a large landowner in Kentucky, reported that it took him ten days in April 1780 to get from the Holston River to Harrodsburg, passing "through an uninhabited Country the most rugged and dismal I ever passed through, there being thousands of dead Horses & Cattle on the Road Side which occasioned a continual Stench; and one Half the way there were no Springs, which compelled us to make use of the water from the Streams in which many of these dead animals lay: and what made the Journey still more disagreeable was, the continual apprehension we were under, of an Attack from the Indians, there not being one Day after we left Holston, but News was brought us of some Murders being committed by those Savages."[11]

Early in 1781 Boone went to Virginia as Fayette County's elected representative to the Virginia Assembly. The frontier clothes he wore made a lasting impression: "He was dressed in real backwoods stile, he had a common jeans suit, with buckskin leggins be[a]ded vary neatily, his leggins were manufactured by the Indians."[12] Because of the British army's advances in Virginia, the legislature had moved from Richmond to Charlottesville, but Tory rangers under the formidable Colonel Banastre Tarleton managed to raid Charlottesville and seize many of the legislators. The raiders arrived at Monticello only minutes after Thomas Jefferson, having been warned of their approach, took off through the woods.[13] Boone himself, though dressed in frontier clothes, was taken into custody when one of Tarleton's dragoons heard a younger man address Boone as "Colonel" or "Captain." Boone was brought before Tarleton but was soon released.[14]

Why the quick release? Boone's son Nathan believed his father, to explain his rank, had shown Tarleton his commission from Lord Dunmore.[15] But the Dunmore commission of Boone was as a captain, and Boone by that time was a colonel. Or would Boone have shown the British commission, as he had to Hamilton in Detroit, to evidence his sympathy with the British cause? Had one of Boone's Tory Bryan relatives intervened on Boone's behalf? Did Boone give his captors his parole, at least not to fight the British? He certainly continued to fight their Indian allies and the British if they were with the Indians. But William Christian wrote to William Preston in June 1781 that "Boone, who was with Lord Cornwallis, is since paroled," and Nathan believed that his father had been released after promising "not to take up arms any more."[16] Exactly how he gained his quick release from British custody is unclear—but all likely explanations involve Boone's willingness to be "a trying to fool" the British (as Boone had said at his Boonesborough court-martial), to be able to go free to fight again in the future. He was evidently willing to stretch the truth to deceive his wartime enemies.

By the end of June 1781 Boone was back with the Virginia Assembly, which had reconvened at Staunton. As was true throughout his life, he did not stay still for long. He went back to Kentucky during the summer, then up the Ohio River and into Pennsylvania to see relatives there, and returned to Virginia for the fall session of the Virginia Assembly. Never a man for routine, Boone appears to have been remiss in his legislative committee work; in

December the speaker of the Assembly ordered the House sergeant-at-arms to take Daniel Boone and other absent members into custody.[17]

Indian raids and white counterraids continued. In the first nine months of 1781 Indians killed or captured 131 in Jefferson County, the county that included Louisville. That number represented about one-eighth of the county's population.[18] In May 1781 Indians led by Simon Girty attacked Squire Boone's settlement near Shelbyville and inflicted three wounds on Squire Boone, including a broken arm. The broken arm, badly set, ended up an inch and half shorter than the other arm. When Squire Boone's family abandoned the settlement in September 1781, they were ambushed, and many in the group were killed.[19] When John Floyd took a party out to bury the dead, Indians killed 16 of Floyd's men. Earlier in 1781 Floyd had written to General Clark that the only reason the settlers had not completely deserted his area of Kentucky "is the inability of the Settlers to remove, having already lost most of their horses, and the Ohio River only runs one way."[20] After his defeat in September 1781, even the resilient Floyd despaired: "I fear our destruction is inevitable—the attention of near 6,000 Savage Warriors is now fixed upon Kentucky. . . . I am greatly perplexed and embarrassed about our situation."[21]

Although fighting between British and Americans ended in the east after Cornwallis's surrender at Yorktown in October 1781, the pace of fighting between Indians and whites in the Ohio Valley quickened. In March 1782 rangers from the Monongahela Valley attacked the Moravian Christian Indian villages on the Muskingum River in Ohio, took ninety captives, and killed them by crushing their skulls with clubs and mallets—twenty-nine men, twenty-seven women, and thirty-four children.[22] That white massacre of peaceful Indians did not make the Delawares, Shawnees, and other Ohio Indians more pro-American. In June 1782 Indians on the Sandusky River in Ohio routed a force of hundreds of Pennsylvania militiamen under Col. William Crawford. The Indian victors, wrongly believing that Crawford had been involved in the slaughter of the Moravian Indians a few months earlier, tortured him to death at the stake. They stripped Crawford, tied his hands behind his back, tied his bound wrists to the stake with enough scope to permit him to walk around it once or twice, fired some seventy charges of gunpowder into his naked body, cut off his ears, applied burning sticks to his flesh, and threw hot coals and hot ashes at him. After two hours, when Crawford fell forward on his stomach, the Indians scalped him. An old squaw took hot coals from the fire on a board and poured them on his bleeding head until he died.[23] Simon Girty was said to have watched Crawford's lingering death and, when Crawford asked Girty to shoot him, to have told Crawford he could not because he had no gun.[24]

Kentucky's turn had already begun to come. In May 1782, near Boonesborough, Wyandots from the west killed Capt. James Estill and twenty-two of his men. In July Boone's longtime associate and friend Nathaniel Hart was killed on his farm outside of Boonesborough. By August 1782 several hundred Indians from different tribes—Ottawas, Wyandots, Shawnees, Delawares, and Cherokees—had already crossed into Kentucky from Ohio, led by Capt. William Caldwell and, under him, the half-Shawnee Capt. Alexander McKee and the Indian agent Matthew Elliott, who had gone over to the British side in 1778, along with McKee and Simon Girty. Girty accompanied the 1782 invading force as an interpreter and was said to have incited the Indians at Chillicothe with Indian-style eloquence before the assembled tribes crossed the Ohio in the summer of 1782 for their massive raids into Kentucky: "Brothers: The Long Knives have overrun your country, and usurped your hunting grounds. They have destroyed your cane, trodden down the clover, killed the deer and the buffaloes. . . . Unless you rise in the majesty of your might, and exterminate the whole race, you may bid adieu to the hunting grounds of your fathers—to the delicious flesh of the animals with which it once abounded—and to the skins with which you were once enabled to purchase your clothing and your rum."[25]

The Indians began their attack with an attack south of the Kentucky River. Close to seventy Indians captured two boys at Hoy's Station, some distance south of Lexington. When Capt. John Holder (who called out at the siege of Boonesborough, "I've no time to pray, goddammit") went off in pursuit, he and his men were lured into ambush by one Indian running away from them at top speed near the Upper Blue Licks, and four of his men were killed.[26] The raid on Hoy's Station may have been intended to cause stations north of the Kentucky River to weaken their defenses by sending reinforcements south. On August 15–17, 1782, the Indians attacked what was probably their prime target, Bryan's Station, north of the Kentucky River and northwest of Lexington. The Indians, who greatly outnumbered the forty-two or forty-four men defending the station, burned outlying cabins and crops, slaughtered the livestock, and killed a handful of defenders. They also attempted to storm the stockade itself but lacked artillery and had limited time before relief arrived from the settlements to the south.[27] Simon Girty reportedly tried to talk Bryan's Station into surrendering by threatening that artillery was on the way and that if the Indians stormed the fort, no one would be able to control them. A defender called back that the Kentucky militia was on its way: "If you and your gang of murderers stay here another day, we will have your scalps drying in the sun on the roofs of these cabins"—adding that his station still had plenty of powder and lead "to beat such a son of bitch as Girty." Girty broke off the shouted exchange, and the Indians resumed their firing at the station.[28]

Relief came to Bryan's Station far more quickly than it had to Boonesborough in 1778, no doubt because there were now many more settlers in Kentucky than there had been four years earlier. Men came from Boone's Station, Harrodsburg, Lexington, and other stations. Forty-five men came from Fayette County alone. By the morning of August 18 a total of 182 men had assembled at Bryan's Station—but the attacking Indians were no longer there. There was just a battered station, surrounded by burned crops and dead livestock already starting to bloat and stink in the summer heat. Alexander McKee reported to De Peyster that the Indians had "killed upwards of 300 hogs, 150 head of cattle, and a number of sheep."[29]

More relief was on its way from the south in the form of several hundred men led by Col. Benjamin Logan. Should the Kentucky militiamen at Bryan's Station wait to be reinforced by Logan's men, or should they go after the attackers immediately, before the Indians could cross the Ohio back into Indian country? That was the question the militia leaders discussed on August 18. Col. John Todd of Lexington, who had fought at Point Pleasant, and Lt. Col. Daniel Boone, of Boone's Station, led the Fayette County militia. Col. Stephen Trigg led the Lincoln County men, assisted by Maj. Hugh McGary of Harrodsburg. This was the same McGary who in 1777, after discovering that a Shawnee warrior he had killed outside Harrodsburg was wearing the shirt of his stepson, who had just been killed by the Shawnees, had cut up the Indian's body and fed the pieces to his dogs. McGary had not become more stable since then. He had yelling fights with his new wife and with her brother.[30] An early Boone biographer who interviewed Boone reported that descriptions of McGary "concur in representing him to have been a man of fierce and daring courage, but of a fiery and ferocious temper, void of humane and gentle qualities, a quarrelsome and unpleasant man in civil life."[31] At the August 18 officers' meeting, however, McGary sensibly advised waiting for Logan's hundreds of men before pursuing the large body of Indians who had attacked the station. Colonel Todd claimed that guesses about the Indians' numbers were exaggerated, described McGary's advice as "timidity," and said they could not afford to let the Indians escape.[32]

In the culture of the frontier—and the frontier had a strong culture, even if it was without the learning and manners that the word *culture* sometimes connotes—to question one's bravery was to question one's manhood. Such an imputation tended to shorten any rational discussion of pros and cons, much as the discussion at the besieged Boonesborough of the Indians' offer had been cut short by Colonel Callaway's vowing to kill the first man who proposed surrender. The officers gathered at Bryan's Station decided to go after the Indians the next morning, without waiting for Logan and his men. It is easy to imagine that Hugh McGary did not like being publicly accused of timidity.

Under Colonel Todd's overall command the Kentucky militiamen set out after the Indians, who were heading toward to the Lower Blue Licks on the Licking River. Boone did not like what he saw. All the signs pointed to a very large force. On the one hand, the Indians seemed to be going out of their way to make their trail easy to follow—leaving trash behind, breaking off branches. On the other hand, it looked to Boone as if the Indians were "concealing their numbers by treading in each other's tracks."[33] Why would the Indians do that unless they were seeking to cause the whites to underestimate their strength? Were the Indians luring the Kentuckians into an ambush, the way the fleet-footed Indian had lured Holder's men onward after the attack on Hoy's Station? Other signs told Boone that many Indians were in front of the Kentuckians. One militiaman remembered that Boone, "by counting the Indian's fires, concluded there were at least 500 Indians."[34] That was about three times as many fighters as were in the pursuing Kentucky militia. The estimate was high. Captain Caldwell soon after the battle reported his force consisted of 300 Indians and rangers.[35] Even so, Caldwell's men outnumbered the Kentucky militiamen nearly two to one.

By the following morning, Monday, August 19, 1782, the Kentuckians were at the Licking River. They could see several Indians on the top of a hill across the water. Colonel Todd asked Boone for his views. "Colonel, they intend to fight us," Boone said, summarizing the signs he had seen along the way of the Indians' superior numbers. "They wish to seduce us into an ambush."[36] Boone knew the Lower Blue Licks intimately, having rescued Jemima and the Callaway girls near there in 1776 and having been there

with the salt-boilers in 1778. Boone knew that the far side of the river had ra-
vines that could conceal hundreds of Indians. "I say not follow," Boone said
"they largely out-number us, and it is not prudent to pursue."[37] What was
more prudent was to wait for Logan's powerful reinforcements, particularly
because the British and Indians were in an excellent defensive position—on
high ground and with the ability to retreat if need be, while the Americans
would have to ford the Licking River to attack then charge uphill in rugged
terrain, and, if defeated, they would find retreat made difficult by the river
they had just crossed.

McGary said, "We have force enough to whip all the Indians we will
find."[38] According to some accounts, Boone suggested that if an attack were
made, half of the Kentuckians should ford the river upstream and attack the
Indians from the flank, while the rest attacked from in front. That in itself
was a risky maneuver. To split your force in front of a much larger enemy
force was what Gen. George Armstrong Custer was to do, with notable lack
of success, at the Little Big Horn.[39] McGary shouted out, "By Godly, what did
we come here for?" "To fight Indians," someone replied. "By Godly," McGary
called, "then why not fight them?"[40] Turning to Boone, he said: "I never saw
any signs of cowardice about you before."[41] "No man before has ever dared
to call me a coward," Boone said.[42] "I can go as far in an Indian fight as any
other man."[43]

McGary spurred his horse into the water of the river, calling out, "All
who are not damned cowards follow me, and I'll soon show you the Indians."[44] Even though the colonels in charge had made no decision, the Kentuckians rode into the river, rather than be thought cowards. "The contagion
was irresistible," Boone's nephew Samuel Boone later said, for "the taunt of
cowardice was unpalatable to a Kentuckian and stung them on to reckless-
ness."[45] Todd and Trigg ordered their men to join the charge, and Boone
joined his men in the river. "Come on," Boone is said to have called out, "we
are all slaughtered men."[46]

The Kentuckians advanced up the ridge after crossing the river. On the
left of the uneven charge Boone led the men from Fayette County, including
Boone's son Israel, Boone's nephew Squire Boone, and two Scholl relatives.
Colonel Todd and Major McGary commanded the center, Colonel Trigg the
right. The Kentuckians went for the summit of a ridge a half-mile from the
river, with McGary leading. Like most of the militia officers, McGary was
still mounted. As the Kentuckians neared the top, the Indians began a terrific

fire, particularly from concealment along the Kentuckians' right. Many of the Kentuckians in front were cut down in the opening fire. McGary was untouched. Within minutes Colonel Todd and Colonel Trigg were both mortally wounded. The Indian left turned and broke the Kentuckians' right flank.

McGary and his surviving men, having fired their guns, turned and ran back toward the river. An Indian rose from behind a stump in front of Boone, who was carrying not a rifle but a long English fowling piece, loaded with three or four rifle bullets and sixteen or eighteen buckshot. Boone shot the Indian dead and kept advancing. McGary rode up and shouted: "Boone, why are you not retreating? Todd and Trigg's line has given way, and the Indians are all around you."[47] Boone looked down the hill and saw Indians rushing for the Americans' horses and standing between his men and the river.

Boone ordered his men into the woods on their left, for better cover as they retreated to the river. He told them to hold their fire, so as to be able to keep the Indians off as the Kentuckians recrossed the river. Boone's oldest surviving son, Israel, twenty-five years old, stayed close to his father. Israel "had been sick with the slow fever, but was recovering." His neck was still badly stiff. Boone got a horse for Israel, but the young man said, "Father, I won't leave you." Boone went to get another horse and, "amid the cracking of the guns, heard some struggling on the ground. He turned to find that Israel had fallen with blood gushing from his mouth, obviously a mortal wound." Israel's "arms were stretched out and shivering."[48]

Boone mounted the horse he had wanted Israel to take and rode west to a different place to cross the river, not the ford where the Americans had crossed to make their attack. The main body of Kentuckians struggled to make it back across the river near where they had crossed before. They were pursued by Indians who, having fired their rifles, were closing in with knives and tomahawks and clubs. As Boone told Filson: "When we gave way, they pursued us with the utmost eagerness, and in every quarter spread destruction. The river was difficult to cross, and many were killed in the flight, some just entering the river, some in the water, others after crossing in ascending the cliffs."[49] More would have died had the Indians not paused for plunder and for scalps of the fallen Kentuckians and had not one of Boone's men, once he was across the river, formed up some of the fleeing men and had them fire a volley to give pause to the oncoming Indians.

On the retreat Boone encountered Colonel Logan, riding up from Bryan's Station with hundreds of additional Kentucky militiamen. Logan turned

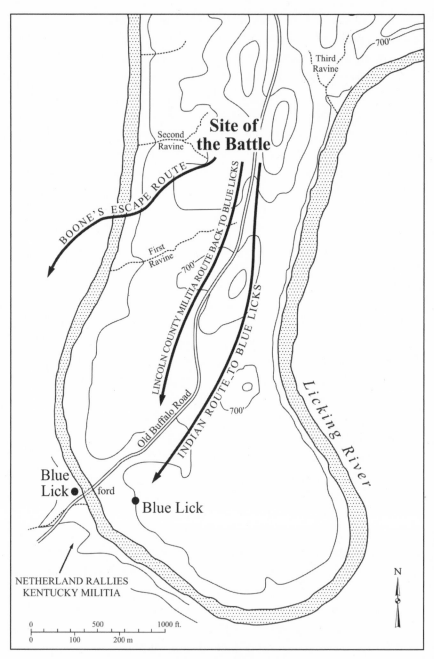

The Battle of the Blue Licks
Courtesy of Neal O. Hammon, redrawn by Mary Lee Eggart

back and waited for a few days for an attack that never came. On August 24 Boone rode with Logan's men back to the Blue Licks to bury the dead Kentuckians. Five hot August days had gone by since the fighting. Boone later recalled finding "their bodies strewed every where, cut and mangled in a dreadful manner. This mournful scene exhibited a horror almost unparalleled: Some torn and eaten by wild beasts; those in the river eaten by fishes; all in such a putrefied condition, that no one could be distinguished from another."[50] Vultures circled in the air above the bodies, many of which had been scalped. One witness said "the smell of a human was the awfullest smell he ever had in his life."[51] Nathan Boone said that, though Israel's "face was blackened and swollen," Boone was able to recognize him "from the locality and some marks." Boone was never able to remember the Blue Licks battle and the death of Israel without being deeply affected, often to tears.[52]

Boone "blamed himself to some degree for the Blue Lick battle." He had not been able to prevent the Kentuckians' charge into the Indians' ambush, and "he let his zeal get the better of his judgment."[53] There was a more personal cause for remorse. Just as Boone had exposed his oldest son, James, to hazards that led to his being killed by Indians in 1773 at the age of sixteen, Boone now must have felt responsible for the death of his next oldest son, Israel, at age twenty-five. While Boone's daughter-in-law Olive said that Boone had tried to persuade Israel not to go, Boone's granddaughter Delinda Boone Craig said that Boone had told her that he had made Israel go. Israel, confined by sickness to his bed, had not volunteered with the other young men at Boone's Station to ride to the relief of Bryan's Station. Boone reproved Israel, saying: "I did not hear your name when they were beating up for volunteers—I had expected to hear it among the first. I am sorry to think I have raised a timid son." Israel enrolled. According to Delinda: "Boone always blamed himself for the loss of his son. . . . Israel, he said, ought not to have gone, and would not have gone but for his chiding."[54] Whichever version is correct, there is no dispute about Boone's lasting remorse at Israel's death. Nor can it be denied that Boone had led his first two sons to their early deaths.

The fighting on the far side of the Licking River had not lasted much more than fifteen minutes. It resulted in the worst defeat Kentuckians suffered during the Revolution. Over sixty Kentuckians were killed, more than a third of the militiamen who had gone into the fight. Boone wrote to Virginia governor Benjamin Harrison that "sixty six of our Brave Kanetuckians fell the matchless Masscraed victoms of [the Indians'] cruelty."[55] Another six or eight Kentuckians were taken prisoner. Many of the surviving Kentuckians were badly wounded, including Boone's nephew Squire Boone, whose thigh bone was shattered. Of the two dozen militia officers fifteen of them, well over half, were killed. Many of the officers had remained on their horses during the battle and had made fine targets as a result. The dead American officers included Col. John Todd, the commanding officer, and Col. Stephen Trigg, who had commanded the Kentuckian right. The Indians lost no more than eleven killed.[56]

Less than two weeks after the battle, an unusually low-spirited Boone wrote urging Governor Harrison to send relief quickly or risk seeing the settlements melt away: "I have Encouraged the people here in this County all I Could, but I Can no longer Encourage my Neighbours nor my Self to risque our Lives here at Such Extraordinary hazards. the Inhabitants of these Counties are very much alarmed at the thoughts of the Indians bringing another Campaign into our Country this fall, which if it Should be the Case will Break these Settlements, So I hope your Excellency will take it into Consideration and Send us Some Relief as quick as possaple."[57]

Relief came, but largely in the form of Kentuckian self-help. Virginia did not send troops. Instead, George Rogers Clark, who had been criticized for weakening the defenses of the bluegrass country by moving much of Kentucky's militia west to the Falls of the Ohio, and militia leaders such as Boone assembled a force of Kentucky militia for a punitive expedition into Ohio. By late October 1782 between one thousand and eleven hundred men had assembled at the mouth of the Licking River. Clark led the overall force, assisted by John Floyd and Benjamin Logan. Boone, who on September 25 had been promoted by the Virginia Council to full colonel and made the lieutenant of Fayette County in place of the slain John Todd, commanded the Fayette County militia.[58] The men crossed the Ohio River on November 1, 1782, and for close to three weeks went through Indian country north of the river. The Indians receded before them to the north. The Kentuckians killed only twenty Indians but plundered Old Chillicothe, Piqua, and four other villages on the Miami and Little Miami rivers, and destroyed an estimated ten thousand bushels of corn. As part of the campaign, Boone led a detachment of one hundred men to a village called Willstown, at the junction of the Miami and Stillwater Creek. Finding that the Indians had fled, his men took what they could carry, including pelts, and burned all the cabins in the village. Benjamin Logan, leading a separate detachment, plundered and burned the trading post run by the French-Canadian trader Lorimier, who had helped to outfit expeditions against the white settlers in Kentucky and who had been with Blackfish when Boone was taken captive in 1778.[59]

As Boone put it, the Kentuckians on Clark's expedition "burnt [the Indian towns] all to ashes, entirely destroyed their corn, and other fruits, and every where spread a scene of desolation in the country. . . . This campaign in some measure damped the spirits of the Indians, and made them sensible of our superiority. Their connections were dissolved, their armies scattered, and a future invasion put entirely out of their power."[60] According to Clark, "The quantity of provisions burned surpassed all idea we had of the Indian stores."[61] The Kentuckians also took, to exchange for white captives held by the Indians, a number of captives—including, one Kentuckian later remembered happily, a young woman he described as the "most splendid looking squaw I ever saw."[62] Governor Harrison, who initially had been irritated at Clark for launching the expedition without consulting with him, was delighted with the results. He wrote to Clark, "Your expedition will be attended with good consequences; it will teach the Indians to dread us, and convince them that we will not tamely submit to their depredations."[63]

After the Clark expedition the Shawnees remaining in Ohio moved their towns farther north, farther away from Kentucky. The move made it harder for whites to kill the remaining Shawnees but also made it harder for Shawnees to mount large attacks into Kentucky. The peace between the Americans and the British also reduced the chances of major Indian attacks in Kentucky. While the fighting in the thirteen colonies had already virtually ended with the surrender of General Cornwallis at Yorktown in October 1781 and preliminary articles of peace were signed in November 1782, the signing of the peace treaty in September 1783 enabled the Americans to point out to the Indians in the Ohio Valley that the Indians should not expect any more military support from the British against the American settlements.

Filson's telling of Boone's life through 1783 ends with Boone saying: "My footsteps have often been marked with blood. . . . Two darling sons, and a brother, have I lost by savage hands. . . . But now the scene is changed: Peace crowns the sylvan shade. . . . I now live in peace and safety, enjoying the sweets of liberty, and the bounties of Providence, with my once fellow-sufferers, in this delightful country, which I have seen purchased with a vast expence of blood and treasure."[64] The lushness of the prose is certainly attributable to Filson, not Boone. Filson, having invested heavily in warrants to buy land in Kentucky, was writing to lure settlers into Kentucky and so had a strong economic interest in describing Kentucky as a land of "peace and safety." Even in Filson's telling, however, Boone noted that after Clark's expedition the Indians "continued to practice mischief secretly upon the inhabitants, in the exposed parts of the country."[65]

Violence and killings between Indians and whites in Kentucky persisted for more than a decade after the Battle of the Blue Licks. In that period there were also to be battles in Ohio between Indians and whites that were much larger than the Blue Licks battle—but the battles were not in Kentucky; they occurred, rather, as allied Indian groups sought to defend their lands north and west of the Ohio River. Apart from an attack on Kincheloe's Station a few weeks after the Blue Licks battle, there were no more large-scale Indian attacks on white settlers in Kentucky. The Kentuckians began to leave their stockaded stations—to "settle out" and work their own land and, at least in the inner bluegrass area, to live in cabins that looked more like houses than forts.[66] A settler who reached Boonesborough in May 1784 reported that "the picketing of the fort was gone, but the cabins were occupied and the bast ends [bastions] stood. . . . That fall they began to move out."[67]

Settlers were to pour into Kentucky in ever-greater numbers. Even during the fierce fighting of the Revolution, Kentucky's population had grown from about two hundred in the settlements at the start of 1776 to an estimated thirty thousand in 1783.[68] By 1790 Kentucky's population would more than double, to seventy-four thousand.[69] The growth in the number of settlers in Kentucky mirrored the overall growth in the number of settlers coming down the Ohio after 1783.[70] In the economy of Kentucky, as the number of settlers soared, farming and trade were far outstripping hunting and trapping in importance, to the benefit of Kentucky's economy but to the detriment of the frontiersman lifestyle that Boone enjoyed and excelled in. In all these ways the success of the 1782 Clark expedition, in which Boone played an important part as commander of the Fayette County militia, marked a turning point for Kentucky and for Boone.

Matthew Harris Jouett, *George Rogers Clark*, based on a portrait
by John Wesley Jarvis painted after Clark's death. Clark captured Vincennes,
and Lt. Col. Henry Hamilton, from the British.
Filson Historical Society, Louisville

Eighteenth-century surveying instruments from the Smithsonian Museum
of American History—theodolite, chain, compass, Jacob's staff,
chaining pins, and drafting instruments
Photograph by Adam Jones

John Filson's purported self-portrait. Collector and Filson biographer Reuben T. Durrett
"discovered" this sketch in a book believed to have once been owned by Filson.

Filson Historical Society, Louisville

THE
DISCOVERY, SETTLEMENT
And prefent State of
K E N T U C K E:
A N D

An ESSAY towards the TOPOGRAPHY, and NATURAL HISTORY of that important Country:

To which is added,

An A P P E N D I X,

C O N T A I N I N G,

I. The ADVENTURES of Col. *Daniel Boon*, one of the firft Settlers, comprehending every important Occurrence in the political Hiftory of that Province.

II. The MINUTES of the *Piankafhaw* council, held at *Poft St. Vincents, April* 15, 1784.

III. An ACCOUNT of the *Indian* Nations inhabiting within the Limits of the Thirteen United States, their Manners and Cuftoms, and Reflections on their Origin.

IV. The STAGES and DISTANCES between *Philadelphia* and the Falls of the *Ohio*; from *Pittfburg* to *Penfacola* and feveral other Places. — The Whole illuftrated by a new and accurate MAP of *Kentucke* and the Country adjoining, drawn from actual Surveys.

By *J O H N F I L S O N.*

Wilmington, Printed by JAMES ADAMS, 1784.

Title page of John Filson's *The Discovery, Settlement and Present State of Kentucke* (1784), which included as an appendix "The Adventures of Col. Daniel Boon." Boone vouched for the accuracy of Filson's book.

Filson Historical Society, Louisville

LE SOLDAT DU CHÊNE,
AN OSAGE CHIEF.

Charles Balthazar Julien Fevret de Saint-Mémin (1770–1852), *Le Soldat du Chêne,
an Osage Chief,* from McKenney and Hall, *History of the Indian Tribes of
North America* (Philadelphia: Frederick W. Greenough, 1838–44)

Courtesy of University of Cincinnati Digital Press

"Col. Daniel Boon." Daniel Boone.
Stipple engraving by J. O. Lewis after Chester Harding, 1820.

Missouri Historical Society Photographs and Prints Collections. NS 34096.
Scan © 2006, Missouri Historical Society.

The home of Nathan Boone in St. Charles County, Mo., in which Boone died in 1820

Photograph by the author

Thomas Cole, *Daniel Boone at His Cabin at Great Osage Lake*, c. 1826.
Oil on canvas, 38 ¼" x 42 ⅝".
Courtesy of Mead Art Museum, Amherst College. Accession number AC P.1939.7.

George Caleb Bingham, *Daniel Boone Escorting Settlers through the Cumberland Gap*, 1851–52. Oil on canvas, 36 ½" x 50 ¼". *Mildred Lane Kemper Art Museum, Washington University in St. Louis. Gift of Nathaniel Phillips, 1890.*

Daniel Boone Protects His Family. Color lithograph by H. Schile, 1874. Based on Horatio Greenough's monumental sculpture *The Rescue* (1836–53). *Missouri Historical Society Photographs and Prints Collection. NS21599. Scan © 2007, Missouri Historical Society.*

H. D. Nichols, daguerreotype of Lyman C. Draper, c. 1858. Draper spent decades gathering the world's largest collection of interview notes and other materials relating to Boone.

Courtesy of Wisconsin Historical Society (WHi 35)

Monument at Boone's tomb in Frankfort

Photograph by the author

15

WHITES AND INDIANS

THE POST-1782 RAIDS BY INDIANS IN KENTUCKY AND THE EXCHANGES of prisoners taken in the raids tell us much about relations between whites and Indians in frontier Kentucky—relations that were complex and far from uniform. The raids and the prisoner exchanges also illustrate how Boone dealt with the Indians.

The post-1782 raids took a large toll on Kentucky settlers, in lives lost and in property taken. In 1790 Harry Innes, who as a member of Kentucky's Board of War had a significant role in Kentucky's defense against Indian attack, estimated that in the less than seven years he had been in Kentucky, Indians had killed at least fifteen hundred settlers in or on the way to Kentucky, had stolen no fewer than twenty thousand horses, and had taken or destroyed other property worth some fifteen thousand pounds.[1] During the same period stories of Indian raids filled the pages of the *Kentucky Gazette*. The accounts were terse but impressive by their recurrence. For example:

On the 4th Dec. 1787 an Indian fired on a whiteman on Bear Grass near Louisville, who being wounded fell; with his loaded rifle in his hand, which he laid across his breast; the Indian ran up to scalp him, when the wounded man fired and wounded the Indian in turn. The Indian was so badly wounded that he dropped his gun and blankett and ran off. The whiteman lived but a short time.

About the 28th January 1788, the Indians stole twenty five horses from Col. Johnston's at the Great Crossings, Scott County, and made their escape with them.

On the night of the 21st of February 1788, five men who were encamped at the Sinkhole Spring on the road from Lexington to

Nashville, were fired on whilst asleep by a party of Indians, two of them were killed, two escaped unhurt, and one ran off and was not heard of afterwards. The two who escaped came to the nearest settlements in Kentucky, when a party of men immediately collected and went in persuit of the Indians. After several days travel they overtook the Indians in the night at their camp and fired on them, at which they were so alarmed that they ran off naked, without their guns or any part of their baggage.

At about the same time three boats, in descending the Ohio river, were taken by Indians near the mouth of the Big Miami, and the whole of the crews as well as passengers were indiscriminately murdered.[2]

And so forth, in issue upon issue of the newspaper. Anyone reading these accounts might well believe that Kentucky must be doomed—but the total number of settlers killed, even if one credits Judge Innes's estimate of fifteen hundred settlers killed (elsewhere, for a somewhat shorter period, he estimated that only three hundred were killed in Kentucky), was a very small fraction of the number of settlers who came to Kentucky during the same period.[3] As early as 1787, John Brown, then a congressman from the Kentucky part of Virginia, was willing, in proposing that Congress admit Kentucky as a state, to condition Kentucky's statehood on its having at least sixty thousand inhabitants.[4] Brown must have thought that threshold would be met handily, and it was. By 1790, two years before Kentucky's admission as a state, there were seventy-four thousand settlers living there.[5]

Why did the Indians continue with the raids, given the ever-growing disparity of numbers between whites and Indians? One reason doubtless was the Indians' desire—however more and more unlikely that desire was to be fulfilled—to drive whites out of Kentucky. Another motive may well have been the Indians' growing dependence on the market economy. The Indians needed white goods—guns, gunpowder, knives, traps, ornaments, rum, horses, and kettles, for example. The increased killing of game by Indians and whites alike made it harder and harder for Indians to hunt enough animals to produce enough pelts to buy the goods they wanted. Raiding, however, was still a way for the Indians to get those goods. That had to have been a reason for Indian attacks—among them the repeated attacks by Chickamaugas on settlements in southern Kentucky and on pack trains of settlers coming into

Kentucky on the Wilderness Road and by Shawnees on the heavily laden boats of settlers coming down the Ohio River from Pittsburgh.

Was it pure coincidence that several of the Indian attacks were on leading Kentuckians? Just as in earlier years Indians had killed Col. James Patton, twice attacked Boone and his parties of settlers, scalped and mutilated Col. Richard Callaway, and tortured Col. William Crawford to death, Indians after the peace treaty with the British killed many Kentucky leaders—among them John Floyd, William Christian, and John May. A review of those killings suggests that Floyd may have been deliberately targeted; not so, Christian and May.

John Floyd, who in 1774 had surveyed thousands of acres for settlers, around the Falls and in the bluegrass country, had risen rapidly in Kentucky after he returned in 1779 from privateering, imprisonment by the British, and escape to France. He became a substantial landowner, one of the original trustees of Louisville, and in 1780 the county lieutenant (the head of the militia) for Jefferson County. As part of Clark's retaliatory expedition in November 1782 after the Battle of the Blue Licks, Floyd had led battalions from Jefferson and Fayette counties in destroying Shawnee villages. Floyd continued as a surveyor of lands around Louisville. Surveying was a risky occupation because, as a white captive of the Shawnees recorded, Indians "feel the deepest hatred" for surveyors and considered them "the agents who take their lands from them, because they are invariably the forerunners of settlement by the whites."[6]

Floyd knew how vulnerable he was to Indian attack. In March 1783, after reporting that Indians had just killed his wife's brother, Floyd told Col. William Preston: "I have long expected something like this to be my own lot, & if the war is continued much longer I can hardly escape, tho' I am now determined to be more cautious than I have been heretofore, yet every man in this country must be more or less exposed to danger." Floyd ended his letter saying that he did not expect to have the pleasure of seeing Preston again "till the War is ended, if ever I should survive that time. But let me see you or not, or let me enjoy all the Blessing of peace or be involved in every calamity of war & distress, I shall ever remain your very affectionate Friend & Servt."[7]

Within days Floyd's expectation came to pass. On April 8, 1783, Indians shot Floyd as he was riding to a salt lick with his brother and a friend, Alexander Breckenridge, from Floyd's station on the Beargrass near Louisville. Floyd was wearing his favorite coat, a bright scarlet coat he had brought back from Paris to wear at his wedding. He died of his wounds two days later. His wife married Breckenridge—but when she died in 1812, at her request Floyd's scarlet coat was placed in her coffin. Perhaps Floyd was shot simply because his scarlet coat made him a highly visible target for Indians who did not know who he was. One suspects, however, that the Indians may have been lying in wait for him because of his prominence as a militia officer and local official.

In April 1786 Indians killed Col. William Christian, brother-in-law of three prominent Americans: Patrick Henry, Col. William Fleming, and Col. Stephen Trigg (one of the militia leaders killed at the Battle of the Blue Licks).[8] Christian had commanded the Fincastle County militia in Lord Dunmore's War, owned substantial acreage in Kentucky (some of it had been surveyed by Floyd), and had moved from Virginia to Kentucky in 1785. After Indians stole horses near Bear Grass Creek, Christian led a party of pursuers across the Ohio and caught up with the Indians—but Christian himself was killed in the shoot-out.[9] Christian's death sounds like a result of a melee, rather than of a targeted killing.

John May, after whom the town of Maysville (previously known as Limestone) was named, was an early and large investor in Kentucky land. In 1780 alone he had entered claims for seventy-five thousand acres in forty different locations in Kentucky.[10] It did not hurt him that his brother George was the county surveyor for Kentucky County. Early in 1790 John May chartered a flatboat on the Kanawha and set off down the Ohio River from Point Pleasant for Kentucky. Indians used white captives to lure the boat within gunshot. The whites on May's boat were outgunned and outnumbered. After several whites were killed or wounded, the firing died down. John May stood up in the boat holding his nightcap in the air as a signal of surrender. He was shot dead through the forehead, scalped, and thrown into the river. The Indians were manifestly looking for goods and plunder on the boat, but there is no evidence they were deliberately going after May.[11]

Another killing by the Indians did not involve a leading settler but, in the way in which it was carried out, sounds like an instance of score settling. This was the killing of a white man named Greathouse, who in 1774, with several other whites, at Yellow Creek on the Ohio River, had killed several relatives of the Mingo chief Logan and in doing so had slit open the belly of Logan's pregnant sister and impaled her unborn child on a stake. In late March 1791 Indians from the north bank of the Ohio, near Limestone, seized Greathouse's flatboat as it came down the river. According to the captain of another flatboat that had passed Greathouse's boat and that itself was attacked, Greathouse and his group were roaring drunk. Simon Kenton and others from Limestone went to the site of the attack and found on the shore of the river the naked bodies of a woman and of a big man, Greathouse, lying by a sapling with intestines wrapped around its trunk. Both bodies had been cut open below the navel. The Indians had cut the intestines of Greathouse and of the woman, tied the severed ends to the sapling, and forced the two to walk around the sapling, winding their intestines around it, until they died.[12] The manner of Greathouse's death may have been a coincidence, but it smacks of payback for the killing of Chief Logan's sister. Indians had killed white captives in this manner before. A white captive reported that in 1757, near where Braddock had been defeated, Indians took one of their prisoners, "ripped open his belly with a knife and took one end of his guts and tied it to a tree. Then they whipped the miserable man round and round till he died," obliging the captives who survived "to dance while they had their sport with the dying man."[13] But this manner of killing was not common, and it bore an eerie resemblance to what Greathouse's party had done to Logan's sister.

Score settling went both ways. In the autumn of 1786 Boone and Simon Kenton were part of an expedition led by Col. Benjamin Logan north of the Ohio to attack Shawnee villages. Boone and Kenton rode into one village on the heels of Indians, who were running off. One of the Indians kept looking back over his shoulder. Boone recognized him at once. "Mind that fellow!" Boone called out. "I know him—it's Big Jim, who killed my son in Powell's Valley!" Big Jim was the Indian who had tortured and killed young James Boone in 1773, during Boone's first attempt to settle Kentucky. Hearing Boone call out his name, Big Jim turned and fired, killing one of the mounted Kentuckians, before he was hit and fell wounded. Big Jim reloaded and fired again, felling another ranger. As Big Jim reloaded, Kenton ran up and stabbed him dead. The rangers scalped Big Jim and mutilated his body.[14]

Not all the white score-settling killings were as warranted as the killing of Big Jim was. The killing in 1786 of the Shawnee chief Moluntha was as unjustified—and went almost as unpunished—as had been the killing of the Shawnee chief Cornstalk in 1777. Moluntha was taken captive by Kentuckians in Benjamin Logan's 1786 expedition to the Shawnee villages, soon after Big Jim was killed. After the capture Moluntha and his captors were sharing a pipe. According to some accounts, Moluntha was holding an American flag and a copy of a treaty with the Americans—the January 1786 Treaty of Fort Finney, by which Shawnees agreed to cede lands in Ohio east of the Great Miami River.[15] Hugh McGary, whose rashness had helped bring about the settlers' disastrous defeat at Blue Licks, rushed up and asked Moluntha if he had been at Blue Licks. Moluntha said something McGary took to mean yes—although Moluntha had not been at Blue Licks, may not have understood McGary, and may simply have been greeting McGary. "Damn you," McGary cried. "I'll give you Blue Licks play!"[16] McGary pulled out his tomahawk, split the chief's skull, and turned to attack another Shawnee captive, Cornstalk's sister, a Shawnee leader in her own right. He cut off three of her fingers with his tomahawk before other Kentuckians stopped him. McGary's only punishment was to be reprimanded and stripped of his commission.[17]

Much of the brutal violence on both sides did not involve score settling. Indians not infrequently tortured captives to death. In January 1791 they raided Dunlap's Station on the north side of the Ohio River. Simon Girty forced a white captive to beg the settlers in the station to surrender. They did not, and the Indian attackers slowly killed the white prisoner within sight of the station. According to one of the defenders, the Indians "stripped [the prisoner] naked, pinioning his outstretched hands and feet to the earth, kindling a fire on his naked abdomen, and thus, in lingering tortures, they allowed him to die. His screams of agony were ringing in our ears during the remainder of the night, becoming gradually weaker and weaker till toward daylight, when they ceased."[18]

Whites were brutal too. Indians scalped whites—but whites also scalped Indians, as whites had done at least since the late seventeenth century.[19] George Rogers Clark believed "that to excel them in barbarity was and is the only way to make war upon Indians and gain a name among them."[20] Clark acted on this belief, tomahawking prisoners in sight of others, and ordered his reluctant men to scalp a living French civilian captive.[21] Ordinary soldiers, motivated by the hope of profit from sharing in plunder, killed Indians or mutilated dead ones for their jewelry. A Kentuckian on Clark's 1782 campaign into the Shawnee towns saw a militiaman running back from the first wave of assault "with his fingers all bloody . . . he had cut off their fingers and noses and earbobs to get their trinkets. . . . Had a whole handful of trinkets that he got."[22] Some whites—not, so far as is evident, in Kentucky—engaged in biological warfare in the Ohio Valley. In 1763 the British commander Sir Jeffery Amherst suggested to Col. Henry Bouquet, the commanding officer at Fort Pitt, that blankets from military hospitals be given to "Disaffected

Tribes" in order "to Send the Small Pox among" them and so "Exterpate this Execrable Race"—a suggestion that apparently led to Indians being given, at a parley at Fort Pitt, "two Blankets and a Handkerchief out of the Small Pox Hospital."[23] Even before that, a trader at Fort Pitt, after noting in his diary an attempt by two Delawares to induce the whites to surrender the fort, wrote: "Out of our regard to them we gave them two Blankets and a Handkerchief out of the Small Pox Hospital. I hope it will have the desired effect."[24] Similarly, in 1777 an American captain abandoning the fort at Kittanning wrote to General Hand that he had left behind some flour after putting in it some "medesion [medicine]" that he hoped "may be of Some Service to the blks [blacks—that is, Indians]."[25]

Despite the violence between the two, whites and Indians interacted and borrowed from each other's cultures. Indian leaders such as Neolin and Tecumseh's brother the Prophet had visions that Indian power would be restored if Indians abandoned white ways and weapons and hunted only with bows and arrows, but that was not going to happen, so long as the Indians had access to guns, shot, and powder. Indians, having learned how well they could hunt with long rifles, were not about to abandon the practice. As the senior Spanish official in Missouri put it in 1793, speaking of the Little Osages: "It is impossible for [them] to subsist without our arms and ammunition. . . . [Bows and arrows] do not provide them with game as easily as do guns."[26] By the 1760s Indians in the Ohio Valley were increasingly using metal kettles in place of pottery and white artifacts (silver jewelry and glass beads) as status symbols.[27] Similarly, many white soldiers and hunters on the frontier used tomahawks (witness McGary's killing of Moluntha), and white frontiersmen like Boone used Indian medicines that worked for some ailments better than white medicines. The whites also grew crops they had learned about from the Indians, including corn, squash, pumpkins, beans. The Ohio Valley Indians grew crops that they had learned about from the whites—cabbage, turnips, and cucumbers—and raised hogs, horses, and cattle. The Ohio Valley Indians also learned how to forge iron and how to build log cabins with stone chimneys and were increasingly wearing clothing made of textiles, rather than of animal hides.[28] For example, Boone's adoptive father, the Shawnee war chief Blackfish, sold to a Kentucky settler a broadcloth "cappo" (a European cloak or coat with a hood).[29] The Delaware chief White Eyes and Oconostota, war leader of the Cherokees, both wore eyeglasses.[30]

Boone and other frontiersmen saw that for use in the woods, deerskin made better clothing than homespun, and they dressed accordingly. The Spanish governor of St. Louis described the arrival of Clark and his men into his town in July 1778: "The commanding general arrived . . . in a hunting shirt and breechcloth, naked of foot and limb and with his bed, powder horn and gun on his shoulder. The troops had no other equipment than breech-cloth, powder horn, gun, and knapsack."[31] It was hard to tell a woodsman like Boone from an Indian by the clothing, which is why Boone in 1778 cried out to identify himself to the settlers when he made it back to Boonesborough after his escape from the Shawnees.

Assimilation and cultural exchange on the frontier went well beyond weaponry, food, and clothing. Many Indians learned English. Many whites, Boone among them, picked up more than a smattering of an Indian lan-guage. Some whites, having spent years in captivity, spoke at least one Indian language fluently. Simon Girty, adopted by the Senecas when he was fifteen, spoke Delaware, Seneca, and probably Shawnee. There were also intermar-riages. Several Indian chiefs were part white. John Floyd was part Catawba.

Some whites hated Indians indiscriminately—Hugh McGary, for exam-ple. White hatred of Indians had grown more widespread as a result of wide-spread Indian attacks on frontier settlers—in the French and Indian War (1755–63), in Pontiac's War (1763–64), and before and after the Revolution (1773–94)—though many British settlers had viewed Indians as godless sav-ages long before those attacks.[32] It is also possible that many whites tended to demonize Indians to justify their taking of Indian lands. Other whites, often ones who had been taken captive in childhood and who had grown up as Indians, assimilated completely into Indian society. Numerous captives became comfortable in the Indian world and did not want to go back to the white world.[33] Some stayed in the Indian community and, when they saw a white man come to their village, would run away, fearing that the white visitor had come to take them "home."[34] Some came back and reentered the white world. The reentry was not always easy, either for the white captives or for their Indian adoptive parents, particularly if the captives had lived long among the Indians. When the Shawnees at the end of the French and Indian War gave up their white captives, the Shawnee spokesman said to the white leaders: "They have all been tied to us by adoption, and altho' we now deliver them up to you, we will always look upon them as our relations whenever the Great Spirit is pleased that we may visit them. . . . We have taken us much care of these Prisoners as if they were our own Flesh and Blood; they are now become unacquainted with your Customs & manners, & therefore, Fathers, we request that you will use them tenderly & kindly, which will be a means of inducing them to live contentedly with you."[35]

Thomas Ingles, taken captive by the Shawnees in 1755 at the Draper's Meadow attack in which James Patton was killed, lived among the Indians until 1768. He had forgotten much of his English when he rejoined his white family. John Slover, taken by the Miamis when he was eight, lived as an Indian until he was twenty, when he was taken to a parley with the whites in 1773. There he saw some of his white relatives, who, as he told it, "urged me to give up the life of a savage": "I did so with some reluctance—this manner of life had become natural to me, for I had scarcely known any other."[36] John Tanner, about nine when he was taken captive in 1789 in Kentucky, lived among the Indians until 1817, by which time he had married twice and had forgotten not only most of his native language but also his English name. Known as "the white Indian," Tanner, a violent man, disappeared in 1846, perhaps after killing a white man, perhaps having been killed by the white man's murderer in an attempt to cover up the crime.[37] One suspects that Tanner's violence was caused by his uncertainty about who he was.

Straddling the cultural divide could invite lethal hatred. Witness the example of William Wells, a white who had been captured and adopted by the Miamis when he was a child. Wells married Sweet Breeze, a daughter of the Miami war chief Little Turtle. After fighting with the Indians against General Harmar's army, Wells went over to the American side and became a lead scout for Gen. Anthony Wayne. After the wars he went back to live among the Miamis. Wells was an Indian agent for the Americans among the Miamis, the Potawatomis, and the Delawares for most of the years between the Treaty of Greenville in 1795 and the War of 1812. In 1812 the Indians who attacked Chicago killed Wells, ripped out his heart, divided it among themselves, and ate it.[38]

Boone and the salt-boilers who were taken captive with him in 1778 illustrate many of the possible outcomes of Indian captivity and the extent to which the white and Indian worlds interacted on the frontier.[39] Of those whose subsequent history has been reconstructed, a dozen or so were not adopted but were delivered by the Shawnees to the British in Detroit within two months of being captured. The son of one of these captives wrote that "they were treated much better by the Indians than by the British."[40] About ten of the salt-boilers were adopted by the Indians. Of these five—Boone, Arabia Brown, Ansel Goodman, William Hancock, and Andrew Johnson—escaped within months. Their captivity was short enough to mean they had not fully assimilated with the Indians.

Other salt-boilers, who lived for a longer time with the same tribe, adapted more completely to Indian ways. One example was Col. Richard Callaway's nephew Micajah (known as Cage) Callaway, who lived over five years as an Indian. Some of the salt-boiler prisoners said that Cage Callaway was along at the raid in which Shawnees killed his uncle and that he had threatened revenge on his uncle for whipping him before he was taken prisoner.[41] In 1781 a white saw Cage Callaway fighting alongside the Indians in an attack near the Ohio River that killed forty settlers. He acted as interpreter for the Shawnees at a prisoner exchange at Louisville in July 1783 and at Clark's request was released by the Indians. He subsequently served Boone as a chainman on several of Boone's surveys in 1785 and 1787 and as an interpreter at a prisoner exchange at Limestone in 1787; later he scouted for General Wayne against the Indians. Cage Callaway managed to straddle the white and Indian worlds fairly comfortably. When he died in 1848, at the age of ninety-four, he was the last surviving salt-boiler from Boone's group.[42]

Another salt-boiler, Jack Dunn, escaped from the Shawnees around 1779, joined a Kentucky militia expedition against the Shawnees, but then reportedly deserted and warned the Shawnees that the whites were coming.[43] The salt-boiler George Hendricks was a captive until April 1780 but among four different tribes. Adopted by the Shawnees, he escaped from them in September 1778 but was captured by the Wyandots. After living with them for two years, he lived among the Miamis, before being sold to the Kickapoos and by them in 1780 to the British at Detroit. His movement from tribe to tribe probably prevented his developing an allegiance to any of them. He later acted as a guide for George Rogers Clark on several of his expeditions.[44]

Of all the salt-boilers adopted by the Indians, the most miserably conflicted in his loyalties was Joseph Jackson, who lived with the Indians from 1778, when he was in his early twenties, to 1799 and then again after 1802. Jackson, whose Indian name was Fish, married an Indian woman and had children by her. Draper, who interviewed Jackson late in Jackson's life, was convinced that he (though he denied it) had fought against the Americans at the Battle of the Blue Licks in 1782, against General Harmar in 1790, against General St. Clair in 1791, and against General Wayne at the Battle of Fallen

Timbers in 1794. In 1800 Jackson went to see his brother in Kentucky, where he bought a farm and two slaves and married into a rich family—and was deeply unhappy. After fighting repeatedly with his white wife, he moved to Missouri to be with his Shawnee friends and relatives. Boone saw him at a Shawnee hunting camp in 1802, a few years after Boone and his family had moved to Missouri.[45] More than forty years later Jackson was to tell Draper that "the Indians ruined him." A few months after Draper interviewed him, Jackson, aged eighty-eight, hanged himself.[46]

Boone, on the spectrum of different ways of interacting with Indians and their way of life, was neither a blind hater of all things Indian nor a renegade. He had Indian friends. During his seven months as a Shawnee captive, Boone, as we have seen, learned some Shawnee, became friends with his adoptive father Blackfish and some members of that family, and may have taken up with an Indian woman. One of his granddaughters, who saw him with Shawnee visitors years later in Missouri, said Boone could speak and understand Shawnee well enough for ordinary conversation.[47] Boone liked to do many of the same things Indian men traditionally did—hunting and trapping in the wilderness. A young English traveler who met Boone in 1797 and heard him talk about "the disadvantages of great improvements in society" and his desire to "enjoy the pleasures arising from a secluded and solitary life" concluded that Boone was "one of that class of men, who, from nature and habit, was nearly allied in disposition and manners to an Indian."[48]

Boone, however, was not about to give up the white way of life and become an Indian at the cost of his leadership role among the whites and at risk to his hopes of land ownership. He recognized that Indians would fight to defend their land and, as Boone told Filson, were "determined utterly to extirpate the whites out of Kentucke" to prevent the whites from taking their "desirable habitations."[49] That being the case, the whites had to fight the Indians until the Indians relinquished their efforts to hang onto the land, and Boone would and did fight hard with the whites in that struggle. But Boone "fought the tribes fairly, on terms that made him respected among the tribes."[50] Peck, who knew Boone, wrote, "He never delighted in shedding human blood, even that of his enemies in war, and avoided it whenever he could."[51]

Boone in 1809 gave the following advice on how to deal with Indians: "Always meet them frankly and fearlessly, showing not the slightest sign of fear or trepidation. By kind acts and just treatment, keep on the friendly side of them. Bestow upon the squaws small presents, however short you may be of them, which will conciliate them and secure their good will of friendship against any hostile designs, and command their aid and sympathies in case of sickness while among them."[52] Boone lived by this code, which may have derived in part from the Quaker principles he had imbibed as a child. There is no evidence that Boone was gratuitously violent against Indians, nor that he was brutal in his treatment of Indians in an effort to impress them. On the contrary, as the warfare subsided in Kentucky, Boone was trusted by Indians and whites alike to play a central role in prisoner exchanges.

Early in 1786, while peace-seeking Shawnees were negotiating with whites at the mouth of the Great Miami downstream from Limestone, some Kentuckians stole horses from the Indian encampment and brought them to the American settlements. Boone ordered the militia to take the horses back to the Indians, even though the settlers' opposition was so great that he could not return all of the horses.[53] After Colonel Logan's 1786 expedition to the Shawnee villages, in which many Indian prisoners were taken, Logan appointed Boone, who by this time had moved to Limestone, as a commissioner to exchange Indian captives for whites held by the Indians. Limestone was a likely place for the exchanges to occur, being so close to the Shawnee territory. Boone housed the Indian prisoners and set up a special account labeled "Daniel Boones Indan Book" to keep track of the expenses. The Indians were kept under guard, as much to protect them against vigilante attack by Kentuckians who had lost relatives to Indians as to prevent their escape. Boone apparently also sought to keep the Indians happy. His first bill to Virginia included a charge of "£3/0/0" "for 19 galons of Whiskey delivered to the Indins priseners on there first arrival at Limeston."[54] The provisions Boone eventually bought for the prisoners included 900 pounds of flour, 15 bushels of corn, 48 quarts of salt, 350 pounds of bacon and dried beef, 70 pounds of tobacco, and 82 gallons of whiskey and brandy. Col. Benjamin Logan certified that all of the "artickels was nessasary for the Indiens & I think the Accounts is just," and Virginia reimbursed Boone for the full amount he had charged for provisions (£101.1.6).[55]

Boone did more to facilitate prisoner exchanges than act as tavern keeper for the Indian prisoners. He went out of his way to return exchanged white prisoners to their families, and he put his own honor on the line in negotiating with the Indians for prisoner exchanges. Traveling in the Shawnee country north of the Ohio River, Boone found a young white girl named Chloe Flinn, about seven years old, a recent captive not yet attached to her adoptive family. The girl could tell Boone her name but not where her home had been or where her relatives were. He took her home to Rebecca. The Boones reared her as part of their family until he was able to locate her relatives and return her to them. Indians had raided the Flinn family farm in western Virginia, killed her father, and taken the children as captives. Chloe's sister and brother stayed with the Indians. The sister married a Shawnee; the brother became an interpreter and trader. Chloe stayed with the whites and grew up so grateful to Boone that she gave one of her own sons the first name Boone. Another of Chloe's sons, as a Virginia legislator, introduced the bill that named a new county in the western part of Virginia (now part of West Virginia) as Boone County.[56]

In March 1787 a Shawnee chief arrived at Limestone with three white prisoners. He proposed to exchange them and to bring all the Shawnees' white captives to Limestone if the whites would release Cornstalk's sister Nohelema, who had been taken captive on Logan's expedition and was being held by the settlers at Danville. Boone agreed. When the militia colonel at Danville refused to give up Nohelema, Boone wrote to him with the exasperation of the man on the front line being second-guessed from afar: "I am hire With my hands full of Bisness and No athoraty and if I am Not indulged in What I Do for the best it Is Not worth my While to put my Self to all this trubel." Boone noted he had pledged himself to the Shawnee chief as "Spisel [special] Security for the Complyance" with the proposed exchange and that his request was being made "to Clear me of my obligation that I Come under to the Chief."[57] The Danville colonel acceded. Nohelema was returned to the Shawnees, and the prisoner exchange began in earnest.

In April 1787 a Shawnee named Captain Wolf brought nine more white captives, and Boone arranged another exchange of prisoners. In August of that year close to seventy-five Shawnee warriors led by a Shawnee chief known to the whites as Captain Johnny appeared on the north side of the Ohio across from Limestone (by this time officially named Maysville, but both names continued to be used interchangeably well into the next century) with a larger group of American captives. To start discussions, Boone sent two young Indian captives across the river, accompanied by Boone's son Daniel Morgan Boone, then seventeen years old. Boone, Colonel Logan, and other whites then crossed the Ohio to meet with the Shawnees. Captain Johnny, who had succeeded Moluntha as leader of the peace faction within the Shawnees, explained he had been trying to round up all of the

Shawnees' white captives, but the Shawnees on the Wabash River would not give up their captives and were still for war. Captain Johnny said five Shawnee towns—the ones closest to Limestone—were for peace. Logan took the opportunity to remind the Indians that they had not been able to defeat the whites even when the British were fighting as allies of the Indians and said it would be in vain for the Indians to continue a war by themselves. This was a variation of what an American spokesman had told Shawnees during a prisoner exchange in July 1783: "Your Fathers the English have made Peace with us for themselves, but forgot you their Children who fought with them, and neglected you like Bastards."[58] Logan agreed to exchange many Indian prisoners but said he could not release them all as long as some Americans were still captives. Logan, Boone, Captain Johnny, and others signed English transcriptions of the speeches of Captain Johnny and Logan, and prisoners were exchanged. An all-night feast of celebration followed near Boone's tavern in Limestone.[59]

During the prisoner exchanges Boone and his son Daniel Morgan Boone became friends with Blue Jacket, then a young war leader of the Shawnees. In the fall of 1787 Daniel Morgan Boone went hunting north of the Ohio River with Blue Jacket, who said he would not hurt Limestone's residents and in fact freed at least one local resident who had been captured by Shawnees. In 1788 Kentuckians pursuing Indians who had stolen horses from Strode's Station captured Blue Jacket and recovered the stolen horses. The Kentuckians started beating Blue Jacket, but because he claimed to be a friend of Boone, he was taken to Limestone and locked up in a cabin pending trial. Someone (could it have been Boone?) left a knife in the cabin, stuck in the logs near Blue Jacket. The Indian "worked around till he got it, cut the rope with which he was bound, and cleared out just about day."[60] Blue Jacket made his way back to the Shawnees and lived to be a commander in the allied Indian forces that defeated the Americans, first under General Harmar and then under General St. Clair, before finally being beaten by the Americans under General Wayne.

Is it possible to impose an order on the wide range of white attitudes toward Indians? Historians have tried to do so. Richard White, in his magisterial survey of white-Indian interactions in the Great Lakes region between 1650 and 1815, contends that Europeans and Indians initially viewed each other as alien and nonhuman, then reached accommodations and some common understandings, and as the American push for land became ever more aggressive and the Indians more desperate, once again tended toward mutual demonization.[61] There is much in this thesis—but it also true that throughout this time period one can find whites who hated all Indians, whites raised from childhood among Indians who became Indians culturally, and whites who respected and liked some Indians and parts of Indian culture. It stands to reason that white demonization of Indians increased as whites took more and more Indian lands and needed to justify the taking, but much depended on the experiences and mind-set of the individual.

Daniel Boone was vividly aware of the dangers of Indian attack. Indians killed his two oldest children, his brother, and many of his friends; Indians had taken Boone himself captive and made him run the gauntlet. Despite these experiences, Boone did not become an Indian hater like McGary or Clark. In part this may have been because Boone had positive experiences with Indians as well as horrifying ones. It is clear that Boone, in his Shawnee captivity, liked Blackfish and his family and enjoyed hunting with the Shawnees. It is likely that Boone also was influenced by his Quaker upbringing and in the Quaker teaching that all men carry within them some spark of the spirit of God. It is also true that Boone was a realist and a pragmatist. He recognized that the Indians who attacked him and his family and friends were fighting to defend their lands and that he and his fellow white frontiersmen were fighting for the same lands. Boone evidently realized there was a time for fighting and a time for peaceful interaction, much like the Shawnee who had questioned him in 1778 before the Shawnees decided to adopt him: "When we in war you kill me, I kill you. All right!"[62] Boone also distinguished between individual Indians—the straightforward war leader Blackfish, for example, and Big Jim, who ripped out the fingernails of Boone's son James before tomahawking him to death. In his dealings with Blue Jacket, as in the prisoner exchanges and in so many of his dealings with Indians, Boone proceeded not as an ideologue—an Indian lover or an Indian hater, an American patriot, an expansionist—but instead as a pragmatic individual looking to treat people fairly, and to do right by those who did right by him and his neighbors.

16

TRADING AND LAND SPECULATION
Master of All He Surveyed?

WHAT COLONEL LOGAN HAD TOLD CAPTAIN JOHNNY AND HIS SHAWNEE
warriors at the Limestone parley in 1787 was right, and Boone must have
known it. It was much the same as what the U.S. commissioners had told the
Seneca chief Cornplanter in 1783: "You are a subdued people. . . . We shall
. . . declare to you the condition on which, alone, you can be received into
the peace and protection of the United States."[1] Kentucky's Indian neighbors
were still able to mount occasional raids into Kentucky, but they no longer
had any prospect of waging a successful war against Kentucky and its tens
of thousands of settlers. There was a resurgence of fighting between Indians
and whites in the early 1790s, as the U.S. government sought lands north and
west of the Ohio River, by diplomacy and by armed force, and as the Indians joined forces in defense of their lands and won impressive victories over
General Harmar in 1790 and over General St. Clair in 1791, before being finally beaten at Fallen Timbers in 1794—but the battles were in Ohio, where
Indians still had villages. The fighting in Kentucky after 1782 involved only
small-scale raids.

What was Boone to do with the balance of his life? In 1784 he turned
fifty, a considerable age to achieve on the frontier. He bore scars from past
wounds. He was heavier than he had been. Many of his longtime colleagues
had already died. In 1783, for example, two months after John Floyd was
struck down by an Indian bullet, Col. William Preston, who had survived
fighting Banastre Tarleton's rangers in North Carolina in 1781, died at age
fifty-three, felled by a stroke while reviewing his county militia.[2] Moreover,
Kentucky was far different in 1784 than it had been when Boone first hunted
in it, one of the only white men in the country, surrounded by game that appeared to be limitless. Now game was scarce, and settlers were plentiful. The

need for Indian fighters had dwindled, in large part because of the efforts and successes of Boone and other frontier leaders.

Boone did what many do when they realize they are no longer young and will not live forever: he sought to make money. He tried a variety of means, including surveying and speculating in land, tavern keeping, trading, ginseng gathering, and government contracting. For a time it looked as if Boone would become lastingly rich, but ultimately none of his ventures paid off, and his reverses embittered him.

Boone's longest-lasting efforts related to land. The hope of getting rich by buying and selling land was what drove most settlers west to the frontier, as it had driven the Boones and the Bryans to the Yadkin Valley. Nathan Reid, who in his early twenties at Boonesborough had helped Boone and John Floyd rescue Jemima Boone and the Callaway girls from the Indians, described the kind of hope that he and Floyd (and presumably Boone) had in the 1770s for making a fortune from land in Kentucky: "Frequently have Floyd and I sat down on a log, or at the foot of a tree, and giving a free rein to our heated imaginations, constructed many a glorious castle in the air. We would, on such occasions, contrast the many discomforts that then beset us, with the pleasures of boundless wealth. Spread out before us lay the finest body of land in the world, any quantity of which, with but little exertion, we could make our own. We clearly foresaw that it would not be long before these lands would be justly appreciated, and sought after by thousands. Then we should be rich as we cared to be."[3]

The whites' interest in Kentucky land grew as the Indian threat receded and the Virginia land laws provided a mechanism for resolving conflicting claims to land in Kentucky. By the early 1780s, as one visitor to Kentucky put it, "The spirit of speculation was flowing in such a torrent that it would bear down every weak obstacle that stood in its way."[4] William Preston's nephew John Breckenridge, who was to move to Kentucky and become attorney general and speaker of the House there before being elected to the U.S. Senate, in 1786 wrote, "Kentucky is the greatest field for Speculation, I believe, in the World."[5] Boone had seen others—on a grand scale George Washington, on smaller scales William Preston and John Floyd—make fortunes out of western land. Unlike Washington, Preston, and Floyd, however, Boone failed to accumulate substantial land ownership. Their successes and Boone's failure tell us much about how wealth was created through land ownership and trading on the frontier as well as about Boone's character, strengths, and weaknesses.

At the age of seventeen George Washington, after a summer surveying Lord Fairfax's vast land claims in Virginia, noted: "The greatest Estates we have in this Colony were made . . . by taking up & purchasing at very low rates the rich back Lands which were thought nothing of in those days, but are now the most valuable lands we possess." He acted on this insight. At age twenty he bought 1,459 acres in the Virginian piedmont.[6] He also acquired significant land ownership by inheritance and by marriage (Martha Dandridge Custis owned 18,000 acres when Washington married her), but much of his acreage came from land to the west of the established settlements, claimed based on explorations and surveys made by him (as a young man) or by others, including John Floyd, on his behalf.[7] As George Washington wrote in 1771, "What Inducements have Men to explore uninhabited Wilds but the prospect of getting good Lands?"[8] Eventually, Washington came to own over 52,000 acres across six different states.[9]

William Preston, whom Boone knew personally, may also have served as a role model for Boone. Although not a land speculator on Washington's scale, Preston did remarkably well for himself. He was already an important official in western Virginia and a substantial landowner when he commissioned Boone as a captain in the militia in 1774, but he did not start with much. Preston's father, who began life as a ship's carpenter, received 4,000 acres of land in western Virginia for settling a tract in which Preston's uncle James Patton had an interest. William Preston may have received some share of this acreage when his father died in 1748, but it is likely that at least part of the estate would have gone to Preston's mother and to his three sisters. From this moderate start Preston built up a fortune. When he died in 1783, he owned 17,251 acres—19 tracts in Virginia, and 3 tracts aggregating 3,000 acres in what is now Kentucky, including valuable lands that were to become a large part of Louisville and a choice tract that Floyd had surveyed for him near Lexington.[10] As with Washington, Preston was a surveyor, and that position helped him amass his acreage. For all the other civil and military positions Preston amassed over his long career, he never lost sight of the importance of surveying. He started as deputy surveyor of Augusta County in 1752, when he was only twenty-two. He became surveyor of Botetourt County in 1769 and surveyor of Montgomery County in 1780. When Preston died, the inventory of personal property in his estate included not only forty-two Negroes valued at $4,431.65 and 273 books valued at $194.60 but also "surveyor's instruments."[11]

John Floyd, close to twenty years younger than Boone and Preston, was only in his early thirties when he was killed by Indians in 1783, but he was already well-off in Kentucky land. Floyd's land acquisitions included a thousand acres around a large spring near Georgetown, a tract of comparable size on Beargrass Creek, on the outskirts of Louisville, and two hundred acres in what was to become downtown Lexington. Like Preston, while he gained many other titles and positions, Floyd's position as a surveyor was important in helping him to acquire land. Preston had made Floyd a deputy surveyor for Fincastle County before Floyd led the surveys in Kentucky in 1774 that led to large land claims for Preston and for Floyd.

Surveying was important in part because without a survey by an official surveyor, land would not be allocated and registered. Surveying was also highly profitable. George Washington, surveying Fairfax claims as a young man of seventeen, earned a doubloon a day, sometimes six pistoles—roughly $15–$22.50 a day, or about $100 a week—close to what he would earn forty years later as president of the United States. Charles Mason and Jeremiah Dixon in 1763 were paid £3,500 by the Calverts of Maryland and the Penns of Pennsylvania to survey the boundary between Maryland and Pennsylvania—the Mason-Dixon Line.[12] That was a princely sum, but without an accurate survey the proprietors of Maryland and Pennsylvania could not convey clear title to land on either side of the boundary and therefore could not realize the value of their land ownership. The surveyor's fees prescribed in the Virginia land laws were generous, relative to the amount of work involved. In some instances landowners paid surveyors by allocating part of the land in question to the surveyors. In addition, surveyors of unsettled frontier were in an ideal position to spot what land tracts were most promising and to file claims to those tracts for themselves or as jobbers for others (as John Floyd and George May did in Kentucky). As Nicholas Cresswell wrote in 1775 wrote, explaining why he wanted a surveyor's license before he went west down the Ohio River, "The place of Surveyor will be worth some hundreds a year, exclusive of the opportunities a Surveyor has of taking up lands for himself."[13]

By the early 1780s Boone had important attributes for investing in land in Kentucky. No white man had seen more of Kentucky or for a longer period of time. Boone knew where the good land was, where the springs were, where the salt licks were. His visual memory was remarkable. He could orient himself within country he had not seen for fifteen or twenty years. He had made land claims himself at Colonel Henderson's since-defunct Transylvania land office in 1775 and, in 1779, under the Virginia land laws.[14] He had also made claims as a locator or jobber for others. But Boone was not a licensed surveyor and did not know how to make and write up a survey. He set out to remedy these lacks. He worked with other surveyors, including acting as a "land marker" for James Shelby, brother of Isaac Shelby, who was to become Kentucky's first governor. Boone also learned more about surveying—doing the measurements, doing the notes, writing the survey reports—from his son-in-law Will Hays, who was a deputy surveyor and who had helped Boone improve his reading and writing. Boone became an authorized deputy surveyor for Fayette County in 1782 and for Lincoln County in 1783. He spent much of the next several years surveying and building up his own land claims. Unlike William Preston and John Floyd, however, Boone was not able to parlay his surveying into lasting ownership of substantial acreage.

The painstaking efforts of historians Neal O. Hammon and James Russell Harris, based on an exhaustive review of Kentucky land records, show how active Boone was as a surveyor. He did some 172 surveys, of 394,093 acres, with by far the greatest part of his surveys being done in 1784 and 1785.[15] The table that follows shows that Boone covered thousands of miles, surveying a sizable chunk of Kentucky—about 2 percent of the total area of the state. The essence of surveying in Boone's day was measuring and recording distances, directions, and angles from identifiable markers. Distances were measured by using metal chains of standardized length. Each chain measured four perches, or twenty-two yards, divided into one hundred equal links. Ten square chains equaled one acre. That meant that a surveyor could compute the area of a parcel of land in square chains and then divide by ten to come up with the area in acres.[16]

Compasses gave directions; theodolites gave angles. Typically, Boone would take one marker and two chainmen with him on his surveys. Among those used as chainmen and markers were his relatives (for example, his sons Daniel Morgan, Jesse Bryan, and Nathan, who were taken on Boone's surveys starting when they were as young as eleven or twelve; five other relatives named Boone; and Boone's sons-in-law Flanders Callaway and Joseph Scholl) and also colleagues from Boonesborough days, including the former salt-boiler and Indian captive Micajah Callaway.[17]

Opinions vary about how good Boone was as a surveyor. Several considered him about average for the time and location. One Kentucky settler

Summary of Boone's Surveys

YEAR	ACRES SURVEYED	NUMBER OF SURVEYS	MINIMUM DAYS	TRIP MILES
1783	17,305	24	30	256
1784	138,375	54	97	1,138
1785	159,806	59	122	1,642
1786	38,733	10	31	548
1787	4,400	5	17	290
1788	10,400	2	11	240
1796	19,175	9	16	190
1797	5,900	6	18	340
TOTALS	393,094	169	342	4,644

Source: Based on Hammon and Harris, "Daniel Boone the Surveyor."

remembered that "all Boone's entries were mighty vague."[18] Willard Rouse Jillson, after reviewing Boone's many surveys, wrote: "Boone's handwriting, including his signature, is always very readable. His spelling is generally poor, a trait that was not uncommon among many Virginians of his day, but his written or surveying record and his surveyed plats are as good as the average—certainly better than some that were made at the same time, if not quite the equal of others. . . . Many of the surveyors contemporary with Boone excelled him in spelling, in neatness and in general surveying precision, particularly in the matter of the presentation of the platted survey."[19] Boone's own son Nathan, for many years a successful surveyor himself, said that his father's "knowledge of surveying was limited" and that he "could survey square or oblong bodies"—suggesting that Boone lacked some of the skills needed to deal with more irregularly shaped tracts.[20]

Boone's surveys indicated corners by reference to ephemeral features (for example, "SW Corner at a Honey Locus [sic] thence west 200 poles to a White Walnut hickory"), but that was normal for surveys at the time, and Hammon found that Boone's surveys were "precise in the direction and measurement of the sides."[21] It is also true that some of Boone's surveys of irregular shapes do not close—that is, do not end up exactly where they started. But according to Hammon and Harris, "Many experienced surveyors of the day seldom experienced better results."[22] Moreover, Boone, like other surveyors in the thirteen colonies (including others working in the Kentucky district of Virginia) did not have the benefit of the accurate grids contemplated by the Land Ordinance of 1785, a law that provided the groundwork for sound surveys and land allocations of the new land acquired in the wake of the Revolution.[23] Hammon and Harris concluded that Boone was no worse at surveys of irregular tracts than his contemporaries and was skillful at surveys of conventional tracts.

In any event the surveying business produced good fees for Boone, as it had for Washington. Boone was averaging an estimated ten pounds in net profits per survey.[24] In 1784 and 1785 that would mean he was making over five hundred pounds a year—at a time when typical Pennsylvania farmers were earning around twenty-five pounds per year and established merchants perhaps one hundred pounds per year.[25] And Boone was also profiting by using his incomparable knowledge of Kentucky to locate lands for others to claim, sometimes (but probably infrequently) in return for a piece of the located tract. Thomas Logwood, for example, for whom Boone had located and surveyed over fourteen thousand acres, assigned five thousand of those acres to Boone.[26] Boone used his income from surveying and locating lands fees in part to invest in more real estate in Kentucky and in part to buy a tavern/inn in Limestone. Neither venture made Boone rich.

In the land business Boone added to his existing claims by buying warrants for thousands of acres and entering claims under those warrants for himself or for others. The land record databases are incomplete, but Hammon's review of them has uncovered that on just one day (December 21, 1781) Boone paid £61,970 to acquire warrants for a total of 38,750 acres.[27] Although the galloping inflation in Virginia's currency made the purchase price much less formidable than its face amount suggests, it is hard to see where Boone would have acquired this sum on his own, particularly less than a year after a large amount of money was stolen from him near Williamsburg. The size of the purchase suggests that Boone was buying many of the warrants on behalf of others—as a jobber, as part of a land investment partnership, or because others in Kentucky, far from the land office in Richmond, entrusted funds to him to be used to buy warrants at the land office when he was in Richmond as a legislator.

Boone filed many land claims, though far fewer than the largest speculators, such as John May. Boone's son Nathan said that even after losing some land in litigation and title fights, "he still had claims to well-nigh 100,000 acres" in the late 1790s, "but most of it was also claimed by others."[28] The 100,000-acre figure is probably hyperbole. A recent review of all Virginia

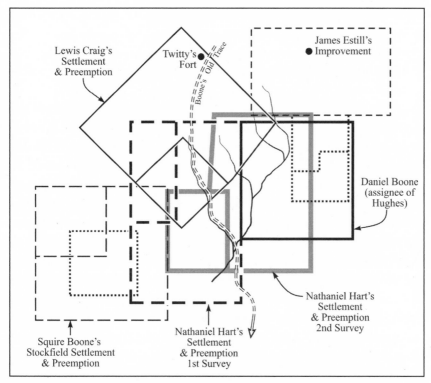

Shingled Land Claims in Madison County, Ky., including one by Daniel Boone,
from records in *Heirs of Nathaniel Hart v. Samuel Estill* lawsuit.
Courtesy of Neal O. Hammon, redrawn by Mary Lee Eggart

land grants and deeds showed that Boone entered claims for 27,969 acres
(17,500 of which he had surveyed), sold 19,588 acres, and secured grants
(patents) for 8,379 acres.[29] But even at this level Boone was seeking to own
acreage that would rival or exceed Preston's land claims. As Nathan put it,
at about the time Boone moved to Limestone "he thought himself worth a
fortune in the undeveloped lands of Kentucky," but "little by little his wealth
melted away," and "when he finally left Kentucky in 1799 he was poor."[30]

What happened? Part of the problem was that land title in Kentucky was
plagued by uncertainties, which were caused by the huge number of treasury warrants sold by Virginia in its efforts to pay down its Revolutionary
War debts, the requirement under the Virginia land laws that warrants could
only be used for land not previously claimed, the imperfect surveys, and
the resulting conflicting claims to the same land. The overlapping claims—
called "shingled" claims because they overlaid one another like shingles

on a roof—gave rise to extensive and long-lasting litigation over land titles in Kentucky.

These land title uncertainties, however, applied also to other investors in Kentucky land, such as Preston and Floyd. Boone knew the lands of Kentucky and was a deputy surveyor. He clearly knew what land was desirable. Boone was able to provide some land for his many children. Why, then, did he not build up a lasting fortune in land, as Preston had done and as Floyd was well on his way to doing when he was killed? One problem was that Boone was less well connected than Preston and Floyd. For one thing, Boone did not always choose the right patron. His initial hopes for substantial acreage in Kentucky were based on promised grants in the mid-1770s from Henderson's Transylvania Company, whose pretensions to own most of Kentucky and a large chunk of Tennessee proved to be baseless. Moreover, Boone's positions in government were not as central as those of other leading land accumulators. Boone became the head of the militia of Fayette County and was authorized to be a deputy surveyor in Fayette County and Lincoln County—and probably in Bourbon, Madison, and Mason counties as well and perhaps in Clark County and at least one county in what was to become West Virginia.[31] In each county, however, there were many deputy surveyors but only one surveyor.[32] To be *the* surveyor of a county—as William Preston and George May were—was to be far more centrally located in claiming and properly registering land than to be one of a great many deputy surveyors. The county surveyor, not a deputy surveyor, was responsible for seeing to it that surveys were registered in his office, copied in the county survey book, and forwarded to the land office in Richmond for registration and for the issuance of patents. The county surveyor also collected fees whenever claims and surveys were entered, without having to do the survey work. It also did not hurt to be, or (like William Preston) to be close to, a land commissioner such as William Fleming, empowered to settle disputed land claims in Kentucky. Nor, so long as Kentucky was part of Virginia, did it hurt to have extensive dealings (as William Preston and John Floyd had and Boone did not) with leading figures in Richmond and eastern Virginia.

A shortage of cash also cramped Boone's ability to buy and to register claims. In 1785, for example, he wrote to Col. William Christian that he had filed some registration relating to "the Land Bissness that your father Left in my Hands" and "Requst the faver of you to Send me by the bearer ... ten pound and this Shall be your Resite [Receipt] for that Sum and you Will oblyge your omble Sarvent." Boone noted, "I have a Number of plots to Register at the general Cort and am Scarse of Cash[.] plese to oblyge me if possible."[33]

Boone also suffered in his land dealings from overpromising and trusting too much. At least when he sold a tract of land, he warranted that he had good title to it and agreed to "forever Defend the land and premises hereby bargained"—a rash promise to make, given the confused state of title to Kentucky land. Apart from warranties in deeds, Boone as jobber or locator of land under warrants presumably undertook that the location was properly made, on a tract of land of specified acreage, none of which had been previously claimed. In either case, when conflicting claimants to the land surfaced, as they did all too frequently, the purchaser would ask Boone to indemnify him against the conflicting claims or to provide him with good title to the same amount of land of comparable value and location.[34]

In addition, Boone was burned by trusting in crooks and deadbeats. An outstanding example was Gilbert Imlay, formerly an American officer in a New Jersey regiment, who possibly served as a double agent and British officer during the Revolution and who was to engage with James Wilkinson (American general and secret agent of the Spanish) in various schemes with the Spanish and the French involving Louisiana. Imlay, who appeared in Limestone in 1783, agreed to buy from Boone what Nathan Boone described as "a splendid tract" not far from Limestone, on the road to Lexington. Imlay agreed to pay for the land in installments or to forfeit a bond of two thousand pounds. When Boone filed the survey of the ten thousand–acre tract in 1785, he endorsed on the survey, "I do hereby assign my right and title of the within survey to Gilbert Imlay and his heirs and assigns"—even though Boone had not yet been paid for the land. Imlay fled from Kentucky to escape his many creditors there and wrote Boone to say that he was "sincerely sorry it is not in my power to give you any Assistance, for Such is the embarrassing State of Affairs in this Country that I have not been able to recover a pound from all the engagements that have been made me." Imlay's sorrow did not prevent him, before he took off for England, from assigning the tract to his friend Wilkinson for an undisclosed sum, so that when Boone attempted to sell the tract to a solvent buyer, he could not do so because the land had already been sold. Boone received nothing for the "splendid tract," and Wilkinson had the gall to demand from Boone compensation for part of the tract that was lost to prior claims and, when seeking to sell the tract, to promote it as having been "located and surveyed by Col. Dan Boone."[35]

Imlay, with comparable gall, included in his book on the American West Boone's narrative from Filson's *Discovery of Kentucke*.[36]

Boone was also plagued by troubles with the accurate record keeping needed to perfect and defend title to land. In part this was because Boone was far less educated in reading and writing than men like John Floyd and Boone's own son-in-law Will Hays, as can be seen at a glance by comparing surveys prepared by the three men. The handwriting and spelling in the surveys by Floyd and Hays are elegant, not so in Boone's. Boone also had little interest in record keeping and bad luck in safeguarding such records as he had. One acquaintance said that Boone "was indifferent in the affairs of the world, and told me that he intrusted to Col. Floyd all his lands, contracts, and rights, to perfect" and that "the Colo's death caused the loss of papers, and that he never looked after them."[37] The loss of records resulting from the Indians' killing of Floyd made it hard for Boone to perfect a number of his claims.

In addition, Boone's strategy for getting rich through land investments was fundamentally flawed. As Faragher has pointed out, Virginia was assessing property taxes not only on perfected titles but also on land held under unperfected claims. To obtain the money Boone needed to pay property taxes to hang onto claims he thought promising, he was selling at low prices—often, according to his son Nathan, "for a trifle"—tracts to which he had already title patents. Some of his land was sold in sheriff's sales to satisfy claims for unpaid land taxes.[38] Boone may have thought he was making a profit on land sales, without taking adequate account of the galloping inflation going on in Virginia. His strategy might have worked if Boone had been able to obtain valid patents for his recently claimed land, but frequently he could not do so or he sold the land before a patent had been issued. Even if Boone had waited to obtain patents, that would not have assured perfect title, since Virginia at the time not infrequently issued patents to more than one person covering more or less the same tract of land.

Finally, by the mid-1780s gaining good title to land in Kentucky often required having the bankroll, the stomach, and the skills to engage in protracted litigation, and Boone had none of them. The Land Commission helped to resolve conflicting claims to land in Kentucky, but often litigation was needed to settle title. As a visitor to Kentucky in 1797 wrote, "The uncertainty of titles to Kentucky lands is become quite a proverb, and arises from the negligent and careless way in which the government suffered the first emigrants to settle the country," creating conflicting claims to the same land that were "the cause of your buying, almost universally, with every tract of land a lawsuit with some prior claimant."[39]

Boone found himself embroiled in suits so often that in 1785 he engaged a lawyer in Lexington who agreed to "appear for him the sd Boone in all actions at Law brought by or against him"—and "not to take any cause . . . except where I may have been previously retained by others, against him."[40] One notoriously protracted litigation, *Boofman v. Hickman*, relating to land located by Boone in 1774, lasted twenty-three years before it was finally resolved, after Boone apparently gave the plaintiff six hundred acres of land for a nominal price.[41] Boone must have incurred substantial obligations for legal fees in connection with these suits.[42] He was subjected to many depositions, and his character was called into question.[43] In 1791, for example, Nathaniel Hart, Jr., son of Boone's old friend and colleague Nathaniel Hart, wrote to his uncle, "Boone I believe has acted like a scoundrel" in surveying Boone's own preemption claim on land that the Hart family believed belonged to them. Hart alleged that in 1784 Boone caused entries made by Hart "to be surveyed in some manner contrary to locations in order to avoid an interference with a claim of his own." The dispute gave rise to yet another suit, in which Boone was ultimately vindicated but only after public accusations of fraudulent conduct.[44] Boone hated all the litigation, regardless of its outcome.[45] His life was also threatened by litigants who had lost cases because of his testimony, until Boone said "he could not travel with safety": "Even in time of peace he felt his own Kentucky was as dangerous to him as in the time of the Indian wars. In addition to premeditated personal injury, he felt he was a target for assassination."[46]

So Boone's interests in land melted away. Boone did little better in his other post-Revolution ventures in Kentucky. Sometime in the mid-1780s he bought property in Limestone, where he set up a store and tavern. Judging by the extent of his surveying in 1784 and 1785 in areas considerably to the west of Limestone, it is likely that Boone did not make Limestone his main home until 1786. Limestone's location was promising. The young town offered a sheltered landing on the south (non-Indian) side of the Ohio River. The thousands of settlers and traders coming down the Ohio from Pittsburgh each year, seeking access to the rich bluegrass country around Lexington, could save hundreds of miles by landing at Limestone, hiring wagons, and going southwest on the road toward Lexington, instead of floating farther down to the mouth of the Kentucky and traveling southeast back to

Lexington. Limestone was unprepossessing and small, squeezed between a steep hill and the river. One visitor called it "the fag end of Kentuckey," and another described it as "a muddy hole of a place with two or three log houses and a tavern."[47] But its location caused Limestone to be known as "the landing place to Kentucky," and Filson described it as "a fine harbour for boats coming down the Ohio."[48] And if Boone was looking for trade with Indians and with Indian traders, Limestone was not far from the Shawnee towns. Its central location as a point of contact with the Indians was demonstrated in 1787, when Boone housed the Indian hostages at Limestone, and the captive exchanges with the Indians were negotiated near Limestone and celebrated at Boone's tavern there.

It was not unnatural for Boone to keep a tavern. That was something that substantial citizens did, though perhaps it was not considered an elegant way of making a living.[49] In 1754 Boone's father, after becoming a sizable landowner on the Yadkin in North Carolina and a justice of the peace, was licensed to run a public house. Similarly, William Preston's father, John Preston—while owning many hundreds of acres in western Virginia and while being a pillar of the Tinkling Spring Presbyterian Church—in 1746 obtained a license to keep an "ordinary" (an inn and tavern).[50] To be sure, tavern keepers were obliged to comply with conditions contained in their licenses (for example, the tavern keeper was required not to "Suffer or permit any unlawful gaming in his House nor on the Sabbath day Suffer any person to tipple & drink more than is necessary"), but these conditions were not onerous, and some had a pleasing subjectivity (for example, how much drinking was "necessary" on the Sabbath?).[51] Outweighing the burdens of complying with tavern regulations were the facts that tavern keeping could be profitable as well as a fine way to hear of other possible commercial opportunities.

At Limestone, Boone had military responsibilities as colonel of the local militia. Among other things he wrote to Gov. Patrick Henry requesting more troops because there were two killings by Indians, "A Deale of Sine Seen in Different Places, in purtikuler Limeston," and "in Short An Inden Warr is Expected."[52] A grandson remembered that whenever there was an Indian alarm near Limestone, everybody would run into the tavern, shouting: "Where's Colonel Boone?" One old slave complained: "Why de debil don't dey go to doing something, and not be asking all the time for Colonel Boone?"[53] But Boone's military duties did not keep him from exploring many different ways of trying to make a dollar, in addition to surveying and tavern keeping. He also kept a warehouse at Limestone, supplied trappers, and even went into the ginseng business in a sizable way.

In his businesses Boone made use of slave labor when he could afford slaves. The Bourbon County tax roll for 1787 showed that he then owned seven slaves. There are records of Boone buying three African-American young women between 1781 and 1786. Faragher suspects that at least some of the other Boone slaves in the 1787 tax roll were children. As Boone's funds dwindled, so did his slaveholdings. A letter of his from 1791 appears to reflect the sale of a slave woman and her child and Boone's need for funds: he wrote that his son Daniel Morgan Boone "Wates on you for the Balance Due me for Rose and her Child Which is 32 pounds virganea money Besides the Intrust."[54]

Boone's ginseng efforts reflected that Kentucky, though on America's western frontier, was part of a global economy. The Chinese treasured ginseng, which was believed to increase mental activity and potency—perhaps because its forked root, to one possessed of a strong imagination, looked vaguely like a two-legged human (its Chinese name, *jen-shen*, means "man-shaped"). Ginseng roots that were old and wrinkled were particularly esteemed because the plant's long life was thought to be transferable to its consumer. For many years wild ginseng root had been exported from North America, much of it ultimately for the Chinese market, ever since a French Jesuit priest reported his discovery of ginseng in the woods near Montreal. The total recorded amount of ginseng shipped from Britain's continental American colonies in 1770 was over thirty-seven tons.[55] In February 1784 the *Empress of China*, the first American ship to trade with China after the Treaty of Paris was signed, sailed from New York harbor with almost thirty tons of ginseng in her cargo. The backers of the voyage, including the American merchant Robert Morris, made a fortune, selling to the Chinese primarily ginseng from western Virginia and Pennsylvania and selling to the Americans Chinese tea, silk, cotton, and porcelain. After the ship returned to New York in May 1785, the success of the venture was widely reported in the American press. The Chinese had paid five dollars a pound for the ginseng that made up most of the ship's cargo.[56]

Ginseng grew wild near Limestone, and Boone saw an opportunity to buy cheap and sell dear. According to his son Nathan, during the fall and winter of 1787 and the following winter, Boone employed several hands to dig ginseng and bought more from others. Nathan (though only around seven) was old enough to help with the digging. The crew washed the roots and strung them up to dry in the sun. By the spring of 1788 they had some 12 or 15 tons of dried ginseng. That would be close to half the total number of tons that the *Empress of China* had carried to China. If Boone could sell the root for $1 a pound, Boone would receive gross proceeds of $24,000 or $30,000—well over $500,000 in today's dollars. It is not possible to be precise in this calculation because we do not know whether the "tons" to which Nathan referred were units of weight (2,000 or 2,240 pounds), units of volume (35 or 40 cubic feet), or perhaps "tuns" (large casks).[57]

The Boones loaded their precious cargo onto a keelboat to take it up the Ohio from Limestone (by this time officially known as Maysville) on its way ultimately to Philadelphia. Three miles short of Point Pleasant the current pushed the boat onto driftwood at the head of an island, and the boat filled with water. With the help of people from Point Pleasant, including John Van Bibber (whom Boone had saved from starvation in the woods some years earlier), the Boones raised the boat, spread the wet ginseng out on the shore to dry, and reloaded the vessel. They pushed on upriver past Pittsburgh, repacking the ginseng onto horses near Redstone on the Monongahela for an overland trip to Hagerstown, Maryland, and from there to Philadelphia. But the ginseng was damaged, and Boone ended up getting only half the price for undamaged ginseng. By the time the ginseng got to Philadelphia, after the delay caused by the boat swamping, the price of ginseng (even in good condition) had dropped. One can imagine that hundreds of frontiersmen, hearing of the profits made by Morris and others, had done exactly what Boone had done and that the ginseng market in Philadelphia was as swamped as Boone's boat had been. Boone, who had incurred large costs in wages, freight, and buying ginseng from other diggers, ended up losing money on his ginseng venture.[58]

On the trip Boone traveled with Rebecca, Nathan, and two other sons and took the opportunity to visit relatives near Exeter, Pennsylvania. One woman in Pennsylvania remembered that Rebecca "was very pleasant and sociable, and spoke very freely of their affairs" but that Boone himself was "stern looking—very taciturn and gloomy."[59] And why not? He had flailed about in a variety of attempts to become rich and had succeeded only in losing his land, owing money, and being sued repeatedly.

After seeing his relatives, Boone headed back west. He decided to move to Point Pleasant, rather than returning to Maysville. A traveler in 1789 noted in his journal that at Point Pleasant, "I took Breakfast with Colo. Boon and his family being the best I had Eaten for many days," and then put his family and his horse in Boone's boat, fastening his own small boat to Boone's before continuing all through the night down the Ohio to Maysville.[60] By July 1789 Boone was giving "Grate Conhowway" (Kanawha) as the address on a letter, in which he wrote that he "cannot help Reflecting a Litel on the Downfall of ginsagn. This ware a Litel unfortenet Last fall But I doubt it will be worse this But the information Come to me in Tolerable good Time although I had took in a goodel."[61]

Point Pleasant had a good commercial location, where the Kanawha flowed into the Ohio, and military significance, being the site of Fort Randolph. Boone knew some people there, including the Van Bibbers. But the overwhelming reason for the move must have been that Boone had had it with Maysville. His commercial ventures had failed. His real estate had largely "melted away." The only thing that had grown for Boone was his exposure to litigation. By the time he left Maysville, he was far from master of all he had surveyed. He still owned or claimed some land, but it was fast disappearing in continuing disputes. Boone went back to Maysville to wind up his business in the town and to sell a few more parcels of land, but he filed no new claims of ownership of land in Kentucky.

17

LIVING LEGEND, SHRINKING FORTUNE

BOONE LEFT MAYSVILLE A BADLY BATTERED MAN. HIS FORTUNES DID not improve in the next decade, as he moved his home from place to place, generally downward economically and farther away from towns and commerce (and courts and creditors). But while his fortunes declined, his reputation grew. Boone was becoming a legend in his own lifetime—a legend that helped to draw settlers and to transform Kentucky from the unpopulated wilderness that had so entranced Boone when he first hunted there.

In 1784, the year Boone turned fifty, the first book extolling him appeared in print. John Filson, who had interviewed Boone at length the previous year, included "The ADVENTURES of Col. *Daniel Boon*" as the first appendix to Filson's brief book grandly entitled "THE DISCOVERY, SETTLEMENT And present State of KENTUCKE: and An ESSAY towards the TOPOGRAPHY, and NATURAL HISTORY of that important Country." The book included a reasonably good map of Kentucky (Filson had been trained as a surveyor and had spoken to Boone and others in Kentucky), a description of Indian tribes east of the Mississippi, and an appendix listing the stages and distances of going from Philadelphia to the Falls of the Ohio by land through the Cumberland Gap and from Philadelphia to Pittsburgh and down the Ohio River to the Falls and beyond. The appendix on Boone's adventures purported to be a first-person recounting by Boone of his hunts, settlement, and Indian fighting there, from Boone's trip with John Finley in 1769 through the Battle of the Blue Licks and Clark's expedition into the Shawnee villages in 1782. Right after the title page was a written endorsement, signed by Boone, Levi Todd, and James Harrod, recommending the book as "containing as accurate a description of our country [Kentucky] as we think can possibly be given."

The American edition of Filson's book sold out. John Trumbull of

Connecticut took the Boone narrative out of Filson's book, stripped it of florid Filsonisms, and published it as a pamphlet, which remained in print for many decades. Filson's book (borrowed without payment of royalties, there being no copyright protection) became a hit in Europe—translated into French by 1785, published in at least three editions in Germany (a source of many immigrants to Kentucky), and reprinted in England and Ireland during the 1790s.[1] Boone came to realize the international reach of the book and of his fame. In 1797, for example, when he was canoeing alone on the Ohio River with his dog and his gun, a young English traveler on a flatboat haled him aboard. On hearing Boone's name, the Englishman, "extremely happy in having an opportunity of conversing with the hero of so many adventures," produced a copy of Filson's book (in the pilfered version appended to Gilbert Imlay's *Topographical Description*) and began to read it aloud to Boone. Boone "confirmed all that was there related of him." The Englishman, Francis Baily, twenty-one years old at the time, wrote in his journal that he "could observe the old man's face brighten up at the mention of any of those transactions in which he had taken so active a part."[2]

Why had Boone in 1783 spent hours talking to Filson? The two men could hardly be more different—the tough old frontiersman and the bookish young tenderfoot. Filson was in his early thirties when he arrived in Kentucky around 1782 from Pennsylvania. Filson must have come across as the former schoolteacher he was. Judging from his pencil sketch of himself, he was small, balding, and unprepossessing. But Boone liked to talk to a sympathetic hearer. Francis Baily wrote that when he mentioned to Boone the siege of Boonesborough, Boone "entered upon the subject with all the minuteness imaginable, and as descriptively as if it had recently happened," and went on to describe his captivity by the Indians and to trace with a moistened finger on a board a map of where the Indians took him on the lakes, "and the old man interspersed his tale with many a pleasing anecdote and interesting observation."[3] Moreover, Filson and Boone shared a common objective: to become rich through a rise in the price of land in Kentucky. Boone still had significant Kentucky land claims when Filson interviewed him. So did Filson, in a smaller way.

Filson proclaimed in the preface to his book that, "incredible as it may appear to some," his book on Kentucky "is not published from lucrative motives, but solely to inform the world of the happy climate, and plentiful soil of this favoured region."[4] That assertion was, and is, incredible. Like Boone,

Filson had invested heavily in warrants to buy land in Kentucky. With the proceeds from his share of his father's estate, he had entered claims for more than twelve thousand acres in Kentucky,[5] and he had ample reason to promote immigration to Kentucky and the demand for its land by extolling Kentucky's wonders. He did so exuberantly. Kentucky, Filson wrote, was "the best tract of land in North-America, and probably in the world." The one hundred square miles from the heads of the Licking, Kentucky, and Dick's rivers and down the Green River to the Ohio make up "the most extraordinary country that the sun enlightens with his celestial beams." "The soil of Kentucke is of a loose, deep black mould, without sand, in the first rate lands about two or three feet deep, and exceeding luxurious in all its productions." And so on, in a similar vein, for over a hundred pages. Even if a particular kind of treasure was lacking in Kentucky, Filson made it sound as if it was just a question of time before it would be found there in abundance. He reported, for example, "Iron ore and lead are found in abundance, but we do not hear of any silver or gold mine as yet discovered." After the first-person narrative of Boone and the other appendices, Filson ended his little book with a peroration "upon the happy circumstances, that the inhabitants of Kentucke will probably enjoy, from the possession of a country so extensive and so fertile"—a region "abounding with all the luxuries of nature, stored with all the principal materials for art and industry, inhabited by virtuous and industrious citizens," which "must universally attract the attention of mankind" and where "government, so long prostituted to the most criminal purposes, establishes an asylum in the wilderness for the distressed of mankind." Filson predicted confidently that to Kentucky "innumerable multitudes will emigrate from the hateful regions of despotism and tyranny."[6]

Filson clearly did not believe in selling by understatement or in using colors other than purple in his prose. Filson's Boone appendix, purportedly a record of Boone telling his own story, overflows with locutions that bear no resemblance to anything Boone ever wrote in his own hand. It is hard to imagine Boone describing himself as "an instrument ordained to settle the wilderness" or saying of the Cumberland Gap: "The aspect of these cliffs is so wild and horrid, that it is impossible to behold them without terror. The spectator is apt to imagine that nature had formerly suffered some violent convulsion; and that these are the dismembered remains of the dreadful shock; the ruins, not of Persepolis or Palmyra, but of the world!"[7] But if the language is often Filson's, it is clear that Boone spent time with Filson on the facts—the early hunts, the blazing of the trail, the killing of James Boone, the history of the fights with the Indians. Boone was never loath to disclaim exaggerated accounts of his deeds, but there is no record that he ever criticized the accuracy of what Filson wrote about them. In addition to confirming to the English traveler what Filson had said about Boone, Boone, after hearing someone else read about him from Filson's book, declared: "All true! Every word true! Not a lie in it!"[8]

After 1783 Filson's path diverged from Boone's, even as Filson's book was working to draw settlers to Kentucky and to build Boone's reputation. Filson bounced around much as Boone did, and with no greater success. He went to Delaware to arrange for the book's publication, taught school in Wilmington, and came back to Louisville to try fur trading. Like Boone, he borrowed and had trouble repaying what he had borrowed. At the end of 1785 Filson wrote in a note in favor of my ancestor John Brown of Louisville: "I acknowledge myself indebted to John Brown the amount of sixty-one dollars or sixty-one pounds of beaver, which I promise to pay him upon demand next spring." Filson never paid the note, despite repeated requests. Brown obtained judgment in a suit in Louisville in 1787, but the only property he could attach in execution of the judgment was one old sickle belonging to Filson. In 1787 Filson announced in the *Kentucky Gazette* a proposal to establish a seminary to teach French and "all the arts and sciences used in academies," but nothing came of the project. In Louisville he studied "physic" with a view to becoming a doctor. He proposed to become cotenant of a tract in Powell's Valley that purportedly had a silver mine. He had an unhappy attempt at love near Louisville. In mid-1788 he wrote in a poem, "adieu Amanda," saying that "one leap in yonder gulf shall end my pain" and that in Elysian fields he would "forget the pains of love."

In the event Filson did not need to leap into a gulf to end his pain. In 1788 he proposed with others to develop a tract of land in Ohio opposite the mouth of Kentucky's Licking River, although he never paid his share of the tract's purchase price. To lure settlers, Filson drew up a plat for the town, to which he gave the fantastically multilingual name Losantiville (as Filson explained it: "L is for Licking River; os, Latin for mouth; anti, Greek for opposite; and ville, French for city").[9] In the fall of 1788, within weeks of crossing the Ohio to explore the tract with his co-venturers, Filson disappeared. Having become nervous about Indian sign, he made the fatal mistake of leaving his co-venturers and setting off alone back toward the white settlements.

He was almost certainly killed by the Indians; in any case his remains were never found. But he and his partners had picked a promising site for a city. It exists to this day under the name Cincinnati, given to it in 1790 by Gen. Arthur St. Clair, the governor of the Northwest Territory.[10]

Filson was probably dead by the time Boone left Maysville and moved to Point Pleasant—but Filson's book and his account of Boone's role in defending Kentucky and defeating the Indians were very much alive and drawing settlers to Kentucky. Would-be land buyers poured into Kentucky, down the Ohio, and across the Cumberland Gap, in the full grip of a land boom frenzy. Moses Austin, who went through Kentucky on his way to Missouri, described his conversation with the ill-clad emigrant horde he encountered on the Wilderness Road in December 1796: "Ask these Pilgrims what they expect when they git to Kentuckey and their Answer is Land. have you any. No, but I expect I can git it, have you any thing to pay for land, No. did you Ever see the Country. No but Every Body says its good land. Can any thing be more Absurd than the Conduct of man, here is hundreds Travelling hundreds of Miles, they know not for what Nor Whither, except its to Kentucky, passing land almost as good and easy obtain.d, the Proprietors of which would gladly give on any terms, but it will not do its not Kentuckey its not the Promis.d land its not the goodly inheritance the Land of Milk and Honey."[11]

But the land boom did not help Boone. By 1789 he had given away to relatives, sold, or lost to stronger claimants most of his land claims in Kentucky and was in the process of disposing of most of the balance, in large part to meet claims against him. Upon his arrival in Point Pleasant he turned to other ways of seeking to make a living. He started a store in town, buying skins, furs, and bear bacon from hunters and trappers and selling them supplies. From time to time Boone would send his sons Daniel Morgan and Jesse upriver to Maryland to buy new hunting and trapping supplies in exchange for the pelts that Boone had bought from the hunters and trappers. Boone also continued to ship ginseng east. His shipments were sizable. A Maryland merchant wrote in April 1790 to let Boone know that one of the Boone sons had delivered at Hagerstown two barrels of ginseng, 1,790 deerskins, 129 bearskins, and a number of fox and otter skins, to be sold and the net proceeds applied to Boone's account—and to let Boone know that he had been "rather long" in paying off his obligations for the trade goods he had bought on credit and that the merchant could not "want our money longer," being himself "in great want" of funds to remit to his suppliers in Philadelphia.[12] Boone also tried buying horses in the bluegrass country and selling them in the east. Two Boone sons, Daniel Morgan and Jesse, drove the horses for sale in Hagerstown to Boone's trading partner Thomas Hart, but many horses escaped along the way, and Boone was not able to cover the cost of the horses he had bought.[13]

Boone's commercial activities epitomize failure as a merchant: buying high, selling low, and sinking further and further into debt in the process. But Boone was still a man of some property. On the list of tithables for his county in 1792, he showed up as owning two horses, one slave, and five hundred acres of land.[14] The list shows Boone's continuing slave ownership, though down, as Boone's economic circumstances had plummeted, from the seven he owned in Bourbon County in 1787. Boone still also had a personal following, which translated into military and political office. In October 1789 the court of the newly created Kanawha County, Virginia—Point Pleasant's county—recommended to the governor of Virginia that Boone be appointed lieutenant colonel, the head of the county's militia, and by 1791 the commission was issued.[15] Being the militia leader was not an empty honor. Shawnees were still raiding the neighborhood—killing and scalping one Van Bibber girl, for example, and capturing three members of her family.[16]

Boone also was elected to be a delegate to the Virginia Assembly in 1791, where he served on a committee on religion and a committee on propositions and licenses. While in Richmond as a delegate in December 1792, Boone asked the governor of Virginia to award him the contract to take ammunition to the post at Redstone along the Monongahela (now Brownsville, Pa.) and to carry food to the garrison at Fort Randolph on the Kanawha at Point Pleasant. The spelling is vintage Boone: "As sum purson Must Carry out the armantsion to Red Stone if Your Exclency should have thought me a proper purson I would undertake it on Conditions I have the apintment to vitel the Company at Kanhowway so that I Could take Down the flowre as I paste the place. I am your Excelencys most obedent omble servant Dal Boone."[17]

Boone was granted the contract, but he was no more successful as a government contractor than he had been as a merchant and as a land speculator. He did deliver ammunition—some four hundred pounds of gunpowder, sixteen hundred pounds of lead, and a kegful of flints—to posts down the Monongahela and the Ohio, but by the time he reached Point Pleasant he did not have enough rations for the garrison, and his outstanding debts made it impossible for him to buy anything on credit from local merchants. The captain of the Kanawha rangers, Hugh Caperton, also thought that Boone was bringing ammunition. Boone had no such understanding. After a yelling match in which Caperton accused Boone of incompetence, Boone picked up his rifle and left for the woods. When the county sheriff finally found him, all Boone would say was that "Captain Caperton did not do to his liken."[18] The garrison's colonel, who may have approved the formation of Caperton's unit without due authorization, accused Boone to the governor of "total non-compliance" with what Boone had undertaken to do, bought the necessary rations for the garrison out of his own pocket, and replaced Boone as the garrison's supplier.[19]

By the end of 1792, the year in which Kentucky became a state, Boone was not only entangled in debt but charged with incompetence and disregard of contractual obligations. On top of the continuing lawsuits and creditor claims and commercial losses, the unpleasantness associated with the provisioning contract may have been the last straw for Boone in his attempts to prosper in the mainstream of the growing economy of western Virginia and Kentucky. The following year Boone closed the store in Point Pleasant and moved with Rebecca into the backcountry, to a small squatter's cabin sixty miles upriver on the Kanawha.[20] He had found game near the cabin a year or two earlier. After the 1797 legislative session, Boone had gone by himself up the river and killed two buffalo, an animal that was becoming increasingly hard to find in western Virginia. Boone and young Nathan went back with some friends to bring back the buffalo meat. Nathan saw great numbers of well-fed possums coming down to the water to drink and killed several to render for their oil.[21] Based on these experiences, upcountry on the Kanawha must have looked to Boone like a place where he could live off the land hunting and trapping, out of reach of lawsuits.

It was a tough life, and Boone was no longer young. He turned sixty in 1794. By then, for the first time in the nearly forty years he and Rebecca had been married, none of their many children was living with them.[22] Boone and Rebecca moved from hunting camp to hunting camp. Boone's rheumatism made it painful for him to get about, so he spent more time tending beaver traps than ranging in the woods for deer or bear. One rheumatism attack in the 1793–94 winter was so bad that one of the men he hunted with carried Boone out to his trap line in the morning and back again in the evening. But even though Boone could not move readily, a neighbor said that he still "would kill more deer than any of his neighbors, he so well knew the deers' haunts and habits."[23]

Boone and Rebecca spent several winters in a hunter's camp on the Levisa Fork of the Big Sandy River in eastern Kentucky, at a site he and his son Jesse had discovered around 1790. They had half-faced camps, like the ones Boone and his brother Squire had used in their long hunts in Kentucky in the late 1760s. A visitor said they "ate their meals from a common rough trough, very much like a sap trough, ... each using as needed a butcher-knife to cut the meat, & using forks made of cane." Skins and bear meat hung from tree boughs all around the camp. Boone claimed that he had killed "the master bear of the Western country," two feet across the hip bones, which must have weighed five or six hundred pounds in its prime.[24] He told someone else he had taken 155 bears near the camp during one three-week period and on one morning had "killed eleven by late breakfast time."[25] Boone and Rebecca, with two married daughters and their husbands, one fall rendered their kill of bear into several dozen barrels of bear grease, which they floated downriver and sold at a dollar a gallon.[26] Bear meat was worth more rendered into oil than it was as meat, and a bear's carcass would yield from ten to twenty gallons of oil.[27]

We can only guess how Rebecca viewed this life. She was well into her fifties, and the life was rough—no solid house, no town or store or station. But she stayed with Boone. Perhaps for the first time, she was with him regularly on his hunts, keeping camp, carrying his rifle when his rheumatism was so bad that he could not carry it himself. During his rheumatism attacks Boone could not move, could not trek to Lexington or to Hagerstown, could not dig ginseng. The couple, through spending long stretches of time together, through Daniel's need for Rebecca's help and Rebecca's skill in the camp and on the hunts, may have grown closer together than they ever had been.

Boone also was getting close to his youngest son, Nathan, then in his mid-teens. In 1794 Boone took Nathan hunting near the Ohio, and Nathan killed his first deer. They killed a dozen more, and Boone killed two or three bears, before Boone one midnight heard a chopping noise, which he believed was Indians making a raft to cross the river to get to their camp. Boone and Nathan loaded their canoe with meat and skins and paddled down the river in the foggy night. They heard Indians paddling across the river behind them before they finally were far enough away to be safe.[28] Indian attacks near the Ohio were still frequent enough that Nathan in 1795 encouraged his parents to move back to Kentucky, on Brushy Creek near what is now Carlisle, on land owned by Daniel Morgan Boone. There the Boones built a small cabin and continued to hunt and to trap, with some surveying, mostly in Mason County.[29]

In 1796 Boone made his last attempt in Kentucky at a large-scale business venture—the reconstruction of the Wilderness Road. The trail Boone and his axemen had blazed in 1775 through the Cumberland Gap and into the center of Kentucky was still a major route for immigrants to Kentucky, though it was ill maintained, too narrow for wagons, and often bordered by rotting horse and cattle corpses. In November 1795 Kentucky's first governor, Isaac Shelby, signed an act for building a good wagon road between Kentucky and Virginia. Boone had known Shelby for decades—at least since Henderson's treaty with the Cherokees at Sycamore Shoals in 1775—and had surveyed two tracts of land for him in 1782.[30] Boone, aged sixty-two, applied to Governor Shelby for the contract to rebuild the road:

feburey the 11th 1796

Sir

after my Best Respts to your Excelancy and family I wish to inform you that I have sum intention of undertaking this New Rode that is to be Cut through the Wilderness and I think My Self intiteled to the ofer of the Bisness as I first Marked out that Rode in March 1775 and never Re'd anything for my trubel and Sepose I am No Statesman I am a Woodsman and think My Self as Capable of Marking and Cutting that Rode as any other man. Sir if you think with Me I would thank you to write mee a Line By the post the first oportuneaty and he Will Lodge it at Mr. John Miler son hinkston fork as I wish to know Where and When it is to Laat So that I may atend at the time.

I am Deer Sir your very omble Sarvent.
Daniel Boone[31]

There is no record of a reply from Governor Shelby, who appointed colonels James Knox and Joseph Crockett to make the improvements on the road. What the governor was looking for, no doubt, were managers who could supervise a large engineering and construction project and its financial aspects, prepare or review budgets and reports, and let subcontracts. These were skills quite different from those that Boone possessed and had displayed in blazing the road in 1775—woodsmanship and raw courage. Knox and Crockett improved the road in an impressively short time while also changing the route substantially in many places. On October 15, 1796, they placed an announcement in the *Kentucky Gazette* that ran across all four columns of the newspaper's front page: "THE WILDERNESS ROAD from Cumberland Gap to the settlements in Kentucky is now compleated. Waggons loaded with a ton weight, may pass with ease, with four good horses,—Travellers will find no difficulty in procuring such necessaries as they stand in need of on the road; and the abundant crop now growing in Kentucky, will afford the emigrants a certainty of being supplied with every necessary of life on the most convenient terms."[32]

Colonels Crockett and Knox exaggerated the comforts of the rebuilt road. When Moses Austin traveled on it in December 1796, he reported that "although the road has been lately opend for wagons and much work don on it much more must be don to make it tolerable."[33] A few years later, in 1803, the Methodist bishop Francis Asbury noted in his journal both how bad the road was and how heavily it was traveled: "What a road we have passed! Certainly the worst on the whole continent even in the best weather; yet bad as it was there were four or five hundred crossing the rude hills whilst we were." The bishop also noted: "I found amongst my other trials I have taken the itch; and, considering the filthy houses and filthy beds I have met with, in coming from the Kentucky conference, it is perhaps strange that I have not caught it twenty times. I do not see that there is any security against it but by sleeping with a brimstone shirt."[34]

But it would have been little consolation to Boone to hear that the Wilderness Road, as rebuilt by others, was far from comfortable. The galling fact was that Boone, who had blazed the road, was not chosen to improve it. By the time the bishop traveled the road, Boone was many hundreds of miles away. In 1799, disgusted with Kentucky, plagued by claims and disputes, largely landless, Daniel Boone had moved out of the United States to what was then a Spanish territory: Missouri.

18

OUT TO MISSOURI

IN 1799, WHEN BOONE AND HIS FAMILY MOVED THERE, MISSOURI WAS still part of the Spanish territory of Upper Louisiana, but Spain's grasp on that territory was far from strong, and Spain knew it was vulnerable to attack. The whole of Upper Louisiana had few non-Indian occupants—only perhaps four thousand in 1799, consisting almost entirely of settlements clinging to the Mississippi River and a few on the lower Missouri.[1] Many of the whites in Upper Louisiana were French, not Spanish—descendants of the French who had moved into the region before and after France ceded Upper Louisiana to Spain in the 1763 Treaty of Paris. The Spanish garrisons were small and isolated. Traders from Canada were taking an ever greater share of the Indian trade in the Upper Louisiana. Moreover, after Spain broke with Great Britain by making peace with revolutionary France, Spain in 1796 found itself once again at war with Great Britain. The British had seized all of Canada from the French in 1763, had forts down into the Illinois country, had besieged St. Louis in 1780, and in the 1790s had opened trading posts with the Mandans and other Indian groups on the Missouri. Senior Spanish officials worried that there was little to prevent the British from taking Upper Louisiana—and by gaining control of the mouth of the Missouri, gaining control of the fur trade with the entire Missouri River basin—and then coming down the Mississippi in strength, seizing the vital port of New Orleans, and pressing on to the rich silver mines of Mexico. The Spanish also feared that the British in Canada might effect a rapprochement with the Americans and act jointly against the Spanish in Louisiana and perhaps beyond.

The Spanish saw no way to prevent these dire outcomes by themselves. Spain's navy was no match for Britain's, and the few Spanish troops in Missouri were not equal to America's Illinois garrisons, particularly if coupled with the veteran British regiments in Canada. What to do? The Spanish sought

to encourage immigration into Upper Louisiana of French Canadians—
fellow Catholics, after all—but not many came.[2] The Spanish also encouraged
Shawnees and Delawares to settle, but there were limited numbers of them.
The only large buffer the Spanish could think of interposing was frontiersmen from America—people who were hardy, scrappy, anti-British (having
just fought the British for eight years to gain their country's independence),
and hungry for the sparsely populated land west of the Mississippi.

With hindsight the Spanish were inviting the fox into the chicken coop,
as much so as when the Romans hired Goths as mercenaries to defend the
Roman Empire's eastern borders from barbarian hordes. The Spanish were
aware of the American risk. As early as 1792, the governor-general of Louisiana had warned Lt. Gov. Zenon Trudeau, in charge of Upper Louisiana,
that the Americans are "much more terrible at present for the Dominions
of His Majesty than the English."[3] But the Spanish had limited military resources of their own to devote to North America. Even though they realized
that the Americans themselves posed a grave threat to continued Spanish
control of Upper Louisiana, they had few other ways of keeping the British
out of Louisiana. In 1798 Trudeau wrote the governor-general of Louisiana
that to increase the population of the settlements on the western bank of
the Mississippi in Upper Louisiana, "I see no other means than that of the
United States, who alone can supply a great number of families." Trudeau
recognized that bringing settlers up from New Orleans was impracticable,
the trip being too great and costly, and said that the American immigrants to
Missouri "have behaved very well, for since they have found lands superior
to those of the Ohio, they are earnestly beginning to improve them."[4] So the
Spanish, starting in 1796, encouraged, by word of mouth and by circulating
handbills in Kentucky, American frontiersmen to come to Missouri, offering land grants and no property taxes. Those inducements were greater than
what had induced tens of thousands of Americans to come to Kentucky—
where the best land was already taken, the remaining land was being sold
(not granted for free) to settlers, and game had become hard to find.

Boone's oldest surviving son, Daniel Morgan Boone, in 1797, then in his
late twenties, decided to take a look at land prospects in Missouri. Boone
told him to meet the Spanish governor and to find out "the quantity of land
granted to new settlers, heads of families and servants" and also "if settlers
were required to embrace the Catholic religion." Daniel Morgan found land
to his liking on the Femme Osage Creek on the north side of the Missouri

River, about fifty miles upstream from St. Louis and west of almost all white settlements in Missouri. He then called on Lieutenant Governor Trudeau, who seemed pleased with the idea of having the famous Daniel Boone lead a new colony of immigrants to settle on the Missouri River. Trudeau wrote Boone to say that if he came to Missouri, he would have 1,000 arpents of land (about 850 acres) for himself and something like 600 arpents per family who came with him. Boone was also given to understand that, although citizens in the Spanish dominions were meant to be Catholics, that was not enforced so far as American emigrants to Upper Louisiana were concerned and that American settlers were "left to enjoy their own religious views but without attempting their own propagation."[5]

Trudeau's letter, coupled with Daniel Morgan Boone's enthusiastic report about the Femme Osage land, convinced Boone and his family to go with Daniel Morgan to Missouri and build a settlement. In the fall of 1798 Boone had moved from Brushy Creek to a small cabin near the mouth of the Little Sandy, in what is now Greenup County, in the northeastern corner of Kentucky, on land that had been cleared by Nathan Boone. That move may have been so that Boone could stay a step ahead of his creditors. In November 1798 the Fayette County court issued a warrant directing the Mason County sheriff to take Boone into custody, after Boone had ignored a summons in a suit based on a £3,000 bond relating to a promised conveyance of six thousand acres of land not far from Lexington. The warrant was endorsed on behalf of the Mason County sheriff, "Not Found."[6] Up on the Little Sandy, Boone and his sons found a huge poplar tree, felled it, and worked throughout the summer of 1799 hollowing it out to make a large dugout pirogue. By the fall the boat was ready—over fifty feet long, five feet wide, and able to hold five tons of freight. The Boones set off downstream in September.

The party was neither small nor inconspicuous. Daniel Morgan Boone and Nathan Boone were in charge of the big pirogue. Boone's brother Squire came in a separate boat. He was willing to give Missouri a try because he was looking for a chance to recoup his fortunes. Squire Boone was to tell Congress that among the "many misfortunes" that had befallen him from "constantly living on the Frontier," he had received "Eight bullet holes through him and had been in seventeen engagements with the Indians in support of his country and lost his property by unforeseen accidents."[7] Like Daniel Boone, Squire had failed in land speculation in Kentucky and had been besieged by creditors and lawyers. He then tried unsuccessfully to settle in

Mississippi and in Spanish Florida and lived with relatives in Pennsylvania. Squire summarized his own career by saying that he had fallen from dining with the governor of Virginia, "as high a grade of honour as I ever hope to," to having to steal hominy from a slave to live on, "as low a grade as I ever have been reduced to."[8] Other Boone relatives joined the party at Limestone or elsewhere along the way—among them Will Hays and Susannah, Flanders Callaway and Jemima, Isaac Van Bibber, and some seventeen Boone grandchildren. Boone, sixty-four years old, made the long trip to Missouri on land, driving the cattle, helped by a young man named George Buchanan, by a slave owned by one of Boone's sons, and, downstream, by Will Hays and Flanders Callaway.

Along the way Nathan stopped at Limestone to pick up a marriage license and went back upstream by himself to marry Olive Van Bibber on the Little Sandy. As Nathan remembered it, "It grieved the old colonel [Boone] that he had nothing to give me and my wife with which to start our new life" because of "his losses and misfortunes."[9] The young couple followed the main party on the land by themselves, subsisting on parched corn and the game Nathan killed. As Olive later remembered it: "It was rather a perilous trip for so young a couple. I was just sixteen, my husband eighteen."[10]

The Boone family move to Missouri has an Old Testament aspect—the patriarch taking with him to the new land his wife, his extended family, his and their servants and kin, like Abram on his journey to the land of Canaan. In October 1799 Boone led his family into St. Louis. Founded in 1764, St. Louis had become the center of Upper Louisiana's large fur trade, thanks to its location near where the Missouri flows into the Mississippi. Two years before Boone's arrival, Moses Austin had described St. Louis as "better built than any Town on the Missisipi," with "a Number of welthey Merch.t and an Extensive Trade, from the Missouri Illinois and upper parts of the Missisipi. Its fast improveing and will soon be a large place; the Town at this time Contains about 2000 Houses, most of which are of Stone, and some of them large but not Elegant." By contrast, Austin called Louisville "a detestable place," with only about "30 Houses but there is not an Elegant Hous in the place" and without "a Tavern in the place that deserves a better name than that of Grog Shop."[11]

The entrance of Boone and his relatives and friends into St. Louis was not stylish. One observer remembered that Boone "rode a sad looking horse [with] saddle bags, with Rifle on his shoulder, leather hunting shirt, and a couple of hunting knives in his belt" and was "accompanied by 3 or 4 hunting dogs."[12] But the officialdom at St. Louis greeted Boone in style. Trudeau was there, as was the French aristocrat who had succeeded him as lieutenant governor, the imposingly named Pierre Charles Dehault Delassus et de Deluzière, Knight of the Grand Cross of the Royal Order of St. Michael. The town garrison paraded in Boone's honor, with drums rolling and sabers drawn. While the Boones and their companions may have looked ragged, there were a lot of them. Trudeau's hope that Daniel Boone would be able to bring with him a large number of settlers, with more to follow, was being fulfilled. The Boone group looked like backwoodsmen—but that was what the Spanish needed as settlers. Boone and many of those with him were experienced hunters, fighters, and Indian traders, and they were willing to settle farther west on the Missouri than any existing settlement. The Femme Osage area was still wilderness when the Boones moved there. It was more than twenty-five miles west of St. Charles, which Trudeau had described as too far from St. Louis for any priest to offer to go there and as the residence of "savages, mongrels and the worst scoundrels" in the territory.[13] But Femme Osage's wild and western location made it an excellent place to attract trade with western Indians that would benefit the merchants of St. Louis and that might otherwise be siphoned off by the increasingly intrusive traders from Canada.

After the ceremonies Boone met privately with Delassus, giving him a list of fifteen American heads of family in his party. Delassus in turn promised not only to honor the commitments that Trudeau had made but also to make the Femme Osage area a separate administrative district, with Boone as its commandant and "syndic"—in effect, at once civil administrator, military leader, and judge of the district (or as Boone described himself in his official signatures, "Commander of the District of the femme Osage").[14] Boone's formal appointment as syndic was issued on June 11, 1800.[15]

Why did Boone, in his mid-sixties, undertake a move of hundreds of miles, to land that was still wild, still subject to Indian raids, and in Spanish territory? Legendary reasons are based on the myth of Boone as a loner, a noble savage who was happy only in remote wilderness. Boone was also undoubtedly bitter about his treatment and his failures in Kentucky. But there were also sound economic reasons as well as Boone's desire to continue doing what he did best and liked best.

Boone is said to have visited Cincinnati on his way out to Missouri and, when asked why he was leaving, to have replied: "Too many people! Too crowded! Too crowded! I want more elbow-room!"[16] One wonders why

Boone, driving cattle along the southern bank of the Ohio, would have crossed to Cincinnati on the north side—but the "more elbow-room!" cry sounds similar to what Boone had told an English traveler in 1797, that he was "unwilling . . . to live among men who were shackled in habits, and would not enjoy uncontrolled the free blessings which nature had bestowed upon them." Boone told the Englishman that he "was going to hunt for beavers in some unfrequented corner of the woods, where undisturbed he might pursue this amusement, and enjoy the pleasures arising from a secluded and solitary life."[17] Throughout his life Boone liked wilderness and hunting, and game was easier to come by in Missouri than in increasingly populated Kentucky. By the time he moved to Missouri, Kentucky's population (thanks in part to Boone's actions and example) had climbed over 200,000.[18] Game in Kentucky was much harder to find in 1799 than it had been in 1770, when Boone believed he was the only white man in all of Kentucky.

Boone's bitterness and the economic reasons for his move were intertwined. By 1799 he no longer owned more than a small fraction of the land he had claimed in Kentucky. His prospects of starting over again looked much better in Missouri than in Kentucky. Litigation against him in Kentucky was continuing, as evidenced by the 1798 warrant to take him into custody. Boone had appointed his nephew John Grant as an attorney-in-fact to defend lawsuits and conveyed to Grant his interest in a remaining tract on the Licking River, with instructions to sell it or deed it piecemeal to those with honest claims against him. Exhausted and embittered by litigation and by allegations that he had been incompetent or even fraudulent in his land dealings, Boone advised his children never to contest claims by others against the land he had thought was his, saying that "the suits, even if successful, would cost more time, money, and vexation than they would be worth."[19]

Boone moved to Missouri in part because of his desire to get away from his ongoing problems in Kentucky ("law-suits—sheriffs—and pressing demands") and his bitterness at his many failed ventures there.[20] He may also have resented the new generation of leaders in Kentucky. As the Indian threat receded, there was less need for the skills of frontiersmen such as Boone and Kenton. Many of the rich and well-educated Virginians who had conceived and sponsored the settlement of Kentucky and had claimed land there had prudently remained in Virginia during the fighting but moved out during the 1790s to develop their land and take up positions of leadership, while many of the old frontiersmen died off, emigrated farther west, or sank into relative obscurity.²¹ Some of those new leaders looked down their noses at frontiersmen. One of the gentry observed, when frontiersmen began to move from Kentucky to Missouri in the late 1790s, that "the rage among the poorer class of people here appears to be for the Spanish settlements"; another in the early 1800s said that the out-migration from Kentucky would "improve the morals of the state, as it will purge it of many of the *pioneers*."²² Boone may well have been aware of similar attitudes. He certainly knew that Governor Shelby had chosen men more prosperous than Boone to improve the Wilderness Road.

Boone also had strong economic inducements on the upside to make the move to Missouri. The Spanish were offering him a substantial amount of excellent land—land that should appreciate in value as Missouri, like Kentucky before it, became more settled. At a time when Boone was in no position to pay for land, the Spanish authorities told him they would grant him land for free. That price (or absence of price) must have sounded as right to Boone as it had been over thirty years earlier, when the British governor of West Florida was offering land for free to induce immigrants. There was also the opportunity to make a good living once Boone reached the Femme Osage—at the very least from hunting and trapping the game Daniel Morgan had told him about and perhaps, if licensed, by trading with the upstream Indians for the pelts they could harvest on the vast reaches of the Missouri's watershed. If the fur-trading families in St. Louis could get rich from the Indian trade, why not the Boones, who could set up a trading post closer to the Indians than St. Louis? As Jemima Boone was to tell her daughter, after the Spanish promised her father "ample Portions of Land for himself and family," he "pilled up Stakes, hearing of the Game and Indians in Misoura."²³

There was another economic inducement to the move: by moving to Missouri, Boone would gain clear and unfettered access to major markets, through the Mississippi and New Orleans. He knew from his own searing experience how hard it was, west of the Alleghenies, to bring goods to America's eastern towns and cities. He had lost a hoped-for fortune in 1788 trying to take ginseng up the Ohio River to get it to Philadelphia and the China trade. He knew how much it cost to haul peltry upriver on boats or on packhorses to the east. The logical way for a trans-Allegheny settler or hunter in or south of the Ohio Valley to get his goods to major markets was down the Mississippi to New Orleans. In an age before railroads or steamboats, in the words of Gen. Thomas Gage, "trade will go with the Stream."²⁴ But would

Boone, as an American, be free to ship to New Orleans? Filson in his *Discovery of Kentucke* said it would "be absurd to expect a free navigation of the Mississippi whilst the Spaniards are in possession of New Orleans," though the Spanish "may perhaps trade with us upon their own terms, while they think it consistent with their interest."[25] In 1780 the Kentucky land investor John May noted that "the Value of the Land here will much depend on the Convenience of Navigation," which was uncertain, "as the Spaniard are in Possession of all the lower Parts of the Missippi."[26] Unfettered access to trade at New Orleans was worth a great deal of money. In the late 1780s, for example, tobacco that sold for $2.00 or $2.50 per hundred pounds in Kentucky sold in New Orleans for $9.00 per hundred pounds.[27]

When Boone decided to move to Missouri, the trans-Allegheny Americans had recently seen how vulnerable their trade was to Spanish wishes. The Spanish closed the Mississippi to American navigation in 1784 and after several years allowed American boats to use the Mississippi only upon payment of a duty of 15 percent. In 1786 John Jay, the American secretary of foreign affairs, had reported to Congress that it should be possible to arrange a commercial treaty with Spain, if the United States would agree to give up the privilege of navigating the Mississippi for twenty-five or thirty years. Kentucky erupted in protest against this prospect. Some even discussed whether Kentucky should separate from the United States as a way of gaining untrammeled access to the Mississippi and New Orleans. James Wilkinson, who was a highly paid secret agent of the Spanish at the same time he was a general in the United States Army, urged the Spanish to close the Mississippi to the Americans, as a way of inducing Kentucky to separate from the United States and ally itself with Spain. The denial of navigation rights to Americans had the effect of further enriching Wilkinson, who had obtained from the Spanish an exemption from the denial.[28] Spanish officials in Louisiana used the threat of closing navigation rights as a lever "to negotiate secretly with the western people, their entire separation from the other states" and then to place the Kentuckians and the other westerners "under his Majesty's protection," with mercantile privileges at New Orleans.[29]

Not until 1795 did Spain, in the Treaty of San Lorenzo, covenant to give the United States free navigation on the Mississippi and the right of deposit at New Orleans—and even after that treaty was signed, the Spanish intendant in New Orleans in 1802 withdrew from American traders the right of deposit at New Orleans.[30] There would be no clearly lasting right to free trade down the river so long as New Orleans was in non-American hands. New Orleans was, as Thomas Jefferson put it, a place "the possessor of which is our natural and habitual enemy."[31] By becoming a settler in Spanish Upper Louisiana, Boone stood to be able to trade down the Mississippi whether Missouri stayed Spanish (even if Spain were to repudiate the 1795 treaty) or whether it became part of the United States.

The move to Missouri had important noneconomic benefits for Boone as well. Instead of running from creditors, moving from hunting camp to hunting camp in the backwoods of Kentucky and of what was to become West Virginia, Boone would be the respected head of a community, as he had been at Boone's Station years before, and a patriarch surrounded by relatives and descendants. The greater amount of wildlife on the Missouri River than in Kentucky meant not only economic benefits—game to eat and pelts to trade—but also that Boone would be able to continue the hunting and trapping he had loved since he was a child. In addition, moving had been part of Boone's life since his first moves in childhood from eastern Pennsylvania into the Shenandoah Valley of Virginia and out to the Yadkin Valley in North Carolina.

Was Boone, by moving to Spanish territory and becoming an official in the Spanish administration of Upper Louisiana, repudiating the United States? He probably was seeking to separate himself permanently from Kentucky. According to Nathan Boone, his father said "that when he left Kentucky, he did it with the intention of never stepping his feet upon Kentucky soil again; and if he was compelled to lose his head on the block or revisit Kentucky, he would not hesitate to chose the former."[32] But deciding not to go back to Kentucky was quite different than deciding to renounce the United States. Boone told one of his early biographers that he never would have thought to settle in Missouri "had he not firmly believed it would become a portion of the American republic."[33] This might be after-the-fact thinking, reflecting the biographer's desire, writing after Boone's death, to glorify the man. But U.S. policy at the time of Boone's move was not against Americans moving to Missouri. Thomas Jefferson, hearing of the Spanish handbills inviting American settlement, said, "I wish a hundred thousand of our inhabitants would accept" because "it may be the means of delivering to us peaceably what may otherwise cost a war."[34]

In fact, Boone was one of many thousands of Americans who moved to Missouri between 1784 and 1804.[35] Moses Austin in 1797, traveling to

Missouri to consider developing "the Richest Lead Mines in the World," noted that "the great advantages held out by the Government of Spain will soon make the Settlements on the Missouri Formidable. Land have already been granted to 1000 Famelies Near four Hundred of which have arrived from different parts of the United States."[36] Austin concluded his journal with a prophecy that in not many years "the Country I have pass.d in a state of Nature will be overspread with Towns and Villages, for it is Not possible a Country which has with in its self everything to make its settlers Rich and Happy can remain Unnoticed by the American people."[37]

When Austin arrived in Missouri, two years before Boone's arrival, some settlements in Missouri were already primarily American. An English traveler reported in April 1797 that at New Madrid, for example, under the "flattering temptation" of free land "many Americans have been induced to come and settle . . . and were it not for a few French and Spanish that are mixed with them, it might easily be mistaken for an American settlement."[38] The flood of American settlers into Missouri continued after Boone's arrival and after Spain in October 1800, drained by the expense of administering Louisiana and doubtless foreseeing the increasing difficulty of retaining it, agreed to transfer Louisiana to France, an arrangement not actually effected until 1803.[39] By 1804, the year in which Capt. Amos Stoddard arrived in St. Louis to take over the administration of Upper Louisiana from the French, under the terms of the 1803 Louisiana Purchase, American settlers made up about 60 percent of the population of Upper Louisiana.[40] Napoleon and his advisers must have felt pleased to have been able to get $15 million (over $280 million in today's money) from the United States for the province of Louisiana, much of which was already occupied by Americans. As the French foreign minister Talleyrand put it in 1803, the sale was "an advantageous arrangement for the inevitable loss of a country which war was about to place at the mercy of another nation [Great Britain, with which France was at war]."[41] The transaction was also advantageous to the United States. The purchase doubled the country's area, with acreage so vast that selling a small portion would fund repayment of borrowings to make the purchase. It also ensured American navigation of the Mississippi, ended the threat to American expansion posed by French ownership of Louisiana, and, as Jefferson saw it, provided a depository for Ohio Valley and other Indian tribes from east of the Mississippi.[42]

The Americans at the time of Boone's move to Missouri did not view

Boone as a traitor. In 1804 the perfidious Gen. James Wilkinson, while serving as one of the two United States commissioners for Louisiana, was to suggest to the Spanish authorities that as one of the steps to retain their territory west of the Missouri they should take prisoner the settlers with Boone or force them to leave Spanish territory. The Spanish governor of West Florida, paraphrasing Wilkinson's advice, warned his government that it was "a matter of the greatest importance for the American settlements in the Missouri River to be driven from it, even those which have been indirectly permitted"—noting in particular that "a person named Boone, who is the same one who first penetrated the wilderness of Kentucky, is at present settled on the Missouri, at a distance of fifty leagues from its confluence with the Mississippi, with a number of his adherents."[43] Moreover, when the Americans implementing the Louisiana Purchase took over the administration of Upper Louisiana, they appear not to have replaced Daniel Boone as commandant and syndic of the Femme Osage District for a time, which suggests they did not view him as a turncoat or enemy of the United States.[44] In 1804 Lieutenant Governor Delassus wrote to Capt. Amos Stoddard, his American successor, an evaluation of his subordinates, in which he described "Mr. Boone" as "a respectable old man, just and impartial": "He has already, since I appointed him, offered his resignation owing to his infirmities— Believing I know his probity I have induced him to remain in view of the confidence I have in him for the public good."[45] The Americans took control of Louisiana in ceremonies at New Orleans in December 1803, and Stoddard took over for the Americans at St. Louis on March 10, 1804.[46] Boone appears not to have been replaced in his position at Femme Osage until 1805, when the new American officials took office—among them Boone's son Daniel Morgan Boone, who became a justice of the peace and a judge on the Court of Quarter Sessions and Common Pleas.

Following the Louisiana Purchase, Boone was still regarded as the leader of his community. In May 1804 the Lewis and Clark expedition left St. Louis on its great journey to explore the vast lands the United States had purchased from France. Early on the expedition passed Boone's settlement, not far from St. Charles. Meriwether Lewis commented in his journal for May 20, 1804, on the extent of Boone's influence, saying the people "yeald passive obedience to the will of their temporal master, the Commandant."[47] A private in the expedition, Joseph Whitehouse, wrote three days later in a way that, while overblowing Boone's role in the opening of Kentucky, shows how

Boone was viewed by the general public: "Passed some Plantations, which is called Boons settlement lying on the North side of the River. This settlement was made by Colonel Daniel Boone, the person who first discover'd Kentucky, & who was residing at this place, with a number of his family and friends."[48]

Boone's move to Missouri and his change from Kentucky militia colonel to a syndic in the Spanish administration in Upper Louisiana once again illustrate how fluid and changing were the dynamics and loyalties on the frontier in Boone's time. We think of Missouri as completely American—and centrally American, at that. In 1799, however, the United States as a whole was new, and its jurisdiction did not extend beyond the Mississippi River. Missouri was still Spanish, and it was not clear who would end up controlling it—Spain, France, Britain, the United States, or perhaps the powerful Indian tribes still living in Missouri. In considering Boone's move to Missouri, as in considering many of his decisions, it does little good to think of Boone acting to fulfill some overriding political or philosophical objective such as to further the cause of America's westward expansion or, conversely, to repudiate America in the same way that he separated himself from Kentucky. It is more profitable to analyze the move in light of Boone's pragmatism and his predilections. The move to Missouri gave Boone chances to start over, to get some land for himself and his family, to lead a community, and to hunt and trap in the wilderness.

19

BOONE IN MISSOURI

ONCE IN MISSOURI, BOONE, AS SYNDIC, DID SOME JUDGING. MUCH more of his time was spent hunting and trapping and in the quest to perfect title to the land he thought he had been granted by the Spanish. Boone was growing older and frailer, but his reputation continued to grow across America and Europe.

The fragments that survive of Boone's work as syndic convey the roughness of the frontier and of the justice Boone dispensed. As his son Nathan put it, he "governed more by *equity* than by *law*."[1] Boone held court out in the open, under the shade of an elm that came to be known as the Judgment Tree. For petty offenses, according to one of Boone's nephews, Boone often gave the defendant a choice of being whipped on the spot and set free or being sent to the more settled and larger (though still small) community of St. Charles for trial in court. Many chose to be "whipped and cleared," as one story has it.[2]

Months after the Americans had assumed control over Lower and Upper Louisiana, in a case that presumably was sent on for trial at St. Charles, Boone signed a deposition that gives a flavor of frontier life in Missouri:

June 30th, 1804

This Day came before me Justice of the Peace for the District of the Femme Osage, Francis Woods Peter Smith & John Manley and made oath that on the 29th of June of said Month at the house of David Bryan a Certain James Meek and the Bearer hereof Bery Vinzant had some difference Which Came to blows and in the scuffle the said James Meek bit of a piece of Bery Vinzants Left Ear, further the

Deponent saith not Given under my hand and seal the day and Date
above written

Daniel Boone [seal][3]

One case too serious to be heard by a syndic in Femme Osage involved the
December 1804 killing of Will Hays, husband of Boone's daughter Susannah. Susannah had died in 1800 soon after the Boone party came to Missouri, felled by a "bilious fever" at the age of thirty-nine. One of her daughters married James Davis, and it was Davis who killed Will Hays, at Hays's
place on the Femme Osage Creek, not far from where Boone and Rebecca
lived. For decades Boone had worked closely with Hays, who had helped to
teach Boone writing and arithmetic and how to survey. Hays had become,
however, in Nathan's words, "a bad tempered, drinking man." After Susannah's death Hays drank even more heavily and had wild rages, including
ones directed at Davis. When Davis came on Hays's place to borrow a horse
in December 1804, Hays came out with a loaded rifle, and Davis went behind a tree. "All the trees in the world shan't save you," Hays said, aiming toward Davis and daring him to shoot. Davis jumped out from behind the tree
and fired. Hays, shot in the chest, died several hours later. One of the Hays
children, Daniel Boone Hays, the only witness to the killing, reported it to
Boone, who took Davis into St. Charles, posted bond for his release, and tes-
tified at the trial about Hays and his character. Davis was acquitted.[4]

Even after Boone ceased to be an official at Femme Osage, he continued to be a significant local figure—chosen as executor of estates and as a
resolver of disputes. He also played an ongoing role in defending the settlements. After the Louisiana Purchase, the territory of Louisiana in 1804 organized local militia. In 1806 James Wilkinson, the governor of the territory,
appointed Boone as the captain of the Sixth Company of the militia, in the
District of St. Charles. Nathan Boone was appointed an ensign, the third-
ranking officer in the company.[5]

Much of Boone's time in Missouri before 1813, when he was not out hunting, was spent on land on the Femme Osage Creek that had been granted to
his son Nathan, though Boone and Rebecca also lived for a time at their son
Daniel Morgan's house in the Femme Osage District. Nathan started with a
cabin in 1800, followed later that year by a "good substantial log house," and
several years later by a "commodious stone building," still standing in what

is now Defiance, Missouri—a house that was "built of hewn lime stone and offers the comforts of a city residence."[6] Boone and Rebecca moved in with Nathan and his family, before building, around 1805, a small house in Nathan's yard that was Boone's home until early 1813. Boone traded lead, powder, and dry goods for trappers' peltry, which he then sold in St. Louis.[7] He also helped Nathan on his building projects. Boone built himself a shop and did "all the needed smith work for the family" as well as making and repairing traps and guns, before he tired of it, disposed of his tools, and concentrated on hunting.[8]

Boone never stopped hunting and trapping, though his ailments and age restricted him more and more as the years went by. When he was at the Femme Osage, he hunted around home. In the late summer of 1801 or 1802 he joined his sons Nathan and Daniel Morgan on a deer hunt, getting skins for sale at St. Louis. He then went beaver trapping on the Bourbeuse River, perhaps twenty miles south of Nathan's house, with Derry Coburn, a Negro slave in his early twenties who belonged to Daniel Morgan. Boone enjoyed being with Derry. According to a Boone relative who knew them both, Derry "was a man of the same peculiar disposition which characterized Daniel Boone, non-communicative on the subject of his exploits."[9] That only partly describes Boone's loquacity. Boone liked to talk, to Derry and to friends and to sympathetic strangers, and he liked to reminisce. One visitor to Boone in Missouri said that "though at first reserved and barely answering questions respectfully, he soon became communicative, warmed up, and became animated in narrating his early adventures in the west."[10] But Boone talked when he felt like it, and unnecessary talking in the woods was not good for hunting or trapping. On a hunt or setting or checking traps, Boone and Derry could understand what each other was thinking without saying much. Boone did most of the trapping. Derry stretched the skins and was the cook and camp tender.[11] The trapping was good. In September 1802, for example, Nathan and another man, trapping perhaps 150 miles west of Nathan's house, caught nine hundred beaver.[12]

In October 1802 Boone, Derry, and Will Hays, Jr., went trapping on the Niangua River, over a hundred miles southwest of the Boone settlement on the Femme Osage. The farther west they went, the better the hunting and the trapping—and the more they intruded into Osage hunting grounds and threatened Osage profits as middlemen in the fur trade with tribes farther west. As the Shawnees had fought to keep intruders out of their hunting

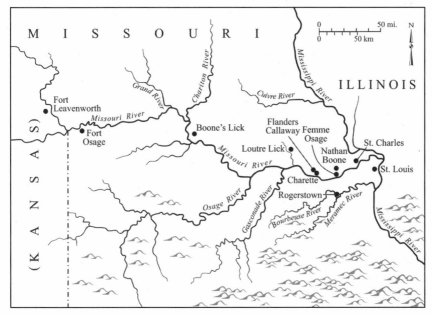

Boone Country in Missouri
Map by Mary Lee Eggart

grounds, so did the Osages, who were a mightier nation in Missouri than the Shawnees had been in Kentucky when Boone first hunted there. Thomas Jefferson, who had authorized the Louisiana Purchase and commissioned Lewis and Clark to explore the new American territory, said of the Osages: "The truth is they are the great nation South of the Missouri, their possession extending from thence to the Red River."[13] The Osages in 1804 numbered about sixty-three hundred, including some fifteen hundred warriors and were in firm control of the southern prairie–Plains—most of Missouri, except its eastern quarter; all of northwestern Arkansas; and most of Oklahoma, apart from the panhandle.[14] Their men were proud, well proportioned, and tall—six feet or more. Washington Irving described the Osages as "the finest-looking Indians in the West."[15] Until the early nineteenth century whites came to Osage country to trade but did not control Osage territory.[16]

The Osages were well armed from trading furs for guns, powder, and shot with French traders in St. Louis. Warfare was central to their way of life. Osages believed that "after death they will go to another village. If they die on the battlefield they will go to a village where they will find plenty of horses and game. If they die of illness they are relegated to a miserable village."[17] These were the people on whose hunting lands Boone and his companions were intruding in 1802. The result was foreseeable, particularly since the Osages at the time were facing incursions into their hunting grounds not only from whites like Boone but also from other tribes, including Shawnees, Cherokees, Chickasaws, Choctaws, Delaware, and Illinois, driven out of the east by the ever-expanding American settlements, as well as from northern tribes such as the Sauks, backed by Canadian fur traders.

One day when Derry was cooking a venison stew, Hays was out trapping, and Boone had just left the camp to look at his traps, eight or ten Osages ran into camp, yelling and shooting off their guns. Derry ran. Boone, seeing the Indians firing into the air, figured they were not seeking to kill him and his companions but to scare them away and take the goods from the camp. So Boone, by this time sixty-seven years old, rode back into camp. The Indians pulled him from his horse and took his coat. Boone called Derry back to the camp. The Indians took their furs and the powder in Boone's horn, tasted the venison Derry was cooking but found it way too peppery for their liking, and rode off. Boone had concealed some powder, and Derry had secreted a chunk of lead. They had enough ammunition to continue trapping until spring (though they had to hide in a snowed-in cave for days to avoid a large party of Indians, and at one point a steel trap sprang shut on one of Boone's hands and mangled it; the hand nearly froze before Boone got back to his hunting camp and, with Derry's help, was able to get the trap off). When Boone and Derry finally returned home, they brought with them about two hundred beaver skins.[18] The incident with the Osages must have reminded Boone of the time in 1769 when Captain Will and his Shawnees took the pelts from Boone's hunters and told them to go home and never come back to Shawnee hunting grounds.

For a time Boone, old and subject to crippling rheumatism, did not hunt or trap much in Osage territory. In 1808, however, he went on a fall and winter beaver hunt with Will Hays, Jr., and Derry, going almost two hundred miles upriver on the Missouri, not far from what was to become Kansas City. A solitary Indian invited them to his camp, rode ahead of them, and came back with twenty or thirty whooping Indians—presumably Osages, it being Osage country. Boone and his companions wheeled their horses and rode off in a hurry but had to cut loose their traps and the skins and furs they had taken.[19]

Nathan Boone, who hunted often in central and western Missouri, also had unpleasant encounters with Indians. In 1803 Indians took from him and his fellow hunters most of their furs as well as four horses. In November 1804 Osages took from Nathan and his brother-in-law Matthias "Tice" Van Bibber their horses, blankets, coats, and all of their furs (Nathan alone had caught fifty-six beavers and twelve otters), and within minutes another group of Indians—Osages, Nathan believed—forced them to turn over most of their powder, balls, and flints. Nathan and Tice traveled back east on foot for seventeen days in bitter cold, often knee-deep in snow, with no meat, before they came upon the salt spring that was to become known as Boone's Lick. Nathan managed to kill and roast a huge panther and make vests for himself and Tice out of the skin. They finally found a camp of white hunters, including Nathan's nephew James Callaway. Nathan and Tice thawed themselves out and ate up, before walking the rest of their hundred-mile trip home. They arrived on Christmas Eve. Olive Boone told Draper, with an evident edge, "It was the first Christmas [Nathan] had spent at home since our marriage, and I had to thank the Indians for that." Nathan suffered from the effect of the exposure on that trip for the rest of his life. He and Tice had been obliged to cut up their deerskin leggings to patch the ice-worn holes in their moccasins, until their leggings were nearly gone and their legs were exposed to the snow and the cold. Tice Van Bibber never recovered from the ordeal and died within two or three years.[20]

Nathan Boone realized there was a significant commercial opportunity at the salt licks he had encountered on that cold trek. Starting in 1805, he and his brother Daniel Morgan Boone began large-scale salt-boiling operations at Boone's Lick, ultimately producing a hundred bushels of salt a day—with frequent interruptions from Indians stealing and killing the beef cattle that were being driven to the works to feed the salt-boilers. The saltworks, which the Boone brothers sold around 1811, helped to encourage a flood of white settlement around Boone's Lick, more than a hundred miles west of Femme Osage. The trail worked into the ground between Boone's Lick and St. Charles ultimately grew into the Boone's Lick Road, a main route for settlers moving into central Missouri after the War of 1812.[21] Timothy Flint, in St. Charles at the time, reported that from 1816 through 1819 "the whole current of immigration set towards . . . Boon's Lick. . . . Boon's Lick was the common centre of hopes, and the common point of union of the people. Ask one of them whither he was moving, and the answer was, 'To Boon's Lick, to be sure.'"[22] The Boone name and reputation contributed to what Peck, an early Boone biographer who interviewed Boone in 1818, described as an "an avalanche": "It seemed as though Kentucky and Tennessee were breaking up and moving" into the lower Missouri Valley, with the Boone's Lick country as the new promised land—with many of the newcomers, according to Peck, "drawn by [Boone's] example and influence."[23] Once again, the Boones were spearheading the westward drive of American settlement.

The Osages' fight against incursions into their territory was as destined to failure as had been the Shawnees' efforts in Kentucky and Ohio. The flood of intruders—white settlers and Indians driven out of the east—was overwhelming, and the Osages were weakened by disunity, fostered in part by whites. The main trading houses in St. Louis, led by the Chouteau family, backed the northern branch of the Osages; white traders on the Arkansas River backed a southern, or Arkansas, branch. The fragmented Osages ended up agreeing to give up their claims to lands in Missouri, in successive treaties in 1808, 1818, and 1825, and moved west into Oklahoma.[24] Nathan Boone, though only twenty-seven, played a key role in the 1808 treaty. As a captain in the St. Charles militia, he guided the American troops under Gen. William Clark (the Clark of Lewis and Clark) to a site almost 250 miles west of St. Charles, where the Americans built a fort and trading post that came to be called Fort Osage. There Nathan met with the Osage chief White Hair and encouraged the Osages to come to the fort to agree to the treaty and to receive trade goods.[25]

The Shawnees were one of the many Indian groups intruding into Osage territory in the 1790s and early 1800s. Louis Lorimier, who had been part of the Shawnee raid that had taken Boone and the salt-boilers captive in 1778, in the early 1790s led a group of Shawnees and Delawares to Cape Girardeau, a hundred miles or so south of St. Louis on the Mississippi, where the Spanish gave them a large land grant. By the late 1790s there were some twelve hundred Shawnees and six hundred Delawares on the grant. Like Boone, Lorimier became an official in the Spanish administration in Louisiana.[26] Other Shawnees moved into Missouri, until soon after the War of 1812 there were an estimated fourteen hundred Shawnees in Missouri—far more than the roughly eight hundred still in Ohio.[27]

It is possible that Lorimier and Boone, the old adversaries, crossed paths in Missouri. It is certain that Boone saw other Shawnees who had been at

Old Chillicothe during Boone's captivity there and who had since moved to a village across the Missouri River from St. Charles. Boone also met with the salt-boiler captive Joseph Jackson, who had rejoined these Shawnees under his Shawnee name Fish after his unhappy attempt to reenter the white world in Kentucky. Boone visited the Shawnees and Fish at their hunting camp and at their village near St. Charles.[28] The Shawnees visited Boone at Femme Osage from time to time. A Boone granddaughter remembered seeing unfamiliar horses tied up in front of the house. "Your grandfather has got some visitors, old friends," Rebecca told her, "some of the identical old Shawanoes with whom he was a prisoner."[29] The granddaughter remembered that the Indians gave Boone a pony that became a great favorite with the granddaughters.[30] Boone and the Shawnees went on local hunts together and reminisced about old times. "Dan," one of them said, "you remember when we had you prisoner, and our chief adopted you as his son, and you and he made an agreement that we would all go to Boonsburrow, and you would make them all surrender, and, all bury the Tomahack & all live like Brothers & Sisters." Boone did not deny any of it.[31]

Boone got on well with the Indians. Like many Indian men, he liked hunting and roaming the woods more than farming. Boone would have agreed with much of what the Osage chief Big Chief said in 1820, declining to adopt the whites' farming life:

I see and admire your manner of living, your good warm houses, your extensive fields of corn, your gardens, your cows, oxen, workhouses, wagons, and a thousand machines, that I know not the use of. I see that you are able to clothe yourself, even from weeds and grass. In short, you can do almost what you chose. You whites possess the power of subduing almost every animal to your use. You are surrounded by slaves. Everything about you is in chains. I hear I should exchange my presents for yours. I too should become a slave. Talk to my sons, perhaps they may be persuaded to adopt your fashions, or at least to recommend them to their sons; but for myself, I was born free, was raised free, and wish to die free. I am perfectly content with my condition. The forests and rivers supply all the calls of nature in plenty.[32]

Yet while Boone liked hunting in the wilderness in Missouri, he also pursued land ownership—with results almost as disappointing as they had been in Kentucky. Lieutenant governors Trudeau and Delassus had promised Boone 1,000 arpents, about 850 acres, of land in the Femme Osage District. After the United States acquired Louisiana, however, Congress in 1805 created a Board of Commissioners to determine land title in Louisiana, under a law promising to honor grants for "actual settlers on the land." Boone, never fond of farming, had never farmed his grant and had stayed with his sons Daniel Morgan and Nathan, rather than building a house on his own tract. When Boone appeared before the commissioners in February 1806, his excuse for not having farmed the tract he claimed was that Lieutenant Governor Delassus had told him that "being commandant of the said district, he need not trouble himself about the cultivating" requirement, because "by the commission he held (of commandant of said district), he was not considered as coming within the meaning of said laws." But Boone produced no writing from Delassus to verify this claimed waiver. Nor did it help him that Delassus had made many grants of Louisiana land, totaling over a million acres, to himself, his relatives, and his friends, after Spain had ceded Louisiana to France, and that many of the grants had been backdated to before the cession. The board had been set up in part to undo such grants and by doing so to free up acreage for sale to other settlers.

In 1809 Boone heard from John Coburn, whom he had known back in Kentucky in the 1780s and who now was a judge and influential political figure in the territory of Louisiana, that the board would not grant an exception to the requirement that the granted tract had to have been occupied and improved. In December 1809 the board formally rejected Boone's claim.[33] Several of his relatives fared better. Daniel Morgan Boone was confirmed in his ownership of six hundred arpents, Squire Boone of seven hundred arpents, and Flanders Callaway of eight hundred arpents.[34] Once again, the prospect of substantial land ownership was slipping from Boone's grasp. Judge Coburn and others worked on a petition to Congress for a bill to grant him land in Missouri (despite the board's conclusion), based on all Boone had done to open up the west for American settlement, and on a similar memorial seeking the Kentucky legislature's support of the petition to Congress. To assist this effort, Boone dictated the story of his life to his grandson John Boone Callaway, a son of Flanders and Jemima Callaway.

Boone kept on hunting and trapping—more trapping than hunting, because his eyesight was not as good as it had been. He was frequently stricken with bouts of rheumatism, at times so badly that, as he wrote Judge Coburn,

he was "Deep in Markury"—presumably meaning that he was dosing himself with mercurous chloride, or calomel, in an attempt to lessen the pain of
his rheumatism.[35] His relatives sought to dissuade him from the woods. His
nephew Daniel Boone Bryan told him he was "too old to be going any more a
trapping, and ought now to be staying with his family." Boone replied: "Dan'l,
you know I have never been a farmer, and I cannot make anything by cultivating the soil. My wife is getting old and needs some little coffee and other
refreshments, and I have no other way of paying for them but by trapping."[36]

So Boone went out again with Derry. This may well have been the winter
hunt in 1808–9 when the Indians took his traps and furs. Boone became so
sick that he thought his time had come. With Derry's help he walked to the
crest of a hill and "marked out the ground in the shape and size of a grave."[37]
He gave Derry detailed instructions on how to bury him if he died. His body
was to be washed and laid straight and "wrapped up in one of the cleanest
blankets." He told Derry how to dig the grave and mark it and asked him to
cover it with wood poles laid sidewise, to keep the animals from getting him.[38]
Perhaps Boone was thinking of how the wolves in 1773 had gotten at the body
of his dead son James. According to Derry, Boone gave these instructions
"with entire calmness, and as if he was giving instructions about ordinary
business."[39] But Boone got better and made it home and lived to hunt again.

Reminders of mortality were pressing on him. More and more of Boone's
close kin were dying. His daughter Susannah—the frisky untamable Susannah, mother of ten children—had died in 1800. In 1802 his daughter Levina,
Joseph Scholl's wife, died in Kentucky at thirty-six, leaving eight children,
who came out with Scholl to Missouri. Boone's youngest daughter, Rebecca,
who had been weak and consumptive, died in 1805 in Kentucky, at thirty-
seven, the mother of seven children. Her husband, Philip Goe, drank himself to death soon thereafter.[40] It was hard to be cheerful, but Boone kept going. His spirits were lifted by a visit from his old Kentucky friend, the giant
woodsman Simon Kenton, who came out to Missouri to see him. Boone was
chopping wood when Kenton came by. Boone burst into tears when he saw
him. Kenton had lost all of his land after protracted litigation in Kentucky
and had even spent time in debtor's prison. But the two spent a happy week
or two together—as Nathan Boone put it, "The old pioneers seemed to enjoy
themselves finely in recounting their old Kentucky troubles and hardships."[41]

In 1810 two other old companions from Kentucky, Michael Stoner and
James Bridges, stopped by Boone's place on their way to hunt farther up

the Missouri—and Boone could not resist joining them. They set out in the fall, accompanied by Flanders Callaway and his slave Mose, Will Hays, Jr., and Derry, and came back down the river in early 1811 with a load of beaver pelts. Derry was rowing one of the boats, with Boone at the tiller, bound for St. Louis to seek a decent price for their furs. It is not clear how far up the Missouri the party had gone. Stoner's son said they went "high up the Missouri." Hays's son said his father and Boone went as far as the Yellowstone— which would have meant all the way to what is now the eastern part of Montana, a trip of improbable length and hardship for a man of Boone's age. But even if the boats made it no farther than Kansas, that was a long haul for a man in his mid-seventies.[42] ·

An officer stationed at Fort Osage, near Missouri's western border, in 1816 wrote to the newspapers: "We have been honored by a visit from Col. Boone, the first settler of Kentucky; he lately spent two weeks with us. . . . The colonel cannot live without being in the woods. He goes a hunting twice a year to the remotest wilderness he can reach; and hires a man to go with him, whom he binds in written articles to take care of him and bring him home, dead or alive." According to the officer, Boone left Fort Osage bound upstream to the Platte River. The account jibes with Peck's report that Boone in April 1816 went to Fort Osage and on to the Little Platte, as well as with Nathan Boone's account that in April 1816 Boone hired a woodsman known as Indian Philips to go on a hunt up the Missouri. Looking for beaver, they got as far as twenty miles above Fort Leavenworth before Boone fell ill and had to return home. At about the same time Boone reportedly said he planned to take "two or three whites and a party of Osage Indians, and visit the salt mountains. lakes and ponds, and see the natural curiosities of the country along the mountains. The salt-mountain is but 5 or 600 miles west of this place."[43] At eighty-one or eighty-two Boone was apparently still thinking of new lands to the west—and perhaps of getting back into the salt business.

Yet age and frailty were finally catching up with Boone. When the British during the War of 1812 stirred up the Indians in Missouri and several settlers were killed by Indian raids, Boone played only a spectator's part in the fighting. His sons Nathan and Daniel Morgan both served as captains—Nathan leading a company of mounted rangers in the U.S. Army, Daniel Morgan a militia company that built fortified posts to protect the settlers—but Boone himself was too old. There are stories that he volunteered for service at the beginning of the war and was turned down (being seventy-eight years old at the time).[44] In 1815, however, when a nearby cabin was attacked, with three children mortally tomahawked and the father badly wounded with a ball in the groin, Boone, aged eighty, came over, probed for the bullet, extracted it, dressed the wound, and went outside to scout if the Indians were still in the area.[45] And Boone did have to "fort up" several times during the War of 1812, on rumors of imminent Indian attack. On one of those hurried trips down-river to Daniel Morgan's fortified station, a boat holding the autobiography that Boone had dictated to his grandson overturned, and the book and most of Boone's other records were lost in the waters of the Missouri River.[46]

But if the actual Daniel Boone was growing frailer, his reputation and his legend were continuing to grow. Pirated versions of Filson's book were still selling in Europe. In America Daniel Bryan, who may have been a cousin of Boone's wife, Rebecca, in 1813 published a 250-page epic poem, *The Mountain Muse: Comprising the Adventures of Daniel Boone and the Power of Virtue and Refined Beauty.* In 1816 Boone's great-niece Harriet Boone read Boone the poem, which depicts him as having been selected by an angel of God to settle the American frontier:

> With meteor-swiftness, from the council-dome,
> High through the azure heights of Atmosphere,
> His lofty way the mission'd Seraph winged;
> Till poised above the Carolinian hills,
> He sought with searching view, th'adventurous Boone.[47]

Bryan's endless iambic pentameter rolls on with an extravagance that makes even Filson's prose seem restrained. He depicts, among other scenes, the one in which Boone and his traveling companions for the first time look out on the rolling plains of Kentucky's bluegrass country:

> Lo! Now the farthest mountain-ledge they scale,
> And from its breezy summit raptured see,
> Kentucky's rolling Hills and broad Campaigns!
> Prophetic transports thrill'd their kindling hearts,
> Unwonted ebullitions warm'd their blood,
> And God's Omnipotence and Wisdom waked
> Profoundest adoration of their souls;
> As in continued prospect they beheld
> Green-mantled Groves and blossom-tinted Knolls,

Of their wide-ranging Vision, and survey'd
Through prescient Fancy's telescopic tube,
Republic-institutions rising round
The rich Expanse, beneath the angelic aid,
Of Conquest-crown'd Columbian Liberty.[48]

Having heard Bryan's poem, Boone said he regretted that he "could not sue him for slander." He added that all such works "ought to be left until the person was put in the ground."[49] But the growing Boone legend—however distasteful its excesses may have been to Boone—did not hurt the ongoing efforts of his allies in Washington and elsewhere to further his petition to Congress for a land grant in Missouri. The petition, presumably written primarily by Boone's friend Judge Coburn, was far from understated:

> Your petitioner has spent a long life in exploring the wilds of North America, and has, by his own personal exertions, been greatly instrumental in opening the road to civilization in the immense territories attached to the United States. . . .
>
> But, while your petitioner has thus opened the way to thousands, to countries possessed of every natural advantage, and although he may have gratified to excess his thirst for discovery, he has to lament that he has not derived those personal advantages which his exertions would seem to have merited. . . .
>
> He approaches the august assemblage of his fellow-citizens with a confidence inspired by that spirit which has led him so often to the deep recesses of the wilds of America, and he flatters himself that he, with his family, will be induced to acknowledge that the United States knows how to appreciate and will encourage the efforts of her citizens, in enterprises of magnitude, from which proportionate public good may be derived.

The petition, coupled with Boone's extraordinary achievements in opening up the American west, did the trick. The bill granting Boone land in Missouri was reported out of the Senate committee favorably in January 1810. The House Committee on Public Lands in December 1813 recommended that the House confirm Boone's ownership of 1,000 arpents of land in the Femme Osage District, noting that Boone had "rendered to his country arduous and useful services." It may be that the petition was originally for 10,000 acres of the finest land in Missouri, but the delegate from Missouri told Congress that all Boone wanted was for Congress to confirm the original grant of 1,000 arpents. That was what Congress did. On February 10, 1814, President James Madison signed the bill into law. For a brief time Boone owned about 850 acres of Missouri land. By May 1815, however, he had sold the land off, with most of the proceeds going to Kentuckians who had read about the grant to Boone and came to Missouri to assert claims relating to Boone's title warranties on Kentucky land conveyed by him.[50] Boone was punctilious about paying his debts, no matter how old and stale—if the debts were real ones and if he had funds. The last claimant from Kentucky alleged that Boone had given his wife, when she was an orphan child, some land that she eventually had to relinquish because of an earlier or more precise entry by someone else. Boone said he had no land or funds and told the claimant: "[You have] come a great distance to suck a bull and I reckon you will have to go home dry."[51]

20

LAST DAYS

TOUGH AS BOONE WAS, HE WAS MORTAL. AFTER 1800 HE MUST HAVE been increasingly aware of his mortality. By 1805 three of his daughters had died. He was dealt a harder blow in 1813, when Rebecca, his wife for fifty-six years, died. For seven years Boone and Rebecca had shared a cabin on Nathan's land, and Boone's age and rheumatism kept the two of them close together for a longer period than ever before. As in past winters, Boone and Rebecca early in 1813 traveled together to the Callaways' sugar maple grove to join in the sugar making. Rebecca—the robust Rebecca, the mother of ten, the care provider—fell ill. Boone took her to the Callaways' house, but she died within a week, on March 18, 1813, aged seventy-three.[1] Boone often described her death as an "inexpressible loss."[2] It may have been that it took Rebecca's death to make Boone, who had traveled so far away from Rebecca so often and for so long, aware of how much he loved and relied on her—for family, common sense, warmth, humor, support, and partnership.

Boone's growing infirmities limited what he could do. He wanted to keep on with hunting and trapping, but rheumatism cramped his ability to get about. His hearing was going too, and his eyesight was no longer keen. In 1818 newspapers all over the country, as well as in Europe, copied a bogus story reporting that Boone had been found dead at a deer lick, kneeling by a stump on which he had rested his cocked rifle, poised for firing. Told about the story, Boone said the whole thing was impossible—his eyes were not good enough for hunting, though he could still trap.[3]

Boone kept on thinking about more hunting, of the long trips he had taken with rifle and powder horn. In November 1817, at the age of eighty-three, he set off on horseback with Nathan's son James on a hunting trip, packing a gun, a kettle, traps, and provisions. On the first day they went about thirteen miles from the house of Flanders and Jemima Callaway before making a shelter in the dark. Two inches of snow fell overnight. Young James managed to catch bare-handed a wild duck that landed near their campfire. They ate the duck for breakfast and pushed on another thirty miles to the northwest over the next two days, in biting cold, to Loutre Lick. Boone had intended to go on another thirty miles to the south fork of the Salt River, with the hope of camping for a few weeks and going after bear, deer, turkey, beaver, and perhaps an occasional buffalo. But the cold was too much for him. He stayed at the home of a granddaughter on Loutre Lick, while James Boone went back home to Nathan and Olive. Hearing that Boone was sick to the point of dying, Nathan ordered a coffin to be built and set off to Loutre Lick in a light carriage, to take his father's body back. He was "agreeably surprised" to find that his father was alive, recovering, and able in a few days to ride home.[4]

Boone's physical limitations did not keep him from talking about going out hunting again. As John Mason Peck, who interviewed Boone in 1818, put it, "Hunting was a ruling passion" for Boone.[5] Even after the aborted hunt with his grandson, Boone kept working on a powder horn, scraping it thin with a piece of glass so the level of the powder inside could be seen. He told a visitor he would need the horn for his fall hunt. When he put the horn aside, the master of the house, out of Boone's hearing, told the visitor that Boone had been working on that powder horn for five years, for a fall hunt "still in the future."[6] According to one of Boone's friends in Missouri, Boone's "friendship for the gun, & trap, & scouring the woods for discovery, continued till the last; and his friends, by stratagem, had to prevent his indulgence, when too debilitated to encounter them."[7]

But if Boone talked of hunting, he also prepared for his own end. When he came back with Nathan from his aborted hunt with his grandson James, Boone, according to Nathan, "went to see the coffin that had been hastily provided for him. He thought it too rough and uncouth, and soon after he had a much better one made of cherry, according to his own directions": "He took it to my house and kept it in the attic, greatly to the fear of all the little folks in the house. He would frequently visit and inspect it to see that no accident or injury befell it."[8] Boone directed that the new coffin be identical to the one he had ordered for Rebecca and had it built by the man who had built Rebecca's. A Boone granddaughter remembered that Boone would get his coffin "down from the garret, where it was kept, and examine it frequently, rub and polish it up, and coolly whistle while doing so." He scared a young girl in the neighborhood by lying down in the coffin "to show how well it fit him" and told people he "had taken many a nice nap in it." The rougher coffin that Nathan had ordered when Boone fell ill on Loutre Creek was put into service to bury a Boone relative who died on a visit to Missouri.[9]

Boone probably never returned to Kentucky in his old age. There are stories that he went back there to pay off his remaining debts, after he sold off the land Congress had awarded him in Missouri. Peter Houston said old Boone in Kentucky repaid two pounds that Houston had given him just before Boone moved to Missouri.[10] Houston's grandson in 1887 said he had been told over fifty years earlier that Boone forced on a man named Joseph Trotter money that Boone had borrowed from Trotter's father, saying, "I have come here to pay my debts and I will not leave here indebted to any man."[11] These stories, recited decades after Boone's death, sound mythical. After 1815 Boone was not often well enough for long trips, and he had unhappy memories of Kentucky, of litigation and lost land claims. Nathan Boone, a man of precise memory befitting his training as a surveyor and topographer and his years leading a company of dragoons through unmapped Indian country, was adamant that his father not only never went back to Kentucky but also said he would rather lose his head on the block than do so.[12] Boone told Judge David Todd in Missouri "that he abandoned Kentucky in despair of ever enjoying any land there, and declared, on this side of the Mississippi, he would never recross it."[13]

One who claimed to have seen Boone in Kentucky, after the War of 1812, was John James Audubon, who described Boone as "stout, hale and athletic": "The stature and general appearance of this wanderer of the western forests approached the gigantic. His chest was broad and prominent; his muscular powers displayed themselves in every limb."[14] Audubon, however, often said things that were more colorful than true. The illegitimate son of a French sea captain and a chambermaid in Saint-Domingue, he claimed to be the son of a French admiral and a Spanish lady who owned a plantation near New Orleans. He also had told a bemused group of Edinburgh naturalists that American rattlesnakes could travel on the ground as fast as squirrels, climb to the highest branches of trees, and kill by constricting their prey—all interesting, none of it factual.[15] By the time of Audubon's purported meeting with Boone in Kentucky, Boone was not the robust giant whom Audubon described and painted but was rheumatic, frail, had poor vision, and weighed only about 155 pounds.[16]

More likely than not, Boone as an old man stayed in Missouri. Bits of Kentucky land litigation followed him there. Twice in 1817 his deposition was taken in Missouri in cases involving land in Kentucky. He was eighty-two, but his depositions reveal a remarkable recall, in one case about trails near the Blue Licks that he had taken in 1776 and 1780, in the other about a salt lick he had seen in 1775.[17] He still did some trapping and shot deer that blundered into range. Much of his time was devoted to being a patriarch to many children and far more grandchildren and great-grandchildren. The young, when they were grown up, remembered old Boone, his hair white, still able, even after his short-term memory had faltered, to recall the old days in Pennsylvania, North Carolina, and Kentucky. Peck, who several times interviewed Boone as an old man , reported that his clothes were homemade, "his manners were gentle," his "voice was soft and melodious," a smile "frequently played over his features in conversation," and "an irritable expression was never heard" from him.[18] Boone, who had sung songs as a young man when he believed himself completely alone in the wilderness of Kentucky, now sang songs to his great-grandchildren such as this one:

> Possum up a gum tree
> Raccoon in the hollow
> Pretty girls at our house
> As fat as they can wallow.[19]

The old country song tells of abundance—of game, of girls. Was Boone also thinking of the beauty and buxom abundance of Rebecca, as she had been years ago?

After Rebecca's death Boone read the Bible more. According to Nathan: "In his latter days my father was a great student of the Bible. He was seldom seen reading any other book and fully believed in the great truths of Christianity. He seemed most partial towards the Presbyterians, although he disliked the unkind differences too often manifested by different Christian sects. . . . His worship was in secret. Whenever preaching was in the neighborhood, he made it a point to attend and well remembered what he had heard and read."[20] "His worship was in secret" sounds like a nice way of saying that Boone was not a regular and demonstrative churchgoer.

There were few regular churchgoers in Kentucky when Boone lived there. One historian estimates that by the late 1790s only about 5 to 10 percent of Kentuckians belonged to a Christian church. David Barrow, a Baptist preacher in Kentucky, noted in his journal in 1795, "Of all the denominations, the Deists, Nothingarians and anythingarians are the most numerous."[21] But interest in religion grew in Kentucky and Missouri in the early nineteenth century, thanks in part to the torrent of settlers and the influx of preachers, including spellbinding revivalists. Religion on the frontier received a further boost from the enormous earthquakes, starting on December 16, 1811, centered near New Madrid, Missouri. One of the quakes, felt as far away as Boston, had an estimated magnitude of more than 8 on the Richter scale. A New Madrid resident described being awakened at 2 a.m. by a "very awful noise, resembling loud but distant thunder, . . . followed, in a few minutes, by the complete saturation of the atmosphere with sulphurious vapor, causing total darkness," and then hearing "the screams of the affrighted inhabitants, running to and fro, not knowing where to go, or what to do—the cries of the fowls, and beasts of every species—the cracking of falling trees, and the roaring of the Mississippi—the current of which was retrograde for a few minutes."[22] A quake big enough to make the Mississippi flow upstream was big enough to put the fear of God in many Missourians. According to a writer who came to New Madrid a few years later, the people of New Madrid "had been noted for their profligacy and impiety. In the midst of these scenes of terror, all, Catholics and Protestants, praying and profane, . . . betook themselves to the voice of prayer."[23]

Although Boone did not mention the New Madrid quakes in his few surviving writings from this period, the deaths of family members and friends and his own debility gave him plenty of other reasons to ponder last things. His interest in religion was not new. Years before he had even experimented a little with spiritualism but found it did not work. According to Nathan, Boone and his friend William Hill, who had gone with Boone to Florida and later into Kentucky, "made an agreement that whoever should die first would return and give the other information about the spirit world. Hill died first, but Father used to say he never received the promised intelligence from the spirit world."[24]

Boone's was a steady and straightforward religious belief, though not that of a regular churchgoer. His early biographer Timothy Flint, a clergyman by training, who interviewed Boone in Missouri in 1816, wrote: "It is due to truth to state, that Boone, little addicted to books, knew but little of the bible. . . . He worshipped, as he often said, the Great Spirit—for the woods were his books and his temple; and the creed of the red men naturally became his."[25] Another early biographer, the Baptist minister Peck, who interviewed Boone two years after Flint, wrote similarly: "In a general sense [Boone] was a believer in Christianity as a revelation from God in the sacred Scriptures, but never joined any church. His habits of mind were contemplative, and he reverenced the Deity in his works."[26]

Nor was Boone a revivalist. Other Boones and Bryans got caught up in the "Come to Jesus" excitement of the camp meetings and the surge of revivalism in Missouri in Boone's last years. Jemima and her husband, Flanders Callaway, helped to found the Friendship Baptist Church in Charette, Missouri. Nathan's daughter Delinda married a "hardshell" Baptist preacher. Boone's nephew Squire was a Baptist lay preacher who organized churches in Virginia and Kentucky. There are no stories, however, of Boone getting the jerks or speaking in tongues at a camp meeting or undergoing a conversion experience. Instead, when a Baptist preacher asked Boone, "[Had there not come a time] when you experienced a change in your feelings towards the Savior?" Boone answered, "No, sir, I have always loved God ever since I could recollect."[27]

In 1816, three years after Rebecca died, Boone heard of the death of his older brother Samuel, husband of Sarah Day Boone, who had taught Boone to read and write years ago back in Pennsylvania. Boone wrote Sarah Boone a letter that sums up his religious and ethical beliefs: "How we Live in this World and what Chance we Shall have in the next we know Not[.] for my part I am as ignerant as a Child [.] all the Relegan I have [is] to Love and fear god, beleve in Jesus Christ, Dow all the good to my Nighbour and my Self that I can, and Do as Little harm as I Can help and trust on gods marcy for the Rest, and I Beleve god never made a man of my prisipel to be lost."[28] The spelling in the letter—one of Boone's last writings—may be in part phonetic, but the words were words to live by, even in the midst of change.[29]

And the changes Boone was seeing around him were immense. The population of Missouri grew tenfold from the time Boone arrived in 1799 to when he died in 1820. Many of the settlers in Missouri by 1820 lived well west of where Boone lived, which had been the westernmost edge of settlement when he arrived. Kentucky's population—only perhaps 200 settlers in 1775—was over a half-million in 1820. Indians had been forced west, not only out of Kentucky and Ohio but largely out of Missouri—a relocation made much more feasible by America's acquisition of vast western landholdings in the Louisiana Purchase. By 1820 in Missouri non-Indians outnumbered

Indians more than three to one, the once-fearsome Osages had lost most of their land, and there was increasing pressure to force the Shawnees to trade their Spanish land grant in eastern Missouri for land west of Missouri.[30] Game in Missouri and east of the Mississippi had been largely killed off, and wilderness had become farmland and towns. Kentucky had been a state since 1792, Ohio since 1803. Missouri was on the verge of statehood in 1820, its admission delayed primarily by a bitter fight in Congress over the extent to which slavery was to be permitted in Missouri and other new western states. That issue was solved for the time being by the Missouri Compromise, under which Missouri was to be admitted as a slave state and Maine as a free state, and thereafter slavery was not to be permitted west of the Mississippi north of latitude 36°30'—but the aging Thomas Jefferson saw the question as "a fire bell in the night," sounding "the knell of the Union," and the compromise as "a reprieve only," not a final resolution.[31] All in all, the whole country differed vastly from the one Boone had known in his prime.

But Boone was no longer in his prime. Boone's name and reputation encouraged countless immigrants into Missouri from the upper south, especially from Kentucky, North Carolina, and Tennessee, many of whom brought slaves with them, laying the groundwork for the poisonous polarization over slavery that was nearly to rip the young United States apart—but one wonders how aware old Boone was of these issues, apart from his understanding that there were far more settlers and far less game.

A few months before Boone died, the young painter Chester Harding sought him out to paint his portrait. Harding asked directions of a woman, who described Boone as "that white-headed old man who lives on the bottom, near the river," and steered Harding to where Boone lived, in a cabin behind the home of Jemima and Flanders Callaway. Boone did not want his portrait painted, "being governed by feelings of modesty and a strong dislike to anything approaching display or public attention."[32] But Jemima persuaded Boone to sit for the picture. Harding found Boone "rather infirm; his memory of passing events was much impaired, yet he would amuse me every day by his anecdotes of his earlier life." A friend had to steady Boone's head as he sat. Harding's original oil sketch shows a gaunt old man but with a frank and steady gaze. Nathan told Draper, "Everyone thought [the portrait] good, except that it didn't show his plump cheeks, a sign of the broad face he had in his robust days." The sketch, now in the Massachusetts Historical Society, is the only surviving picture of Boone painted from life.[33]

After Harding left, Boone had an attack of fever and wanted to go to Nathan's substantial stone house. Nathan took him there in a carriage. Neighbors, thinking the end was near, jostled to see Boone, who asked that his coffin be brought down and placed near him. He thumped it with his cane to satisfy himself that it was still sound. Boone's fever came back, and "he began to complain of an acute burning sensation, such as he had never before felt, in his breast, which continually grew worse." Boone may well have been undergoing a heart attack. "When he was advised to take medicine, he declined, as he thought it would do no good. He said it was his last sickness, but, he said calmly, he was not afraid to die. He recognized all his relatives who came to see him . . . and talked within a few minutes of his last breath."[34] Boone made clear he wanted to be buried next to Rebecca. He said he "was about worn out" but that he had tried to do right, had struggled to pay his debts, and now trusted in God's mercy. Jemima Callaway arrived, and he recognized her too. Nathan and Jemima, on either side of the bedside, held Boone's hands. A slave shaved him, and Jemima cut his hair. "I am going," he said at last; "my time has come." He died soon after sunrise on September 26, 1820, a little more than a month before what would have been his eighty-sixth birthday.

The funeral was at the Callaways' home on the rich bottomland near Charette. The service was in the barn because the house was not big enough to hold all the people who were there. Boone was buried next to Rebecca, in the coffin that matched hers, on a hill a mile from the Missouri River.[35] The Missouri legislature adjourned in Boone's honor and wore mourning badges for twenty days.[36]

21

LIFE AFTER DEATH

ALREADY MYTHIC DURING HIS LIFE, BOONE AFTER HIS DEATH NOT only survived but evolved in countless stories, biographies, novels, poems, and paintings. That survival and evolution continues to this day, assisted both by the magnitude and drama of what Boone did and by the scarcity of autobiographical material that survived him. Tellers of the Boone story have each been able to fashion a Boone to their own liking because they have been little constrained by the man's own words. Filson's account of Boone was no more than a short sketch, ending in 1783. After the loss in the Missouri River during the War of 1812 of the autobiography that Boone had dictated to a grandson, Boone had tried again, dictating his life and adventures to a grandson-in-law named Dr. John Jones. The idea was that Jones would prepare the narrative for press, with the profits to go to Boone. Nathan said the narrative was never completed because of Boone's Loutre Lick trip and his subsequent sickness and changes of residence among his children. Jones promised to give Nathan the incomplete narrative, but it was never found after Jones died suddenly in the early 1840s.[1] So people recounting Boone's story after his death were left largely unfettered by Boone's own telling of his story. They took full advantage of their liberty to shape their picture of him to their own purposes.[2]

Some presented Boone as a child of nature, an exemplar of the earthly Rousseau-like Paradise of life in the wilderness. This was how Lord Byron presented him in his book-length *Don Juan,* a poem begun in 1818 as a picaresque ramble that was "meant to be a little quietly facetious upon everything."[3] For more than sixteen long cantos Byron follows the Spanish lover Don Juan—whose amorous entanglements bear more than an occasional resemblance to those of Byron—from his childhood in Spain, to Turkey (where he is sold into slavery), to joining the Russians in their siege of the Turkish-held city Ismail at the mouth of the Danube, to Russia (where Catherine the Great takes him as a lover), and to England (sent on an embassy by Catherine). The preceding sentence may give the impression that *Don Juan* is tightly plotted—but as Virginia Woolf said, it has "an elastic shape which will hold whatever you choose to put into it . . . [Byron] could say whatever came into his head."[4] Byron wrote to a friend: "You ask me for the plan of Donny Jonny: I *have* no plan—I *had* no plan, but I had or have materials . . . . Why, Man, the Soul of such writing is its licence; at least the *liberty* of that *licence,* if you like."[5] In *Don Juan* itself the poet wrote, without embarrassment, "Note or text / I never know the word which will come next."[6]

What came next, in the middle of canto 8, were stanzas describing Boone in idyllic terms. The canto, published in 1823 (three years after Boone died), tells of the Russians' siege of Ismail. After describing the Turks' defeat and before recounting the bloody sack of the city, Byron pauses to praise the God-made country over the man-made (and man-destroyed) city, by pointing to Daniel Boone and his progeny:

> LXI
> Of all men, saving Sylla the man-slayer,
>   Who passes for in life and death most lucky,
> Of the great names which in our faces stare,
>   The General Boon, back-woodsman of Kentucky,
> Was happiest amongst mortals anywhere;
>   For killing nothing but a bear or buck, he
> Enjoy'd the lonely, vigorous, harmless days
> Of his old age in wilds of deepest maze.

> LXII
> Crime came not near him—she is not the child
>   Of solitude; Health shrank not from him—for
> Her home is in the rarely trodden wild,
>   Where if men seek her not, and death be more
> Their choice than life, forgive them, as beguiled
>   By habit to what their own hearts abhor—
> In cities caged. The present case in point I
> Cite is, that Boon lived hunting up to ninety;

LXIII

And what's still stranger, left behind a name
    For which men vainly decimate the throng,
Not only famous, but of that *good* fame,
    Without which glory's but a tavern song—
Simple, serene, the *antipodes* of shame,
    Which hate nor envy e'er could tinge with wrong;
An active hermit, even in age the child
Of Nature, or the man of Ross run wild.

LXIV

'Tis true he shrank from men even of his nation,
    When they built up unto his darling trees,—
He moved some hundred miles off, for a station
    Where there were fewer houses and more ease;
The inconvenience of civilisation
    Is, that you neither can be pleased nor please;
But where he met the individual man,
He show'd himself as kind as mortal can.

LXV

He was not all alone: around him grew
    A sylvan tribe of children of the chase,
Whose young, unwaken'd world was ever new,
    Nor sword nor sorrow yet had left a trace
On her unwrinkled brow, nor could you view
    A frown on Nature's or on human face;
The free-born forest found and kept them free,
And fresh as is a torrent or a tree.

LXVI

And tall, and strong, and swift of foot were they,
    Beyond the dwarfing city's pale abortions,
Because their thoughts had never been the prey
    Of care or gain: the green woods were their portions;
No sinking spirits told them they grew grey,
    No fashion made them apes of her distortions;

Simple they were, not savage; and their rifles,
Though very true, were not yet used for trifles.

LXVII

Motion was in their days, rest in their slumbers,
   And cheerfulness the handmaid of their toil;
Nor yet too many nor too few their numbers;
   Corruption could not make their hearts her soil;
The lust which stings, the splendour which encumbers,
   With the free foresters divide no spoil;
Serene, not sullen, were the solitudes
Of this unsighing people of the woods.

LXVIII

So much for Nature:—by way of variety,
   Now back to thy great joys, Civilisation!
And the sweet consequence of large society,
   War, pestilence, the despot's desolation,
The kingly scourge, the lust of notoriety,
   The millions slain by soldiers for their ration,
The scenes like Catherine's boudoir at threescore,
   With Ismail's storm to soften it the more.

Byron's Boone stanzas stretched facts for effect. Boone becomes a general, not a mere colonel, and lives "hunting up to ninety." Byron had to force rhymes to meet the demands of the ottava rima form—eight lines in a stanza, with a strict *abababcc* rhyme scheme. So "buck, he" rhymes with *Kentucky*—but try yourself to come up with two (printable) rhymes for *Kentucky*. The reaching for rhymes may well have led to the sharp changes in mood and direction that give the poem its unique impromptu quality. Overall, Byron painted in the Boone verses a sylvan and free heaven on earth—a basic theme for Byron, who admired Rousseau and made a pilgrimage to places associated with him—in contrast to the tyranny and cruelty of the old world, exemplified in the brutality of the siege and sacking of Ismail.[7]

It is a measure of Boone's international fame that Byron, writing in Italy, saw Boone as one of "the great names which in our faces stare," and chose him to be the recognizable emblem of the happy backwoodsman. That may have happened because Byron had read a version of Filson's account of Boone or Henry Marie Brackenridge's book, published in 1814, of his travels in Louisiana and up the Missouri River. Brackenridge included a description of Boone as patriarch presiding over an extended family that "retired through choice," burying themselves "in the midst of the wilderness," to place themselves at "a distance from the deceit and turbulence of the world" and to be "truly free."[8] But Byron's knowledge of Boone may also have come, indirectly, from Gilbert Imlay, the rogue who cheated Boone out of a large tract of prime Kentucky land and who included a pirated version of Filson's account in his own book on the American west. Byron's circle, in his self-imposed exile in continental Europe, included several people with connections to Imlay, including Percy Bysshe Shelley, Shelley's lover (and eventual wife) Mary Godwin (the author of *Frankenstein; or, The Modern Prometheus*), and Mary Godwin's young stepsister, Claire Clairmont. Mary Godwin was the daughter of Mary Wollstonecraft, who had lived for years with Imlay and who had borne his daughter, Fanny Imlay. Claire Clairmont threw herself at Byron when she was only seventeen and within a year bore him a daughter in Italy.[9] This complicated and sexually intertwined Imlay-connected network bears no resemblance to the idyllic simplicity of Boone and his family that Byron depicted—but may well have helped Byron learn about Boone.[10]

Like Byron, James Fenimore Cooper also showed Boone as a child of nature, in Cooper's depiction of the Boone-like Natty Bumppo in the Leatherstocking novels—*The Pioneers* (1823), *The Last of the Mohicans* (1826), *The Prairie* (1827), *The Pathfinder* (1840), and *The Deerslayer* (1841)—all portraying the hero as a "philosopher of the wilderness." In *The Prairie* Bumppo crosses the Mississippi as an old man—"The sound of the ax has driven him from his beloved forests to seek a refuge . . . on the denuded plains that stretch to the Rockies"—much as Boone did. Cooper expressly noted, at the beginning of *The Prairie,* that "the adventurous and venerable patriarch" Boone placed the Mississippi between him and the multitude, "seeking for the renewal of enjoyments which were rendered worthless in his eyes, when trammeled by the forms of human institutions."[11] The same view, of Boone as child of nature, was presented by Thomas Cole in *Daniel Boone at His Cabin at Great Osage Lake*, painted around 1826. Cole shows Boone as a frowning old man, alone in front of a cabin in a wilderness with a lowering sky, dressed in a buckskin hunting shirt, holding a rifle, a dead deer at his feet.

Other writers and artists presented Boone not as a natural philosopher but as a heroic slayer of Indians, often engaged in hand-to-hand combat. Timothy Flint, a clergyman before he became a popular writer, went to Missouri as a missionary and interviewed Boone there, planning to write about him—but Flint's goal in his book on Boone was "not to bury the memory of our pioneer in that most revolting of all sepulchers, a dull biography." When a historian chided him for writing a book so lacking in fact, Flint said his book "was made not for use but to sell."[12] Flint succeeded; *Biographical Memoir of Daniel Boone, the First Settler of Kentucky*, published in 1833, went through fourteen editions by 1868. Accuracy was not Flint's strong suit. In Flint's telling, for example, Boone's year of birth is twelve years after the actual date, Boone's year of death two years too early, and the number of Indians who took the girls captive near Boonesborough balloons to nineteen. Flint was more interested in tales of derring-do, however unlikely, than in dry facts. Flint's Boone: comes close to shooting Rebecca, mistaking her for a deer at night; kills a wound-maddened she-bear by pointing his knife at the bear's heart as she hugged him (the bear "fell harmless to the ground"); and kills many panthers, one by lodging a bullet "in the heart of the fearful animal, at the very moment it was in the act to spring upon him."

Boone's most amazing feats, in Flint's book, involve fighting and evading Indians, depicted as fearsome foes (in the attack on Bryant's Station "the mass of biped wolves raised their murderous yell"; in torturing white captives, Indian women "appear to surpass the men in the fury of their merciless rage, and the industrious ingenuity of their torments"). Pursued by Indians, on two separate occasions, Flint's Boone swings on a grapevine to make his path hard for his enemies to follow. Hearing that the Indians have captured his daughter, Boone swears, "By the Eternal Power that made me a father, I will either bring her back, or spill my life blood." Before being taken captive by the Shawnees, Flint's Boone, attacked by two Indians, kills one with a rifle shot and then fights the other Indian over the slain Indian: "Boone, placing his foot on the dead body, dexterously received the well-aimed tomahawk of his powerful enemy on the barrel of his rifle, thus preventing his skull from being cloven by it. In the very attitude of firing [*sic*] the Indian had exposed his body to the knife of [Boone] who plunged it in his body to the hilt."[13]

Flint's portrayal of Boone as Indian slayer reflected his own beliefs that there was an innate "repulsion between the Anglo-Americans and them [the Indians]"—an "antipathy between the two races that seems fixed and unalterable" —and that Indians "are a cruel people by nature" in whom "the writhing of their victims inspires a horrible joy."[14] Others also portrayed Boone, who rarely killed Indians, as a mighty Indian killer. The same improbable scene of Boone standing on one slain Indian while sinking a knife into another one was carved in stone in 1826–27 by Enrico Causici in his heroic sculpture *The Conflict between Daniel Boone and the Indians,* which for years appeared over the south door of the Rotunda in the Capitol in Washington, D.C.

Flint was writing and Causici was sculpting at a time when Indians were being removed by force and threat of force to enable white settlement to continue to expand westward. As the art historian J. Grant Sweeney has observed, portrayal of Indian ferocity was "iconic justification for the aggressive expansion of the nation into Indian territories."[15] A similar theme, coupled with concepts of white racial superiority, underlay many dime novels about Boone as well as Horatio Greenough's monumental sculpture *The Rescue* (1836–53), designed for the steps of the Capitol, in which an oversized Boone-like figure is shown staying the hand of a muscular, breechclout-wearing Indian about to tomahawk a terrified settler mother and child. Greenough said his purpose was "to convey the idea of the triumph of the whites over the savage tribes."[16] Once again, tellers of the Boone story were presenting a different aspect of Boone, to further their own objectives.[17]

Flint portrayed Boone not only as an Indian fighter but also as an opener of the wilderness—a man "formed to be a woodsman, and the adventurous precursor in the first settlement of Kentucky," a man whose name will be recorded "in all future time, and in every portion of the globe . . . as the patriarch of Backwoods Pioneers."[18] The theme of Boone as the spearhead of America's westward expansion, already present in Filson's book, was repeated in Judge Coburn's 1820 eulogy, describing Boone as "the instrument of opening the road to millions of the human family from the pressure of sterility and want, to a land flowing with milk and honey."[19] That theme became more central in later portrayals of Boone, made as America swept westward across the continent, settling the Louisiana territory, defeating Mexico, pushing on to California—fulfilling what came to be known as the country's "manifest destiny," a phrase first used in an 1845 newspaper article by John L. Sullivan, editor of the *New York Morning News,* stating that America's claim "is by right of our manifest destiny to overspread and possess the whole of the Continent which Providence has given us for the development of . . . a noble young empire."[20]

Peck, in his 1847 biography, had as his main theme Boone as agent of America's westward drive—as evident from the subtitle, "The Pioneer of Kentucky." Peck said Boone "spoke feelingly, and with solemnity, of being a creature of Providence, ordained by Heaven as a pioneer in the wilderness, to advance the civilization and the extension of his country," although Peck also showed Boone as "an enthusiastic admirer of nature in its primeval wildness."[21] The same theme of Boone as pathfinder, as "Columbus of the woods," underlies paintings of Boone in the 1840s and 1850s—above all, George Caleb Bingham's *Daniel Boone Escorting Settlers through the Cumberland Gap* (1851–52).[22] Bingham shows Boone leading settlers through the mountain pass into the promised land of Kentucky, like Moses leading the children of Israel through Sinai. Boone stands looking at us, in unsoiled buckskins, his clean-shaven face a younger version of the face in Harding's portrait—not surprisingly, since Bingham as a boy had helped Harding in Missouri make a finished portrait of Boone from Harding's portrait sketch. Rifle on shoulder, Boone leads a horse on which sits a shawl-wearing woman, presumably Rebecca. In the background sunlight is breaking through dark clouds over the Cumberland Mountains. As Sweeney observed, "No single work of art has contributed more to establishing Daniel Boone as the quintessential symbol of westward expansion in mid-nineteenth century America."[23]

After 1860, with the continental United States occupying all of its present limits, there was less need for images of Boone as pathfinder or as slayer of demonic Indians. Rousing popular biographies of Boone continued, but there was also a diligent effort to record the historical Boone. That effort was led by Lyman Copeland Draper, who in 1838, when only twenty-three years old, decided his life's work would be to research and write the history of the American frontier through a series of lives of the pioneers, beginning with Daniel Boone, who, as Draper put it, "is generally acknowledged to be the pioneer of the West." The first task, in Draper's view, was to gather materials before they were lost and to compile the "precious historical incident" still "treasured up in the memory of aged Western Pioneers, which would perish with them if not quickly rescued." The task was immense. On his own and later as secretary of the State Historical Society of Wisconsin, Draper— all five foot one and 101 pounds of him—traveled over fifty thousand miles,

much of it on foot or on horseback, talking to old-timers, copying or purchasing manuscripts, interviewing and corresponding with Nathan and
Olive Boone and countless other Boones and Bryans. His tenacity and prodigious research resulted in the assembly of the world's largest collection of
manuscripts relating to the Ohio Valley and the Northwest Territory.

Writing was much harder for Draper than compiling data. He took co-
pious notes—over three hundred pages on his interviews with Nathan and
Olive Boone, for example—and started a massive biography of Boone, which
he even advertised prematurely when he heard that a competing one was
about to be published.[24] Yet he could not finish his Boone book. He could not
go down a path without pursuing byways that led to other smaller byways,
in fractal profusion. He stopped working on the book in 1856, having completed over eight hundred pages of manuscript and having taken Boone's life
as far as the siege of Boonesborough in 1778. Draper continued to collect
materials about Boone and other frontier figures and corresponded with
potential sources of Boone information until not long before he died, in
1891. Draper even turned to spiritualism, to ask questions of what he hoped
were the astral presences of George Rogers Clark and Simon Kenton. He
wrote no more of the Boone book, however, after 1856. Toward the end of
his life Draper made a desperate utterance with which many historians will
sympathize: "I have wasted my life in puttering. I can write nothing so long
as I fear there is a fact, no matter how small, as yet ungarnered." Draper's
successor as secretary of the State Historical Society of Wisconsin, Reuben
Gold Thwaites, who was to write a fine biography of Boone (and many other
excellent books on frontier history, in large part by mining Draper's collections), said of Draper's writing: "It was ever the same story. Ever planning,
never doing."[25] But if Draper completed only an unfinished discursive start
of a Boone biography, he also left behind, as part of the huge mass of frontier
history documents that he bequeathed to the Wisconsin historical society,
a monumental collection of documents and interview notes that has un-
derlain all subsequent biographies of Boone—though each biographer has
brought to the task his own interests and insights.

Thus, the portrayal of Boone, in literature and the visual arts, has evolved
and changed in the years since Boone died. Draper's document trove (although it included many folkloric reminiscences compiled decades after the
events) had put some limits on the historians in their depiction of Boone.

No such limits have restricted poets or the makers of movies and television shows. Some readers will remember Fess Parker in the 1960s TV series on Boone, wearing a coonskin cap of the sort the real Boone despised ("From the coonskin cap on the top of ol' Dan / to the heel of his rawhide shoe; / the rippin'est, roarin'est, fightin'est man / the frontier ever knew").[26] Nor have Draper's documents prevented the manufacture of spurious Boone relics— including trees blazoned with inscriptions to the effect that "D. Boon cilled a Bar on this Tree" (though Boone always spelled his name with an *e* at the end).[27]

Daniel Boone is hard to pin down. Even his physical remains may—or may not—have moved after Boone's death. In 1845, twenty-five years after he died, the founders of a new cemetery in Frankfort, Kentucky's capital, sought to honor Boone—and to promote their cemetery—by moving (with considerable fanfare) the remains of Boone and Rebecca from the Bryan family graveyard in Missouri to the Frankfort cemetery. One of the organizers of the proposed reinterment was an ancestor of mine, Mason Brown, a judge on the circuit court and a son of Kentucky's first U.S. senator, John Brown.[28] Brown was chairman of the Frankfort Cemetery Company, which pledged to erect over Boone's remains "a monument . . . to which every Kentuckian can point with pride, as marking the spot where the ashes of this pure, noble and fearless pioneer have been placed by the descendants of his early friends and comrades."[29]

The cemetery organizers wrote to Nathan Boone, promising the Frankfort cemetery would be "the most beautiful cemetery in the West" and sending letters in support of the proposed move from a slew of dignitaries— among them U.S. Senator John J. Crittenden and the governor, two former governors, and the attorney general of Kentucky. The cemetery engaged Boone's nephew William Linville Boone, a Kentuckian, to negotiate with Boone descendants. William Boone went out to Missouri with Crittenden's son Thomas and Jacob Swigert (clerk of Kentucky's Court of Appeals) and told the owner of the farm where Boone and Rebecca were buried that the Boone family had consented to the move. Three local men were hired to dig up the remains. Word spread, and a few dozen people, many of them Boones and Bryans, gathered at the graveyard. The family graves were ill marked, though in the mid-1830s small gravestones with the names of Daniel and Rebecca had been inscribed and erected. According to Swigert, "There were 30 or 40 persons standing around, who identified the grave of Boone, where they got his body."[30] A St. Louis newspaper reported that the "coffins were entirely rotten." Many bones crumbled on touch, but the workers put what they could in pine boxes, which were taken to Frankfort.[31]

The cemetery organizers and Frankfort's leaders held an elaborate procession and ceremony for the burial of the Boone remains. The night before the reinterment, in the presence of Mason Brown, William Boone, and other Kentucky dignitaries, Boone's bones were taken out of a pine box and placed in a fancier coffin. Also present was Mason Brown's son, my father's grandfather John Mason Brown, then only a boy. Years later he described the scene to Lyman Draper:

> Though I was but eight and a half years old, I have still a most vivid and accurate remembrance of all that occurred—It was my first sight of a skeleton, and I shall never forget how Dr. Snead arranged the bones in order upon a bed of shavings that quite filled the coffin—
>
> The skull of Boone was handled by the persons present and its peculiarities commented upon—My father placed it in my hands that I might say that I had lifted it—A cast of Boone's skull was then taken by a person named Davis. . . . He poured wax until a mold was formed and then made two plaster casts therefrom.

Mason Brown sent one of the two casts to the Smithsonian, where it was destroyed in a fire. After John Mason Brown was sent the other cast in 1882, he had three or four copies made, one of which he sent to Draper. A cast (or a copy of a cast) ended up at the Kentucky Historical Society, where it is still on display with other Boone relics.[32]

The procession and reinterment ceremony took up much of Saturday, September 13, 1845. The *Frankfort Commonwealth* exuberantly estimated the crowd at between fifteen and twenty thousand—a remarkable number for a town that at the time had a total population of about three thousand. There were twenty-one groups in the order of procession. After military companies and a band came the hearse, drawn by four white horses, and accompanied by old surviving pioneers, serving as pallbearers. Then came the orator (Senator Crittenden), the clergy, the president and members of the Frankfort Cemetery Company, the governor of Kentucky, judges, congressmen and state legislators, the clergy of the Methodist Episcopal Conference (meeting in Frankfort that week), Masons, Odd Fellows, fire companies, schools and teachers, militia, another band, and finally "No. 20. Strangers and

Citizens in Carriages" and "No. 21. Strangers and Citizens on Horseback."

In addition to the old white settlers, in the procession there "also tottered along the first black man who ever trod the soil of Kentucky, and his steps were sustained by another, also of African descent, who was the first child of other than Indian parentage ever born in what now is a Commonwealth of nearly a million souls." The newspaper account hastened to add: "Of the people who composed the great body of the Procession, it may well be said that the Saxon race, in no clime or country, could have been more nobly represented—whether for the brave appearance of the men or the splendid beauty of the women. They seemed indeed the suitable inheritors of this goodly land." Following a hymn and a prayer, Senator Crittenden orated and "enchained attention by the spells of his magic eloquence" (the substance of which went unreported). After a closing prayer and a benediction, the coffins were lowered into the graves, the aged pioneer pallbearers threw dirt on the coffins, others helped to fill in the graves, and the crowd dispersed.

The same issue of the Frankfort paper went on to report that the Kentucky Annual Conference of the Methodist Episcopal Church, presided over by a bishop who had delivered a prayer at the Boone ceremony earlier that week, in a meeting "conducted in the spirit of christian kindness," had voted ninety-eight to five to join the Methodist Episcopal Church, South, the proslavery southern section of the church. The Methodist Church in the United States was being torn apart on the issue of slavery. The issue that had delayed Missouri's admission to the Union in 1820, the year of Boone's death, was rending American Christian denominations in the year that Kentucky sought to honor Boone by his reinterment.[33]

The Frankfort cemetery began selling lots briskly after the reinterment. The Boone ceremony must have been good for business. Despite what the cemetery organizers had said to the Boone family and the owner of the Missouri graveyard, however, the Frankfort cemetery did not fund a monument honoring the Boones. The state of Kentucky in 1860 finally paid for a four-sided stone monument, fifteen feet high, with bas-relief panels on each side illustrating different aspects of Boone—among them the natural philosopher in the woods and the Indian fighter who wielded rifle butt and hunting knife against a bare-chested muscular Indian with raised tomahawk.

At the time of the reinterment the study of phrenology—the analysis of mind and character by studying the relative development of different parts of the brain, as indicated by the shape of the skull—was still in vogue. A few months after the reinterment the *Frankfort Commonwealth* published a report of a phrenological analysis of the skull, by the man who had taken a cast of the skull. The examiner listed a variety of "admeasurements" (for example, "From Philoprogenitiveness to Individuality—8 inches") and noted: "Relative sizes of the organs—all the affective faculties—with one exception (Inhabitiveness) very large. Conclusion: very strong; always on the alert; the highest degree of courage; he had no affinity for society—he fled from it." According to the examiner, the subject "was passionately fond of traveling; had great perception of courses and distances, and could not be lost in the woods. Such is the character which I deduce from his head."[34] It is remarkable what the phrenologist could discern from careful measurement of the skull—with the benefit of knowing whose skull it was and what had been that person's outstanding strengths.

Or was the skull in fact Boone's? Missourians over the years have claimed the Kentuckians took the wrong bones out of the ill-marked graveyard in which many Boones, Bryans, and slaves were buried and have argued that Boone is still buried in Missouri (and that tourists therefore should go to the Missouri graveyard, not the Frankfort cemetery). Kentuckians have argued in reply that the Boone relatives in Missouri consented to the removal and that bystanders had pointed out the location of Boone's grave to those exhuming the bones. In 1983 Kentucky's forensic anthropologist Dr. David Wolf looked at the plaster cast of the skull now at the Kentucky Historical Society and declared that the skull might well not be Boone's. According to Dr. Wolf, the forehead did not slope as much as that of the usual Caucasian male skull, the general shape of the brow ridges was more black than white, an indentation of the frontal bone tended "to be more of a black feature than a white," and the occipital bone at the back of the head was more protruding and bun-shaped, which he said was a black feature. "Boy, this could really be the skull of a Negro," Dr. Wolf said—though he admitted that the cast was a poor one, giving him little to go on, and that the skull could be of a Caucasian. He told the *National Geographic*: "The cast was poorly made and was only of the cranium. But the round forehead and long, narrow head are typical of Negroids, and the apparent young age at death certainly casts doubt that it was Boone's."[35]

Dr. Wolf was not infallible, however. In 1988 he concluded that human remains found in Jefferson County, Kentucky, were those of an African-American girl who had been killed in the 1970s. In 2004 Dr. Emily Craig,

Dr. Wolf's successor as Kentucky's forensic anthropologist, studied the same bones and determined they were at least a hundred years old and that the case "was not a 'modern' homicide of a teenager" but "a disturbed grave, most likely from the mid or late 1800s." Asked how Dr. Wolf had reached his very different conclusion, Dr. Craig said, "Mistakes happen, that's all I know how to say it."[36] In 1995 Dr. Craig said that the plaster cast in the Kentucky Historical Society, purportedly of Boone's skull, had "negligible" scientific worth, being only of the top half of the skull: "I can tell it is a male. But I would be very reluctant to make a determination of race. It was altered. It was filed down to make it look nice. As a scientist, I can't in good conscience make a determination."[37]In Dr. Craig's view an exhumation and an examination of the actual remains would be needed to determine if the bones in Frankfort are Boone's. No one is pushing for that to happen.[38]

One suspects that Boone would have been amused by the whole thing—the ceremony in Frankfort, the dispute over the location of his moldering bones, the racial identification of the skull.

22

CODA

A CLOUD OF MYTH AND LEGEND SURROUNDS BOONE. THERE ARE
contemporary accounts and letters (including several from Boone himself),
but many of the stories about Boone were gathered decades after he died,
from very old pioneers and from the children or grandchildren of pioneers.
Many of the biographies contain more folktales than facts. There are physical Boone relics, but many are no more convincing than pieces of the True
Cross. The myths, the legends, the dubious relics, are not Boone's legacy. His
legacy consists of the reality of his achievements, the strength of his character and principles, and the transformation of America that he helped to
bring about.

Consider Boone's actual achievements. On foot, on horse, or by boat
Boone traveled from eastern Pennsylvania down to Florida, across much
of Virginia, Maryland, Tennessee, North Carolina, and Kentucky, into what
is now Ohio and Michigan, across the Mississippi and well up the Missouri
River. He blazed what became the Wilderness Road, from the Cumberland
Gap up to the Kentucky River—the route on which hundreds of thousands
of settlers were to travel on their way to Kentucky. He led settlers into Kentucky in 1775 to build Boonesborough, even after Indians killed several in
the group he led. He was a leader in Boonesborough's successful defense in
1778, which did much to prevent American settlers from abandoning Kentucky during the bloody years of the Revolution. He brought many settlers
into Kentucky, and later into Missouri, both in person and by his example
and the strength of his reputation.

Boone's achievements were based on the strengths of his character and
principles. He had stamina and remarkable courage, sometimes to the point
of excess. His formal education was minimal, but he had suppleness and

quickness of mind in dealing with changing circumstances—for example, his captivity by the Shawnees. His humor and self-deprecation were engaging. So was his nondoctrinaire religious outlook "to Love and fear god, beleve in Jesus Christ, Dow all the good to my Nighbour and my Self that I can, and Do as Little harm as I Can help, and trust on gods marcy for the rest."[1] He dealt fairly with others, Indians as well as whites.

Boone had weaknesses and deficiencies. He was not a good businessman. His scant formal education showed up in his phonetic spelling. He had little taste for large organizations or for regular attendance on legislative committees. His family connections were not grand. But in tight spots people looked to Boone. It was no accident that the frontiersmen on the Clinch River in 1774 wanted him as their captain, or that the station built in the wilderness for Col. Richard Henderson's Transylvania Company was called Boonesborough, not Hendersonville. In addition to his skills as a woodsman and scout, Boone was a decent man, not the coonskin cap–wearing near-brute of the dime novels. Someone who knew him in Boonesborough described him as "a remarkably pleasant good natured mannerly man."[2] Judge David Todd, a member of a leading family of Kentucky settlers, who like Boone had moved to Missouri from Kentucky, said Boone "was a plain, gentlemanly man, good memory, mild, and equable. No ruffian, nor did he partake near as far as I have seen of the slovenly backwoods character."[3]

Boone's achievements, character, and principles helped to bring about the enormous transformations in America that happened during Boone's long life: the westward expansion, the explosive growth in population of Kentucky and Missouri, the decline of game, the Indians' dwindling power, the changes in the American economy, the nascent threat that slavery posed to the American Union, and the development of a sense of American national identity.

In 1750, the year of Boone's first long hunt, the total non-Indian population in the British colonies in what became the United States was 1.1 million.[4] That population was located primarily within a hundred miles of the Atlantic coast. The U.S. Census Bureau keeps track of the population center of the United States. By the bureau's definition the population center of the United States is the point at which an "imaginary, flat, weightless and rigid map of the U.S. would balance perfectly" if every person—counted where they lived on the day of the census—weighed the same. The earliest year for which the Census Bureau has calculated the country's population center is

1790, fifteen years after Boone led the blazing of what became the Wilderness Road and helped to found Boonesborough. By 1790 hundreds of thousands had settled in Kentucky and elsewhere in the Ohio Valley, but the center of the American population—which had jumped to 3.9 million—was still in an Atlantic Coast state, near Chestertown, Maryland, on the eastern side of the Chesapeake Bay. By 1820, the year of Boone's death, the total U.S. population had grown to 9.6 million (not a great deal less than the approximately 13.9 million who then lived in Great Britain), and the center of population had shifted well to the west, in the Shenandoah Mountains in what is now West Virginia, where Boone had hunted often.[5] As Frederick Jackson Turner, the great historian of the American frontier, noted, "By the census of 1820 the settled area included Ohio, southern Indiana and Illinois, southeastern Missouri, and about one-half of Louisiana."[6] Thanks to the Louisiana Purchase, U.S. territory in 1820 extended west to the Rocky Mountains. That, too, was in some part attributable to Boone and others like him: Napoleon and Talleyrand were more willing to sell the Louisiana territory to the United States because they recognized that the territory would be increasingly hard to hold in light of the immigration into Upper Louisiana of thousands of Americans—and many of those Americans went to Missouri following the example of Daniel Boone.

If the population of America as a whole grew impressively during Boone's lifetime, the population of Kentucky and Missouri exploded. In Kentucky there were only about 200 American settlers in the beginning of 1776. The numbers grew to 74,000 in 1790 and to 564,000 in 1820, the year Boone died. The growth in Missouri was similar—from fewer than 5,000 non-Indians in 1800, to 20,000 in 1810 and over 60,000 in 1820. A significant part of the growth of the non-Indian population in Missouri was in the Boone's Lick country (opened up in large part by Boone's sons Nathan and Daniel Morgan), where 20,000 people lived by 1820.[7] Boone and his children were remarkably fecund, but Boone was not, of course, the progenitor of all of the new Kentuckians and Missourians. Many hundreds of settlers followed Boone directly into Kentucky and Missouri. Many tens of thousands more came into Kentucky and Missouri at least in part because of Boone's reputation and example and, in the case of Kentucky, because of the defense of Boonesborough against the Indians and the success Boone, Benjamin Logan, George Rogers Clark, and others had in raiding the Shawnees in Ohio and pushing them westward.

The huge population growth in Kentucky and Missouri during Boone's lifetime contributed to other vast changes in Kentucky, Missouri, and throughout what had been the frontier. Game was killed or driven westward, away from the settlements. Farms replaced forests. Clapboard houses and plowed fields replaced seasonal hunting camps in the wilderness. Roads capable of bearing laden wagons replaced the narrow horse paths Boone and others had blazed. The entire economy and way of life in Kentucky and Missouri were radically different in 1820 than in 1750, and Boone had contributed to that change. Turner summarized the change in his essay on the passing of the frontier: "Stand at Cumberland Gap and watch the procession of civilization, marching single file—the buffalo following the trail to the salt springs, the Indian, the fur-trader and hunter, the cattle-raiser, the farmer— and the frontier has passed by."[8] Boone would not have liked those economic changes—in particular the diminishing of the game, the replacement of forests by farmland, the far denser population, or lack of "elbow-room"—but he helped to bring each of them about. Boone and his followers killed game with great efficiency. As a trader, Boone helped to equip white and Indian hunters and trappers with guns, powder, shot, and traps and purchased the pelts they brought in trade. He and his family and companions cut down forests to make cabins and stockades and firewood, including the enormous amounts of wood needed to boil salt from weakly saline springwater. Boone surveyed thousands of acres of land for settlers in Kentucky and helped to popularize to prospective settlers the advantages of settling in Kentucky and in Missouri.

The power of the Indians, relative to the white settlers, had dwindled to near-insignificance in Kentucky and Missouri by the time Boone died. In the early 1770s the Shawnees to the north and the Cherokees to the south far outnumbered the whites in what was to become Kentucky, and Boone was able to hunt there only on sufferance and by concealing himself from the Indians. By the mid-1790s few Indians remained in Kentucky, the risk of significant Indian attack was minimal, and many Shawnees and Cherokees had left Kentucky for the west—many of them going, as Boone would go, across the Mississippi into Missouri. The pattern recurred in Missouri. The Osages, in number and military strength, were far greater than the small Spanish garrison in Upper Louisiana when Boone and his family arrived in 1799. By 1808, under pressure from a flood into Missouri not only of white settlers but also of Shawnees, Cherokees, Choctaws, and other Indians who had been driven west across the Mississippi, the Osages had given up much of their claims to land in eastern Missouri—through a treaty orchestrated in part by Boone's son Nathan. By the time Boone died in 1820, Osage power was broken, the Osages were moving west out of Missouri, and whites greatly outnumbered Indians in Missouri.

The dwindling of Indian power was largely a result of the enormous growth in white settlement as well as the debilitating effect of smallpox, measles, and other white-introduced diseases, and, after 1803, the U.S. government's ability to relocate eastern Indians to western lands it had acquired in the Louisiana Purchase. But Boone—though not an Indian hater—played a significant part in the relative decline of Indian power in Kentucky and Missouri. In Kentucky he led the blazing of a main route for immigrants, was himself among the first American settlers, guided subsequent parties of settlers, and encouraged others to come by his example. He also led the defense of Boonesborough that kept settlers in Kentucky and played an important role in the American raids on the Shawnee towns north of the Ohio River that broke the Shawnees' power and contributed to their migration across the Mississippi. In Missouri Boone led a sizable party of Americans to settle up the Missouri in the Femme Osage District, and his example encouraged a flood of Americans coming into Missouri. In both places Boone's hunting and trapping—and that of other Americans—helped to decimate the game. In these ways Boone, although he had Indian friends, helped to destroy the traditional Indian way of life and to force the Shawnees across the Mississippi and eventually to push them and the Osages out of Missouri. A vignette illustrates the extent of the Shawnee removal to the west: in 1809 Hugh McGary, the Indian hater who had fed the body of one Shawnee to his dogs and who had murdered Shawnee chief Moluntha, died peacefully in a town in southeastern Illinois called Shawneetown. The town, the site of what had been a Shawnee village, had no Shawnees in it by the time of McGary's death.[9]

In short, by the time Boone died, Kentucky and Missouri—and the old frontier in general—had been transformed to such an extent as to be barely recognizable by pioneers of Boone's generation. Around 1820 Boone's old friend the illiterate giant Simon Kenton, who had moved to Ohio in 1798, came back to Washington, Kentucky, where he had lived for many years before he left the state. One day Kenton saw a boy riding to take a bag of corn to be ground at a new mill. Curious to see the new mill, Kenton rode his horse alongside the boy. They stopped at a ridge not far from Limestone, overlooking the countryside. Kenton said, as if talking to himself: "What a change! What a change!" He told the boy that in the old days what had since become the main road between Lexington and Limestone was only a buffalo trace, with impenetrable cane-brake on either side of it. Now there were clapboard houses, barns, and fenced fields. There was a big spring on the boy's father's farm. Kenton told the boy that years earlier, in the 1770s, Kenton and Boone had come upon that spring after they had hidden from a large party of Indians hunting buffalo and elk nearby. The Indians left so much dung at the site that Kenton and Boone named it the "Shitting Spring." Kenton said that for some years afterward "many a claim was entered such a course and distance from 'the Sh-ting Spring.'" The spring now was on well-kept farmland.[10]

It simply was not the same world. Boonesborough, which Boone had helped to found and to build in 1775, had been one of Kentucky's larger towns when Kentucky became a state in 1792. By 1810 it was an obscure hamlet. Soon it was only the site of a ferry crossing on the Kentucky River. In 1838 Boonesborough's most notable landmark, the giant elm Judge Henderson had called "the most beautiful tree that imagination can suggest"—the tree under which the Transylvania legislative convention met in May 1775—was cut down.[11]

Instead of log cabins huddled together in stockades, by 1820 Kentuckians and Missourians were building houses of stone and brick. Timothy Flint, who had found on the Ohio Valley in 1815 "log-houses, and wooden benches," ten years later saw there "brick houses, ornamented court-yards, trellis-wrought summer-houses, fruit-gardens, and within, carpets, sideboards, and sofas."[12] At least until the credit crunch and financial panic of 1819, there was money enough in Kentucky's bluegrass towns—and, for that matter, in the Boone's Lick region in Missouri—for conspicuous consumption. Lexington, in the heart of the bluegrass country, did not exist when Boone first came to the area. By 1810 Lexington had a population of 4,300 (a jump from 1,800 ten years earlier), of whom 1,509 (35%) were slaves, a burgeoning economy built on hemp (surrounding hemp plantations as well as factories turning the hemp into rope and bagging material) and buzzing commerce, and many substantial brick townhouses.[13] Four years later an article in the *Niles' Weekly Register* noted about Lexington: "They have a theatre; and their balls and assemblies are conducted with as much grace and ease as they are anywhere, and the dresses of the parties tasty and elegant.

Strange things these in the 'backwoods!'—The houses are mostly of brick, and some of them splendid edifices—one or two of the inns yield to none in America for extensiveness, convenience and good living."[14]

Frankfort, the state capital, which had only a cabin or two in 1780, soon boasted its own array of showy brick houses, including one that Senator John Brown built in the 1790s. By 1802 formal balls were being held in Frankfort houses.[15] Two years later Brown's wife, Margaretta, wrote to a friend that Frankfort "commands a very considerable trade" and "contains about eight hundred inhabitants, one-third of whom are black; and more neat and convenient dwelling-houses than could have been expected" given how recently Frankfort was settled (less than twenty years). She described her own house as "commodious, and even elegant."[16] Margaretta, writing her husband in 1811 while visiting her native New York City, described "a very brilliant party" she had enjoyed there, saying that she would "be proud to introduce the most distinguished amongst them to our Frankfort Assemblies, or private parties, confident that we should lose nothing by the comparison, either in point of tasteful dresses, genteel arrangements, or choice of refreshments."[17] In 1819 Margaretta Brown wrote to their son Orlando, then a student at Princeton, that Kentuckians are "so far . . . from being free of ostentation, that the profusion and display at our entertainments, has ever been a matter of astonishment to strangers," but no one has the courage to set a better example "for fear of being thought mean . . . . We could not invite a friend to dinner, but 'the table must groan with costly piles of food.'" Only changed circumstances (presumably Margaretta had in mind the 1819 panic and the closing of many western banks) caused Kentuckians to be pursuing a more moderate course "from necessity, which we never would have adopted by choice."[18]

Thomas Hart, a relative by marriage of Senator Brown, expressed what his group liked to do: "What a pleasure we have in raking up money and spending it with our friends!"[19] A visitor from New England, Rev. Timothy Flint, who was to interview Boone in Missouri and pen a Boone biography, noted of Frankfort at about this time that "the inhabitants, male and female, were remarkable for their display in dress" and wrote that Lexington "has taken on the tone of a literary place, and may be fitly called the Athens of the West."[20] None of this sounds like the wilderness of Kentucky in which Boone hunted alone in 1770, or the Missouri frontier to which Boone led his family in 1799—but whether or not Boone would have liked the changes, he had helped to bring them about by what he had done to open up Kentucky and Missouri to farming and commerce.

Another transforming change was the development of American national identity and a reduction of the conflicting loyalties that had existed when what became America was claimed by Britain, British colonies, France, Spain, and different Indian tribes. When Boone was born in 1734, there was little sense of unity among the disparate British colonies along the Atlantic coast, from Georgia to the Maine district of Massachusetts. Different colonies—notably Virginia and Pennsylvania—asserted their separate claims to the Ohio Valley and competed bitterly for the Indian fur trade. During the Revolution Indians, Americans, and British vied for control of the Ohio Valley, and Spain struggled to keep the Louisiana Territory. The Revolution gave birth to a new nation, the United States of America, with a national government that became stronger with the adoption of the Constitution—but there were still conflicting loyalties. The British sought to keep control of as much as possible of the Indian fur trade, supplying Indian forces until the British garrisons in Detroit and elsewhere in the Northwest Territory were finally removed in 1796, and even thereafter stirring up Indian resistance to America in the War of 1812. Prior to the Louisiana Purchase, the Spanish sought to use their control of New Orleans as a lever to detach from the new United States the westerners seeking to trade down the Mississippi. By the time of Boone's death, however, there was a far greater sense of American unity and identity. The Louisiana Territory had become part of the United States, the Indians were no longer effective fighting forces in Missouri or in the Ohio Valley, and the Americans had fought the British to a standstill in the War of 1812.

Boone both exemplified the conflicting loyalties that existed on the frontier and worked to build the new American nation. He had become an adopted son of a Shawnee chief and had told the British commandant in Detroit that he would seek to have the settlers at Boonesborough pledge allegiance to the British Crown. Boone had gone to Missouri when it was still Spanish territory and had held office under the Spanish administrators of Upper Louisiana. But he also fought the British-supported Indians in Kentucky and played a key role in keeping American settlers in Kentucky during the Revolution, as well as in breaking Indian power in the Ohio Valley. The migration of Boone and his family across the Mississippi led many other Americans to settle in what became Missouri and made more likely the eventual cession of the Louisiana Territory to the United States.

This is not to suggest that the United States in 1820 was monolithic. The bitter issue of slavery was already festering, as shown by the fight over Missouri's admission to the Union. In a way Boone contributed to this issue, too—not knowingly and not as a zealot on either side of the issue. Boone owned a few slaves from time to time, in his moments of prosperity, but no surviving writing by or story about Boone indicates that he was wedded either to slavery or to its abolition. Just as Boone had friends among the Shawnees, Boone appears to have respected and valued individual African-Americans—among them Derry Coburn, Boone's preferred companion on many of his hunting trips in Missouri. Like much of what Boone did, his closeness to Derry seems to have been based on pragmatism rather than ideology: Derry was skilled at hunting and woodcraft, and the two men got along together well in the wilderness. But Boone's career inadvertently furthered the spread of slavery, and so contributed to the issue that nearly destroyed the Union forty years after Boone's death.

Boone helped to open up the bluegrass country of Kentucky. While he himself was conspicuously uninterested in farming, the land he opened up in Kentucky lent itself to growing hemp, which was a labor-intensive crop. Hemp cultivation in Kentucky was a principal reason for the growth of the state's slave population and for the pro-slavery views of many of Kentucky's leaders. In 1792, when Kentucky was drafting a constitution as part of becoming a state, the delegates (many of whom owned hemp plantations) voted twenty-six to sixteen to defeat an antislavery plank. More than 90 percent of the delegates owned slaves, although only 23 percent of the electorate were slaveholders.[21]

Again inadvertently, Boone helped the spread of slavery into Missouri. His family's move to Missouri encouraged many from states in the Upper South in which Boone had lived—Kentucky, Tennessee, North Carolina, and Virginia—to follow suit. Many of these emigrants had been slave owners before moving to Missouri, and they brought slaves with them, in part because many moved to the Boone's Lick region, which was well suited for labor-intensive hemp and tobacco cultivation. To a large extent the emigrants had chosen to acquire land in Missouri, where slavery was permitted, rather than in the Northwest Territory, in which slavery was forbidden by the Northwest Ordinance. By 1820 there were nearly two thousand slaves in the Boone's Lick country, many owned by immigrants from Kentucky and Tennessee. In

Missouri as a whole in 1820 there were some ten thousand slaves, about 15 percent of the territory's population.[22]

Daniel Boone contributed to the transforming changes in America during his long career—the birth of the nation, the westward growth of American territory and of the American settlers, the shrinking of Indian power, the shift from hunting to farming and commerce, the increasing sense of national identity—not because of any ideological conviction but because of what he liked to do and did well. His interviewer and biographer Peck viewed Boone as God's instrument in building America, but Peck, despite his theological bent as a Baptist minister, was obliged to report that Boone "appeared to have entered into the wilderness with no comprehensive views or extensive plans of future improvements" and that Boone's aim was "not to lay the foundations of a state or nation."[23]

Boone liked to explore new lands, to scout, to hunt, to trap. He was outstandingly good at these things, so people trusted him and followed him. The more that Boone succeeded in hunting and trapping and leading settlers to new lands and the more that people followed him, the harder it was for him to remain a successful hunter and trapper and scout while staying in the same place, and the more he was driven to new lands, with ever more people following in his wake. By doing what he did best, Boone helped to bring about the birth and transformation of America.

Acknowledgments

The notes that follow, along with the bibliographical note, demonstrate my indebtedness to the many who, starting during Boone's lifetime, have studied and written about Daniel Boone. I am also indebted to the Kentucky Historical Society (in particular to Kenneth H. Williams for his guidance and to Beth Shields, Diane Shelton Meister, and Don Rightmyer for their research in the Draper manuscripts), the Filson Historical Society (special thanks to James J. Holmberg, curator of special collections, and Jacob Lee and Pen Bogert), the Virginia Historical Society, Liberty Hall Historic Site (notably Sara Harger Elliott, now at the Kentucky Historical Society, and Randy Huff), and many libraries—including the Library of Congress (thanks in particular to Bonnie Coles), Yale University Library, the Library of the University of Cincinnati (thanks to Linda Newman, digital projects coordinator, University Libraries), Westerly Public Library (particular thanks to Caroline Kreck, reference librarian), and Stonington Free Library. For records relating to Boone in Missouri that are in the archives of the St. Charles County Historical Society, I am grateful to William Popp, the society's archivist, and to John Korasick, administrative archivist, State Archives, Local Records, in Jefferson City. Neal O. Hammon has been extremely generous in sharing his deep knowledge of history, surveying, and land records in Kentucky during the Revolutionary and post-Revolutionary periods. Ken Kamper, historian for the Boone Society, kindly guided me around Boone sites in Missouri and shared his extensive learning about Boone and the Boone family in Missouri. Mary Lee Eggart, research assistant in the Cartographic Section of Louisiana State University's Department of Geology and Anthropology, prepared most of the maps for this book. My thanks also to Rand Dotson at

Louisiana State University Press for his patience and skillful guidance and to Elizabeth Gratch for her wise and careful copyediting. In addition, I am grateful to Bertram Wyatt-Brown, Stephen Aron, Neal Hammon, Richard Taylor, and an unnamed reader for Louisiana State University Press for their very helpful comments on drafts of this book. I alone am responsible for any errors in it.

Notes

Bakeless   John Bakeless, *Daniel Boone* (1939; rpt., Harrisburg, Pa.: Stackpole Books, 1965)

Cresswell   Nicholas Cresswell, *The Journal of Nicholas Cresswell, 1774–1777* (New York: Dial Press, 1924)

CVSP   William R. Palmer, ed., *Calendar of Virginia State Papers and Other Manuscripts*, 11 vols. (1875–93; rpt., New York: Kraus Reprint Corp., 1960–69)

DHDW   Reuben Gold Thwaites and Louise Phelps Kellogg, *Documentary History of Dunmore's War, 1774* (Madison: State Historical Society of Wisconsin, 1905)

DM   Draper Manuscript Collection, State Historical Society of Wisconsin, Madison

Dorman   John Frederick Dorman, *The Prestons of Smithfield and Greenfield in Virginia* (Filson Club, 1982)

Downes   Randolph C. Downes, *Council Fires on the Upper Ohio: A Narrative of Indian Affairs in the Upper Ohio Valley until 1795* (Pittsburgh: University of Pittsburgh Press, 1940)

Draper   Lyman C. Draper, *The Life of Daniel Boone*, ed. Ted Franklin Belue (Mechanicsburg, Pa.: Stackpole Books, 1998)

Drimmer   Frederick Drimmer, ed., *Captured by the Indians: 15 Firsthand Accounts, 1750–1870* (New York: Dover Publications, 1961)

Faragher   John Mack Faragher, *Daniel Boone: The Life and Legend of an American Pioneer* (New York: Henry Holt, 1992)

FCHQ   *Filson Club Historical Quarterly*

FDUO   Reuben Gold Thwaites and Louise Phelps Kellogg, *Frontier Defense on the Upper Ohio, 1777–1778* (Madison: State Historical Society of Wisconsin, 1912)

FHS   Filson Historical Society, Louisville, Ky.

Filson   John Filson, *The Discovery, Settlement and Present State of Kentucke: and An Essay towards the Topography, and Natural History of that important Country: To which is added An Appendix Containing, I. The Adventures of Col. Daniel Boon, one of the First Settlers, comprehending every important Occurrence in*

287

the political History of that Province (Wilmington, Del.: James Adams, 1784; facsimile reprint by Heritage Books, 2004)

Flint, *Boone* Timothy Flint, *The Life and Adventures of Daniel Boone, The First Settler of Kentucky, Interspersed with Incidents in the Early Annals of the Country* (New York: U. P. James, 1868). First pub. (1833) as *Biographical Memoir of Daniel Boone, the First Settler of Kentucky.*

Historical Statistics Bureau of the Census, *Bicentennial Edition: Historical Statistics of the United States—Colonial Times to 1970* (Washington, D.C.: Department of Commerce, 1975)

Houston Peter Houston, *A Sketch of the Life and Character of Daniel Boone,* ed. Ted Franklin Belue (Mechanicsburg, Pa.: Stackpole Books, 1997)

JDS John Dabney Shane

KHS Kentucky Historical Society, Frankfort

Lofaro Michael A. Lofaro, *Daniel Boone: An American Life* (Lexington: University Press of Kentucky, 2003)

MFDB Neal O. Hammon, ed., *My Father, Daniel Boone: The Draper Interviews with Nathan Boone* (Lexington: University Press of Kentucky, 1999)

Mereness Newton D. Mereness, ed., *Travels in the American Colonies* (1916; rpt., New York: Antiquarian Press, 1961)

Morgan Robert Morgan, *Boone: A Biography* (Chapel Hill, N.C.: Algonquin Books, 2007)

Peck John Mason Peck, *Life of Daniel Boone, the Pioneer of Kentucky* (1847; rpt., New York: University Society, Inc., 1905)

Ranck George W. Ranck, *Boonesborough: Its Founding, Pioneer Struggles, Indian Experiences, Transylvania Days, and Revolutionary Annals* (Louisville, Ky.: Filson Club, 1901)

RKHS *Register of the Kentucky Historical Society*

RUO Reuben Gold Thwaites and Louise Phelps Kellogg, eds., *The Revolution on the Upper Ohio, 1775–1777* (Madison: Wisconsin Historical Society, 1908)

Trabue Chester Raymond Young, ed., *Westward into Kentucky: The Narrative of Daniel Trabue* (Lexington: University Press of Kentucky, 1981)

PREFACE

1. *Historical Statistics,* pt. 1, 8; pt. 2, 1168.
2. Ibid., pt. 1, 28.
3. Ibid., pt. 1, 30.
4. Filson.

1. OLD BOONE

1. Bakeless, 360.

2. Chester Harding, *My Egotistigraphy* (Cambridge, Mass.: John Wilson Press, 1866), 35–36, qtd. in Lofaro, 174–75.

3. John C. Boone to Draper, Nov. 20, 1890, DM 16C132.

4. *MFDB*, 138.

5. "A Traveller," in the *New-York Statesman,* copied in the *Cincinnati National Republican,* Aug. 19, 1823, DM 16C67.

6. Ralph Clayton to the *St. Louis Christian Advocate,* May 30, 1877, DM 7C43[1–3].

7. Peck, 186–89.

8. Draper interview with Delinda Boone Craig, 1866, DM 30C79.

2. QUAKERS IN PENNSYLVANIA, SETTLERS IN
BACKCOUNTRY NORTH CAROLINA

1. Between 1661 and 1685 historians estimate that at least fifteen thousand Quakers were jailed in England for their religious beliefs, and over four hundred died because of those beliefs. David Hackett Fischer, *Albion's Seed: Four British Folkways in America* (Oxford: Oxford University Press, 1989), 598.

2. Fischer, *Albion's Seed,* 459–62, 598.

3. Jean R. Soderlund, ed., *William Penn and the Founding of Pennsylvania, 1680–1684* (Philadelphia: University of Pennsylvania Press, 1983), 5.

4. The Nov. 2 birth date is under the New Style calendar. Under the Old Style calendar Boone was born on Oct. 22. *MFDB,* 10.

5. For a map showing the British settlements in America before 1760 and their expansion between 1760 and 1769 and between 1770 and 1776, see Bernard Bailyn, *Voyagers to the West: A Passage in the Peopling of America on the Eve of the Revolution* (New York: Vintage Books, 1986), 9.

6. For an example of a deed from the Delawares to Penn and for a map of his purchases from the Delawares between 1682 and 1684, see Soderlund, *William Penn and the Founding of Pennsylvania,* 156–62.

7. James H. Merrell, *Into the American Woods: Negotiators on the Pennsylvania Frontier* (New York: W. W. Norton, 1999), 161–62; Faragher, 18–19.

8. Merrell, *Into the American Woods,* 35–36.

9. Draper, 110–11.

10. Margaret H. Bacon, *The Quiet Rebels: The Story of the Quakers in America* (New York: Basic Books, 1969), 47.

11. Soderlund, *William Penn and the Founding of Pennsylvania,* 41.

12. Penn to the "King of the Indians," Oct. 18, 1681, Richard Dunn and Mary Maples Dunn, eds., *The Papers of William Penn,* 5 vols. (Philadelphia: University of Pennsylvania Press, 1981–86), 2:128–29.

13. Bacon, *Quiet Rebels,* 59. In a 1683 letter Penn wrote, "I have made it my business to understand [the Indians' language], that I might not want an interpreter on any occasion." Qtd. in Soderlund, *William Penn and the Founding of Pennsylvania,* 313, 316.

14. Randall M. Miller and William Pencak, eds., *Pennsylvania: A History of the Commonwealth* (University Park: Pennsylvania State University Press, 2002), 77; Paul A. W. Wallace, *Conrad Weiser, 1696–1760, Friend of Colonist and Mohawk* (Philadelphia: University of Pennsylvania Press, 1945), 96–99.

15. For a skeptical look at how the Penn family claimed title to lands in Pennsylvania, see Eric Hinderaker, *Elusive Empires: Constructing Colonialism in the Ohio Valley, 1673–1800* (Cambridge: Cambridge University Press, 1997), 101–5, 127–28.

16. Fischer, *Albion's Seed,* 485–86.

17. Ibid., 681.

18. Bailyn, *Voyagers to the West,* 129–30, shows that between Dec. 1773 and Mar. 1776, of the emigrants from England and Scotland whose sex is known, about three-quarters were males.

19. Fischer, *Albion's Seed,* 498–99.

20. *MFDB,* 11; Draper, 111.

21. *MFDB,* 11.

22. Flint, *Boone,* 15–19.

23. Faragher, 15–16.

24. *MFDB,* 11, 45.

25. A leading historian of the Old Northwest who had to translate Clark's memoir before publishing it wrote that "Clark's spelling and syntax were as original as was his military genius; even the trained scholar finds difficulty at times in determining his meaning." Milo M. Quaife, *The Capture of Old Vincennes: The Original Narratives of George Rogers Clark and of His Opponent Gov. Henry Hamilton* (Indianapolis: Bobbs-Merrill, 1927), xvii.

26. Excerpts from the minutes of the Exeter meeting appear in John Joseph Stoudt, "Daniel and Squire Boone," *Historical Review of Berks County* (July 1936): 111–12. See also Faragher, 23–26.

27. Stoudt, "Daniel and Squire Boone," 112.

28. *MFDB,* 139.

29. Houston, 30.

30. The basis of Quaker dealings with other men was that "men will reciprocate if treated fairly and kindly." William Comfort, *The Quakers, A Brief History of Their Influence on Pennsylvania* (Gettysburg: Pennsylvania Historical Association, 1948), 6.

31. Bailyn, *Voyagers to the West,* 16.

32. For a map of the areas of North Carolina settled by 1759, in 1760–69, and in 1770–76, see Bailyn, *Voyagers to the West,* 17.

33. Faragher, 27–30; Lofaro, 7–8.

34. George Boone Moffitt to Draper, June 14, 1853, DM 2C11 ("went on a general jamboree"); Faragher, 28–29.

35. Daniel Boone Bryan to Draper, Feb. 27, 1843, DM 22C5; Faragher, 31.

36. *MFDB,* 13.

37. Draper, 126.

38. Faragher, 31.

39. Bernard Bailyn, *The Peopling of British North America: An Introduction* (New York: Vintage Books, 1986), 111.

40. Faragher, 31–32.

41. William P. Boone to Draper, Apr. 27, 1846, DM 19C1; Draper interview with Isaiah Boone, 1846, DM 19C61.

3. BRADDOCK'S DEFEAT

1. For the increasing westward reach of the Pennsylvanian Indian trade, see generally Hinderaker, *Elusive Empires*, 40–44.

2. See Richard White, *The Middle Ground: Indians, Empires, and Republics in the Great Lakes Region, 1650–1815* (New York: Cambridge University Press, 1991), 224.

3. Céloron's name is sometimes given as Céleron and as de Bienville, rather than de Blainville.

4. Hinderaker, *Elusive Empires*, 128–38; Michael N. McConnell, *A Country Between: The Upper Ohio Valley and Its Peoples, 1724–1774* (Lincoln: University of Nebraska Press, 1992), 15–54.

5. "The Speech of Ackowanothio, an old Indian on the Ohio, on behalf of the Delawares and others living on the Ohio. September 1758," Provincial Papers, Department of Archives, Harrisburg, 27:69, qtd. in Wallace, *Conrad Weiser*, 529.

6. Lois Mulkearn, ed., *George Mercer Papers relating to the Ohio Company of Virginia* (Pittsburgh: University of Pittsburgh Press, 1954), 39.

7. George Croghan to governor of Pennsylvania, May 14, 1754, *Pennsylvania Archives* (Philadelphia: Joseph Severns; Harrisburg: Commonwealth of Pennsylvania, 1852–1949), ser. 1, 2:144–45.

8. Lofaro, 11.

9. Petition of John Hanbury on behalf of the Ohio Company to the king in council, reprinted in Kenneth P. Bailey, *The Ohio Company of Virginia and the Westward Movement, 1748–1792: A Chapter in the History of the Colonial Frontier* (Spokane: Arthur H. Clark, 1939), 299.

10. McConnell, *Country Between*, 92.

11. R. Douglas Hurt, Jr., *The Ohio Frontier: Crucible of the Old Northwest, 1720–1830* (Bloomington: Indiana University Press, 1998), 33–39; White, *Middle Ground*, 230–32; Matthew C. Ward, *Breaking the Backcountry: The Seven Years' War in Virginia and Pennsylvania, 1764–1765* (Pittsburg, University of Pittsburg Press, 2003), 29–30.

12. For the increasing French influence in the Ohio Valley from 1750 to 1754, see generally Hinderaker, *Elusive Empires*, 135–40; Downes, 54–71; Bailey, *Ohio Company*, 25–31, 183–93; Ward, *Breaking the Backcountry*, 29–35; and McConnell, *Country Between*, 98–105.

13. Joseph J. Ellis, *His Excellency George Washington* (New York: Alfred A. Knopf, 2004), 5.

14. Ward, *Breaking the Backcountry*, 32–33.

15. Conrad Weiser on Sept. 3, 1754, reported Tanacharison's impressions. Downes, 70–71, citing *Pennsylvania Colonial Records*, 6:151. Weiser's journal is also printed in Wallace, *Conrad Weiser*, 366–67. Tanacharison's name is also sometimes spelled "Tanaghrisson."

16. White, *Middle Ground*, 40–41 (25–90%); Miller and Pencak, *Pennsylvania*, 35 (95%).

17. Peter Wraxall, "Thoughts upon the British Indian Interest in North America," Jan. 9, 1756, *New York Colonial Documents* 7:18, qtd. in Downes, 79.

18. Shamokin Daniel to Christian Frederick Post in 1758, in Downes, 88.

19. *Historical Statistics*, 2, 1168 (estimated population of American colonies was 1.17 million in 1750 and 1.59 million in 1760); Colin G. Calloway, *The Scratch of a Pen: 1763 and the Transformation of North America* (Oxford: Oxford University Press, 2006), 24, 113 (total French

population in North America in 1763 was about 80,000, with the majority settled in the St. Lawrence Valley).

20. Wallace, *Conrad Weiser,* 530.

21. Draper, 47.

22. Bailey, *Ohio Company,* 24. Patton had initially petitioned the Virginia government in 1743 for "200,000 acres of land on three branches of the Mississippia and the Waters thereof, on which I proposed to settle one family for each 1,000 acres." The Virginia council awarded Patton 100,000 acres in Apr. 1745. Patton to John Blair, Jan. 1753, DM 1QQ75.

23. Robert D. Mitchell, *Commercialism and Frontier: Perspectives on the Early Shenandoah Valley* (Charlottesville: University of Virginia Press, 1977), 82; Peter J. Sehlinger, *Kentucky's Last Cavalier: General William Preston, 1816-1887* (Lexington: Kentucky Historical Society, 2004), 2.

24. For Patton's inept preliminaries at Logstown, see McConnell, *Country Between,* 94.

25. Letitia Floyd to Benjamin Rush Floyd, Feb. 22, 1843.

26. Ward, *Breaking the Backcountry,* 104-6; Robert L. Kincaid, *The Wilderness Road* (Indianapolis: Bobbs-Merrill, 1947), 62.

27. Benjamin Franklin, *Autobiography,* 152-53.

28. Shingas in Nov. 1755 told his captive Charles Stuart about his conversation with Braddock. Beverly W. Bond, Jr., "The Captivity of Charles Stuart, 1755-1775," *Mississippi Valley Historical Review* 13 (1926-27): 63-65. On Shingas's decision to join with the Shawnees and to make war against the English, see McConnell, *Country Between,* 119-20. For the number of Indian scouts with Braddock's army, see Ward, *Breaking the Backcountry,* 42.

29. Message of Scaroyady conveyed by Conrad Weiser to the governor of Pennsylvania, "Memorandum of Conrad Weiser," Aug. 23, 1755, Penn MS, Large Folio, II, Historical Society of Philadelphia, qtd. in *Conrad Weiser,* 390.

30. Ellis, *His Excellency,* 21.

31. Ward, *Breaking the Backcountry,* 7, 42-43.

32. Drimmer, 29.

33. Ward, *Breaking the Backcountry,* 43-44; John Grenier, *The First Way of War: American War Making on the Frontier, 1607-1814* (New York: Cambridge University Press 2005), 111-13; Armstrong Starkey, *European and Native American Warfare, 1675-1815* (Norman: University of Oklahoma Press, 1998) 94-96.

34. Maj. Robert Orme to Robert Dinwiddie, July 18, 1755, Great Britain Public Records Office, Colonial Office, Class 5 Papers, 5:46.

35. Robert Orme, "Journal of General Braddock's Expedition," British Library, 102-7; Ward, *Breaking the Backcountry,* 44.

36. *MFDB,* 13.

37. Draper, 132.

38. The captive was James Smith, then eighteen years old. Drimmer, 30.

39. Ellis, *His Excellency,* 22.

40. Cresswell, 65 (Sunday, Apr. 16, 1775). The Presbyterian minister David McClure reported similarly in his journal for Aug. 31, 1772: "It was a melancholy spectacle to see the bones of men strewed over the ground, left to this day, without the solemn rite of sepulture. . . . The

bones had been gnawed by wolves, the vestiges of their teeth appearing on them, I examined several, & found the mark of the scalping knife on all." *Diary of David McClure, Doctor of Divinity, 1748–1820* (New York: Knickerbocker Press, 1899), 48.

41. *MFDB,* 13.

42. In 1753, as the French and their Indian allies moved aggressively to seize control of the fur trade in the Ohio Valley, one of the attacks on associates of the leading Pennsylvania trader George Croghan was an attack by Miamis on a trading party of John Findley that killed three of Findley's men. Downes, 65. For a summary of attacks by French soldiers and allied Indians from the Great Lakes post on British traders in the Ohio Valley between 1740 and 1753, see Hinderaker, *Elusive Empires,* 139.

43. Draper interview with Edward Coles, 1848, DM 6S309.

44. Ralph Clayton to the *St. Louis Christian Advocate,* May 30, 1877, DM 7C43[1–3], 7C44. Clayton, who told the story on his ninety-fifth birthday, claimed to have heard it from Boone in Missouri in 1818.

4. A GOOD WIFE

1. Draper interview with Joseph Scholl, 1868, DM 24S217.

2. Faragher, 42–43.

3. *MFDB,* 19.

4. Draper, 141.

5. G. Hedrick to Draper, June 26, 1866, DM 28C67.

6. Draper interview with Peter Smith, 1863, DM 18S113.

7. Houston, 36.

8. *MFDB,* 140; Faragher, 30–31. Descriptions of Boone vary. Josiah Collins, who was with him in Boonesborough in 1778, said Boone "didn't exceed 5 ft. 10 ins. Very well set, well made man. . . . Hair, reddish sandy. Complexion, fair. High fore-head—hollow-eyed—middling long nose, and that bowed over a little wide mouth—and a good set of teeth—of remarkable pleasant temper, nothing appeared to ruffle his mind, or make him uneasy, & of a pleasant countenance." JDS interview with Josiah Collins, c. 1840s, DM 12CC76. Timothy Flint, who interviewed Boone in 1818, said Boone had "a mild clear blue eye." Elijah Bryan said Boone's eyes "were deep blue, and very brilliant, and were always on the alert." According to Houston, whose account has been questioned, Boone had dark eyes and was "dark complected." Elijah Bryan said that until the last year or two of his life Boone was inclined to corpulency. Note by T. F. Belue, Houston, 70. A nephew described Boone as "about five feet 8 or 9 inches high stout strong made light hair blue eyes yellow eyebrows wide mouth thin lips fair complexion Nose a little on the Roman order." Daniel Boone Bryan to Draper, Feb. 27, 1843, DM 22C5. A visitor to Boone in Missouri described him as "about five feet 10 inches in height—of fair, light complexion—and one of the finest forms and noblest foreheads [he] ever saw." Draper interview with Edward Coles, 1848, DM 6S311.

9. *MFDB,* 36–37.

10. *MFDB,* 19, DM 6S41.

11. R. G. Prunty to Draper, Jan. 26, 1883, DM 57[3]. Prunty said he got the story from his mother-in-law, the wife of Boone's son Nathan.

12. Draper, 140–41.

13. See Joseph Doddridge, *Notes of the Settlement and Indian Wars of the Western Parts of Pennsylvania and Virginia* (1824), in Samuel Kercheval, *A History of the Valley of Virginia* (Strasburg, Va.: Shenandoah Publishing Co., 1925), 251.

14. Draper, 143, 146–47.

15. Faragher, 52.

16. Governor Pierre de Rigaud de Vaudreuil to Jean Baptiste de Machault, June 8, 1756, in *Documents Relating to the Colonial History of the State of New York*, ed. Edmund B. O'Callaghan and Berthold Fernow, 15 vols. (Albany, Parson's Weed, 1853–87), 10:413; Ward, *Breaking the Backcountry*, 46.

17. Miller and Pencak, *Pennsylvania*, 112; Ward, *Breaking the Backcountry*, 64–70.

18. Downes, 80–82; McConnell, *Country Between*, 121–22.

19. Capt. Jean-Daniel Dumas, July 24, 1756, Wallace, *Conrad Weiser*, 395.

20. Washington to John Robinson, Nov. 9, 1756, in *The Papers of George Washington, Colonial Series*, ed. W. W. Abbot and Dorothy Twohig, 10 vols. (Charlottesville: University Press of Virginia, 1983–95), 4:16–17; Ward, *Breaking the Backcountry*, 57 and, for the effectiveness of raids in Virginia and Pennsylvania, 60–73.

21. Downes, 88–92. For the negotiation of the treaty of Easton, see Wallace, *Conrad Weiser*, 520–52.

22. Bakeless, 31, 438 (referring to a deed in book 3 of the Rowan County records dated Oct. 12, 1759, with an added note that Boone bought the tract for fifty pounds); Morgan, 65, 468 n.65 (referring to a deed of gift dated Oct. 18, 1759, from Squire and Sarah Boone to Daniel Boone, citing Rowan County *Minutes, Court of Pleas and Quarter Sessions*, 2:277).

23. *MFDB*, 14.

24. Bailyn, *Peopling of British North America*, 116.

25. Lofaro, 18–19.

26. Silas W. Parris, writing for Thomas Norman to Draper, Nov. 3, 1884, DM 2C53.

27. Stephen Hempstead to Draper, Feb. 15, 1863, DM 16C76[2]. In Hempstead's version, the incident happened on Boone's return from Shawnee captivity (in other words, in 1778). In another version of the story the child was born in 1771, and Daniel's brother Squire Boone was said to be the father. JDS interview with Josiah Collins, 1840s, DM 12CC97. Neither of these versions makes sense, since Rebecca Boone bore no children in 1778 or 1771.

28. Draper interview with Stephen Cooper, 1889, DM 11C101.

29. Cf. *Journal of Nicholas Cresswell*, 103, 105.

30. JDS interview with Josiah Collins, 1840s, DM 12CC97. The word Shane left blank presumably was *cuckold*.

31. Daniel Boone Papers, Archibald Henderson Collection, University of North Carolina, qtd. in Faragher, 67. For a slightly different translation, see Morgan, 128–29.

32. Draper, 403.

33. Filson, 73.

34. Draper interview with Edward Byram, Oct. 2, 1863, DM 19S170.

35. Eviza L. Coshow to Draper, May 29, 1885, DM 21C45[2].

5. LONG HUNTS

1. Stephen Aron, *How the West Was Lost: The Transformation of Kentucky from Daniel Boone to Henry Clay* (Baltimore: Johns Hopkins University Press, 1996), 13. See generally Ted Franklin Belue, *The Hunters of Kentucky: A Narrative History of America's First Far West, 1750–1792* (Mechanicsburg, Pa.: Stackpole Books, 2003).

2. In 1768, e.g., the Philadelphia firm of Baynton, Wharton, and Morgan planned to send out sixty hunters in four boats; at least two boats made the trip. Otis K. Rice, *Frontier Kentucky* (Lexington: University Press of Kentucky, 1993), 23.

3. Downes, 13–14. Other hunters in Kentucky whose peltry was taken by Indians included Caspar Mansker and Abraham and Isaac Bledsoe, who started out from New River in June 1769 and were robbed by Cherokees; a party in 1772 from the Yadkin Valley, under Benjamin Cleveland, also robbed by Cherokees; and a large party in 1771 under Joseph Drake and Henry Skaggs, robbed by Shawnees (on the discovery of the loss Skaggs carved on a tree: "fifteen hundred skins gone to ruination").

4. See Belue, *Hunters of Kentucky,* 206–8, for a description of Pennsylvania or Kentucky rifles and their history.

5. The rifle came down in the Floyd and the Preston families to my great-uncle Preston Brown, who noted on a label attached to the rifle that he had inherited it from his great-aunt Susan Hepburn. Susan Preston Hepburn (1819–97) was a granddaughter of Colonel William Preston. Dorman, 60.

6. Draper, 208, 212–13, 224.

7. For the steps to load a Kentucky rifle, see Belue, *Hunters of Kentucky,* 207–8.

8. Belue, *Hunters of Kentucky,* 92; Shepard Krech III, *The Ecological Indian: Myth and History* (New York: W. W. Norton, 1999), 160, 163.

9. *Historical Statistics,* pt. 2, chap. Z—Colonial and Pre-Federal Statistics, 1184. The British colonies in the analysis of exports included Newfoundland, Bermuda, and Bahamas.

10. Draper interview with Edward Byram, Oct. 2, 1863, DM 19S170.

11. *MFDB,* 33.

12. Draper, 229.

13. Krech, *Ecological Indian,* 154.

14. *MFDB,* 33.

15. *MFDB,* 33.

16. Belue, *Hunters of Kentucky,* 91.

17. *MFDB,* 33.

18. Houston, 21.

19. *MFDB,* 35.

20. Belue, *Hunters of Kentucky,* 151.

21. Col. William Fleming, "Journal of Travels in Kentucky, 1779–1780," in Mereness, 640.

22. Filson, 51.

23. JDS interview with William Clinkenbeard, c. 1840s, DM 11CC61.

24. See generally Andrew C. Isenberg, *The Destruction of the Bison: An Environmental History, 1750–1920* (Cambridge: Cambridge University Press, 2000), 93–163.

25. *Journal of Nicholas Cresswell,* 85.

26. Cf. comments of Kentucky hunter Hugh Bell on how to cook buffalo tongue, in Belue, *Hunters of Kentucky*, 161.

27. Ibid., 161.

28. Ibid., 219; Narrative of Spencer Records, DM 23CC37.

29. "Journal of Col. William Fleming," Mereness, 628–29.

30. Belue, *Hunters of Kentucky*, 219.

31. Ibid., 160.

32. *Journal of Nicholas Cresswell*, 89.

33. Trabue, 72.

34. *MFDB*, 34; Draper, 233–35, 251.

35. *MFDB*, 35.

36. *MFDB*, 33.

37. A folkloric-sounding panther story occurs in a suspect memoir said to have been written by a Boone acquaintance, Peter Houston, when over eighty. Before Boone left for Kentucky, he and Houston, while carrying a deer ham at night, heard the screams of an approaching panther, dropped the deer ham, and went to Houston's cabin. Houston's dogs treed the panther. Boone and Houston went to the tree in the dark. Boone had Houston strike flint and steel to light the tinder and shavings in a tinder-box. Boone fired at the glint in the panther's eyes, bringing down one of the largest panthers Houston had ever seen. (Boone said, "I have killed many such.") Boone's shot in the dark had struck the panther between the eyes. Houston, thirty-four. Peter Houston's grandson in 1887 sent Draper a purported copy of a memoir Peter Houston had written in 1842, when he was over eighty. The original, according to the grandson, had been in a satchel that was stolen. Houston, 5–7.

38. Statement of Maj. William Bailey Smith, *Hunt's Western Review*, DM 31C2[85]; Draper, 501.

39. Draper interview with James Boone (son of Nathan), DM 6S294.

40. Draper, 338.

41. Thomas Speed, *The Wilderness Road: A Description of the Routes of Travel by Which the Pioneers and Early Settlers First Came to Kentucky* (Louisville, Ky.: Filson Club, 1886), 22.

42. Draper, 188–90; Lofaro, 21.

43. See Timothy Flint, *Recollections of the Last Ten Years Passed in Occasional Residences and Journeyings in the Valley of the Mississippi* . . . (Boston: Cummings, Hilliard, 1826), ed. George R. Brooks (Carbondale: Southern Illinois University Press, 1968), 68 ("No employment can be imagined more laborious, and few more dangerous, than this of propelling a boat against the current of such a river.")

44. The hunter was the father of the frontier preacher Abraham Snethen. Paul Woehrmann, ed., "The Autobiography of Abraham Snethen, Frontier Preacher," *FCHQ* 51 (Oct. 1977): 315, 316.

45. Draper interview with Edward Byram, Oct. 2, 1863, DM 19S170; JDS interview with Joshua McQueen, c. 1840s, DM 11CC121.

46. Belue, *Hunters of Kentucky*, 163; Krech, *Ecological Indian*, 126 (extinct east of the Mississippi by 1833).

47. William S. Bryan, "Daniel Boone in Missouri," *Missouri Historical Review* 3 (1906–9): 92–93.

48. Samuel Willard to Rev. Thomas P. Hinds, Oct. 14, 1844, DM 24C112. Willard said that

by canoeing thirty miles west, he had at least caught sight of a buffalo cow and calf and of a herd of elk.

49. Isenberg, *Destruction of the Bison,* preface, 27, 143 (estimate that in 1889 only about three hundred buffalo were left).

50. JDS interview with William Clinkenbeard, c. 1840s, DM 11CC61.

51. JDS interview with Joshua McQueen, c. 1840s, DM 11CC121.

52. Eric Hinderaker, *Elusive Empires: Constructing Colonialism in the Ohio Valley, 1673–1800* (New York: Cambridge University Press, 1997), 14–20; White, *Middle Ground,* 1–7.

53. Krech, *Ecological Indian,* 175–77, 181.

54. Archer Butler Hulbert and William N. Schwarze, eds., *David Zeisberger's History of the Northern American Indians* (Columbus: Ohio State Archaeological and Historical Society, 1910), 14; White, *Middle Ground,* 490; McConnell, *Country Between,* 156 (in 1769 the Munsee town of Goschgoching, with perhaps sixty to eighty hunters, killed twelve hundred deer in the fall hunt); Wallace, *Conrad Weiser,* 271 ("A middling good Hunter among the Indian of Ohio Killes for his Share in one fall 150.200 dears").

55. Krech, *Ecological Indian,* 156–57.

56. Ibid., 161–63; Hinderaker, *Elusive Empires,* 68–74.

57. Yakatastanage (the Mortar), proposing trade terms for the Creek-British treaty of Pensacola, May 28, 1765, Dorothy V. Jones, *License for Empire: Colonialism by Treaty in Early America* (Chicago: University of Chicago Press, 1982), 96, citing Dunbar Rowland, ed., *Mississippi Provincial Archives, English Dominion* (Jackson: Mississippi Department of Archives and History, 1911), 204.

58. White, *Middle Ground,* 486, 503–4.

59. Draper, 415, 418.

60. Isenberg, *Destruction of the Bison,* 82, 85 (quoting François-Antoine Larocque's description of a Crow hunt in 1804 and Charles McKenzie's description of Cheyennes cutting out only the tongues of 250 buffalo cows in 1806. See also Krech, *Ecological Indian,* 133 (in 1805 Mandans killed "whole droves" and took only "the best parts of the meat").

61. By the 1840s Plains tribes were bringing traders over 100,000 buffalo robes a year to traders. Isenberg, *Destruction of the Bison,* 93–94. Indian buffalo killing never approached, however, the levels reached by white hunters in the 1870s, who, armed with guns such as the Sharp "big fifty," killed some one million bison a year between 1872 and 1874. One buffalo hunter, Josiah Wright Moar, estimated that he alone killed 20,000 buffalo between 1870 and 1879. Isenberg, 137. As Red Cloud reportedly said, "Where the Indian killed one buffalo, the hide and tongue hunters killed fifty." Krech, *Ecological Indian,* 143. The hides were tanned and often made into industrial belts for America's burgeoning factories.

62. See generally Krech, *Ecological Indian;* and Isenberg, *Destruction of the Bison.*

6. BOONE'S FIRST HUNTS IN KENTUCKY

1. E.g., Gabriel Arthur, captured by the Shawnees in 1673 and taken north to the mouth of the Scioto before being released in 1674. George Morgan Chinn, *Kentucky: Settlement and Statehood, 1750–1800* (Frankfort: Kentucky Historical Society, 1975), 12–13. See David M.

Burns, *Gateway: Dr. Thomas Walker and the Opening of Kentucky* (Middlesboro, Ky.: Bell County Historical Society, 2000), 16.

2. Draper, 49; for the grant to the company, see Rice, *Frontier Kentucky*, 10.

3. Draper, 61; Belue, *Hunters of Kentucky*, 32.

4. Faragher, 66.

5. Draper interview with Nathan and Olive Boone, 1851, DM 6S42.

6. Jethro Rumple to Draper, Aug. 30, 1883, DM 8C190[1].

7. Faragher, 66; Lofaro, 21.

8. Faragher, 63; Lofaro, 21; Filson, 57.

9. *Montcalm and Wolfe: The French and Indian War* (New York: Da Capo Press, 1995), 526. For the impact of the 1763 Treaty of Paris, see generally Calloway, *Scratch of a Pen*.

10. For the efforts of both Florida provinces to encourage settlement, see Calloway, *Scratch of a Pen*, 150–56.

11. Calloway, *Scratch of a Pen*, 12 (Britain's national debt grew from £74.6 million at the start of the Seven Years' War to £122.6 million on Jan. 5, 1763).

12. McConnell, *Country Between*, 182–206; Ward, *Breaking the Backcountry*, 219–35; Calloway, *Scratch of a Pen*, 66–100.

13. See Bailyn, *Voyagers to the West*, 483, noting that one of the first large groups to migrate to West Florida from the eastern colonies were backcountry Virginians for whom the Chesapeake markets were inaccessible and who had moved to the disputed borderland of western Pennsylvania.

14. Just as "Findley" is spelled different ways, so Stewart's name is sometimes spelled "Stuart."

15. *MFDB*, 15.

16. DM 4C75[8]. The entry is undated and occurs after entries from 1775, but Draper argues persuasively that it must be from the Florida trip.

17. Draper, 186–87.

18. *MFDB*, 15.

19. Journal of Capt. Harry Gordon for Sept. 30, 1767, in Mereness, 486.

20. *MFDB*, 16.

21. *MFDB*, 15; Draper, 188.

22. Faragher, 65–66.

23. *MFDB*, 17, 19; Draper, 195–96; Faragher, 71; DM 6S6–7 ("Ketched in a Snow Storm"; sees his first buffalo).

24. Faragher, 68–69. The early Kentucky historian John Mason Brown, the author's great-grandfather, concluded it was an Iroquois word meaning meadowland. John Mason Brown, *The Political Beginnings of Kentucky* (Louisville, 1889), 10.

25. Draper, 522–23; Filson, 8.

26. *MFDB*, 23; DM 6S7–8.

27. Jones, *License for Empire*, 89.

28. Gen. Thomas Gage to Lord Hillsborough, Jan. 6, 1770, Downes, 144–45. For how the Fort Stanwix negotiations infuriated the Shawnees, Delawares, and Mingos, see Alan Taylor, *The Divided Ground: Indians, Settlers and the Northern Borderland of the American Revolution* (New York: Random House, 2006), 42–45.

29. James H. Howard, *Shawnee! The Ceremonialism of a Native Indian Tribe and Its Cultural Background* (Athens: Ohio University Press, 1981), 32; A. Gwynn Henderson, "Dispelling the Myth: Seventeenth- and Eighteenth-Century Indian Life in Kentucky," *RKHS* 90 (1992): 8.

30. Johnson, *License for Empire*, 101–8; Hinderaker, *Elusive Empires*, 168–70.

31. Lofaro, 43.

32. Johnson, *License for Empire*, 218 n. 33.

33. *MFDB*, 23; Draper, 207.

34. Faragher, 76.

35. Draper, 209–10; Faragher, 76–79. See Morgan, 98 (bluegrass may have originated in Pennsylvania).

36. Filson, 51.

37. Ibid.

38. Ibid., 52.

39. *MFDB*, 24; Draper, 213–16; Faragher, 79–80.

40. JDS's interview with Daniel Boone Bryan (c. 1844), DM 22C14.

41. Draper, 216; *MFDB*, 24.

42. *MFDB*, 25–26.

43. Draper, 224 n. 24; Faragher, 82.

44. *MFDB*, 28.

45. Jonathan Swift, *Gulliver's Travels* (Oxford: Oxford University Press: 1999), 97; Daniel Boone's deposition, Sept. 15, 1796, DM 4C93, qtd. in John Mason Brown's *Oration at the Blue Licks*, Aug. 19, 1882, DM 2C80. See JDS interview with Thomas Eaton, c. 1840s, DM 11CC95 (Eaton always understood that Boone had named the place after a town in *Gulliver's Travels*, though the town in that book is spelled differently).

46. *MFDB*, 28–29.

47. *MFDB*, 29, 144.

48. Draper, 265–65, 276; Faragher, 83–84.

49. Filson, 53.

50. Draper interview with George Smith, DM 32S480, 31C1[60].

51. Filson, 54.

52. Filson, 56.

53. Col. William Fleming, "Journals of Travels in Kentucky, 1779-1780," Mar. 5, 1780 (describing a large black and white woodpecker with a bony white wedge-shaped beak and a "bright red head with remarkable large tuft of feathers on the Crown," shot near St. Asaph's settlement), Mereness, 632; John James Audubon, *Ornithological Biography*, describing birds depicted in his *Birds of America*, qtd. in *Harvard Magazine*, July–Aug. 2005, 88.

54. *MFDB*, 31.

55. *MFDB*, 32.

56. Faragher, 86, 375.

57. Chester Harding, *My Egotistigraphy*, 35–36.

58. Draper, 266–67; Faragher, 86–87; *MFDB*, 37.

59. Letter from John B. Roark to Draper, Mar. 30, 1885, DM 16C81.

60. Filson, 56–57.

7. BOONE BEGINS TO OPEN THE WILDERNESS

1. Draper, 284; *MFDB*, 37.

2. Bailey, *Ohio Company*, 138–43. For overviews of the different companies and speculators seeking large land tracts in the Ohio Valley after the treaty of Fort Stanwix, see Hinderaker, *Elusive Empires*, 168–75; and Rice, *Frontier Kentucky*, 7–54.

3. Faragher, 88–89; for Harrod's surveying, see Kathryn Harrod Mason, *James Harrod of Kentucky* (Baton Rouge: Louisiana State University Press, 1951), 36–43.

4. Faragher, 89–90; "gentleman of some distinction," Lord Dunmore to Lord Dartmouth, Dec. 24, 1774, DM 6C16. For a biographical sketch of Russell, see Draper, 551–53.

5. Filson, 57; Lofaro, 41.

6. The Clinch Valley resident was Thomas W. Carter. His recollection is in M. B. Woods's letter to Draper, Apr. 9, 1883, DM 4C26.

7. *New York Colonial Documents*, 8:396, qtd. in Downe, 153.

8. *MFDB*, 39–41; Draper, 287–88; Faragher, 92–93; James William Hagy, "The First Attempt to Settle Kentucky: Boone in Virginia," *FCHQ* 53 (July 1979): 227–33.

9. Draper, 289–90; Faragher, 94; *MFDB*, 39–41.

10. *MFDB*, 41–42.

11. Draper, 290; Morgan, 138.

12. Lord Dunmore to Lord Dartmouth, Dec. 24, 1774, DM 6C16; Maj. Arthur Campbell to Col. William Preston, DM 3QQ40 (includes "it would be easier to find 200 Men to screen him from the Law, than ten to bring him to Justice"), printed in *DHDW*, 39.

13. Lord Dunmore to Lord Dartmouth, Williamsburg, Dec. 24, 1774, DM 15J4–48, printed in *DHDW*, 378.

14. Faragher, 96; Belue, note in Draper, 326; Lofaro, 45. For other accounts of the Yellow Creek killings, see reminiscences of Judge Henry Jolly, DM 6NN22–24; Bazaleel Wells, DM 2S, bk. 2, 5–6; and George Edgington, DM 2S, book 3, 34, printed in *DHDW*, 9–17. Some give Greathouse's first name as Jacob, others as Daniel.

15. Daniel Smith to William Preston, Mar. 22, 1774, DM 3B115, qtd. in Faragher, 98.

16. *New York Colonial Documents*, 8:462, qtd. in Downe, 154.

17. Draper, 559, 563.

18. Ibid., 559.

19. See letter of Alexander Spottswood Dandridge to Col. William Preston, May 15, 1774, DM 3QQ26 ("According to your instructions Mr Floyd Surveyed for Colo. Washington 2000 Acres of Land and Sent a platt of the Same in a letter to you"); and letter of Col. William Preston to Col. George Washington, Fincastle, May 27, 1774, DM 15S79 ("Agreeable to my promise, I directed Mr. Floyd, an assistant to survey your land on Cole river [Coal River, which flows into the Kanawha a few miles below Charleston], which he did"), printed in *DHDW*, 22–24.

20. Washington to William Crawford, in *The Washington-Crawford Letters, 1767–1781* ed. Consul W. Butterfield (Cincinnati, 1877) 3, qtd. in Downe, 156; and in Calloway, *Scratch of a Pen*, 99.

21. Sehlinger, *General William Preston*, 4.

22. Hammon, "The Fincastle Surveyors at the Falls of the Ohio," *FCHQ* 47 (1973): 19, 23.

23. Ibid., 25.

24. Journal of Thomas Hanson, DM 14J58–84, entry for May 26, 1774, printed in *DHDW*, 123–24.

25. Neal O. Hammon, "The Fincastle Surveyors in the Bluegrass, 1774," *RKHS* (Oct. 1972): 277–94.

26. Hammon, "Fincastle Surveyors in the Bluegrass," 283–86.

27. Journal of Thomas Hanson, DM 14J58–84, entry for July 1, 1774, printed in *DHDW*, 129.

28. Abraham Hite to Col. William Preston, Hampshire, June 3, 1774, DM 3QQ35, printed in *DHDW*, 31–32.

29. See Lord Dunmore's circular letter to the county lieutenants, DM 3QQ39, Williamsburg, June 10, 1774, printed in *DHDW*, 33; for "destroy their Towns," Dunmore to Col. Andrew Lewis, *DHDW*, 86.

30. Barbara Rasmussen, "Anarchy and Enterprise on the Imperial Frontier: Washington, Dunmore, Logan, and Land in the Eighteenth Century Ohio Valley," *Ohio Valley History* 6, no. 4 (Winter 2006): 22 and n. 51.

31. Neal O. Hammon, "Captain Harrod's Company, 1774: A Reappraisal," *RKHS* 72 (1974): 227–28.

32. See letters to and from Col. William Preston in June 1774, in *DHDW*, 42–61.

33. Circular letter of Col. William Preston, July 20, 1774, DM 3QQ139, printed in *DHDW*, 91–92.

34. Draper, 306–7, quoting letters of June 26 and July 13, 1774, to William Preston, DM 3QQ46 and 3QQ64. The letters are printed in *DHDW*, 49–51 and 88–91. The "best Hands" description is from the earlier letter.

35. *MFDB*, 42–43.

36. Deposition of Daniel Boone in *Boofman Heirs v. James Hickman*, Circuit Court Records, Fayette County, Fayette County Complete Book A, 604–42, qtd. in Neal Hammon and Richard Taylor, *Virginia's Western War, 1775–1786* (Mechanicsburg, Pa.: Stackpole Books, 2002), xxix. Boone's deposition, taken on April 24, 1794, is also transcribed in *Fayette County Kentucky Records* (Evansville, Ind.: Cook Publications, 1985), 1:178.

37. Journal of Thomas Hanson for July 25 and July 28, 1774, in *DHDW*, 132.

38. Shane interview with Mrs. Samuel Scott, c. 1840s, DM 11CC225–26; Faragher, 103.

39. Letter of Aug. 28, 1774, DM 33S254–56, reprinted in Neal Hammon and James Russell Harris, "'In a dangerous situation': Letters of Col. John Floyd, 1774–1783," *RKHS* 83 (1983): 209; Draper, 277–78, 305–11; Faragher, 100–102; *DHDW*, 168.

40. Lofaro, 47.

41. *DHDW*, 306. In 1772 the Presbyterian missionary David McClure asked Logan how he was doing. "Pointing to his breast, he said, 'I feel very bad *here*. Wherever I go the evil monethoes (Devils) are after me. The house, the trees & the air, are full of Devils, they continually haunt me, & they will kill me. All things tell me how wicked I have been.' He stood pale & trembling, apparently in great distress. His eyes were fixed on the ground, & the sweat ran down his face like one in agony. It was a strange sight. I had several times seen him at Pittsburgh & thought him the most martial figure of an Indian that I had ever seen." *Diary of David McClure*, 56–57.

42. Draper, 313–15; DM 3QQ118, printed in *DHDW*, 246–47. The copy of Logan's letter is torn on the right side; the bracketed words are reconstructions of the missing words. For the Conestoga Massacre, see McConnell, *County Between*, 190–91.

43. Col. James Robertson to Col. William Preston, Aug. 11, 1774, DM 3QQ73–73[1].

44. Aug. 13, 1774; Draper, 311.

45. Arthur Campbell to William Preston, Oct. 1, 1774, DM 3QQ109, *DHDW*, 219–20.

46. Arthur Campbell to William Preston, Royal-Oak, Oct. 12, 1774, DM 3QQ118, *DHDW*, 244.

47. Arthur Campbell to William Preston, Oct. 13, 1774, *DHDW*, 218.

48. Daniel Smith to William Preston, Oct. 4, 1774, DM 3QQ114, *DHDW*, 228.

49. Daniel Smith to William Preston, Oct. 13, 1774, DM 3QQ119, *DHDW*, 248–49.

50. Draper, 550–51 ("not popular with the mass of society"); Arthur Campbell to William Preston, Oct. 13, 1774, *DHDW*, 250.

51. Maj. Arthur Campbell to Col. William Preston, Aug. 28, 1774, DM 3QQ85, printed in *DHDW*, 170–71.

52. *DHDW*, xv.

53. Dorman, 1–3, 14.

54. Faragher, 105.

55. Draper, 328. Although some have questioned whether the words are close to Logan's, they resemble what Logan told Capt. James Wood in July 1775: "Logan repeated in Plain English the Manner in which the People of Virginia had killed his Mother Sister and all his Relations during which he wept and Sung Alternately and concluded with telling me the Revenge he had taken." Journal of Captain James Wood for July 25, 1775, *RUO*, 50.

56. For some of the correspondence dealing with these difficulties, see *DHDW*, 167–79.

57. William Fleming to William Bowyer, undated, DM 2ZZ7, printed in *DHDW*, 256.

58. Lofaro, 49; Bailyn, *Peopling of British North America*, 536; Draper, 321; *DHDW*, 253–97, 368–95.

59. E.g., Boone's certificate of military service in and discharge from Fincastle County Militia for James McCushin [*sic*], Nov. 25, 1774, Manuscript Collections C N, FHS.

60. Lord Dunmore to Lord Dartmouth, Williamsburg, Dec. 24, 1774, DM 15J4–48, printed in *DHDW*, 371–72. The British commander-in-chief in 1769, Gen. Sir Thomas Gage, had expressed a similar thought to Sir William Johnson, the Indian superintendent: "Frontier People" were "too Numerous, too Lawless and Licentious ever to be restrained" by any authority. Gage to Johnson, Apr. 3, 1769, James Sullivan et al., eds., *The Papers of Sir William Johnson*, 14 vols. (Albany: State University of New York, 1921–63), 12:709–10.

8. TRANSYLVANIA, THE WILDERNESS ROAD, AND THE BUILDING OF BOONESBOROUGH

1. Manuscript memoir of Richard Henderson by his brother Maj. Pleasant Henderson, qtd. in Draper, 354.

2. Archibald Neilson to Andrew Miller, Jan. 10, 1775, qtd. in Faragher, 108, 378. Richard Henderson's journals do not suggest that Boone induced him to make the purchase.

3. Aron, *How the West Was Lost*, 59.

4. Faragher, 73; Draper, 331.

5. The original agreement to act together as the Louisa Company to rent or purchase a large "Tract of Land lying on the west side of the Mountains on the waters of the Missisipi River" was dated Aug. 27, 1774. DM 1CC2.

6. The opinion was issued by Britain's solicitor general and attorney general. Jones, *License for Empire*, 116–17. The East Indian context is clearly distinguishable from the American context, in light of the Proclamation of 1763, the trans-Appalachian rights of Virginia, North Carolina and Pennsylvania under their royal charters, and the colonial laws against private treaties with the Indians.

7. *The Colonial Records of North Carolina*, vol. 9: *1771–1775*, ed. William L. Saunders (Raleigh, N.C.: Josephus Daniels, 1890), 1129–30, qtd. in Lofaro, 50.

8. William Preston to George Washington, Jan. 31, 1775, DM 15S100.

9. William Preston to Lord Dunmore, Mar. 10, 1775, DM 4QQ7, *RUO*, 1–6. Portions of the letter qtd. in Draper, 335.

10. Proclamation of Governor Josiah Martin, Feb. 10, 1775, reprinted in Ranck, 147–50.

11. Proclamation of Lord Dunmore, Mar. 21, 1775, reprinted in Ranck, 181–82.

12. Ranck, 162; Calloway, *American Revolution in Indian Country*, 186.

13. Draper, 333, 363 n. q; Ranck, 151.

14. Brent Yanusdi Cox, *Heart of the Eagle: Dragging Canoe and the Emergence of the Chickamauga Confederacy* (Milan, Tenn.: Chenanee Publishers, 1999), 164, 172.

15. John Haywood, *The Civil and Political History of the State of Tennessee* (Knoxville: Heiskell and Brosn, 1803), 58–59.

16. The tract described in the main deed was from the mouth of the Kentucky River on the Ohio, up the Kentucky to its source, southeast to Powell's Mountain, west along the ridge of that mountain, northwest to the head spring of the most southerly branch of the Cumberland, down the Cumberland to the Ohio, and back up the Ohio to the mouth of the Kentucky. The text of the deed is in Ranck, 151–56. A separate deed granted a right of way from the Holston River to the Cumberland Gap. Lofaro, 52.

17. Filson, 80; Draper, 333.

18. Known as Boone's Trace: Hart Litigation, Fayette County Kentucky Records, 1:669 (deposition of Stephen Hancock), 670 (deposition of Squire Boone), 676 (deposition of Jesse Oldham). A typed copy of the record in this litigation was sent to the author by Neal Hammon in Oct. 2007. The depositions are also transcribed in *Fayette County Kentucky Records*, 1:187–92.

19. Walker's narrative of the trip, published in *Debow's Review* in Feb. 1854, was written about 1824. It is reprinted in Ranck, 161–68. For "by general consent" and "every heart abounded," see 163.

20. Ranck, 163–64. Excerpts of Walker's narrative, including these portions, are also reprinted in Draper, 336–40.

21. Draper, 339; Ranck, 168–69.

22. Ranck, 165.

23. For uncertainty as to the identity of the Indian attackers, see Belue, *Hunters of Kentucky*, 99.

24. James Robertson to Col. William Preston, Culberson, Aug. 11, 1774, DM 3QQ73, printed in *DHDW*, 142.

25. Aron, *How the West Was Lost*, 37, quoting letter from Oconestoto to the Delegates in Convention, June 24, 1775, in *Revolutionary Virginia: The Road to Independence*, ed. William J. Van Schreevan (Charlottesville: Virginia Independence Bicentennial Commission (by) University Press of Virginia, 1973–83), 3:219; Draper, 362 n. n.

26. Ranck, 167.

27. The letter is reprinted in Ranck, 168–69; and in Draper, 339.

28. Calk's journal and a transcript of the journal are at the Kentucky Historical Society and are available online at KHS Digital Collections, which can be reached from the society's home page, www.history.ky.gov. The journal has been reprinted, e.g., in Ellen Eslinger, ed., *Running Mad for Kentucky: Frontier Travel Accounts* (Lexington: University Press of Kentucky 2004), 69–74.

29. Journal of William Calk, entries for Apr. 9, 10, 10, 12, 14, 16 and 17, 1775.

30. Ranck, 172. Henderson's journal is reprinted in Ranck, 169–80. Substantial excerpts—including materials not contained in Ranck's book—appear in Draper, 346–53. William Calk noted in his journal for Apr. 20: "We Start Early & git Down to Caintuck [the Kentucky River] to Boons foart about 12 oclock wheare we Stop they Come out to meet us & welcome us in with a volley of guns."

31. Richard Henderson to the proprietors in North Carolina, Boonesborough, June 12, 1775, reprinted in Ranck, 184–87.

32. Ranck, 164–65, 167.

33. Richard Henderson to proprietors remaining in North Carolina, Boonesborough, June 12, 1775, reprinted in Ranck, 187.

34. Ranck, 35. Although Ranck describes the second fort as having 26 cabins and four blockhouses in the summer of 1775, Hammon believes the second fort at Boonesborough was not started until 1776. It was built by March of 1777. Hammon to author, Feb. 25, 2008.

35. See Journal of Thos. Hanson, *DHDW*, 121; Rice, *Frontier Kentucky*, 72.

36. See report of John Williams, Jan. 3, 1776, to the proprietors in North Carolina, reprinted in Ranck, 233 (Williams called a convention to ask for recommendations for the post of surveyor; those present unanimously recommended Floyd); Draper, 390.

37. Ranck, 174–75; Draper, 347.

38. Hammon and Taylor, *Virginia's Western War*, 13.

39. Ranck, 175.

40. Ibid., 176.

41. Ibid., 177.

42. Henderson's journal for Apr. 27, 1775; Ranck, 176.

43. Walker's Narrative, Ranck, 166.

44. Henderson's journal for May 17, 1775; Ranck, 177.

45. Ranck, 29. The documents reprinted in the appendices to Ranck's book spell the name of the attorney-in-fact "Farrow"; Ranck in his book spells the name "Farrar."

46. The text of the compact is reprinted in Ranck, 208–210 and in Draper, 369–70.

47. Richard Henderson to proprietors remaining in North Carolina, Boonesborough, June 12, 1775, reprinted in Ranck, 190.

48. Henderson's journal for May 29, 1775, recorded the arrival of a letter "with an account of the battle at Boston." Ranck, 177.

49. Walker's narrative, Ranck, 167. For Walker's career during the Revolution, see Draper, 356–57 n. 20.

50. Petition of "The Committee of West Virginia" to the Convention of Virginia, Harrodsburg, June 20, 1776, Ranck, 246.

51. Letter to Patrick Henry, Hillsborough, Apr. 26 ,1775, reprinted in Ranck, 194–95. The proprietors sent a copy of the letter to Thomas Jefferson.

52. Rev. John Brown to Col. William Preston, May 5, 1775, DM 4QQ15. The letter is printed in *RUO*, 10–12; and in Draper, 398. Rev. John Brown, an ancestor of the author, had married Margaret Preston, the sister of William Preston, another ancestor. Dorman, 5.

53. Richard Henderson to proprietors remaining in North Carolina, Boonesborough, June 12, 1775, reprinted in Ranck, 193.

54. Ibid.

55. Richard Henderson and John Luttrell to the proprietors in North Carolina, July 18, 1775, in Draper, 378–82.

56. Draper, 389.

57. Richard Henderson to proprietors remaining in North Carolina, Boonesborough, June 12, 1775, reprinted in Ranck, 189–90.

58. Richard Henderson and John Luttrell to the proprietors in North Carolina, July 18, 1775, in Draper, 378–82.

59. Faragher, 126–27; Lofaro, 62.

60. Faragher, 127; Lofaro, 62.

61. For James Hogg's remarkable career, see Bailyn, *Voyagers to the West,* 499–544.

62. The minutes of the Transylvania Proprietors, Sept. 25, 1775, are reprinted in Ranck, 212–19; the memorial to the Continental Congress is reprinted at 214–16. Portions of the minutes are also reprinted in Draper, 387–88.

63. Boone, however, in 1776 had acquired a tract of one thousand acres, which was held to be properly located. *Estill v. Hart's Heirs,* Harding's Reports, 567 (Spring Term 1808).

64. Bailyn, *Voyagers to the West,* 542.

65. James Hogg to Richard Henderson, Jan. 1776, reprinted in Ranck, 224–29.

66. The petition is reprinted in Ranck, 241–44.

67. The petition, headed Harrodsburg, June 20, 1776, is reprinted in Ranck, 244–47.

68. Draper, 410.

69. John Williams to the proprietors in North Carolina, Boonesborough, Jan. 3, 1776, reprinted in Ranck, 232–39.

70. Proclamation of Transylvania Company against settlement of disputed lands, June 26, 1776, reprinted in Ranck, 248–49.

71. John Floyd to William Preston, May 1776, DM 33S294–95.

72. Ibid.

73. Ranck, 54; Rice, *Frontier Kentucky,* 84.

74. Quaife, *Capture of Old Vincennes,* 34. For the protracted parliamentary jockeying that delayed passage of the bill creating Kentucky County, see John E. Selby, *The Revolution in Virginia, 1775–1783* (1988; rpt., Williamsburg, Va.: Colonial Williamsburg Foundation, 2007), 143–44.

75. On Nov. 4, 1778, the Virginia House of Delegates declared that the purchase heretofore made by Richard Henderson and company of that tract of land called Transylvania, within the commonwealth, "is void; but as the said Richard Henderson and Company have been at very great expense in making the said purchase, and in settling the lands, by which this commonwealth is likely to receive great advantage, by increasing its inhabitants, and establishing

a barrier against the Indians, it is just and reasonable to allow the said Richard Henderson and Company a compensation for their trouble and expense." The Virginia Assembly later in 1778 granted a sizable tract to Richard Henderson and Co. and its heirs as tenants in common. Ranck, 253–55; Selby, *Revolution in Kentucky*, 158–59.

76. Bailyn, *Voyagers to the West*, 544.

77. John Williams to the proprietors in North Carolina, Boonesborough, Jan. 3, 1776, Ranck, 237–38.

78. Filson, 60.

79. Draper, 392–93.

9. DARK AND BLOODY GROUND

1. Faragher, 144. In 1782 the commander of Fayette County militia revised upward to 860 the number of settlers in the central bluegrass region killed since 1775. Aron, *How the West Was Lost*, 48, citing Andrew Steel (Fayette County) to the Governor of Virginia, Sept. 12, 1782, *CVSP*, 3:303–4.

2. Quaife, *Capture of Old Vincennes*, 36.

3. Craig Thompson Friend, *Along the Maysville Road: The Early American Republic in the Trans-Appalachian West* (Knoxville: University of Tennessee Press, 2005), 94–96.

4. For an overview of some of the differences among the settlers in Kentucky and the Ohio Valley during the Revolutionary War, see Elizabeth A. Perkins, *Border Life: Experience and Memory in the Revolutionary Ohio Valley* (Chapel Hill: University of North Carolina Press, 1998), chap. 3, 81–115 ("Distinctions and Partitions amongst us").

5. Richard Kluger, *Seizing Destiny: How America Grew from Sea to Shining Sea* (New York: Alfred A. Knopf, 2007), 93–94 (conflicting claims of colonies), 190 (map of conflicting claims of colonies), and 81–83 (Quebec Act).

6. Richard White describes the claimants who pushed west across the mountains after 1763 as a new "village world" made up of white frontiersmen—a world beyond the control of the governments of the eastern colonies and that had been beyond the control of the British posts west of the Alleghenies. White, *Middle Ground*, 315–21.

7. Preston was advised that a resolution had been adopted that until receipt of a report from a committee appointed by the convention to consider whether the king acted properly in increasing the terms for the sale of land, all surveyors "be & they hereby are Directed to make no Surveys under [Lord Dunmore's] Instructions, nor pay any regard to the Said proclamation." Thomas Lewis to Col. William Preston, Richmond, Aug. 19, 1775, DM 4QQ29, printed in *RUO*, 21.

8. John Floyd to William Preston, Apr. 21, 1775; Draper, 385.

9. Filson, 66–67.

10. McConnell, *Country Between*, 190–206.

11. Speech of Cornstalk, Nov. 7, 1776, Morgan letterbook, 1776, qtd. in Colin G. Calloway, *The American Revolution in Indian Country: Crisis and Diversity in Native American Communities* (New York: Cambridge University Press, 1995), 166.

12. Calloway, *American Revolution in Indian Country*, 169–70 (beginning around 1779

or 1780, some twelve hundred Shawnees—mostly from the Kispoki, Piqua, and Thawekila divisions—moved down the Ohio Valley, with most of them eventually moving to Missouri to take up lands near Cape Girardeau, under auspices of the Spanish government; according to Shawnee tradition, Shawnees crossed the Mississippi as early as 1763).

13. Aron, *How the West Was Lost*, 47.

14. White, *Middle Ground*, 351–53.

15. Quaife, *Capture of Old Vincennes*, ix.

16. Lord Germain to Sir Guy Carleton, White Hall, Mar. 26, 1777, sent to Lieutenant Governor Hamilton from Quebec, May 21, 1777, printed in Consul Willshire Butterfield, *History of the Girtys* (Cincinnati: Robert Clarke & Co. 1890), 342–44; Downes, 195.

17. Hamilton to Gen. Sir Frederick Haldimand, dated July 6, 1781, in Quaife, *Capture of Old Vincennes*, 173.

18. Ranck, 75 n. 1.

19. John Williams to the proprietors in North Carolina, Boonesborough, Jan. 3, 1776, Ranck, 237–38. In 1764 the governor of Pennsylvania had proclaimed the Delawares and Shawnees to be "enemies, rebels, and traitors" and offer a bounty of $150 Spanish dollars for an adult male prisoner and $134 for his scalp. Hinderaker, *Elusive Empires*, 160–61. Virginia also offered a bounty for Indian scalps, though the bounty was repealed in late 1758. Virginia's governor, Francis Fauquier, had pointed out that the bounty "was found to produce bad Consequences, by setting our people to kill Indians whether Friends of Enemies," it being "impossible to distinguish the Nations of Indians." McConnell, *Country Between*, 124. Similarly, in 1756 Conrad Weiser had opposed Pennsylvania's adoption of a scalp bounty, seeing it as a menace to friendly Indians, whose scalps were the most easily procurable. Wallace, *Conrad Weiser*, 434.

20. Daniel Sullivan to Colonel John Cannon, Fort Pitt, Mar. 20, 1778, ed. Reuben Gold Thwaites and Louise P. Kellogg, in *FDUO* (Madison: State Historical Society of Wisconsin, 1912), 231–32.

21. Report from Hamilton to General Haldimand, Sept. 16, 1778, qtd. in Quaife, *Capture of Old Vincennes*, 174 n. 3.

22. Bernard W. Sheehan, "'The Famous Hair Buyer General': Henry Hamilton, George Rogers Clark, and the American Indian," *Indiana Magazine of History* 79 (1983): 4–7.

23. Qtd. ibid., 14.

24. Jefferson wrote Hamilton's superior officer: "The known rule of warfare with the Indian Savages is an indiscriminate-butchery of men women and children. . . . [Hamilton] associates small parties of whites under his immediate command with large parties of the Savages, & sends them to act, not against our Forts or armies in the field, but farming settlements on our frontiers." Jefferson to William Phillips, July 22, 1779, *CVSP*, 1:322; Grenier, *First Way of War*, 17.

25. See Hinderaker, *Elusive Empires*, 188–89, 207, 210–11, 225.

26. Draper interview with Moses Boone, 1846, DM 19C8; Draper, 447–48, 457 n. g; Faragher, 150.

27. See chaps. 13 and 14.

28. See generally Grenier, *First Way of War*.

29. JDS interview with William Clinkenbeard, c. 1840s, DM 11CC55. For the Bryans' reputation for being Tories, see Perkins, *Border Life*, 103 and 103 n. 45.

30. The petition, headed Harrodsburg, June 20, 1776, is reprinted in Ranck, 244–47.

31. Patricia Watlington, "Discontent in Frontier Kentucky," *RKHS* 65 (1967): 85–93.

32. George Washington to Francis Fauquier, Dec. 2 1758, in *The Official Papers of Francis Fauquier, Lieutenant Governor of Virginia, 1758–1768,* ed. George Reese, 3 vols. (Charlottesville: University of Virginia Press, 1980–83), 1:117–18; McConnell, *Country Between,* 150.

33. Lord Dunmore to Lord Dartmouth, Williamsburg, Dec. 24, 1774, DM 15J4–48, printed in *DHDW,* 391.

34. Watlington, "Discontent in Frontier Kentucky," 81.

35. Letter from "a gentleman of veracity," July 24, 1780, DM 46J59.

36. DM 33S296–97, reprinted in Lofaro, 75.

37. See White, *Middle Ground,* 433–68, for an overview of the banding together of the Indians, the British support, the Indian victories, and General Wayne's victory at Fallen Timbers.

38. Grenier, *First Way of War,* 198–99; Starkey, *European and Native American Warfare,* 145–48.

39. Brig. Gen. Rufus Putnam, Downes, 320.

40. Belue, *Hunters of Kentucky,* 250–51; Harry G. Enoch, *In Search of Morgan's Station and "The Last Indian Raid in Kentucky"* (Bowie, Md.: Heritage Books 1997).

41. Grenier, *First Way of War,* 202; Taylor, *Divided Ground,* 283–88; Wayne to Secretary Henry Knox, Aug. 28. 1794, *American State Papers, Class II, Indian Affairs,* 2 vols. (Washington, D.C.: Gales and Seaton, 1832–34), 1:490–91.

42. Kluger, *Seizing Destiny,* 223; White, *Middle Ground,* 464–73; Taylor, *Divided Ground,* 293–94.

10. THE CAPTURE AND RESCUE OF THE GIRLS

1. Report by John Williams to the Proprietors, Boonesborough, Jan. 3, 1776, in Ranck, 239.

2. Nancy O'Malley, "Frontier Defenses and Pioneer Strategies in the Historic Settlement Era," in ed. Craig Thompson Friend, *The Buzzel about Kentuck: Settling the Promised Land* (Lexington: University Press of Kentucky, 1999), 71.

3. Peck, *Boone,* 105–6.

4. William Hickman, "Account of Life and Travels"; Nathan Reid's undated ms., DM 31C[24–25]; and JDS's interview with Josiah Collins, 1840s, DM 12 CC74.

5. "Col. William Fleming's Journal of Travels in Kentucky, 1779–1780," in Mereness, 630.

6. James Galloway's narrative, written in 1832 at his dictation by his grandson Albert Galloway, qtd. in Draper, 403. Galloway said Boonesborough had a dozen cabins. According to Ranck, there were twenty-six cabins at Boonesborough. Ranck, 35.

7. Draper, 404, reproduces an early engraving of Boonesborough.

8. Aron, *How the West Was Lost,* 32.

9. Draper, 403, 426.

10. Quaife, *Capture of Old Vincennes,* 37.

11. O'Malley, "Frontier Defenses," 68.

12. Draper, 405, 431–32.

13. Ibid., 408.

14. Ibid., 407; Hammon and Taylor, *Virginia's Western War,* 39.

15. Henry Stuart, brother of the British superintendent on Alabama and Georgia Indians John Stuart, witnessed the visit of the northern Indian delegation to the Cherokees. Calloway, *American Revolution in Indian Country,* 191–96.

16. "Tired of the confinement of the fort": Statement of Nathan Reid, DM 31C2[24–25].

17. William E. Ellis, *The Kentucky River* (Lexington: University Press of Kentucky 2000), 5.

18. JDS interview with Nathaniel Hart, Jr., c. 1843–44, DM 17CC192. Hart described "Simon" as a "a yellow man, who staid at the Fort." He may have been someone who came to Boonesborough to trade with the settlers. Whites on the frontier were in frequent commercial and social contact with Indians, as exemplified by the story of Boone's encounter with Saucy Jack at the shooting match in Salisbury, the Boones' encounters with Big Jim and Hanging Maw, and the story of the Cherokees' attendance at the Watauga Valley horse race at which Crabtree killed a Cherokee. In another account the girls initially mistook the man who "took hold of their canoe" as a Negro who had run away from Boonesborough. JDS interview with Richard French, c. 1840s, DM 12CC203.

19. *MFDB,* 38.

20. *MFDB,* 49.

21. Statement of Nathan Reid, n.d., DM 31C2[26].

22. Statement of Isaiah Boone, n.d., DM 31C2[40].

23. Statement of Nathan Reid, n.d., DM 31C2[26].

24. Ibid. [25–26].

25. *MFDB,* 50.

26. Draper interview with William Phelps, 1868, DM 24C57.

27. Draper interview with Delinda Boone Craig, 1866, DM 30C48–49.

28. Stephen Hempstead to Draper, Feb. 15, 1863, DM 16C76.

29. Draper interview with Jacob Boone, 1890, DM 14C84.

30. JDS interview with Josiah Collins, 1840s, DM 12CC75.

31. *MFDB,* 50.

32. Floyd to Preston, July 21, 1776, DM 33S300–303. The letter has been published a number of times, including in Otto A. Rothbert, "John Floyd—Pioneer and Hero," *FCHQ* (July 1928): 171–72.

33. Richard Holder to Draper, Oct. 8, 1850, DM 24C29[1].

34. Floyd to Preston, July 21, 1776, DM 33S300–303.

35. Samuel H. Dixon to Draper, Feb. 3, 1852, DM 24C30[5].

36. Eviza L. Coshow to Draper, May 2, 1885, DM 21C28–29. The story of the capture and the rescue of the girls has been told many times. Draper gathered some forty accounts of it—most of them furnished decades after the event. See Draper, 429–30 n. 35, for Draper's sources for his version. Not surprisingly, the stories conflict in many details. For excellent efforts to thread the stories into a coherent narrative, see Faragher, 131–39; Draper, 411–21, 428–30, 432–33; Bakeless, 124–39. Boone himself was succinct in what he told Filson about the capture and rescue of the girls: "On the fourteenth day of July, 1776, two of Col. Calaway's daughters, and one of mine, were taken prisoner near the fort. I immediately pursued the Indians, with only eight men, and on the sixteenth overtook them, killed two of the party, and recovered the girls." Filson, 60.

37. Joseph D. Ketner, director of the Washington University Gallery of Art, qtd. in J. Grant

Sweeney, *The Columbus of the Woods: Daniel Boone and the Typology of Manifest Destiny* (St. Louis: Washington University Gallery of Art, 1992), 54.

38. Ibid., 56.

39. JDS interview with Robert Wickliffe Sr., 1859, DM 15CC84.

40. Draper interview with Delinda Boone Craig, 1866, DM 30C49; see also Richard Holder to Draper, Oct. 8, 1850, DM 24C29[2].

41. Draper interview with Delinda Boone Craig, 1866, DM 30C48–49.

42. Drimmer, *Captured by the Indians*, 12–13. See also Reuben Gold Thwaites, ed., *New Voyages to North-America by the Baron de Lahontan*, 2 vols. (Chicago: A. C. McClurg, 1905), 2:453 ("A Young Woman, say they, is Master of her own Body, and by her Natural Right of Liberty is free to do what she pleases"); and Vernon Kinietz and Erminie W. Voegelin, eds., *Shawnese Traditions: C. C. Trowbridge's Account* (Ann Arbor: University of Michigan Press, 1939), 15 (rape is considered criminal, though the woman's relatives do not attempt to punish the offending man).

43. Statement of David Henry, n.d., DM 31C2[40], qtd. in Faragher, 139.

44. Eviza L. Coshow to Draper, June 12, 1885, DM 21C48[1].

45. James Fenimore Cooper, *The Last of the Mohicans* (New York: Modern Library, 2001), 85, 90, 96–101, 328–31.

46. Floyd to Preston, July 21, 1776, DM 33S300–303. Part of the letter is printed in Hambleton Tapp, "Colonel John Floyd, Kentucky Pioneer," *FCHQ* 15 (1941): 9; and in Draper, 423.

11. THE SHAWNEES CAPTURE BOONE

1. Draper, 424.

2. Hammon and Taylor, *Virginia's Western War*, 44; Grenier, *First Way of War*, 152–53; Calloway, *American Revolution in Indian Country*, 197–99; Selby, *Revolution in Virginia*, 186–88.

3. Calloway, *American Revolution in Indian Country*, 198–200.

4. John Bakeless, *Background to Glory: The Life of George Rogers Clark* (Philadelphia: J. B. Lippincott 1957), 36–41; Quaife, *Capture of Old Vincennes*, 29–37.

5. Letter from Carlisle, Pennsylvania, dated July 4, 1774, DM 2JJ63–65, printed in *DHDW*, 66–67.

6. Henry Hamilton to Governor Carleton, Detroit, Nov. 30, 1775, DM 45J101–101(1), *RUO*, 129–30.

7. Henry Hamilton, "Reminiscences," Henry Hamilton Papers (Houghton Library, Harvard University, Cambridge, Mass.) 92–95, qtd. in Sheehan, "'The Famous Hair-Buyer General,'" 11.

8. Lt. Governor Hamilton to the Earl of Dartmouth, Detroit, Aug. 29–Sept. 2, 1776, *Michigan Pioneer and Historical Collections* 10 (1888): 269–70.

9. Lord Germain to Sir Guy Carleton, White Hall, Mar. 26, 1777, sent to Lieutenant Governor Hamilton from Quebec, May 21, 1777, printed in Butterfield, *History of the Girtys*, 342.

10. Faragher, 146; Draper, 442; Rice, *Frontier Kentucky*, 89–90. According to Draper, the census was on May 1, 1777.

11. Draper, 438.

12. Faragher, 146–47; Draper, 398 n. c (Belue's note).

13. JDS interview with Sarah Graham, DM 12CC45.

14. Draper, 439.

15. *MFDB*, 51.

16. For Boone's praise of Kenton, see Draper's 1851 interview with John and Sarah Kenton McCord, DM 5S144. For accounts of the Apr. 24 attack, see JDS interview with John Gass, c. 1840s, DM 11CC12; Draper, 440–441; Faragher, 147–49; Lofaro, 79.

17. Filson, 61.

18. *RUO*, 65 nn. 95–96.

19. Lord George Germain to Sir Guy Carleton, White Hall, Mar. 26, 1777, and sent to Lieutenant Governor Hamilton from Quebec, May 21, 1777, in Butterfield, *History of the Girtys*, 343–44.

20. Extract of a Council held at Detroit, 17 June, 1777, DM 49J13, printed in *FDUO*, 9–10.

21. David Zeisberger to Col. George Morgan, Chuchachunk, July 7, 1777, DM 3NN11–13 (recounting a report from a messenger sent to Pluggy's Town and Sandusky who encountered John Montour after the treaty at Detroit), *FDUO*, 18–19.

22. Extract of a Council held at Detroit, June 17, 1777, *FDUO*, 11–12.

23. Hamilton to American frontiersmen, Detroit, June 24, 1777, DM 45J2-D.S., *FDUO*, 14.

24. *FDUO*, 13.

25. E.g., David Zeisberger to Col. George Morgan—Cuchachunk, July 7, 1977 , DM 3NN11–13, *FDUO*, 18; Capt. Matthew Arbuckle to Col. Wm Fleming, Fort Randolph July 26, DM 1U68, *FDUO*, 25 (reporting intelligence from a friendly Shawnee "that there has lately been a Treaty at Detroit, where all Nations have unanimously agreed to Distress the frontiers as much as in their Power. They accepted of the War Belt & Tomahawk and are so near as the Shawnee Towns, where they are indeavouring to draw over what Shawnees were resolved to remain Neuter they are Invited & Encouraged by a French Man & a Wyndott Chief who accompanys them").

26. Gen. Edward Hand to Jasper Yeates, Fort Pitt, July 12, 1777, in Thwaites and Kellogg, *FDUO*, 20 ("two Tribes of the Shawanese declare for us, two are against us, the Wiandats [Wyandots, an American name for the Huron Indians] also are evidently our Enemies"). According to an editors' note, of the four Shawnee clans—the Chillicothe, Kiscapoo, Piqua, and Mequochoke—the first two, being farthest from American frontier and nearest the British sphere, were already hostile to the American settlers. There are many ways of spelling the names of these clans (sometimes referred to as divisions).

27. David Zeisberger to Gen. Edward Hand, Cuchachunk, July 26, 1777, DM 1U69, *FDUO*, 27–28.

28. Lieutenant Governor John Page to the Delawares, Williamsburg, Sept. 18, 1777, DM 1U97, *FDUO*, 88–89.

29. Gen. Edward Hand to the Delaware Chiefs at Coochocking &c, Fort Pitt, Oct. 1, 1777, DM 1U103, *FDUO*, 113.

30. Draper, 447.

31. Reminiscences by Dr. Joseph Doddridge, DM 6NN123–126, *FDUO*, 54.

32. JDS interview of John Hawks, c. 1840s, DM 12CC138.

33. Governor Patrick Henry to Gen. Edward Hand, Williamsburg, July 27, 1777, *FDUO*,

32. ("Accounts from Kentucki tell me of the most distressing & deplorable condition of the surviving Inhabitants in that Quarter. Your Movements I trust will prove the best Defence to them. Two hundred men are ordered to their Assistance. But it seems to me, that offensive operations can alone produce Defence agt. Indians.")

34. Capt. Samuel Moorhead to Gen. Edward Hand, James McKibbern's House, Sept. 22, 1777, DM 1U101, *FDUO,* 97, 99.

35. Calendar of letters, DM1U127, Nov. 5, 1777, *FDUO,* 148.

36. Gen. Edward Hand to Governor Patrick Henry—Fort Pitt Nov. 9, 1777, DM 3NN 62, 63, *FDUO,* 154.

37. Report by John Williams to the Proprietors of the Transylvania Co., Boonesborough, Jan. 3, 1776, Ranck, 239.

38. For a full account of the efforts to organize the meeting at Fort Pitt, and the proceedings at the meeting (including the speeches of Cornstalk), see *RUO,* 25–127.

39. Gen. Edward Hand to Jasper Yeates, Fort Pitt, Oct. 2, 1777, Hand Papers, New York Public Library, *FDUO,* 119.

40. "Damnd. Savages": Capt. Matthew Arbuckle to Capt. John Stuart, Fort Randolph, Nov. 2, 1776, DM 1U40, *RUO,* 211. Skepticism: Capt. Matthew Arbuckle to Col. Wm Fleming, Fort Randolph, Aug. 15, 1776, DM 2ZZ78, *RUO,* 187.

41. Narrative of Capt. John Stuart, DM 6NN157, *FDUO,* 159–60.

42. Col. William Preston to Col. William Fleming, Smithfield, Dec. 2, 1777, Thwaites and Kellogg, *FDUO,* 169.

43. Gen. Edward Hand to Jasper Yeates, Fort Pitt, Dec. 24, 1777, Hand Papers, New York Public Library, *FDUO,* 188–89.

44. Gen. Edward Hand to Governor Patrick Henry, Staunton, Dec. 9, 1777, DM 3NN69–71, *FDUO,* 175–76.

45. *FDUO,* 177–78 n. 43.

46. Col. John Bowman to Gen. Edward Hand, Harrodsburg, Dec. 12, 1777, DM 3NN192–196, Thwaites and Kellogg, *FDUO,* 182–83, Draper, 449–50.

47. Petition to the Virginia General Assembly, endorsed Nov. 25, 1777, Lofaro, 83, citing James Rood Robertson, ed., *Petitions of the Early Inhabitants of Kentucky to the General Assembly of Virginia, 1769–1792* (Louisville, Ky.: John P. Morton, 1914), 43.

48. Filson, 63; Draper, 459–60.

49. For accounts of Boone's capture, see Filson, 63; Draper, 460–69; *MFDB,* 53–57; Faragher, 155–62; and Lofaro, 84–88.

50. *MFDB,* 55.

51. Ansel Goodman, petition for a Revolutionary War pension, Oct. 29, 1832, DM 11C28–30.

12. BOONE AMONG THE SHAWNEES

1. Draper interview with Joseph Jackson, 1844, DM 11C62[6]-[7], Draper, 465.

2. Statement of Boone Hays, Feb. 1846, DM 23C36[3–4], Faragher, 161; Draper, 466–67.

3. O. M. Spencer, a white held captive by the Shawnees in 1792–93, wrote that the Shawnees' fondness for ornament extended to the men, who wore "heavy pieces of silver in the

ears, the rims of which, being separated from the cartilage by cutting are weighed down two or three inches from the head." Milo Milton Quaife, ed., *The Indian Captivity of O. M. Spencer—1834* (Chicago: R. R. Donnelley, 1917), qtd. in Howard, *Shawnee!* 69.

4. *Diary of David McClure*, Oct. 28 and 29, 1772, 102. McClure said the ear slitting was said to be a preparation "necessary for a warrior."

5. *Journal of Nicholas Cresswell*, 49–50.

6. The Delaware war chief Buckongahelas, whose ring-weighted earlobes reached his shoulders, would suck on his stretched earlobes while listening to others. White, *Middle Ground*, 495.

7. Filson, 63.

8. Draper interview with Joseph Jackson, 1844, DM 11C62[8–10], Draper, 467; Faragher, 161.

9. *MFDB*, 57.

10. Kinietz and Voegelin, *Shawnese Traditions*, 19–21; Howard, *Shawnee*, 120–25. Trowbridge's manuscript is dated July 24, 1824. Trowbridge records that there used to be a hereditary society headed by four old women who, whenever they heard the "prisoners yell" of a returning war party, would paint their lips with red clay and set out to meet the party. If one of these women touched a prisoner before one of the peace women did, the prisoner "was taken to the village & burned and afterwards cooked & eaten" (54–55). According to another informant, the society's members ate the bodies of prisoners who were not adopted by the Shawnees, and did so "as a kind of sacrifice, out of bowls formed of the sculls of former victims" (64).

11. Charles Johnston, qtd. in Drimmer, *Captured by the Indians*, 210.

12. Drimmer, *Captured by the Indians*, 86 (Alexander Henry quoting a Chippewa who, in 1763, brought in cooked flesh from slain captives and said "it had always been the custom, among all the Indian nations when returning from war, to make a war feast from among the slain").

13. Filson, 63.

14. John Warth, qtd. in J. P. Hale, "Daniel Boone, Some Facts and Incidents not Hitherto Published," *West Virginia School Journal* 2, no. 4 (Feb. 1882): 85–86, cited in Faragher, 165. Warth's story, as recounted by Hale, is somewhat garbled, referring to the killing, not of the son but of the father, of a "noted brave named Cat Fish." A transcript of Hale's account is on the West Virginia Archives and History Web site, www.wvculture.org/History/settlement/boonedaniel02.html.

15. Peck, 73.

16. Orley E. Brown, ed., *The Captivity of Jonathan Alder and His Life with the Indians* (Alliance, Ohio: n.p., 1965), 14. James Smith gave a similar description of his adoption by the Caughnawagas in 1755 (though the three squaws washing me "plunged me under water and washed and rubbed me severely, I could not say they hurt me much"). Drimmer, *Captured by the Indians*, 32.

17. Kinietz and Voegelin, *Shawnese Traditions*, 56. See also Jerry E. Clark, *The Shawnee* (Lexington: University Press of Kentucky, 1993), 28–29 (the group that bore the name Turtle had the honor of carrying the Shawnees' sacred bundle).

18. Kinietz and Voegelin, *Shawnese Traditions*, 2. This tradition appears to have been collected by Trowbridge from Tecumseh's brother the Prophet.

19. For a summary of the available information about the salt-boilers—those adopted by

the Indians and those sold to the British—see Ted Franklin Belue, "Terror in the Canelands: The Fate of Daniel Boone's Salt Boilers," *FCHQ* 68 (1994): 3.

20. Governor Henry Hamilton to Sir Guy Carleton, Detroit, Apr. 25, 1778, DM 11C96(3), printed in *FDUO*, 283.

21. Filson, 64.

22. Durrett Collection, University of Chicago, Codex 127B:196–97, qtd. in Faragher, 169.

23. *MFDB*, 57.

24. Trabue, 64.

25. For how each of the prisoners fared, see Belue, "Terror in the Canelands."

26. Filson, 102.

27. Belue, "Terror in the Canelands," 24–27; Draper, 473–74; Draper interview with Delinda Boone Craig (1866), DM 30C54; JDS interview with Josiah Collins, c. 1840s, DM 12CC:76–77 (says *Pequolly* means "Little Shuts-his-eyes").

28. Kinietz and Voegelin, *Shawnese Traditions*, 9, 55, 67 (many Delaware words are like the Shawnee, and "frequent intercourse has enabled them to communicate with each other on ordinary subjects").

29. Filson, 64–65.

30. *MFDB*, 59.

31. Bakeless, 371. (See DM 6S228; 16C28.)

32. *MFDB*, 60.

33. Thomas Wildcat Alford, *Civilization as Told to Florence Drake* (Norman: University of Oklahoma Press, 1936), 20. Alford had gone to a white school, and his rendering of Shawnee ethical principles may have reflected his Christian education.

34. Ibid., 53.

35. Aron, *How the West Was Lost.*

36. Eviza L. Coshow to Draper, May 3, 1887, DM 21C63[1–2]; Coshow to Draper, Mar. 14 and Apr. 23, 1885, DM 21C24[12–13] and 21C33[2].

37. Kinietz and Voegelin, *Shawnese Traditions*, 34.

38. Filson, 105.

39. *Journal of Nicholas Cresswell*, 103, 105 (the youngest of three Indian women Cresswell met at their camp at night "had some amorous design upon me [and] began to creep nearer me and pulled my Blanket. I found what she wanted and lifted it up. She was young, handsome, and healthy. Fine regular features and fine eyes, had she not painted them with Red before she came to bed"), 108, 113–14 ("Our Squaws are very necessary, fetching our horses to the Camp and saddling them, making our fire at night and cooking our victuals, and every other thing they think will please us").

40. *Diary of David McClure*, Sept. 13, 1772, 53. A trader with an Indian consort would benefit by access to Indian kinship networks. White, *Middle Ground*, 324.

41. For how women outnumbered men in some Indian groups, see White, *Middle Ground*, 66.

42. JDS interview with Josiah Collins, Bath County, Ky., c. 1840s, DM 12CC67.

43. Trabue, 47.

44. Col. William Preston and Col. William Fleming to the Chiefs and Warriors of the Shawnese Nation, Va., Apr. 3, 1778, DM 2ZZ44, reprinted in *FDUO*, 258–61.

45. Belue, "Terror in the Canelands," 7, 12–15.

46. See JDS interview with Josiah Collins, c. 1840s, DM 12CC64.

47. Filson, 65.

48. Hurt, *Ohio Frontier*, 29 (reporting killings by Wyandots and Delawares of white captive women who made unsuccessful escape attempts).

49. Ephraim McLain to Draper, May 17, 1884, DM 16C7[1]-7[2]; see also McLain to Draper, June 9, 1884, DM 16C8 ("Boone himself told me about drawing the bullets from the Indians guns").

50. Filson, 65–66.

51. Ibid., 66.

52. DM 4B176, Belue, "Terror in the Canelands," 27.

53. Filson, 66.

54. "You may depend on it": Draper interview with Henry Wilson, n.d., DM 31C2[72]. According to Wilson, Boone shot a deer. In some accounts the animal Boone killed was a buffalo. For the story of Boone's escape, see *MFDB*, 61–62; Draper, 479–81; Faragher, 174–76.

55. Draper, 480. See JDS interview with Josiah Collins, c. 1840s, 12CC64 (around May 1, 1778, "Mrs. Danl. Boone, supposing her husband dead, ret'd w. her family fr. Bh. to Carolina").

56. *MFDB*, 60.

13. THE SIEGE OF BOONESBOROUGH

1. Trabue, 57.

2. Filson, 66.

3. Trabue, 61.

4. For the strengthening of the fort's defenses, see Draper's interview with Moses Boone, DM 19C12; Draper, 495–96; Filson, 66; *MFDB*, 65; Faragher, 177–78.

5. Quaife, *Capture of Old Vincennes*, 40–41.

6. Trabue, 57.

7. Deposition of Capt. William Buchanan, Nov. 26, 1778, DM 14S18–19; Doddridge, *Notes*, 277, qtd. in Faragher, 178.

8. Robert Hancock to Draper, February 26, 1853, DM 24C17(2–3); deposition of William Hancock, July 17, 1778, DM 4B204–5.

9. Boone to Col. Arthur Campbell or Evan Shelby, Boonesborough, July 18, 1778, DM 4B204, printed in Draper, 180.

10. Faragher, 180.

11. Trabue, 57.

12. For the Paint Creek raid, see Filson, 67; Faragher, 181–82; Draper, 498–500.

13. Notice from a Williamsburg paper of Oct. 9, 1778, reprinted in Draper, 522.

14. Felix Walker's narrative of his trip with Boone from Long Island to Boonesborough in Mar. 1775, written about 1824, reprinted in Ranck, 167.

15. For accounts of the siege, see Filson, 67–70; Draper's interview with Moses Boone, 1846, DM 19C10 ff.; Draper, 500–518; *MFDB*, 65–70; Faragher, 182–99; Trabue, 58–59; Lofaro, 96–104. For estimates of the number of attackers, Indians and Canadians, ranging between 338 and 1,000, but clustering in the 400s, see Draper, 522. Filson's Boone names the French

Canadian officer "Capt. Duquesne"; Draper refers to him as "Capt. Isadore DeChaine" and says he was an interpreter for the British among the Wyandots; Faragher gives his name as Lt. Antoine Dagneaux de Quindre. There may well have been two French Canadians, Chêne and de Quindre. Bakeless reports that both were frequently mentioned in official correspondence and carried on Hamilton's strength report for Sept. 5, 1778. Bakeless, 450 n. 202.2.

16. JDS interview with Josiah Collins, c. 1840s, DM 12CC74.

17. The letters have not survived, but settlers who were at the siege remembered their contents. See, e.g., *MFDB*, 65–66.

18. JDS interview with Daniel Boone Bryan, 1844, DM 22C14[12].

19. Trabue, 58; Draper, 501.

20. Filson, 68.

21. JDS interview with John Gass, c. 1840s, DM 11CC13.

22. The boy was Samuel South. JDS interview with Jesse Daniel, c. 1843, DM 11CC94.

23. JDS interview with Nathaniel Hart, Jr., c. 1843–44, DM 17CC198.

24. William Bailey Smith, in *Hunt's Western Review,* clipping in DM 31C2[87].

25. Draper interview with John Gass, 1844, DM 24C73[2].

26. JDS interview with John Gass, c. 1840s, DM 11CC13.

27. Thomas D. Clark, ed., *The Voice of the Frontier: John Bradford's Historical Notes on Kentucky* (Lexington: University Press of Kentucky, 1993), 19.

28. Draper, 502–3; Faragher, 186.

29. Interview with Moses Boone, DM 19C11.

30. Eviza L. Coshow to Draper, Mar. 14 and 28, 1885, DM 21C24[6], 21C27.

31. Filson, 68; see *MFDB,* 66.

32. Filson, 69; *MFDB,* 66.

33. Interview with Nathan and Olive Boone, 1851, DM 6S142; Interview with Moses Boone, DM 19C11–13.

34. JDS interview with Daniel Boone Bryan, 1844, 22C14[12].

35. Peck, 55, 59–60. Peck interviewed Boone several times toward the end of Boone's life. With respect to the agreement to submit to British authorities in Canada and to pledge allegiance to the British Crown, Peck said he relied "on oral testimony to the writer from Stephen Hancock and Flanders Callaway." See also Draper interview with John Gass, 1844, DM 24C73[4] (under the treaty the Boonesborough people were "agreeing to become subject to the British Governor of Detroit").

36. Filson, 69.

37. Ibid.

38. Trabue, 58. For the Indian custom of locking arms at a treaty signing, see Joseph J. Ellis, *American Creation: Triumphs and Tragedies at the Founding of the Republic* (New York: Alfred A. Knopf, 2007), 158 (at the signing in 1790 in New York City of a treaty between the Creeks and the United States, the Creek chiefs at Federal Hall "shook hands with Washington Indian-style, locking arms while grasping elbows").

39. *MFDB,* 67. According to Moses Boone, the blow was with the pipe end, perhaps intended to stun Boone so he could be taken prisoner. DM 19C13[1].

40. Draper interview with Moses Boone, 1846, DM 11CC12–14.

41. Draper interview with Moses Boone, 1846, DM 19C15–16.

42. Draper interview with Richard French, c. 1840s, DM 12CC205.

43. Draper interview with Moses Boone, 1846, DM 19C15.

44. JDS interview with John Gass, c. 1840s, DM 11CC13.

45. DM 6S138, 142; *MFDB*, 69.

46. Note by Ted Franklin Belue, ed., in Draper, 529 n. n.

47. Eviza L. Coshow to Draper, Mar. 28, 1885, 21C27[1].

48. See, e.g., Ward, *Breaking the Backcountry,* 51 (Fort Granville surrenders in 1756 after Indians set fire to the walls of the fort), 224 (Fort Presque Isle surrenders after Indians use fire arrows to set its bastions and buildings on fire).

49. JDS interview with John Rankins, c. 1840s, DM 11CC83. John Dabney Shane, a Presbyterian minister, noted that "habitual swearers think no sentence smooth and euphonious, which is not filled up in their style," but he omitted blasphemous expressions from his retelling of frontier stories on the ground that introducing such expressions "is certainly repugnant to good taste, and renders the narrative obnoxious to persons of refined and Christian feeling."

50. JDS interview with John Gass, c. 1840s, DM 11CC13.

51. JDS interview with Daniel Boone Bryan, 1844, DM 22C10[9]; Samuel Willard to Rev. Thomas P. Hinds, Oct. 14, 1844, DM 24C112[3].

52. Filson, 69–70; JDS interview with John Gass, c. 1840s, DM 24C73[9].

53. *MFDB*, 68–69.

54. Draper interview with Nathan and Olive Boone, 1851, DM 6S138, 6S143; JDS interview with John Gass, c. 1840s, DM 24C73[9], 11CC12–14.

55. M. B. Woods to Draper, Apr. 9, 1883, DM 4C22[11–12]; see Faragher, 196; Draper, 516, 530. Sometimes Boone is said to have killed the saucy Indian.

56. Draper, 513; Trabue, 59.

57. JDS interview with John Gass, c. 1840s, DM 24C73[9], 11CC14, Draper interview with Moses Boone, 1846, DM 19C18. On who killed Pompey, see Ted Franklin Belue, "Did Daniel Boone Shoot Pompey, the Black Shawnee, at the 1778 Siege of Boonesborough?" *FCHQ* 67 (1993): 5–22.

58. Draper interview with Moses Boone, 1846, DM 19D21–22.

59. Trabue, 59.

60. JDS interview with Richard French, c. 1840s, DM 12CC205.

61. John N. James interview with Simon Kenton, c. 1833, DM 11C77–78.

62. Filson, 70.

63. JDS, interview with Daniel Boone Bryan, 1844, DM 22C14[12].

64. For Trabue's account of Boone's court-martial, see Trabue, 63–64.

65. Faragher, 201.

66. John H. James to Draper, DM 11C76.

67. Kincaid, *Wilderness Road,* 158.

68. JDS interview with John Gass, 1840s, DM 11CC15.

69. Draper, 558; DM 50J12.

70. JDS interview with Richard French, c. 1840s, DM 12CC205 (describing views of Callaway's daughter).

71. Filson, 73.

72. Under the new land law those who "have really and bona fide settled themselves or

their families" or bore the cost of settling others "upon any waste or unappropriated lands on the . . . western waters, to which no other person hath any legal right or claim," before Jan. 1, 1778, are entitled to four hundred acres per family settled (the tract to include the settlement that had been made). Settlers seeking additional land would have a preemption on up to one thousand acres of adjoining land at the current state sale price—on land to which no other person has any legal right or claim. No family was to be entitled to the allowance granted to settlers under the act, "unless they have made a crop of corn in that country, or resided there at least one year since the time of their settlement." In addition, persons who before Jan. 1, 1778, "had marked out or chosen for themselves any waste or unappropriated lands, and built any house or hut, or made other improvements thereon" would be allowed to preempt one thousand acres on the same basis as the preemption rights of persons entitled to four hundred-acre settlements. Persons coming to Kentucky after Jan. 1, 1778, were limited to the preemption "of any quantity of land, not exceeding four hundred acres." William W. Hening, *Statutes of Virginia*, 10:39–41. See Charles Gano Talbert, *Benjamin Logan: Kentucky Frontiersman* (Lexington: University of Kentucky Press 1962), 85, for a summary of the law, which is excerpted in Chinn, *Kentucky: Settlement and Statehood*, 225–26.The law also provided for the sale of treasury warrants, initially at the price of £40 per hundred acres, that could be used for the purchase of the unclaimed land.

73. Col. William Fleming, one of the commissioners, noted in his journal for May 5, 1780, how much the land commission had by then accomplished: 1,328 claimers, 1,334,050 acres granted: 140,250 acres to 351 claimers on preemption; 423,000 acres to 423 claimers for improvements before 1778; 770,800 acres to 554 claimants for settlement and preemption before 1778. Mereness, 645–46. Fleming traded on some claims for his own account. He recorded in his journal, e.g.: "Purchased a preemption of 1000 Acres from Henry Bauchman heir at Law to Jacob Bauchman for £200. Sold the above to Jacob Mors for £500." Mereness, 654.

74. Aron, *How the West Was Lost,* 71. Neil Hammon has advised the author that the total amount of acreage entered in Kentucky County, which at the time included all of what is now the state of Kentucky, was for 3.75 million acres. That is more than 14% of the total area of Kentucky.

75. JDS interview with William Clinkenbeard, 1840s, DM 11CC55.

76. Quaife, *Capture of Old Vincennes,* 48–49.

77. Clark used the same threat in convincing Hamilton to surrender that Hamilton had tried without success in his letter to the besieged Boonesborough defenders: if we have to storm the fort, Clark told Hamilton, "many of course would be cut down, and the consequences of an enraged body of woodsmen breaking into the fort must be obvious to him. It would be beyond the power of an American officer to save a single man." Quaife, *Capture of Old Vincennes,* 145.

78. For Clark's campaigns, see Bakeless, *Background to Glory.*

79. Aron, *How the West Was Lost,* 47–48.

80. Ibid., 32.

81. William Fleming, "Journal of Travels in Kentucky, 1779–1780," in Mereness, 626–27.

82. John Floyd to William Preston, evidently June 1780, DM 17CC182–83. These letters from Floyd to Preston are published in Kathleen Jennings, *Louisville's First Families: A Series of Genealogical Sketches* (Louisville: Standard Printing, 1920).

83. Fleming, "Journal of Travels in Kentucky, 1779–1780," in Mereness, 622.

84. Ibid., 641.

85. *The Merck Manual of Diagnosis and Therapy,* 16th ed. (Rahway, N.J.: Merck Research Laboratories, 1992), 974–75.

86. Fleming, "Journal of Travels in Kentucky, 1783," in Mereness, 697.

87. Statement of Mrs. Rachel Denton, n.d., DM 31C2[96].

88. Fleming, "Journal of Travels in Kentucky, 1779–1780," in Mereness, 628, 636.

89. John Floyd to William Preston, Dec. 19, 1779, DM 17CC123.

90. Fleming, "Journal of Travels in Kentucky, 1779–1780," in Mereness, 627, 630.

91. Trabue, 74–75.

92. Fleming, "Journal of Travels in Kentucky, 1779–1780," in Mereness, 647–48.

93. Statement of Mrs. Rachel Denton, n.d., DM 31C2[96].

94. The move to Marble Creek may not have happened until 1783. Neil Hammon has informed the author that the land on Marble Creek, obtained by Boone and William Hays, was surveyed on Jan. 25, 1783.

95. Faragher, 206.

96. Contract between Boone and Geddes Winston, Dec. 17, 1781, DM 25C78, qtd. in Faragher, 207. Neil Hammon has advised the author he has found no record that Boone received the two thousand acres referred to in the contract.

97. *MFDB,* 70–71; Faragher, 207–8; Lofaro, 111. Neal O. Hammon has reviewed a document relating to an Apr. 11, 1781, court hearing in Fayette County, listing the certificates relating to seventeen claims (belonging to fifteen men) taken in the theft, which Boone said occurred at the house of Adam Byrd of James City County on the night of Mar. 20, 1780. Hammon said that the money required to purchase warrants on these claims would have totaled £6,061. Hammon, "The Boone Robbery" (ms., n.d.; copy in the author's possession). Hammon has advised the author that a land certificate, issued by the land commission, would state that a specified person had proved entitlement to a certain amount of land at a specified location. The certificate had to be returned to the land office at Williamsburg (later, at Richmond) and a prescribed amount of money paid for the land warrants, which then were entered in the office of the county surveyor, who would appoint a deputy to survey the tract.

98. Thomas Hart to Nathaniel Hart, Aug. 3, 1780, in Bakeless, 245–46.

99. Faragher, 208–9.

14. INDIAN RAIDS AND THE BATTLE OF THE BLUE LICKS

1. Quaife, *Capture of Old Vincennes,* 204.

2. Ibid., 205–19.

3. Bakeless, 246–47.

4. Ibid., 249; Trabue, 80–81.

5. Butterfield, *History of the Girtys,* 119.

6. JDS interview with Mrs. John Morrison, ca. 1840s, DM 11CC153 ("powder burnt"); Selby, *Revolution in Virginia,* 199.

7. Filson, 72; Faragher, 210; JDS interview with William Clinkenbeard, c. 1840s, 11CC66.

8. Clark to Thomas Jefferson, Aug. 22, 1780, *George Rogers Clark Papers, 1771–1781,* James Alton James, ed. (Springfield: Illinois State Historical Library, 1912), Virginia Series, 3:451.

9. For different accounts of Ned Boone's killing, see, e.g., Filson, 73; *MFDB,* 71–72; Faragher, 211–13; Bakeless, *Boone,* 256–58; Houston, 18–19; E. B. Scholl to Draper, Jan. 5, 1856, DM 23C104; deposition of Peter Scholl (Ned Boone's son-in-law; one of those who pursued the Indians after the killing), Apr. 17, 1818, DM 7 C 84–87. For "we've killed Daniel Boone," see Thomas S. Bouchelle to Draper, July 28, 1884, DM 9C68[5]; and Draper's notes of his interview with Joseph Jackson, 9C68[5]. For the story of Ned's resemblance to Daniel Boone, see Silas W. Parris to Draper, Oct. 15, 1884, DM 2C53.

10. John Floyd to William Preston, May 5, 1780, DM 17CC125.

11. John May to Samuel Beall, Apr. 15, 1780, Beall-Booth Family Papers, Manuscript Collections, Filson Historical Society.

12. John Redd to Draper, c. 1848, DM 10NN101, qtd. in Draper, 181 n. b.

13. Selby, *Revolution in Virginia,* 281–82.

14. Bakeless, 259, 454 ("Colonel"); *MFDB,* 73 ("Captain").

15. *MFDB,* 73.

16. William Christian to William Preston, June 30, 1781, qtd. in Faragher, 213; Draper interview with Nathan and Olive Boone, 1851, DM 6S151.

17. Bakeless, 260; Faragher, 214.

18. John Floyd to Thomas Jefferson, Apr. 10, 1781, *CVSP,* 2: 47–49.

19. Bakeless, 261.

20. John Floyd to Gen. George Rogers Clark, Aug. 10, 1781, George Rogers Clark Papers, Virginia Series, 3:584–85, qtd. by Hambleton Tapp, "Colonel John Floyd, Kentucky Pioneer," *FCHQ* 15 (Jan. 1941): 17.

21. John Floyd to William Preston, Sept. 30, 1781, DM 17CC137–38, Hammon and Harris, "Letters of Floyd," 228.

22. For the personal dynamics underlying the Pennsylvania militia's decision to kill the Christian Indians, see Rob Harper, "Looking the Other Way: The Gnadenhutten Massacre and the Contextual Interpretation of Violence," *William and Mary Quarterly* 54 (July 2007): 621–54.

23. Butterfield, *History of the Girtys,* 176–189, 365–67; Bakeless, *Background to Glory,* 286–87; Bakeless, *Boone,* 264.

24. Butterfield, *History of the Girtys,* 180.

25. Lofaro, 122; Butterfield, *History of the Girtys,* 190–91, 372–73. Butterfield believes the speech was fictitious, noting that Girty was illiterate and that if the speech was had been made, it would have been given in an Indian language. *History of the Girtys,* 191 n.

26. Filson, 74; Bakeless, 269–71.

27. For accounts of the attack on Bryan's Station, see, e.g., Filson, 75; Bakeless, 274–287; Faragher, 216; Lofaro, 123–25; Neal O. Hammon, *Daniel Boone and the Defeat at Blue Licks* (Minneapolis: Boone Society, 2005), 21–28.

28. Bakeless, 285–87.

29. McKee to De Peyster, Shawanese Country, Aug. 28, 1782, qtd. in Bakeless, 291.

30. JDS interview with Sarah Graham, c. 1840s, DM 12CC45.

31. Peck, 91.

32. Bakeless, 288; Hammon, *Daniel Boone and the Defeat at Blue Licks,* 39.

33. Boone, qtd. in Robert Wickliffe, "The Life of Col. John Todd," MS, c 1840s, DM 5C51[8], qtd. in Faragher, 217.

34. Deposition of Benjamin A. Cooper, Nov. 8, 1836, qtd. in Faragher, 217.

35. William Caldwell to Major De Peyster, Aug. 26, 1782, Haldimand Papers, ser. B, 123:127, qtd. in Hammon, *Daniel Boone and the Defeat at Blue Licks*, 90.

36. Boone, qtd. in Robert Wickliffe, "The Life of Col. John Todd," MS, c. 1840s, DM 5C51[8–9].

37. Draper interview with Delinda Boone Craig, 1866, DM 30C61–63. In Hammon's view there was no officers' conference before crossing the river. He notes that many accounts of the conference were written decades after the battle and that accounts written soon after the battle by Daniel Boone and Levi Todd did not mention such a conference. Hammon, *Daniel Boone and the Defeat at Blue Licks*, 50–54. Hammon suggests that McGary was less blameworthy than many have written for urging the Kentuckians to attack across the river. It is significant, however, that McGary himself, in a letter to Colonel Logan written soon after the battle, wrote of being "much sensured for incouraging the men to fight the Indians when we came up with them." McGary to Col. Benjamin Logan, Aug. 28, 1782, DM 12J35–37, qtd. in Hammon, *Daniel Boone and the Defeat at Blue Licks*, 87. In addition, Arthur Campbell within weeks of the battle said the loss of life at the battle was "not a little thro the vain and seditious expressions of a Major McGeary [*sic*]." Campbell to Col. William Davies, Washington County, Va., Oct. 3, 1782, CVSP 3:337, qtd. in Hammon, *Daniel Boone and the Defeat at Blue Licks*, 94–95.

38. Houston, 24.

39. Neal Hammon believes that Boone never made such a suggestion: "The idea that Boone was so foolish as to even suggest that they divide the army is insulting to the old pioneer." Hammon, *Daniel Boone and the Defeat at Blue Licks*, 77.

40. JDS interview with Jacob Stevens, c. 1840s, DM 12CC134–35.

41. Draper interview with Delinda Boone Craig, 1866, DM 30C61–63.

42. Rebecca Boone Lamond to Draper, Aug. 23, 1845, DM 22C36.

43. Draper interview with Joseph Scholl, 1868, DM 24S214.

44. *MFDB*, 76; Houston, 25. Cf. Peck, 86.

45. Draper interview with Samuel Boone, 1868, DM 22S265.

46. Rebecca Boone Lamond to Draper, Aug. 23, 1845, DM 22C36.

47. *MFDB*, 76.

48. *MFDB*, 76–77.

49. Filson, 77.

50. Ibid., 77–78.

51. JDS interview with Jacob Stevens, c. 1840s, DM 12CC134–35, qtd. in Faragher, 222.

52. *MFDB*, 78; Filson, 77.

53. Draper interview with Joseph Scholl, 1868, DM 24S213.

54. Draper interview with Delinda Boone Craig, 1866, DM 30C63.

55. Boone to Governor Benjamin Harrison, Sept. 11, 1782, printed in Lofaro, 130.

56. McKee to De Peyster, Shawanese Country, Aug. 28, 1782.

57. Boone to Governor Benjamin Harrison, Aug. 30, 1782, Virginia State Archives. The letter is qtd. in Bakeless, 308; and in Hammon, *Daniel Boone and the Defeat at Blue Licks*, 88–89.

58. Talbert, *Benjamin Logan*, 168.

59. Ibid., 177–78.

60. Filson, 78–79.

61. Talbert, *Benjamin Logan*, 179.

62. The Kentuckian was Cave Johnson. See Talbert, *Benjamin Logan*, 179–80.

63. Benjamin Harrison to George Rogers Clark, Jan. 13, 1783, DM 52J73(2).

64. Filson, 80–81.

65. Ibid., 79.

66. O'Malley, "Frontier Defenses," 71–72. O'Malley notes that although life became more serene in the central Kentucky region around Lexington, northern Kentucky along the Ohio River continued to be dangerous

67. JDS interview with John Rankins, c. 1840s, DM 11CC81. For the timing of "settling out" at different Kentucky stations, see Perkins, *Border Life*, 161–62.

68. Filson, 28–29. The Census Bureau estimated Kentucky's population in 1780 at forty-five thousand. *Historical Statistics*, pt. 2, 1168.

69. *Historical Statistics*, pt. 1, 32.

70. General Harmar had his men at Fort Harmar, near Marietta, Ohio, count the boats and settlers coming down the Ohio: from Oct. 10, 1786, to May 12, 1787, 177 boats with 2,689 people; from June 1, 1787, to Dec. 9, 1787, 146 boats and 3,296 people; and from Dec. 9, 1787, to June 15, 1788, 308 boats and 6,320 persons. White, *Middle Ground*, 418.

15. WHITES AND INDIANS

1. Harry Innes to Henry Knox, July 7, 1790, Innes Papers. Vol. 19, no. 113, Talbert, *Benjamin Logan*, 247. Parts of the letter are reprinted in Thomas D. Clark, *Voice of the Frontier*, 134–35.

2. Clark, *Voice of the Frontier*, 110.

3. Harry Innes to John Brown, Dec. 7, 1787, reprinted in *RKHS* 54 (Oct. 1956): 369 (between Sept. 1783 and Dec. 1787, three hundred Kentuckians were killed and twenty thousand horses stolen).

4. Clark, *Voice of the Frontier*, 111.

5. *Historical Statistics*, pt. 1, 32.

6. "A Narrative of the Incidents Attending the Capture, Detention and Ransom of Charles Johnston," in Drimmer, *Captured by the Indians*, 197.

7. John Floyd to William Preston, Mar. 28, 1783, DM 17CC144–48, reprinted in Hammon and Harris, "Letters of Floyd," 234.

8. Hammon and Taylor, *Virginia's Western War*, 109.

9. Clark, *Voice of the Frontier*, 86.

10. Hammon and Taylor, *Virginia's Western War*, 126.

11. Charles Johnston, May's assistant, was on the boat and was taken captive. Johnston, recounting in 1827 the capture of the boat and the shooting of May, said they happened in Feb. 1790. Drimmer, *Captured by the Indians*, 184.

12. Belue, *Hunters of Kentucky*, 246; Jemima Hawkins to Draper, c. 1863, DM 19S93.

13. The captive was Thomas Brown. Drimmer, *Captured by the Indians*, 70.

14. *MFDB*, 81; Faragher, 252–53.

15. Account of Col. Josiah Harmar, Nov. 15, 1786, *CVSP*, 4:204–5, qtd. in Downes, 298; Calloway, *American Revolution in Indian Country,* 177.

16. JDS interview with Isaac Clinkenbeard, c. 1840s, DM 11CC3.

17. Faragher, 253–54; Lofaro, 138–39. McGary may have lost his commission for only a year. *CVSP*, 4:258–60.

18. Butterfield, *History of the Girtys,* 252–53.

19. Grenier, *First Way of War,* 39–43 (laws for scalp bounties in Virginia and Massachusetts; bounties paid by Massachusetts to a white woman for the ten Abenaki scalps she took from the Indians whom she killed in escaping from them).

20. Quaife, *Capture of Old Vincennes,* 165.

21. Ibid., 194.

22. William Clinkenbeard to JDS, c. 1843, DM 11CC54–66.

23. McConnell, *Country Between,* 194–95; Grenier, *First Way of War,* 144–45 (quoting Bouquet's reply: "I will try to inoculate the bastards with Some Blankets that may fall in their Hands").

24. Journal of William Trent for June 24, 1763, qtd. in Calloway, *Scratch of a Pen,* 73.

25. Capt. Samuel Moorhead to Gen. Edward Hand, James McKibbern's House, Sept. 22, 1777, DM 1U101, *FDUO,* 97, 99.

26. Lieutenant Governor Zenon Trudeau to Baron de Carondelet, Sept. 28, 1793, qtd. in Gilbert C. Din and Abraham P. Nasatir, *The Imperial Osages: Spanish Diplomacy in the Mississippi Valley* (Norman: University of Oklahoma Press 1983), 249 n. 71.

27. Hinderaker, *Elusive Empires,* 69–70. See A. Gwynn Henderson, "The Lower Shawnee Town on Ohio: Sustaining Native Autonomy in an Indian 'Republic,'" in Friend, *Buzzel about Kentuck,* 35, 38–44, for the increasing use of European artifacts and the importance of trade (first with the French, then with the Pennsylvanians) at the Lower Shawnee Town (where the Scioto meets the Ohio) in the mid-1750s.

28. McConnell, *Country Between,* 211–20; White, *Middle Ground,* 137–38, 482 (by around 1800 most of the Indians in the region were making only their moccasins—and doing so with European awls).

29. JDS interview with Benjamin Stites, 1842, DM 13CC60. Stites, who bought the cappo, said he had to freeze it "to get the lice out." According to Stites, the Indians frequently wore cappos on their raids. The Indian who killed Stites's uncle "had a cappo and a cocked hat, he must have gotten at St. Clair's defeat." DM 13CC65.

30. Calloway, *American Revolution in Indian Country,* 12.

31. Sheehan, "'The Famous Hair Buyer General,'" 18, quoting Fernando de Leyba to Bernardo de Galvez, July 11 and 21, 1778, in Clark-Leyba Papers, ed. Lawrence Kinnaird, *American Historical Review* 41 (Oct. 1935): 95, 98.

32. For increased animosity of Virginians and Pennsylvanians toward Indians as a result of Indian raids during the Seven Years' War and Pontiac's War, see Ward, *Breaking the Backcountry,* 236–40, 256. Grenier argues persuasively, however, that British settlers, from the first settlements of America, waged all-out war against Indians, including destruction of crops and killing of women and children. Grenier, *First Way of War.* See also Richard Slotkin, *Regeneration through Violence: The Mythology of the American Frontier, 1600–1860* (1973; rpt., Norman: University of Oklahoma Press, 2000), 69–93, on the killings of the Pequots in 1637 (76:

Captain Underwood, noting the killing of women and children, said: "We had sufficient light from the word of God for our proceedings"), and on King Philip's War (1675–78).

33. The Presbyterian minister David McClure in 1772, among the Delawares on the Muskingum, had difficulty convincing a young man who had been a captive since he was nine to rejoin his family in Pennsylvania. McClure observed: "There is an unknown charm in the Indian life, which surprisingly attaches white people; those especially who have been captivated in early life. Whether it is, that uncontrouled liberty, which is found among savages, or that freedom from all anxiety and care for futurity, which they appear to enjoy, or that love of ease, which is so agreeable to the indolence of human nature, or all these combined, the fact is established by numerous instances of english & french captives, who have resisted the most affectionate and inviting allurements to draw them and chose to spend their days among their adopted Indian friends." *Diary of David McClure*, Oct. 7, 1772, 88.

34. Merrell, *Into the American Woods*, 94.

35. Remarks of Lawoughwa, May 10, 1763, *Pennsylvania Colonial Records*, 9:259–60, reprinted in Downes, 122. For a summary of how Ohio Valley Indians treated the many captives they took during the French and Indian War—killing some but treating most "very kindly"—and of the reluctance of many of the longtime captives to return to the white world, see Ward, *Breaking the Backcountry*, 52–55, 210–11, 250 (Col. Henry Bouquet reports that the Shawnees returning white captives to him in 1764 "were obliged to bind several of their prisoners and force them along to the camp; and some women who had been delivered up, afterwards found means to escape and run back to the Indian towns").

36. Drimmer, *Captured by the Indians*, 134.

37. For excerpts from *A Narrative of the Captivity and Adventures of John Tanner*, see Drimmer, *Captured by the Indians*, 142–82.

38. White, *Middle Ground*, 500–501.

39. Belue reconstructed the later lives of the captive salt boilers in his article "Terror in the Canelands: The Fate of Daniel Boone's Salt Boilers," *FCHQ* 68 (1994): 3. Belue's account is based in substantial part on Draper, 481–84.

40. DM 24C135(2), Belue, "Terror in the Canelands," 11 n. 22.

41. JDS interview with John Gass, c. 1840s, DM 11CC15.

42. Belue, "Terror in the Canelands," 14–15. For surveys by Boone on which Micajah Callaway was one of the chainmen, see Neal O. Hammon and James Russell Harris, "Daniel Boone the Surveyor: Old Images and New Realities," *RKHS* 102 (2004): 563–66.

43. Belue, "Terror in the Canelands," 16–17; Draper, 482.

44. Belue, "Terror in the Canelands," 22.

45. *MFDB*, 119.

46. Belue, "Terror in the Canelands," 23–24; Faragher, 165, 313.

47. Draper interview with Delinda Boone Craig, 1866, DM 30C67.

48. Francis Baily, *Journal of a Tour in Unsettled Parts of North America in 1796 & 1797*, ed. Jack D. L. Holmes (Carbondale: Southern Illinois University Press, 1969), 116.

49. Filson, 66–67.

50. Draper interview with John Shaw, 1855, qtd. in Faragher, 300.

51. Peck, 138.

52. Draper interview with Joseph McCormick, 1871, DM 30C110–13. The advice is

consistent with the advice of Conrad Weiser, who for many years was Pennsylvania's interpreter and intermediary with the Delawares, Iroquois, Shawnees, and other Indians: "A European who wishes to stand well with them, must practice well the three following virtues. They are—(1) Speak the truth (2) Give the best that he has (3) Show himself not a coward, but courageous in all cases." Wallace, *Conrad Weiser,* 201.

53. Faragher, 250–51.

54. Boone's Indian account books were reprinted in David I. Bushnell, Jr., "Daniel Boone at Limestone, 1786–1787," *Virginia Magazine of History and Biography* 25 (1917): 1–11.

55. *Virginia Gazette* of Apr. 19, 1787, qtd. in Bushnell, "Daniel Boone at Limestone," 1–2.

56. Faragher, 258–59; Bakeless, 318–19. On Boone's telling Chloe Finn that he would take her home, see Boone Ballard to Draper, Dec. 6, 1882, DM 14C50[1].

57. Boone to Col. Robert Patterson, Mar. 16, 1787, DM 26C176–76(1).

58. Major Wall to the Shawnees at a prisoner exchange at the Falls of the Ohio in May 1783, Correspondence and Papers of Governor-General Sir Frederick Haldiman, 1758–91, British Museum, London, Additional Manuscript 21779, 117, qtd. in Calloway, *American Revolution in Indian Country,* 174.

59. Faragher, 256–58; Bakeless, 321; Lofaro, 139; Talbert, *Benjamin Logan,* 219–20.

60. JDS interview with Col. Thomas Jones, c. 1840s, DM 12CC233.

61. White, *Middle Ground.*

62. John Warth, qtd. in J. P. Hale, "Daniel Boone, Some Facts and Incidents not Hitherto Published," *West Virginia School Journal* 2, no. 4 (Feb. 1882): 85–86, cited in Faragher, *Boone,* 165.

16. TRADING AND LAND SPECULATION

1. Downes, 291. Cornplanter had sought more land: "We Indians love our lands, we warriors must have a large country to range in, indeed our subsistence must depend on our having much hunting ground."

2. Dorman, 21.

3. Notes by Nathan Reid, Jr., of conversations with his father Nathan Reid, in Draper, 407.

4. Rev. David Rice, the father of Presbyterianism in Kentucky, writing of his first visit to Kentucky in the early 1780s; Robert H. Bishop, ed., *An Outline of the History of the Church in the State of Kentucky, During a Period of Forty Years: Containing the Memoirs of Rev. David Rice, and Sketches of the Origin and Present State of Particular Churches, and of the Lives and Labours of a Number of Men Who Were Eminent and Useful in Their Day* (Lexington, 1824), 36, qtd. in Aron, *How the West Was Lost,* 80.

5. John Breckenridge to James Breckenridge, Jan. 29, 1786, James Breckenridge Papers, Alderman Library, University of Virginia, Charlottesville, qtd. in Marion Nelson Winship, "Kentucky in the New Republic: A Study of Distance and Connection," in Friend, *Buzzel about Kentuck,* 103.

6. Andro Linklater, *Measuring America: How an Untamed Wilderness Shaped the United States and Fulfilled the Promise of Democracy* (New York: Walker, 2002), 45.

7. Ellis, *His Excellency George Washington,* 10, 35.

8. Washington to George Mercer, Nov. 7, 1771, qtd. in Ellis, *Washington,* 57.

9. Linklater, *Measuring America*, 45.

10. Dorman, 14 n. 14.

11. Ibid., 14 n. 2.

12. Linklater, *Measuring America*, 33, 38.

13. *Journal of Nicholas Cresswell*, 54 (Tuesday, Jan. 5, 1775).

14. Hammon and Harris, "Daniel Boone the Surveyor," 535, 538–39.

15. Ibid., 537, supplemented by the author's correspondence with Hammon in 2006 about nine additional surveys, aggregating 15,237 acres, done by Boone in 1796 that Hammon found after the date of the article. Hammon and Harris estimated the time required for surveying, travel, and the number of trips required based on survey dates, locations, acreage surveyed, distance traveled, and number of assistants used. Their table did not include time and mileage required to register surveys. Hammon has advised the author that there may be other Boone surveys in Kentucky's files because surveys are indexed by the recipients of the survey, not by the surveyor.

16. See Linklater, *Measuring America*, 15–18, for a description of chains and their use.

17. For summaries of the Boone surveys, see Hammon and Harris, "Daniel Boone the Surveyor," 560–66; Willard Rouse Jillson, "Land Surveys of Daniel Boone," *RKHS* 44 (1946): 87–100.

18. JDS interview with William Risk, c. 1840s, DM 11CC87. According to Risk, it was also said that Boone, not being able to find a land entry he had made for someone, made a new entry and rubbed dirt over the new marks "so as to conceal the fraud"—but it was found out, which "caused him to leave the country for Missouri." Another settler remembered that title under many of the surveys Boone undertook for others did not survive challenges in litigation: "Mighty little land ever held under Boon." JDS interview with Maj. Jesse Daniel, c. 1843, DM 11CC93.

19. Willard Rouse Jillson, *With Compass and Chain: A Brief Narration of the Activities of Col. Daniel Boone as a Land Surveyor in Kentucky* (Frankfort: Roberts Printing Company, 1954), 8.

20. Draper's interview with Nathan and Olive Boone, 1851, DM 6S221. For Nathan Boone's career as a surveyor in Missouri, see R. Douglas Hurt, *Nathan Boone and the American Frontier* (Columbia: University of Missouri Press 1998), 111, 144–45 (surveying the boundary between the Creeks and the Cherokees).

21. Indeed, the Virginia land law contemplated that surveys should ordinarily "be bounded plainly by marked trees." 1778 Virginia land law, app. 9. Hammon email to the author, Oct. 2007 ("precise in the direction and measurement of the sides"). The excerpt is from a reproduction of a Boone survey in Faragher, 174 f.

22. Hammon and Harris, "Daniel Boone the Surveyor," 539.

23. See generally Linklater, *Measuring America*.

24. Hammon and Harris, "Daniel Boone the Surveyor," 550–51; Faragher, 240–41.

25. Faragher, 241.

26. Hammon and Harris, "Daniel Boone the Surveyor," 552; Faragher, 241.

27. From tables of warrants purchased by Boone on Dec. 22, 1781, sent by Hammon to the author in Oct. 2007. The database at the office of the Kentucky Secretary of State for Virginia Treasury Warrants, http://apps.sos.ky.gov/land/nonmilitary/LandOfficeVTW, which lists

these warrants, is not yet complete. By December 1781, the price for warrants had been increased to £1,600 per hundred acres. The inflation in Virginia's currency after the Revolution was dramatic. In the last eight months of 1781 alone, the value of Virginia currency relative to specie dropped more than sixfold—from 150:1 in May to 1000:1 in December. Hening, *Statutes of Virginia*, 10:471–73.

28. *MFDB*, 110; DM 6S216.

29. Hammon and Harris, "Daniel Boone the Surveyor," 553–54, including on 554 a listing of all of Boone's land claims.

30. *MFDB*, 110.

31. Hammon and Harris, "Daniel Boone the Surveyor," 555.

32. There were forty-eight deputy surveyors in Fayette County alone. Hammon to the author, Oct. 23, 2007.

33. Boone to Col. William Christian, Aug. 23, 1785, manuscript collection of the St. Louis Mercantile Library Association, University of Missouri, printed in Lofaro, 135. A photocopy is in the manuscripts collection of the Filson Historical Society.

34. Faragher, 247, 399.

35. Imlay to Boone, Dec. 27, 1786, DM 26C152; Faragher, 246–47; *MFDB*, 109; Hammon to author, Oct. 2007 (Wilkinson's claim against Boone). Imlay's bond, dated Mar. 15, 1783, is in DM 25C83. For Imlay's checkered career and double-dealing and his love affair with the early feminist Mary Wollstonecraft, see Lyndall Gordon, *Vindication: A Life of Mary Wollstonecraft* (New York: HarperCollins, 2005). For Imlay's investment in the slave trade, see Wil Verhoeven, "Gilbert Imlay and the Triangular Trade," *William and Mary Quarterly* 43 (Oct. 2006): 827. Verhoeven has written a biography of Imlay, *Gilbert Imlay: Citizen of the World* (London: Pickering & Chatto, 2007).

36. Gilbert Imlay, *A Topographical Description of the Western Territory of North America Containing a Succinct Account of its Soil, Climate, Natural History, Population, Agriculture, Manners and Customs with an Ample Description of the Several Divisions into Which that Country is Divided* (London: J. Debrett, 1792).

37. David Todd to Mann Butler, Mar. 17, 1834, DM 15CC126.

38. *MFDB*, 109. The Draper manuscripts include notes of sheriff's sales in Kentucky in Aug. and Sept. 1798 of three tracts of land owned by Boone, aggregating 10,500 acres. DM 15C51.

39. Baily, *Journal of a Tour*, 122–23.

40. Receipt of T. Perkins, Oct. 26, 1785, DM 26C69.

41. For summaries of this litigation, see Faragher, 242–45; and Morgan, 357–59. Faragher refers (p. 398) to a 1925 article in the *Lexington Herald*. According to Hammon, there is no record of Boone transferring any of his land to Hickman. Hammon to author, Feb. 24, 2008.

42. E.g., the ledger of John Brown, a prominent lawyer in Kentucky who was to become one of Kentucky's first senators when Kentucky became a state, shows in Sept. 1786 a reference to what appears to be a payment by Boone of five pounds "to fee on Caot [?] v. Triplett." Copy of ledger of John Brown, Liberty Hall Historic Site, Frankfort, Ky., 23. Brown's ledger also show substantial fees due from Squire Boone and George Boone.

43. Hammon's compilation of Boone's depositions includes fifteen taken between 1785 and 1799 in what are now Kentucky and West Virginia. Hammon, ed., "Daniel Boone Papers," MS, copy in the possession of the author, chap. 3.

44. Nathaniel Hart to Thomas Hart, Jan. 10, 1791, Manuscript Collection, FHS. The petition is in Fayette County Historical Records, 1:650-85, a transcript of which was sent by Hammon to the author. The Hart family, eventually represented by Henry Clay, brought suit against Boone and others to recover the land, but lost. The court declared there was no evidence to convict Boone of fraud. *Estill v. Hart's Heirs*, Harding's Reports, 1805-1808, Spring Term 1808, 567.

45. Faragher, 248–49; Bakeless, 340–46. The extent to which Boone was named as a party in suits is unclear. Faragher (p. 248) says Boone "was a party to at least ten lawsuits" from 1786 to 1789, but cites none. Hammon says that as far as he can discover, Boone "was never personally involved in any litigation." Hammon to author, Feb. 24, 2008.

46. *MFDB*, 110.

47. Eslinger, *Running Mad for Kentucky*, 19.

48. Baily, *Journal of a Tour*, 87; Filson, 17.

49. In 1804 the somewhat snobbish young wife of Senator John Brown wrote to her husband that she had been to an "Assembly" at Frankfort, attended by, among other people, "Mr. *Pearson* (the *tavern keeper*)": "This *equality*, my Love, is a mighty *pretty* thing upon *paper*, and a very *useful* one in the common intercourses of life, but does not suit a regular Assembly quite so well." She added, "But I will say no more upon this subject; fortunately recollecting, that you once gave me a serious lecture, for some of my aristocratic notions." Margaretta Brown to John Brown, Mar. 8, 1802, Brown Family Papers, FHS.

50. Dorman 4.

51. Bakeless, 332, 359 (citing examples of other licenses in Kentucky, in 1793, 1794, 1797, and 1799).

52. Boone to (by context) Patrick Henry, Aug. 16, 1785, DM 32C81A (a printed article containing what is said to be a copy of a letter "in the Executive Department of the State of Virginia").

53. Draper interview with Joseph Scholl, 1868, DM 24S217.

54. For Boone's ownership and purchase of slaves, see Bakeless, 329 and 329.1 and Faragher at 397. The letter relating to the sale, dated Mar. 3, 1791, and addressed to "William Haris," DM 14C105[1], is printed in Bakeless, 329.

55. *Historical Statistics*, pt. 2, 1184 (74,604 pounds of ginseng were exported in 1770). As early as 1750, Col. William Johnson had been paying the Iroquois for ginseng, which he shipped to London, "and from there it is sent on to China where it is bought as the greatest rarity." Daniel Claus to Conrad Weiser, Aug. 23, 1752, Peters MSS, 3: 61, Historical Society of Philadelphia, Wallace, *Conrad Weiser*, 338.

56. Philip Chadwick Foster Smith, *The Empress of China* (Philadelphia: Philadelphia Maritime Museum, 1984), 155, 206-7 (report in the *New York Packet* of the venture's "very prosperous achievement" and of China's appetite for ginseng), 312 n. 5 (listing of some of the American newspaper accounts of the ship's return); David A. Taylor, *Ginseng: The Divine Root* (Chapel Hill, N.C.: Algonquin Books, 2006), 89–99, 131–34.

57. Morgan, 366-67, believes Nathan was referring to tuns, although that term usually refers to casks containing liquids (e.g., wine).

58. *MFDB*, 81–82.

59. John F. Watson to Draper, Jan. 12, 1853, DM 1C19[2] (reminiscences of Rachael Lightfoot).

60. Journal of Joel Watkins, entries for May 16 and May 17, 1789, in Eslinger, *Running Mad for Kentucky*, 164–65.

61. Boone to Hart and Richardson, July 30, 1789, DM 14C92.

17. LIVING LEGEND, SHRINKING FORTUNE

1. Faragher, 5–6. For the spread of Filson's Boone narrative in Europe, see also Slotkin, *Regeneration through Violence*, 314–20. For the dissemination of Filson's narrative and its off-shoots in America, see 398–400.

2. Baily, *Journal of a Tour*, 115–17.

3. Ibid., 116.

4. Filson, 5–6.

5. Faragher, 2–3. According to John Walton, *John Filson of Kentucke* (Lexington: University of Kentucky Press, 1956), 24–25, Filson on Dec. 19–20, 1782, claimed under treasury warrants three tracts of land containing 5,000, 4922, and 2446.5 acres. Walton cited register of Col. Thomas Marshall, surveyor of Fayette Country, bk. 3, 101, 102, 106.

6. Filson, 7, 21, 22, 25, 107–8.

7. Ibid., 81, 58.

8. John A. McClung, *Sketches of Western Adventure* (Maysville, Ky.: L. Collins, 1832), 79–80, qtd. in Faragher, 7. Richard Slotkin, who has focused on the myth of the frontier, sees Filson's account as "a literary myth," drawing strength in part from its basis in cultural mythology (e.g., how Americans were portraying Indians) and in "archetypal myth"—the hero descends into the world of darkness and death to seek a boon and returns with powers to sustain his people. Slotkin, *Regeneration through Violence*, 278–310. While Filson's telling of the Boone story may sometimes smack of myth (and contains overwriting to promote interest in the purchase of land in Kentucky), many of the facts and chronology in it jibe with other sources.

9. Undated, unsigned MSS in John Filson's handwriting, DM 1MM60, qtd. in Watson, *John Filson*, 113; see Chinn, *Kentucky: Settlement and Statehood*, 588–89.

10. Watson, *John Filson*, 73 (Filson teaching school in Wilmington in 1785), 84, 91–92 (Filson's note to John Brown and Brown's attempts to be repaid), 98–100 (Filson's prospectus for a seminary, from the Lexington *Gazette* of Jan. 19, 1787), 102 (doubtful the seminary ever was launched), 104–5 (Filson and Breckenridge as tenants in common enter one thousand acres in Powell's Valley to include a silver mine), 106 (Filson's letter to his brother Robert—"I resumed my Studies last winter and greatly advanced my latin, and this spring have begun to study Physic with Doctr Slater in this place, an eminent Physician who came here from London last year, two years I study, as soon as my Study is finished I am to be married"), 107–8 (poem written at Beargrass, June 30, 1788), 109–10, 112–20 (plans for Losantiville and probable killing by Indians); Hammon and Taylor, *Virginia's Western War*, 207 (St. Clair names Cincinnati). For a short sketch of Filson, see J. Winston Coleman, "John Filson: Early Kentucky Historian," *Bulletin of the Historical and Philosophical Society of Ohio* 11, no. 1 (Jan. 1953): 58–65.

11. George P. Garrison, ed., "A Memorandum of M. Austin's Journey from the County of Wythe in the State of Virginia to the Lead Mines in the Province of Louisiana West of the Mississippi, 1796–77, *American Historical Review* 5, no. 3 (1900): 525–26. Some discounting of

Austin's acerbic comments may be in order. He could be rude and disagreeable and, to one historian, "was hardly an unbiased, nor a particularly empathetic observer of western life." Perkins, *Border Life*, 56.

12. Matthew Vanlear to Boone, Apr. 27, 1780, DM 27C6.

13. *MFDB*, 85.

14. Faragher, 265.

15. *MFDB*, 87; Lofaro, 143.

16. Faragher, 266; *MFDB*, 87–88, 93–95.

17. Boone to Governor Henry Lee, Dec. 13, 1791, DM 14C105. The letter is reprinted in Lofaro, 144.

18. Qtd. in W. S. Laidley, "Daniel Boone in the Kanawha Valley," *RKHS* 2 (1913): 9–12.

19. Col. George Clendenin to Governor Henry Lee, Sept. 21, 1792, *CVSP*, 6:67.

20. Faragher, 269–70.

21. *MFDB*, 97.

22. Of the three youngest Boone children, Jesse had married a Van Bibber girl and set up house with her; Daniel Morgan was out by himself, hunting and looking for land; and young Nathan had been sent to Kentucky to stay with his married sisters Jemima and Susannah while he went to a school not far from Boone's Station. *MFDB*, 97.

23. Draper interview with Edward Byram, Oct. 2, 1863, DM 19S170.

24. Draper interview with William Champ, 1863, DM 15C31–31[1].

25. Ralph Clayton to Draper, Apr. 10, 1883, DM 16C45.

26. Faragher, 270–71.

27. *MFDB*, 102.

28. *MFDB*, 98–99.

29. *MFDB*, 104; Hammon and Harris, "Daniel Boone the Surveyor," 566.

30. Isaac Shelby was listed as the marker on the two surveys, though this may have been because Shelby held the warrants for the tracts and acted as marker to familiarize himself with the tracts and to save money on the marker's fees. Hammon and Harris, "Daniel Boone the Surveyor," 543 n. 16.

31. Kincaid, *Wilderness Road*, 185.

32. Ibid., 191.

33. Garrison, "M. Austin's Journey," 525.

34. Kincaid, *Wilderness Road*, 202–3.

18. OUT TO MISSOURI

1. The 1795 census listed 2,665 people. Din and Nasatir, *Imperial Osages*, 243. William E. Foley, *A History of Missouri*, vol. 1: *1673–1820* (Columbia: University of Missouri Press, 1999), 46 (Upper Louisiana had scarcely 1,000 inhabitants when France assumed control of it in 1770), 50 (in 1804, when Spain transferred control of Upper Louisiana to the United States, the population of Upper Louisiana was estimated at 10,350, of which an estimated 15% were slaves). See also Jonas Viles, "Population and Extent of Settlement in Missouri before 1804," *Missouri Historical Review* 5, no. 4 (July 1911): 189–213.

2. Stephen Aron, *American Confluence: The Missouri Frontier from Borderland to Border State* (Bloomington: Indiana University Press, 2006), 78–79.

3. Governor-General François Luis Hector Carondelet to Zenon Trudeau, Mar. 28, 1792, in *Before Lewis and Clark: Documents Illustrating the History of Missouri, 1785–1804*, ed. Abraham P. Nasatir (St. Louis: St. Louis Historical Documents Foundation, 1952), 151.

4. Trudeau to Carondelet, Jan. 15, 1798, in *Before Lewis and Clark*, 542.

5. *MFDB*, 107–8.

6. The warrant, dated Nov. 29, 1798, and the endorsement are in Miscellaneous Papers, Manuscripts Department, FHS.

7. Squire Boone's petition to Congress, undated (c. 1812?), Squire Boone Collection FHS.

8. Delinda Boone Bryan to Draper, Feb. 28, 1843, DM 22C6[2].

9. *MFDB*, 112.

10. *MFDB*, 108, 111–13; DM 6S221; Faragher, 274–79; Lofaro, 152.

11. Garrison, "M. Austin's Journey," 527 (Louisville), 535 (St. Louis). Austin may have been high in estimating St. Louis's size. Trudeau, the Spanish commandant at St. Louis, said its population was 948. Trudeau to governor, St. Louis, Jan. 15, 1798, in Nasatir, *Before Lewis and Clark*, 536.

12. John M. Krum to Draper, Jan. 17, 1883, DM 16C54[1]

13. Trudeau to Governor-General Carondelet, Sept. 26, 1795, in Nasatir, *Before Lewis and Clark*, 350. But the land near St. Charles was rich. Timothy Flint, seeing it in 1816, told his companion, "Here shall be my farm, and here will I end my days!" According to Flint, "In effect, take it all and all, I have not seen, before nor since, a landscape which united, in an equal degree, the grand, the beautiful, and fertile." Flint, *Recollections of the Last Ten Years*, 90–91.

14. DM 15C63, 15C66, 16C28, 6S225–36.

15. Faragher, 279.

16. Bakeless, 360; DM 16C4–5, 16C54(1–5). Flint's early biographer Timothy Flint also gives the story of Boone's "more elbow room!" explanation of the move to Missouri. Flint, *Boone*, 238.

17. Baily, *Journal of a Tour*, 116. The words Baily records as Boone's sound suspiciously similar to Baily's own Rousseau-influenced musings on the idyllic virtues of solitary life in the wilderness.

18. In 1800, a year after Boone moved to Missouri, Kentucky's population was 221,000. *Historical Statistics*, pt. 1, 8 (total U.S. population), 33.

19. *MFDB*, 110.

20. Draper interview with Edward Coles, 1848, DM 310–11.

21. See Arthur K. Moore, *The Frontier Mind* (1957; rpt., New York: McGraw-Hill, 1963), 73 ("The real pioneers—Harrods, McAfees, Calloways, Boones, Bryans, Logans and Floyds— figured progressively less in the affairs of the region, gradually giving way before men of wealth and education such as the Browns, Todds, Bullitts, Breckenridges, McDowells, Harts, George Nichols, Harry Innes, Caleb Wallace, Thomas Marshall and James Wilkinson—many of whom had been leaders previously in southwestern Virginia"), 149–60. As Moore put it, "While conditions were heroic, the conceivers prudently stayed at home; when the Indians had been expelled and society stabilized, they asserted their claims and dispossessed the defenders of the forts" (159–60).

22. William Lytle to John Breckinridge, Jan. 10, 1797, vol./container 14, folio pp. 2421–22, Breckenridge Family Papers, Library of Congress ("rage among the poorer class"); Friend, *Along the Maysville Road,* 92.

23. Eviza L. Coshow to Draper, Mar. 14, 1885, DM 21C24[10].

24. Gen. Thomas Gage to the earl of Shelburne, Feb. 22, 1767: "That Trade will go with the Stream is a Maxim found to be true, from all accounts that have been received of the Indian Trade carried on in the vast Tract of Country which lies on the Back of the British Colonies; and the Peltry acquired there, is carried to the Sea either by the River St. Lawrence or River Mississippi." Mereness, 458–59.

25. Filson, 47.

26. John May to Samuel Beall, Apr. 15, 1780, Beall-Booth Family Papers, manuscript department, FHS.

27. Chinn, *Kentucky: Settlement and Statehood,* 372.

28. For summaries of Spain's flirting with closing the Mississippi to Americans as a way to seek to induce the western American settlements to ally themselves with Spain, see Kluger, *Seizing Destiny,* 210–11; Foley, *History of Missouri,* 1:33–42; Chinn, *Kentucky: Settlement and Statehood, 1750–1800,* 464–69, 604–5; James Ripley Jacobs, *Tarnished Warrior: Major-General James Wilkinson* (New York: Macmillan, 1938). By 1794 Spain had sent some $32,000 to Wilkinson. While some was lost on the way, Wilkinson received some $26,000. Jacobs, *Tarnished Warrior,* 135. In 1788 John Brown, Kentucky's representative to Congress, reported to a convention of Kentuckians considering applying for statehood that the Spanish minister to the United States, Diego de Gardoqui, had said he could grant to the westerners the use of the Mississippi—but under Spain's commercial treaties with other nations, not so long as Kentucky is part of the United States. Talbert, *Benjamin Logan,* 232–36. See Bradford, *Notes on Kentucky,* 117, 302–18. The warnings of John Brown, George Nicholas, and John Breckenridge to James Madison about Kentucky's unhappiness concerning loss of navigation on the Mississippi bore fruit. When John Brown returned to Kentucky from Congress in the spring of 1792, he carried letters from Madison and Jefferson to Harry Innes and George Nicholas announcing that foreign control of the Mississippi would no longer be tolerated. Marion Nelson Winship, "Kentucky in the New Republic: A Study of Distance and Connection," in Friend, *Buzzel about Kentuck,* 109; Chinn, *Kentucky: Settlement and Statehood,* 461–62.

29. Governor Manuel Gayoso de Lemos, "Political Condition of the Province of Louisiana," July 5, 1792, J. A. Robertson, *Louisiana under Spain, France, and the United States: 1785–1807* (Cleveland: A. H. Clark Co., 1911), 1:287.

30. David J. Weber, *The Spanish Frontier in North America* (New Haven: Yale University Press, 1992), 289; Kluger, *Seizing Destiny,* 227–28 (Treaty of San Lorenzo), 267–68 (intendant's closing of port facilities to Americans).

31. Thomas Jefferson to Robert Livingston, Apr. 18, 1802, qtd. in Aron, *American Confluence,* 107.

32. *MFDB,* 111; DM 6S221.

33. Peck, 122.

34. Thomas Jefferson to George Washington, Apr. 2, 1791, qtd. in William E. Foley, *The Genesis of Missouri: From Wilderness Outpost to Statehood* (Columbia: University of Missouri Press, 1989), 61.

35. Many other Americans moved into other Spanish-controlled territory near Missouri in the same period. On July 15, 1789, e.g., future U.S. president Andrew Jackson, then in his early twenties, took the oath of allegiance to the Spanish King Carlos III, in Natchez, Miss., then part of Spanish West Florida. Perhaps Jackson was thinking Natchez was far enough away from Tennessee (where he had been living) and Kentucky that he might live there in peace with Rachel Donelson Robards when he eloped with her, though she apparently was still then married to the Kentuckian Robards. Jackson moved back to Tennessee soon after he swore allegiance to the Spanish king. Ann Toplovich, "Marriage, Mayhem, and Presidential Politics: The Robards-Jackson Backcountry Scandal," *Ohio Valley History* 5 (Winter 2005) 3–22.

36. Garrison, "M. Austin's Journey," 535, 540.

37. Ibid., 542.

38. Baily, *Journal of a Tour,* 137–38.

39. As the Spanish ambassador to the United States put it, "That colony cost us heavily and produced very little for us." Marqués de Casa Yrujó to Pedro de Ceballos y Guerra, Aug. 3, 1803, in Robertson, *Louisiana,* 2:70.

40. Faragher, 275.

41. Talleyrand to Duc Denis Decrès, an xi, 4 Prairial (May 23, 1803), Robertson, *Louisiana,* 2:63.

42. Ellis, *American Creation,* 207–34.

43. Robertson, *Louisiana,* 2:342–43.

44. Faragher, 286.

45. DM 15C64. The description of Boone by Delassus is qtd. in a letter to Draper dated Apr. 17, 1885, from St. Louis by Frederick Billon.

46. Foley, *History of Missouri,* 1:70–71.

47. Reuben Gold Thwaites, ed., *Original Journals of the Lewis and Clark Expedition, 1804–1806* (1904–5; rpt., New York: Arno Press, 1969), 1:24.

48. Gary Moulton, ed., *The Lewis and Clark Journals: An American Epic of Discovery* (Lincoln: University of Nebraska Press 2003), 3.

19. BOONE IN MISSOURI

1. Draper interview with Nathan and Olive Boone, 1851, DM 6S225.

2. Bakeless, Boone, 373; Faragher, 285. St. Charles was hardly a metropolis. A visitor in 1811, more than ten years after Boone arrived in Missouri, said St. Charles had three hundred inhabitants (largely French boatmen but with a considerable proportion of Americans), two or three stores, and "several genteel families." Henry Marie Brackenridge, *Views of Louisiana Together with a Journal of a Voyage up the Missouri River* (1814; rpt., Chicago: Quadrangle Books, 1962), 128.

3. A copy of this document is DM 15C65. The document is printed in Bakeless, 373; and in Lofaro, 156.

4. For the killing of Hays, see Draper interview with Abner Bryan, 1890, DM 4C58; Faragher, 286–87; Lofaro, 156–57; Bakeless, 374–75.

5. Hurt, *Nathan Boone and the American Frontier,* 53.

6. William G. Beck, trans., "Gottfried Duden's 'Report,' 1824–1827," *Missouri Historical Review* 12 (1917–18): 262 (sixteenth letter, Dec. 10, 1825).

7. Draper interview with Delinda Boone Craig, 1866, DM 30C66.

8. *MFDB*, 119, 125; for Boone's residing with Daniel Morgan, see a summary of Boone's testimony in 1896 before the land commission, qtd. in Faragher, 281.

9. Dr. S. Paul Jones to Draper, May 13, 1887, DM 21C1[5–6].

10. Draper interview with Edward Coles, 1848, DM 6S311.

11. *MFDB*, 119.

12. *MFDB*, 120, DM 6S229.

13. Donald Jackson, ed., *Letters of the Lewis and Clark Expedition with Related Documents, 1783–1854* (Urbana: University of Illinois Press 1978), 1:200.

14. Willard H. Rollings, *The Osage: An Enthnohistorical Study of Hegemony on the Prairie-Plains* (Columbia: University of Missouri Press 1992), 215. Lieutenant Governor Trudeau in 1793 estimated that the main branch of the Osages numbered 1,250 men, young men, and warriors. Trudeau to Governor-General Carondelet, Apr. 10, 1793, in Nasatir, *Before Lewis and Clark,* 172. For a map of the Osage homelands, see Rollings, *Osage,* 68.

15. Kristie C. Wolferman, *The Osage in Missouri* (Columbia: University of Missouri Press, 1997), 12.

16. See generally Kathleen DuVal, *The Native Ground: Indians and Colonists in the Heart of the Continent* (Philadelphia: University of Pennsylvania Press, 2006).

17. Carl H. Chapman, ed., "Louis Cartambert: Journey to the Land of the Osages, 1835–1836," *Missouri Historical Society Bulletin* 19, no. 2 (Apr. 1963): 221.

18. *MFDB*, 120; DM 230; for the steel trap, see Faragher, 284–85; Bakeless, 365; and DM 6S231.

19. *MFDB*, 127.

20. *MFDB*, 122–24.

21. *MFDB*, 126–27; DM 6S244–46; Hurt, *Nathan Boone,* 47–50; Faragher, 290.

22. Flint, *Recollections of the Last Ten Years,* 146–47.

23. Aron, *American Confluence,* 150, quoting Rufus Babcock, ed., *Forty Years of Pioneer Life: Memoir of John Mason Peck, D.D.* (Carbondale: Southern Illinois University Press, 1965), 146, 121.

24. Rollings, *Osage,* 11–13, 224–39, 240–42, 254–56.

25. Hurt, *Nathan Boone,* 52–77; Foley, *History of Missouri,* 130–32.

26. Zenon Trudeau to governor, St. Louis , Jan. 15, 1798, printed in Nasatir, *Before Lewis and Clark,* 534 (Carondelet appointed Lorimier commandant at Cape Girardeau); Pierre Chouteau to Wilkinson, St. Louis, Apr. 12, 1806, Missouri Historical Society, Pierre Chouteau letterbook, Nasatir, *Before Lewis and Clark,* 767 (as subagent at Cape Girardeau, Laurimier [*sic*] received four hundred dollars per year from the Spanish government); *RUO,* 114 n. 43; Aron, *American Confluence,* 80–82.

27. Stephen Warren, *The Shawnees and Their Neighbors, 1795–1870* (Urbana: University of Illinois Press, 2005), 17.

28. *MFDB*, 119; DM 6S228.

29. Draper interview with Delinda Boone Craig, 1866, DM 30C66–67.

30. Hammon, *MFDB*, 119; DM 6S228; for the Shawnees' visit, Draper interview with Delinda Boone Craig, 1866, DM 30C66–67.

31. John C. Boone to Draper, Nov. 20, 1890, DM 16C132[2].

32. Rollings, *Osage*, 67, quoting Ora Brooks Peake, *A History of the United States Indian Factory System, 1795–1822* (Denver: Sage Books, 1954), 14.

33. The board used its customary terse formulation: "It is the opinion of the Board, that this claim ought not to be confirmed." For Boone's argument in 1806 and for the decision of the commissioners, see *American State Papers: Public Lands* (Washington, D.C.: Gales and Seaton, 1834), 2:736, available online at http://memory.loc/gov/ammem/amlaw/lwsplink .html#anchor8. See also Faragher, 291–94; Bakeless, 375–80. For the Delassus grants after 1800, see Aron, *American Confluence*, 111.

34. Bakeless, 378.

35. Boone to Judge Coburn, Oct. 5, 1809, manuscript collections of the KHS.

36. JDS interview with Daniel Boone Bryan, 1844, DM 22C14[14].

37. Faragher, 292–93; *MFDB*, 127 (my father "became ill and, fearing he might not recover, gave instructions to Hays and Derry to bury him between two certain trees near camp").

38. Bakeless, 407.

39. Peck, 129.

40. Faragher, 287–88; Lofaro, 159.

41. *MFDB*, 47. Nathan Boone put Kenton's visit in the spring of 1805 or 1806. Kenton's children put the visit in 1809. Faragher, 294; Draper interview with John and Sarah Kenton McCord, 1851, DM 5S172; Draper interview with William M. Kenton, 1851, DM 5S125.

42. Stoner's son George W. Stoner in 1868 told Draper they had gone "high up the Missouri." DM 24C55[10–11]. Stephen Hempstead, a neighbor of Boone's in St. Charles, told Draper in 1863 that he saw a boat coming down the Missouri River early in 1811, "with housing over the cargo, a sure sign of fur coming from the upper Missouri," and that Boone was steering in the stern, with the boat holding a considerable value of furs. Hempstead to Draper, Mar. 6, 1863, DM 16C78[2]; Lofaro, 174 (quoting from the letter); Faragher, 295. Wade Hays, son of William Hays, Jr., on Jan. 18, 1889, recorded that "Daniel Boone & My Father and others Made a trip to the Yellow Stone on the hed waters of the Missouri River was in that country about two winters after Furrs." MS 130, Wade Hays Family History, Seaver Center for Western History Research, Natural History Museum of Los Angeles County, Los Angeles, qtd. in Lofaro, 171.

43. The letter from Fort Osage, qtd. in Bakeless, 391–92, was published in *Niles' Weekly Register*, 10:261 [361], June 15, 1816. For the trip with Indian Philips upriver from Fort Leavenworth, see *MFDB*, 136. See also Peck, 135.

44. Bakeless, 387; Lofaro, 166–67.

45. William S. Bryan and Robert Rose, *A History of the Pioneer Families of Missouri* (St. Louis: Bryan, Brand, 1876) 103–4; Faragher, 303–4; Bakeless, *Boone*, 389.

46. *MFDB*, 135.

47. *The Mountain Muse: Comprising the Adventures of Daniel Boone and the Power of Virtue and Refined Beauty* (Harrisonburg, Va.: Davidson & Bourne, 1813), bk. 2, 52. As Arthur K. Moore put it, Bryan cast Boone "in a Miltonic setting—angels and devils and all—to amplify his matter and further to cloak conquest with divine sanction." Moore, *Frontier Mind*, 164. The angels of the Lord sought, as their choice:

> one, in whose expanded breast are found,
> The great, ennobling virtues of the soul;

Benevolence, Mercy, Meekness, Pity, Love,
Benignant Justice, Valor lion-like,
And Fortitude, with stoic *nerves* endow'd.

(1:727–32)

48. *Mountain Muse,* bk. 2, 112. More of Bryan's stanzas can be found in Slotkin, *Regeneration through Violence,* 348–51.

49. DM 7C43[1], qtd. in Lofaro, 167–68.

50. The progress of Boone's petition and of the bill granting him land in Missouri can be tracked in *American State Papers: Documents, Legislative and Executive, of the Congress of the United States in Relation to the Public Lands,* vol. 2 (Washington, D.C.: Gales and Seaton, 1834), available online at the Library of Congress's American Memory Web site, http://memory.loc .gov/ammem/amlw/lwsplink.html#anchor8 (public lands, vol. 2). Boone's petition and the favorable report of the Senate Committee, chaired by Senator Return Jonathan Meigs of Ohio, are at 2:5; the favorable report of the House Committee on the Public Lands in Dec. 1813 (appending a summary of Boone's Feb. 1806 testimony before the board and the board's decision of Dec. 1, 1809) is at 2:736; and a note of President Madison's approval and signature of the bill is at 2:438. Several versions of Boone's petition are cited in Faragher, 396. For the sale of the land and the application of proceeds to pay creditors, see DM 6S251; David Todd to Mann Butler, Mar. 17, 1834, DM 15CC126 (Boone told him he delivered his claim to the land to a Kentuckian, who pursued him on a loss of land in Kentucky, which Boone had warranted); *MFDB,* 116 (the petition was meant to be for a grant of ten thousand acres above the Boone Femme, "one of the finest tracts of land in Missouri"); and Bakeless, 382.

51. *MFDB,* 117.

20. LAST DAYS

1. *MFDB,* 135; DM 6S227.

2. Eviza L. Coshow to Draper, May 24, 1885, DM 21C45[2–3].

3. Bakeless, 396–97. A leader of the German immigration to Missouri had read in Germany a similar story about Boone's purported death. "Duden's Report," 262.

4. *MFDB,* 36–38.

5. Peck, 108.

6. Nathan Kouns to Draper, Jan. 16, 1863, DM 16C36.

7. David Todd to Mann Butler, Columbia, Mo., Mar. 17, 1834, DM 15CC126.

8. *MFDB,* 138.

9. Elizabeth Corbin to M. D. Lewis, *St. Louis Daily Dispatch,* Apr. 2, 1868, DM 16C97 (Boone had his coffin made to be the same as Rebecca's); Draper interview with Delinda Boone Craig, 1866 DM 30C78 (Boone would get the coffin down and polish it); Eviza L. Coshow to Draper, May 29, 1885, DM 21C45[3] (made her mother [one of Boone's granddaughters] shudder "to see him thump around his Coffin [and] whistle so happy and content"); A. J. Coshow, in the *Republic,* 1894 (Boone would lie in it to show how well it fit); Draper interview with Samuel Boone, 1868, DM 22S260 (Boone said he had taken "many a nice nap in his coffin"). For the use of the coffin Nathan had ordered, see *MFDB,* 138.

10. Houston was eighty-one when he told this story. Houston, 36.

11. F. W. Houston to Draper, Nov. 2, 1887, DM 20C:88–88(5), reprinted in Houston, 44–45.

12. *MFDB,* 111.

13. David Todd to Draper, Columbia, Mo., Mar. 17, 1834, DM 15CC126. See also Draper interview with Joseph McCormick, 1871, 30C111 (Boone in 1809 "said he had never returned from Kentucky to re-visit Kentucky"; he "said he had been treated badly in Kentucky—owned not a foot of its soil, after all his early discoveries, trials & dangers?").

14. Maria R. Audubon, *Audubon and His Journals* (New York: Charles Scribner Sons, 1897; rpt., New York: Dover Publications 1994), 2:241, 506.

15. William Souder, *Under a Wild Sky: John James Audubon and the Making of "The Birds of America"* (New York: North Point Press, 2004), 11, 19, 222–24.

16. For Boone's weight in his final years, see *MFDB,* 140.

17. Deposition of Boone, Sept. 22, 1817, St. Charles County, Missouri, DM 7C80-1; Deposition of Boone, Oct. 6, 1817, St. Charles County, Missouri, DM 7C105. See Hammon, ed. *Daniel Boone Papers,* chap. 3.

18. Peck, 7, 137.

19. Eviza L. Coshow to Draper, May 11, 1891, DM 21C70.

20. *MFDB,* 139.

21. Aron, *How the West Was Lost,* 172 (little interest in religion in Kentucky in the 1790s; quote from diary of David Barrow, MS in Western Kentucky University), 173 (estimate of number of church members in Kentucky), 173–88 (revivals, starting south of the Green River; impact of the New Madrid earthquakes). See also Tom Kanon, "'Scared from Their Sins for a Season': The Religious Ramifications of the New Madrid Earthquakes," *Ohio Valley History* 5:2 (Summer 2005), 27 (memberships of the Methodist Western Conference jumped from 31,000 to close to 46,000 after the earthquakes).

22. Stephen Aron, *American Confluence,* 149–50.

23. Flint, *Recollections of the Last Ten Years,* 163.

24. *MFDB,* 17.

25. Flint, *Boone,* 249.

26. Peck, 138.

27. Faragher, 311, The question of whether Boone had ever experienced a change in his feelings toward Jesus was by Rev. James E. Welch, recounted in the Louisville *Christian Repository,* Mar. 1860, DM 16C47.

28. Boone to Sarah Day Boone, Oct. 17, 1816, DM 27C88–88[1]. Transcriptions of the letter appear in Faragher, 312; and Lofaro, 173.

29. A later document signed by Daniel Boone, in context dating from 1818, is a petition to the Hon. B. N. Tucker recommending Absolem Hays as constable for the Femme Osage Township. Over thirty people signed the petition. Boone's signature follows that of his son-in-law Flanders Callaway. More than twice as many—including Boone's son Daniel Morgan Boone—signed a petition recommending the appointment of a contender for the post named Sumner Bacon. Both petitions are in the archives of the St. Charles County Historical Society, St. Charles, Mo.

30. Aron, *American Confluence,* 158–64, 213–15.

31. Ibid., 178–84; Thomas Jefferson to John Holmes, Apr. 22, 1820.

32. William S. Bryan and Robert Rose, *A History of the Pioneer Families of Missouri* (St. Louis: Bryan, Brand, 1876), 2–3.

33. Sweeney, *Columbus of the Woods,* 14–17. In the summer of 1820 Harding produced at least two finished portraits from the oil sketch and from a now-lost pencil sketch—a half-length portrait, in which Boone wears a brown coat with a dark fur collar, and a full-length portrait, painted on a table oilcloth. The full-length portrait was damaged, though Harding was able to salvage the head. An 1820 engraving by James Otto Lewis, now in the St. Louis Art Museum, shows what Harding's full-length picture would have looked like (Sweeney, *Columbus of the Woods,* fig. 7). See Peck, 139; and DM 6S277–78, for the need to steady the feeble Boone as he sat for the sketch.

34. *MFDB,* 139.

35. Excerpts from Harding's account of painting Boone's portrait, in Harding, *My Egotistigraphy,* 35–36, are printed in Sweeney, *Columbus of the Woods,* 14–15; Bakeless, 413; and Lofaro, 175–76. For accounts of Boone's death, see *MFDB,* 138–39; Draper's interview with Delinda Boone Craig, 1866, DM 30C79–83; Faragher, 317–19; Lofaro, 176–77; Bakeless, 412–13. Nathan Boone says that because there were very few Masons in the region, there were no Masonic honors (139), though Boone was a member. Morgan speculates that Freemasonry may have been significant in Boone's life. The paucity of references to Boone as a mason makes this claim unlikely.

36. Peck, 139–40.

21. LIFE AFTER DEATH

1. *MFDB,* 126.

2. For overviews of differing views of Boone after his death, see Slotkin, *Regeneration through Violence,* esp. 268–516; Moore, *Frontier Mind,* 139–48, 164–88, 199–203; Richard Taylor, "Daniel Boone as American Icon: A Literary View," *RKHS* 102 (2004): 513; Faragher, 320–62; Lofaro, 180–83. Moore found it "indicative of nineteenth-century thinking that Boone should have been installed in two different myths—progressivism and primitivism—which, though not in all respects antithetical, clash on several levels and ultimately point in opposite directions." *Frontier Mind,* 188. For different treatments of Boone in paintings and sculpture, see Sweeney, *Columbus of the Woods.*

3. Byron to Thomas Moore, Sept. 19, 1818, in *Lord Byron: Selected Letters and Journals,* ed. Leslie A. Marchand (Cambridge: Harvard University Press, 1982), 180.

4. Benita Eisler, *Byron: Child of Passion, Fool of Flame* (New York: Knopf, 1999), 611.

5. Byron to John Murray, Aug. 12, 1819, Marchand, *Lord Byron: Selected Letters and Journals,* 213.

6. *Don Juan,* ix, xli.

7. See E. D. Hirsch, "Byron and the Terrestrial Paradise," in *Byron's Poetry,* ed. Frank McConnell (New York: Norton, 1978), 448.

8. Brackenridge, *Views of Louisiana,* 116–18.

9. For the Shelley–Mary Wollstonecraft Godwin–Claire Clairmont ménage, see, e.g.,

Eisler, *Byron*, 504, 514–31, 553; Phyllis Grosskurth, *Byron: The Flawed Angel* (Boston: Houghton Mifflin, 1997), 265, 276–78, 287, 294, 304, 309, 312, 396, 409–10, 469.

10. The relationship was complex enough that the poet Robert Southey accused Byron and Shelley of forming a "League of Incest." Byron denied this, pointing out that Mary Godwin and Clair Clermont were not sisters, Mary being Godwin's daughter by Mary Wollstonecraft and Claire being the daughter of a subsequent wife of Godwin by a former husband. Byron also denied there was "promiscuous intercourse" within the group—"my commerce being limited to the carnal knowledge of the Miss C[lairmont]—I had nothing to do with the off-spring of Mary Wollstonecraft." Byron to John Cam Hobhouse, Nov. 11, 1818, in Marchand, *Lord Byron: Selected Letters and Journals*, 182–83.

11. See Cooper's 1851 introduction to *The Prairie* (New York: Signet/New American Library, 1964), vii; *Prairie*, n. 3 and accompanying text.

12. James Hall, *Sketches of History, Life and Manners in the West* (Cincinnati: Hubbard and Edmands, 1834), qtd. in Faragher, 323.

13. Flint, *Boone*, 21, 27–29, 50, 68–71, 75, 87, 113, 123, 143, 190.

14. Flint, *Recollections of the Last Ten Years*, 119, 116, 102.

15. Sweeney, *Columbus of the Woods*, 25.

16. Horatio Greenough to Sen. James Pearce, Mar. 14, 1859, qtd. in Sweeney, *Columbus of the Woods*, 27. The statue was finally removed from the steps of the Capitol after World War II. Faragher, 337.

17. Slotkin, reviewing different American tellings of the Boone story before 1860, suggests that writers from different regions put their own regional slant on the story: westerners emphasized Boone's powers as a man; easterners tended to view him as uncouth (a white Indian) or decked him in social graces; southern writers made him out to be either a disguised aristocrat or a subordinate to a more aristocratic hero. Slotkin, *Regeneration through Violence*, 394–465.

18. Flint, *Boone*, 8, 250.

19. The quote is from Judge John Coburn's eulogy of Boone in 1820, DM 16C85.

20. John L. Sullivan, "The True Title," Dec. 27, 1845. See William Gilpin in 1860: "The untransacted destiny of the American people is to subdue the continent. . . . Divine task! Immortal mission! Let us tread fast and joyfully the open trail before us! Let every American heart open wide for patriotism to grow undiminished, and confide with religious faith in the sublime and prodigious destiny of his well-loved country." *The Mission of the North American People: Geographical, Social, and Political*, 2nd ed. (1860; rpt., Philadelphia: J. B. Lippincott, 1873), 124.

21. Peck, title page, 137, 7.

22. The critic Henry T. Tuckerman in 1852, in *Western Pioneer*, writing about a painting in which Boone points out to his companions the fertile levels of Kentucky, said the picture proclaimed Boone as "the hunter and pioneer, the Columbus of the woods, the forest philosopher and brave champion." See Sweeney, *Columbus of the Woods*, epigraph and 37.

23. Sweeney, *Columbus of the Woods*, 41. The Bingham picture is at Washington University in St. Louis. A theme similar to Bingham's underlies William T. Ranney's *Daniel Boone's First View of Kentucky* (1849), reproduced as color pl. 3 of Sweeney, *Columbus of the Woods*.

24. Draper to Orlando Brown, May 13, 1854, Orlando Brown papers, FHS (asking Brown to solicit the insertion in two newspapers of his Boone project).

25. For Draper's life and work, including the Boone biography, see Draper, 5–16; Faragher, 342–46; William B. Hesseltine, *Pioneer's Mission: The Story of Lyman Copeland Draper* (Madison: State Historical Society of Wisconsin, 1954); Reuben Gold Thwaites, "Lyman Copeland Draper: A Memoir," in *Collections of the State Historical Society of Wisconsin* 1 (1903): ix–xxvi.

26. For a summary of the dime novels, the movies, the TV series, the novels, and the poems about Boone, see Faragher, 338–42.

27. Note by Belue, Draper, 94 n. 99.

28. Dorman, 152.

29. "Daniel Boone and the Frankfort Cemetery," *RKHS* 50 (1952): 207.

30. JDS interview with Jacob Swigert, 1846, DM 11CC289.

31. For a description of the negotiations and the exhumation, see "Daniel Boone and the Frankfort Cemetery," 208–21; Faragher, 356–58.

32. John Mason Brown to Lyman C. Draper, Oct. 4, 1882, DM 16C82.

33. For accounts of the procession and ceremony, see "Burial of Daniel Boone," *Frankfort Commonwealth*, Sept. 16, 1845; J. W. Venable, "The Burial of Daniel Boone," May 5, 1855, autograph file 5, Houghton Library, Harvard; Faragher, 358–59; "Daniel Boone and the Frankfort Cemetery," 200–236; and Michael A. Lofaro, "The Many Lives of Daniel Boone," *RKHS* 102 (1952): 489, 508–9 (the Procession Order is also printed at "Daniel Boone and the Frankfort Cemetery," 225–26).

34. John G. Tompkins, "PHRENOLOGICAL DEVELOPMENTS OF DANIEL BOONE," *Frankfort Commonwealth*, Feb. 9, 1846, reprinted in *RKHS* 50 (July 1952): 231–32. The article indicates that the man who took a cast of the skull was John G. Tompkins—not, as John Mason Brown remembered in 1882, someone named Davis. In 1907 the grandson of Rev. Philip Slater Fall said his grandfather made the cast of the skull and presented it to the society. "Daniel Boone and the Frankfort Cemetery," 223.

35. *Frankfort State Journal*, June 24, 1983; clipping in Boone Biographical File, KHS; *National Geographic*, Dec. 1985. For the competing claims of Missouri and Kentucky, see Faragher, 361–62.

36. *Cincinnati Enquirer*, Aug. 13, 2004, www.enquirer.com/editions/2004/08/13/loc_kyold remains13.html.

37. *Louisville Courier-Journal*, Mar. 5, 1995. Craig has described her work as a forensic anthropologist, without mentioning Boone's skull but noting that Kentucky needed a full-time forensic anthropologist because of its "history of violent crime and 'mountain justice' dating even back before the notorious feuds of the Hatfields and the McCoys"—a "culture of lawlessness" that "has only gotten worse with the rise of illegal drug use and marijuana's dubious honor as one of the Commonwealth's most lucrative cash crops." Emily Craig, *Teasing Secrets from the Dead: My Investigations at America's Most Infamous Crime Scenes* (New York: Crown Publishers, 2004).

38. Perhaps both Kentucky and Missouri have some of Boone's bones. Ken Kamper, historian for the Boone Society, Inc., has sensibly suggested to the author that in 1845 the exhumers from Kentucky could well have dug out and removed the larger bones of Daniel and Rebecca Boone, but the coffins were rotted away and many of the smaller bones, being harder to spot and less well preserved, would likely have been left behind in the Missouri burying ground.

22. CODA

1. Boone to Sarah Day Boone, Oct. 19, 1816, DM 27C88. Transcriptions of the letter appear in Faragher, 312; and Lofaro, 173.

2. JDS interview with Josiah Collins, 1840s, DM 12CC97.

3. David Todd to Mann Butler, Columbia, Mo., Mar. 17, 1834, DM 15CC126.

4. *Historical Statistics*, pt. 2, chap. Z, 1168 (1,170,760).

5. Ibid., pt. 1, 8 (3,929,214 in 1790; 9,638,453 in 1820).The shift of America's population to the west (and generally to the south) has continued ever since Boone's time. Not until 1980 did the center of the country's population cross the Mississippi into Missouri, more than 180 years after Boone had done so. In 2000 the Census Bureau calculated the population center of the country to be in Edgar Springs, in south-central Missouri—less than a hundred miles from where Boone died. After 180 years the country's center had finally caught up with Daniel Boone and his family. For a map showing how the United States population center has migrated steadily south- and westward, see "America Then and Now," supplement to *National Geographic*, June 2005.

6. Frederick Jackson Turner, *The Significance of the Frontier in American History*, ed. Harold P. Simonson (1893; rpt., New York: Ungar, 1963), 31.

7. Aron, *American Confluence*, 165.

8. Turner, *Significance of the Frontier*, 35.

9. Draper, 456 n. a.

10. Col. Charles A. Marshall to Draper, Nov. 21, 1884, DM 10BB48(8)–48(15).

11. Ranck, 133–36.

12. Flint, *Recollections of the Last Ten Years*, 273.

13. Stephen Aron, "'The Poor Men to Starve': The Lives and Times of Workmen in Early Lexington," in Friend, *Buzzel about Kentucky*, 177–78, 183–84. Lexington's economy was soon to take heavy hits from cheaper British products, the western financial panic, and the shifting of regional trade to Cincinnati and Louisville as steamboats proliferated on the Ohio and Mississippi (181–82).

14. *Niles' Weekly Register*, June 11, 1814; Friend, *Along the Maysville Road*, 238.

15. Margaretta Brown to John Brown, Mar. 8, 1802, Brown Family Papers, FHS, described a "tolerably agreeable" assembly she had attended in Frankfort.

16. Margaretta Brown to Eliza S. Quincy, Dec. 22, 1804, in *Memoir of the Life of Eliza S. M. Quincy*, ed. E. S. Quincy (Boston: J. Wilson and Son, 1861), 97. Apart from a few cabins, houses at Frankfort were not built until after James Wilkinson bought much of the town site in 1786.

17. Margaretta Brown to John Brown, New York, Jan. 31, 1811, Brown Family Papers, FHS.

18. Margaretta Brown to Orlando Brown, July 7, 1819, Brown Family Papers, FHS.

19. Aron, *How the West Was Lost*, 133.

20. Flint, *Recollections of the Last Ten Years*, 49, 51.

21. Aron, *How the West Was Lost*, 90–91.

22. Aron, *American Confluence*, 174, 198.

23. Peck, 137.

Bibliographical Note

The manuscripts and secondary materials relating to Daniel Boone are so extensive that a full bibliography would be as long as the text of this book. Accordingly, this note sketches the bibliographical lay of the land. For more complete bibliographies (and information about even more extensive bibliographies), see Michael A. Lofaro, *Daniel Boone: An American Life* (Lexington: University Press of Kentucky, 2003), 197–208; and John Bakeless, *Daniel Boone* (1939; rpt., Harrisburg, Pa.: Stackpole Books, 1965), 425–34.

MANUSCRIPT COLLECTIONS

All writings on Boone ultimately rest on manuscript collections—above all, on the immense collections assembled in the nineteenth century by Lyman C. Draper, whose tireless gathering of materials about the trans-Allegheny frontier is described in chapter 21 of this book. Draper ended up compiling 486 volumes of materials, housed in the manuscript collections of the State Historical Society of Wisconsin—a trove so immense that a 464-page guide to navigating it has been published: Josephine L. Harper, *Guide to the Draper Manuscripts* (Madison: Wisconsin Historical Society Press, 1983). The materials Draper gathered relating to Boone include not only some letters dating back to Boone's lifetime but also letters to Draper from, and Draper's notes of interviews with, relatives and acquaintances of Boone or their descendants—materials gathered as early as the 1840s and as late as around 1890. Boone's contemporaries, when Draper talked or corresponded with them, were old, and their memories were often clouded or infused with hearsay and tall tales, but a picture of Boone emerges that often correlates with earlier accounts.

Draper's collection also contains notes on many interviews of Boone relatives and friends during the 1840s by John Dabney Shane, a Presbyterian minister who intended to write a history of the Presbyterian Church in the West but who did not confine his note taking to that purpose. Like Draper, Shane was much more of an accumulator than a writer. He wrote to Draper on July 9, 1858: "Between 15 and 20 years earnest devotion to historical studies, has thrown into my possession a vast mass of historical matter. . . . And now as the scenes of life are passing rapidly by me, I begin to feel some solicitude that I should do—what if I try, I can do—and not let my life be spent simply in accumulating materials"—but no written history by Shane has surfaced. In an undated memorandum in Draper's collection, Shane wrote that he did not like "to give scope to a lively fancy." In his view "the patient acquisition of the simple facts is the clue to the true spirit of the times; they are that spirit itself." Elizabeth A. Perkins explores Shane's materials and methods perceptively, and with a strong feeling for the importance of vernacular history, in *Border Life: Experience and Memory in the Revolutionary Ohio Valley* (Chapel Hill: University of North Carolina Press, 1998).

One need not go to Madison, Wisconsin, pleasant though that trip would be, to draw on the riches of the Draper collection. Many important Boone-related materials have been printed. Draper's own unfinished biography of Boone through 1778 (ser. B in the Draper collection), edited by Ted Franklin Belue, was published as *The Life of Daniel Boone* (Mechanicsburg, Pa.: Stackpole Books, 1998). Draper's long and informative interviews in 1851 with Boone's youngest child, Nathan, and with Nathan's wife, Olive Van Bibber Boone, lovingly and carefully edited by Neal O. Hammon, are in print as *My Father, Daniel Boone: The Draper Interviews with Nathan Boone* (Lexington: University Press of Kentucky, 1999). What purports to be a transcription of a memoir about Boone written by Peter Houston when he was eighty-one, edited by Ted Franklin Belue, was published as *A Sketch in the Life and Character of Daniel Boone: A Memoir by Peter Houston* (Mechanicsburg, Pa.: Stackpole Books, 1998). Several collections of manuscripts from the Draper collection that give context to Boone's career have been published, including three edited by Reuben Gold Thwaites and Louise Phelps Kellogg: *Documentary History of Dunmore's War, 1774* (Madison: State Historical Society of Wisconsin, 1905); *The Revolution on the Upper Ohio, 1775–1777* (Madison: State Historical Society of Wisconsin, 1908); and *Frontier Defense on the Upper Ohio* (Madison: State Historical Society of Wisconsin, 1912). Also helpful is Chester Raymond Young's edition of the account that Daniel Trabue wrote in 1827 of his adventures as a young man in Kentucky and Virginia from 1778 into the 1790s, *Westward into Kentucky: The Narrative of Daniel Trabue* (Lexington: University Press of Kentucky, 1981). Trabue was at Logan's Station, not Boonesborough, but he describes the 1778 siege of Boonesborough and gives the only surviving account of Boone's post-siege court-martial.

The full Draper collection is available on over one hundred reels of microform at many universities and historical societies—including both the Kentucky Historical Society in Frankfort and the Filson Historical Society in Louisville, each of which has in its own collections manuscripts by or relating to Boone.

BIOGRAPHIES OF DANIEL BOONE

There have been many biographies of Boone, starting with the one John Filson published in 1784 as an appendix to a book with a name as long as many of Filson's sentences: *The Discovery, Settlement and Present State of Kentucke: and An Essay towards the Topography, and Natural History of that important Country: To which is added, An Appendix Containing, I. The Adventures of Col. Daniel Boon, one of the first Settlers, comprehending every important Occurrence in the political History of that Province . . .* (1784; rpt., Westminster, Md.: Heritage Books, 2004). See chap. 17 for more about John Filson and his book. While Filson's prose is much more purple than anything Boone ever wrote, the events described in the Boone appendix jibe for the most part with other accounts and with primary source material.

The nineteenth century saw a flood of Boone biographies, many of them filled with folkloric tales but light on sources and accuracy. Two popular ones are described in chap. 21: Timothy Flint's *Biographical Memoir of Daniel Boone, the First Settler of Kentucky* (1833; rpt., New York: Hurst and Co., 1868); and John Mason Peck's *Life of Daniel Boone, the Pioneer of Kentucky* (1847; rpt., New York: University Society Inc., 1905). Flint's biography has Boone, being pursued by Indians, swing on vines to avoid leaving footprints, yet Flint actually knew Boone in Missouri. Peck, although he portrayed Boone as ordained by God to open up the wilderness for civilization, had interviewed Boone in 1818, and there is useful material in his book.

Not until the twentieth century did Boone biographies tap the riches of the Draper collection. Reuben Gold Thwaites, who succeeded Draper as secretary of Wisconsin's historical society, was the first to do so, in *Daniel Boone* (1902; rpt., Williamstown, Mass.: Corner House Publishers, 1977). While Thwaites used the Draper materials ably, his book is unannotated and skimps on Boone's years in Missouri (1799–1820). John Bakeless wrote the first strong annotated biography of Boone that drew on the Draper and other manuscript collections. His *Daniel Boone* (1939; rpt., Harrisburg, Pa.: Stackpole Books, 1965) is thorough, informative, and fun to read. Lawrence Elliott, in *The Long Hunter: A New Life of Daniel Boone* (New York: Reader's Digest Press, 1976), included many tall tales about Boone and was not always careful. John Mack Faragher's *Daniel Boone: The Life and Legend of an American Pioneer* (New York: Henry Holt, 1992) is an excellent and lively biography. Michael A. Lofaro's *Daniel Boone: An American Life* (Lexington: University Press of Kentucky, 2003), while less extensive than Faragher's book, is also careful and good. Robert Morgan, in *Boone: A Biography* (Chapel Hill, N.C.: Algonquin Books, 2007), covers much the same ground as Bakeless, Faragher, and Lofaro, with some additional research, discursions, and speculations and with more interest in Boone the woodsman and in tales of his deeds than in the historical context of America's transformation during Boone's life.

OTHER SOURCES

The notes give detailed information about other sources I have consulted. A brief review may nevertheless help those looking for guidance for further reading on some of the topics bearing on Boone's long life that are explored in this book.

The Settling of the British Colonies

The best and most thorough study of the kinds of immigrants coming to the British colonies that became America on the eve of the Revolution, and of where they came from, is Bernard Bailyn's *Voyagers to the West: A Passage in the Peopling of America on the Eve of the Revolution* (New York: Vintage Books, 1986). Bailyn combines exhaustive research and statistical analysis with insights and clear writing. David Hackett Fischer's *Albion's Seed: Four British Folkways in America* (New York: Oxford University Press, 1989) complements Bailyn's study by examining different cultures of British immigrants and how those cultures survived and influenced America as it emerged into nationhood. Particularly relevant for understanding Boone's background is Fischer's discussion of the Quakers.

Hunting and Long Hunts

Hunting for food, and hunting and trapping for the market, were central in Boone's life from boyhood to old age. Boone's youngest child, Nathan, who hunted and trapped with his father in Kentucky and Missouri, explained these skills—for example, how to prepare and pack deerskins; how to trap beaver—in his interviews with Draper *(My Father, Daniel Boone).* Ted Franklin Belue—who clearly loves re-creating the life of a long hunter—describes the long hunters and how they operated in *The Hunters of Kentucky: A Narrative History of America's First Far West, 1750–1792* (Mechanicsburg, Pa.: Stackpole Books, 2003). The market hunters transformed America and drove the game and the frontier ever farther west. Among the best books on the hunters' impact is Andrew C. Isenberg's *The Destruction of the Bison: An Environmental History, 1750–1920* (Cambridge: Cambridge University Press, 2000). Indian hunters, particularly as they gained access to rifles, contributed to that impact, as described by Shepard Krech III in *The Ecological Indian: Myth and History* (New York: W. W. Norton, 1999).

The Opening of Kentucky

Journals and memoirs place us vividly in Kentucky in the early days of its settlement. Dr. Thomas Walker in 1750 led the first group of British colonists to cross the Cumberland Gap into Kentucky. In 1888 Little, Brown, and Co. published Walker's journal of that trip, with a preface by William Cabell Rives. The full text of Walker's journal is readily found on the Internet. Much of the journal is in David M. Burns, *Gateway: Dr. Thomas Walker and the Opening of Kentucky* (Middlesboro, Ky.: Bell County Historical Society, 2000).

A memoir and two journals tell us about the 1775 blazing of the trail to, and the founding of, Boonesborough. The memoir was written years later by Felix Walker, who had been in Boone's advance party of axemen, was badly wounded in the Indian attack on the group, and was nursed back to health by Boone. Walker's account of the trip, written in the 1820s, was published in *Debow's Review* in Feb. 1854 and reprinted in George W. Ranck's rewarding *Boonesborough: Its Founding, Pioneer Struggles, Indian Experiences, Transylvania Days, and Revolutionary Annals* (Louisville, Ky.: Filson Club, 1901). The two journals are those of Col. Richard Henderson and of William Calk, part of Henderson's group that followed Boone's axemen. Calk's short journal, which has the unassuming strength of an ordinary man's daily entries, is at the Kentucky Historical Society, available online at KHS Digital Collections (reachable from the society's home page, www.history.ky.gov), and has been printed several times, in, for example, Ellen Eslinger, ed., *Running Mad for Kentucky: Frontier Travel Accounts* (Lexington: University Press of Kentucky, 2004), 69–74. Henderson's journal—informative, though written in Henderson's characteristic grandiloquence—is published in Ranck's *Boonesborough*, as well as in Walter Clark, *The Colony of Transylvania* (Raleigh, N.C.: E. M. Uzell, 1903). Ranck's book contains a great deal of other information and correspondence about the Transylvania Company's attempt to establish a proprietary colony comprising most of what is now Kentucky and part of what is now Tennessee. A good secondary source, which puts in context the blazing and later history of the trail, is Robert L. Kincaid's *The Wilderness Road* (Indianapolis: Bobbs-Merrill, 1947). Otis K. Rice, in *Frontier Kentucky* (Lexington: University Press of Kentucky, 1993), provided a short (but unannotated) history of Kentucky from the time of the first British explorations through 1783, with a good introduction to the land companies as well as to the settlers' stations.

Kentucky in the Revolutionary Era

Eslinger's *Running Mad for Kentucky,* in addition to Calk's journal, includes selections from twelve other journals of travelers to Kentucky between 1775 and 1796. I particularly enjoy that of Nicholas Cresswell, whose journal reflects his inquiring mind and his interest in frontier and Indian culture—and in Indian women. For the full text of that journal, see *The Journal of Nicholas Cresswell, 1774–1777* (New York: Dial Press, 1924). Other journals that describe Kentucky during the Revolution are those of Col. William Fleming, a doctor by training, who had a physician's eye for the vile sanitary conditions and resulting ill health in Kentucky's beleaguered settlements. Fleming's journals of his travels in Kentucky in 1779–80 and in 1783 were published in Newton D. Mereness, ed., *Travels in the American Colonies* (1916; rpt., New York: Antiquarian Press, 1961). Other primary materials relating to Kentucky and the Ohio Valley during the Revolution were compiled and annotated by Thwaites and Kellogg in *The Revolution on the Upper Ohio, 1775–1777* and *Frontier Defense on the Upper Ohio,* mentioned earlier.

American leaders in the fight for Kentucky included Benjamin Logan, portrayed in Charles Gano Talbert's *Benjamin Logan: Kentucky Frontiersman* (Lexington: University of Kentucky Press, 1962); James Harrod, the founder of Harrodsburg, treated lovingly by Kathryn Harrod Mason in *James Harrod of Kentucky* (Baton Rouge: Louisiana State University Press, 1951); and the giant Simon Kenton. Among the Kenton biographies the informal and adventure-filled one by the great Kentucky historian Thomas D. Clark, *Simon Kenton: Kentucky Scout* (1943; rpt., Ashland, Ky.: Jesse Stuart Foundation, 1998), is particularly enjoyable. Neal O. Hammon and Richard Taylor have written a fine overview of the fighting, with excellent maps, in *Virginia's Western War, 1775–1786* (Mechanicsburg, Pa.: Stackpole Books, 2002). Hammon has also provided a thorough and able analysis of the Indians' greatest victory over the Kentucky settlers in *Daniel Boone and the Defeat at Blue Licks* (Minneapolis: Boone Society, 2005). John E. Selby, *The Revolution in Virginia, 1775–1783* (1988; rpt., Williamsburg, Va.: Colonial Williamsburg Foundation, 2007), is a masterly overview of that subject. For further information about the pioneer settlements in the bluegrass region, see Nancy O'Malley's report to the Kentucky Heritage Council, *"Stockading Up": A Study of Pioneer Stations in the Inner Bluegrass Region of Kentucky* (Lexington, Ky.: Program for Cultural Resource Assessment, 1987); and her paper "Frontier Defenses and Pioneer Strategies in the Historic Settlement Era," in *The Buzzel about Kentuck: Settling the Promised Land*, ed. Craig Thompson Friend (Lexington: University Press of Kentucky, 1999), 57–75.

The Fight for Control of the Ohio Valley

The fight for Kentucky must be understood in the context of the larger struggle for the Ohio Valley—among different Indian groups, the French, the British, the competing interests of neighboring British colonies, the frontiersmen from those colonies, and, after the Revolution, the United States. A splendid overview, vast in its research as well as in its chronological and geographical reach, is Richard White's *The Middle Ground: Indians, Empires, and Republics in the Great Lakes Region, 1650–1815* (Cambridge: Cambridge University Press, 1991). White describes the search for accommodation and common meaning in the meeting of European and Indian cultures in the region. He sees the two groups as initially having regarded each other as alien, then constructing a common world, and ultimately once again viewing each other as fundamentally alien. Not surprisingly, given the book's broad scope, it mentions little directly about Boone.

Eric Hinderaker provides a good introduction to the struggle for control of the Ohio Valley among the French, the British, the Indians, and the American settlers in *Elusive Empires: Constructing Colonialism in the Ohio Valley, 1673–1800* (Cambridge: Cambridge University Press, 1997). Hinderaker and Peter C. Mancall provide a clear overview of changes on the western edge of Britain's North American empire between the end of the sixteenth century and the end of the eighteenth century in *At the Edge of Empire: The Backcountry in British North America* (Baltimore: Johns Hopkins University Press, 2003). For a clear (but unannotated) survey of the struggles in and near Ohio, see R. Douglas Hurt, *The Ohio Frontier: Crucible of the Old Northwest, 1720–1830* (Bloomington: Indiana University Press, 1998). Michael N. McConnell also gives a good picture, largely from the point of view of the different Indian groups in the area, of the competing efforts to control the Ohio Valley until the end of Lord Dunmore's War, in *A Country Between: The Upper Ohio Valley and Its Peoples, 1724–1774* (Lincoln: University of Nebraska Press, 1992). His book, like Hurt's, is not focused on the fights for Kentucky.

In *Breaking the Backcountry: The Seven Years' War in Virginia and Pennsylvania, 1754–1765* (Pittsburgh: University of Pittsburgh Press, 2003), Matthew C. Ward points out how the Seven Years' War and the subsequent Pontiac's War in backcountry Virginia and Pennsylvania developed the fighting techniques of the Ohio Valley Indians and increased the antipathy between many backcountry colonists and Indians. Colin G. Calloway, in *The Scratch of a Pen: 1763 and the Transformation of North America* (Oxford: Oxford University Press, 2006), puts Pontiac's War in the context of the overall sweeping changes throughout North America—including in the Mississippi Valley—that flowed from the Treaty of Paris and its aftermath. Paul A. W. Wallace, in *Conrad Weiser, 1696–1760, Friend of Colonist and Mohawk* (Philadelphia: University of Pennsylvania Press, 1945), provides an excellent picture of Pennsylvania's relations with Indians—including the covenant chain with the Iroquois and the Indians' driving out of the whites from western Pennsylvania after Braddock's Defeat.

Two protagonists in the fight for control of the Ohio Valley were Henry Hamilton, the British commandant at Detroit who supported Indian attacks on the American frontier settlements, and George Rogers Clark, who seized several British posts and took Hamilton captive. Milo M. Quaife lets both men tell their own stories in *The Capture of Old Vincennes: The Original Narratives of George Rogers Clark and of His Opponent Gov. Henry Hamilton* (Indianapolis: Bobbs-Merrill, 1927). The clash between the two (in combat and in style) is well conveyed in John Bakeless, *Background to Glory: The Life of George Rogers Clark* (Philadelphia: J. B. Lippincott, 1957); as well as in Bernard W. Sheehan's article "'The Famous Hair Buyer General': Henry Hamilton, George Rogers Clark, and the American Indian," *Indiana Magazine of History* 79 (1983): 1.

Captivity Stories, the Shawnees, and White-Indian Relations on the Frontier

Stories of what it was like to be a white captive of the Indians abounded during the eighteenth and nineteenth centuries. Many are reprinted in Frederick Drimmer, ed., *Captured by the Indians: 15 Firsthand Accounts, 1750–1870* (New York: Dover Publications, 1961). The accounts are absorbing in what they tell about white frontier life and different Indian cultures and in their alternation between quiet adopted family life and terrifying episodes. For information about the Kentucky salt boilers taken captive along with Boone in 1778, see Draper's *Life of Boone* and Belue's lively "Terror in the Canelands: The Fate of Daniel Boone's Salt Boilers," *Filson Club Historical Quarterly* 68 (1994): 3.

Cultural interactions between whites and Indians are addressed in Hinderaker, *Elusive Empires,* and in White, *Middle Ground.* In *Into the American Woods: Negotiators on the Pennsylvania Frontier* (New York: W. W. Norton, 1999), James H. Merrell reviews the important role played by colonist and Indian go-betweens (men such as Conrad Weiser and Scaroyady) in seeking to defuse tensions and how that role became less important as a result both of the increase in hatred engendered by the killings of the French and Indian War and of the Indians' growing realization that the colonists' objective in making treaties was always land. The expanded use by Shawnees of European artifacts and the Shawnees' growing involvement during the 1740s and 1750s in trade with white traders are carefully explored in A. Gwynn Henderson's essay "The Lower Shawnee Town on Ohio: Sustaining Native Autonomy in an Indian 'Republic,'" in Friend, *Buzzel about Kentuck.* Among the better depictions of the Shawnees are: James H. Howard, *Shawnee! The*

Ceremonialism of a Native Indian Tribe and Its Cultural Background (Athens: Ohio University Press, 1981); *Shawnese Traditions: C. C. Trowbridge's Account,* edited by Vernon Kinietz and Erminie W. Voegelin (Ann Arbor: University of Michigan Press, 1939); and Jerry E. Clark, *The Shawnee* (Lexington: University Press of Kentucky, 1993). In *The Shawnees and Their Neighbors, 1795–1870* (Urbana: University of Illinois Press, 2005), Stephen Warren describes the dramatic changes in Shawnee life after the Battle of Fallen Timbers—both among the minority who remained in Ohio and the majority who moved west, including to Missouri (where Boone encountered some of his former captors) and later to Oklahoma. *The Diary of David McClure, Doctor of Divinity, 1748–1820* (New York: Knickerbocker Press, 1899) gives a vivid picture of Maclure's unsuccessful attempt in 1772 to start a mission to the Delawares on the Muskingum River and of the Delawares' resentment of white encroachment on their lands.

Stephen Aron has explored Indian-white relations in Kentucky in *How the West Was Lost: The Transformation of Kentucky from Daniel Boone to Henry Clay* (Baltimore: Johns Hopkins University Press, 1996), as well as in "The Legacy of Daniel Boone: Three Generations of Boones and the History of Indian-White Relations," *Register of the Kentucky Historical Society* 95 (1997): 219–35. Aron has an enviable ability to combine careful research with a panoramic view of the big picture.

In *The First Way of War: American War Making on the Frontier, 1607–1814* (New York: Cambridge University Press, 2005), John Grenier shows how the predominant way of making war against Indians, from the first British settlements in Virginia through the War of 1812, involved, among other things, raids, destruction of villages and crops, scalping, and the taking of captives. Armstrong Starkey's *European and Native American Warfare, 1675–1815* (Norman: University of Oklahoma Press, 1998) explores a similar period but with less emphasis on total warfare. Starkey sees the whites' ultimate success in the struggle as resulting from the use of a combination of regulars, irregulars, and Indian allies, as well as from the lack of unity among the Indian groups. Colin G. Calloway, in *The American Revolution in Indian Country: Crisis and Diversity in Native American Communities* (New York: Cambridge University Press, 1995), analyzes the generally devastating impact of the Revolution on eight different Indian communities, including Cornstalk's division of the Shawnees and Chota, the capital town of the Overhill Cherokees.

In *The Divided Ground: Indians, Settlers and the Northern Borderland of the American Revolution* (New York: Random House, 2006), Alan Taylor explores how the Iroquois, as a result of the Revolution, went from being a powerful force between Britain and the Americans to being dependent on the United States and on the British government in Canada. Taylor ably describes the background of the Fort Stanwix and Greenville treaties and the despair of the Great Lakes and Ohio Indians at the lack of British support against the Americans after the Revolution.

Land Speculation, Surveying, and Trading
in Kentucky in Boone's Day

William Fleming went to Kentucky as part of the Land Commission established by Virginia in 1779 in an attempt to bring order out of the chaos of conflicting land claims in Kentucky. Fleming's journals, mentioned earlier, shed light on the Land Commission's work. Talbert's biography of Benjamin Logan describes Virginia's land law. Neal O. Hammon, the leading expert on surveys in Kentucky in Boone's day, has written informatively both about John Floyd and the other Fincastle County surveyors and about Boone as a surveyor. See Hammon, "The Fincastle Surveyors at the Falls of the Ohio, 1774," *Filson Club Historical Quarterly* 47 (1973): 14; "The Fincastle Surveyors in the Bluegrass, 1774," *Register of the Kentucky Historical Society* (Oct. 1972): 277; and Hammon and James Russell Harris, "Daniel Boone the Surveyor," *Register of the Kentucky Historical Society* 102 (2004): 535. Hammon concludes that Boone was in many ways admirable as a surveyor. As we have seen in chap. 16, Willard Rouse Jillson's earlier study, based on a less complete review of Boone's surveys, found Boone "as good as the average." See *With Compass and Chain: A Brief Narration of the Activities of Col. Daniel Boone as a Land Surveyor in Kentucky* (Frankfort: n.p., 1954), 8. For an overview of surveying at the time of the Louisiana Purchase, see Andro Linklater, *Measuring America: How an Untamed Wilderness Shaped the United States and Fulfilled the Promise of Democracy* (New York: Walker, 2002).

Boone's activities while living in Limestone are described by David I. Bushnell, Jr., in "Daniel Boone at Limestone, 1786–1787," *Virginia Magazine of History and Biography* 25 (1917): 1–11. For information about the ginseng trade, see Philip Chadwick Foster Smith, *The Empress of China* (Philadelphia: Philadelphia Maritime Museum, 1984); Kristin Johanssen, *Ginseng*

Dreams: The Secret World of America's Most Valuable Plant (Lexington: University Press of Kentucky 2006); and David A. Taylor, *Ginseng: The Divine Root* (Chapel Hill: Algonquin Books, 2006).

John Bradford, who in 1787 had launched Kentucky's first newspaper, the *Kentucky Gazette,* in 1826 published a series of notes on Kentucky's history extending from the first explorations by British colonists to Kentucky's statehood in 1792 and the issues surrounding Spanish control of the Mississippi and the resulting threat to Kentucky's trade. Thomas D. Clark knowledgeably edited and annotated Bradford's notes, as *The Voice of the Frontier: John Bradford's "Notes on Kentucky"* (Lexington: University Press of Kentucky, 1993). Aron's *How the West Was Lost,* mentioned earlier, also gives a fine overview of changes in Kentucky between Boone's day and that of Henry Clay. Joan Wells Coward told much about the growth in Kentucky's population and prosperity between 1790 and 1800 in *Kentucky in the New Republic: The Process of Constitution Making* (Lexington: University Press of Kentucky, 1979). George Morgan Chinn describes Kentucky's struggle for statehood and the launching of its state government in *Kentucky Settlement and Statehood, 1750–1800* (Frankfort: Kentucky Historical Society, 1975), 425–581. Craig Thompson Friend, in *Along the Maysville Road: The Early American Republic in the Trans-Appalachian West* (Knoxville: University of Tennessee Press, 2005), uses the history of the road from Lexington to Maysville as a microhistory of the changes taking place in Kentucky between the 1780s and the 1830s.

Boone's Move to Missouri and His Life There

William E. Foley, for many years general editor of the Missouri Biography Series of the University of Missouri Press, included in his able overview *A History of Missouri,* vol. 1: *1673 to 1820* (Columbia: University of Missouri Press, 1999) a thorough bibliographical essay on, as he put it, "the most pertinent primary and secondary sources available for Missouri's early history." I will not replicate here Foley's helpful guide. Stephen Aron, in *American Confluence: The Missouri Frontier from Borderland to Border State* (Bloomington: Indiana University Press, 2006), masterfully surveys the changes occurring in that region from the first European settlers to Missouri's statehood. He notes the controlling importance of the region's location, at a time when travel and freight by river were preeminent, as the place where the Ohio and the Missouri rivers flowed into the Mississippi. Among Abraham P. Nasatir's many books on Missouri history, one, *Before Lewis and Clark: Documents*

Illustrating the History of Missouri, 1785–1804 (St. Louis: St. Louis Historical Documents Foundation, 1952), is an excellent collection of primary materials, including many from the Spanish archives.

Much has been written about Spain's efforts to pry Kentucky away from the new American republic, in exchange for free trade down the Mississippi, and about the duplicitous roles in that effort of James D. Wilkinson, who was at once general in the United States Army and a highly paid secret agent of Spain. Foley provides an introduction in *History of Missouri*, 1:33–42. James Ripley Jacobs's biography of Wilkinson, *Tarnished Warrior: Major-General James Wilkinson* (New York: Macmillan, 1938), while dated, is still valuable. Several of Bradford's *Notes on Kentucky* address the topic, as does Chinn in *Kentucky Settlement and Statehood.*

For information about the once mighty Osages, see Aron's *American Confluence;* Willard H. Rollings, *The Osage: An Enthnohistorical Study of Hegemony on the Prairie-Plains* (Columbia: University of Missouri Press, 1992); and Kathleen DuVal, *The Native Ground: Indians and Colonists in the Heart of the Continent* (Philadelphia: University of Pennsylvania Press, 2006). Gilbert C. Din and Abraham P. Nasatir described Spain's dealings with the Osages in *The Imperial Osages: Spanish Diplomacy in the Mississippi Valley* (Norman: University of Oklahoma Press, 1983).

Jon Kukla gives an excellent account of the Louisiana Purchase in his *A Wilderness So Immense: The Louisiana Purchase and the Destiny of America* (New York: Alfred A. Knopf, 2003). Joseph J. Ellis provides a fine summary of the purchase, and of Jefferson's objectives in making it, in *American Creation: Triumphs and Tragedies at the Founding of the Republic* (New York: Alfred A. Knopf, 2007), chapter six.

For a vivid picture of St. Louis, St. Charles, and the rush of immigrants to Boone's Lick, Missouri, toward the end of Boone's life, see Timothy Flint, *Recollections of the Last Ten Years Passed in Occasional Residences and Journeyings in the Valley of the Mississippi . . .* (Boston: Cummings, Hilliard, 1826), edited by George R. Brooks (Carbondale: Southern Illinois University Press, 1968). Flint's recollections also cover the dramatic growth in Kentucky's settlement and wealth.

Boone's Life after Death

Faragher, in chap. 10 of his Boone biography, describes well how myths and stories about Boone evolved during and after Boone's death. So does Richard

Taylor in "Daniel Boone as American Icon: A Literary View," *Register of the Kentucky Historical Society* 102 (2004): 513. In *Regeneration through Violence: The Mythology of the American Frontier, 1600–1860* (1973; rpt., Norman: University of Oklahoma Press 2000), Richard Slotkin examines exhaustively how the many accounts of Boone's life and adventures, starting with Filson's 1784 narrative in the *Discovery of Kentucke,* became a basic part of the American myth of the frontier. Arthur K. Moore explored the different uses of the Boone narrative in his lively and provoking *The Frontier Mind* (1957; rpt., New York: McGraw-Hill, 1963). Faragher's chap. 10 also tells the story of the 1845 removal from Missouri to Kentucky of what were believed to be the remains of Boone and his wife. Contemporary newspaper articles and other materials relating to the reinterment are in the Boone Biographical File at the Kentucky Historical Society.

In 1992 the Washington University Gallery of Art in St. Louis mounted an exhibition of paintings, prints, and sculpture relating to Boone. J. Grant Sweeney's catalog of that exhibition, *The Columbus of the Woods: Daniel Boone and the Typology of Manifest Destiny* (St. Louis: Washington University Gallery of Art, 1992), shows how artists tailored images of Boone to fit their own purposes—for example, by emphasizing the wilderness, fierce attacks by Indians, Boone alone in the wilds as a Rousseauesque philosopher, or Boone leading settlers through the Cumberland Gap like Moses leading his people toward the Promised Land.

Index

Adam (slave of William Russell), 56–57

American national identity, during Boone's life: and conflict between British and Americans, 94–99, 116–17, 121–23, 135–36, 148, 150, 281; and conflict between British and French, 5, 12–19, 24–25, 41, 226–27, 235, 281; and conflict between British colonies, 12, 92, 100, 281; and conflict between Spanish and Americans, xv, 233–37, 281; and conflict between Spanish and British, 41, 226–27; and conflict between Whigs and Tories, 92, 99; growth in national identity after adoption of Constitution, 281. *See also* Boone, Daniel—conflicting loyalties; Declaration of Independence; Indian-white relations; Louisiana Purchase; War of 1812

American Revolution. *See* Revolutionary War

Anglicans, 6, 79, 83, 110

Arbuckle, Matthew, 124–25

Aron, Stephen, 139, 286, 352, 354–55

Asbury, Francis, 225

Attakullakulla (Cherokee chief), 71–72

Audubon, John James, 51, 254

Austin, Moses: on immigrants to Kentucky and the Wilderness Road, 220, 225, 329n11; on lead mines in Missouri, 234–35; on Louisville, 229; predicts wilderness will be overspread by American towns and villages, 235; on St. Louis, 229

Baily, Francis, 217, 231, 331n17

Bailyn, Bernard, 289n5, 290n18, 346

Bakeless, John, 287, 343, 346, 351

Bear, 10, 31, 35–36, 40, 54, 85, 104–05, 167, 172, 220, 223, 265

Beaubien, Charles, 127, 135

Beaver: abundance of, 10, 49, 85, 242; economic importance of pelts, 33–34, 147, 219; how to trap, 34, 347; products made from fur of, 22; trapped by Boone or Nathan Boone, 30, 127, 222, 231, 240, 242–43, 248, 253,; wars over trade in pelts, 37

Belue, Ted Franklin, 295n1, 295n4, 295n7, 344, 347, 351

Big Jim (Indian), xx, 57, 189, 199

Bingham, George Caleb, 267, 339n23

Biographical Memoir of Daniel Boone . . . (Flint), 256–57, 265–66, 288, 331n16, 345

Bird, Henry, 171

Blackfish (Shawnee chief): Boone's adoptive father, 2, 134–38, 142–43, 154, 195; capture of salt-boilers, 128–31, 183; daughters of, 138; death, 163; leads attacks on Kentucky, 118, 126–27; salt-boiling on Scioto River, 143; and siege of Boonesborough, 2, 133, 149–55; son possibly killed by Boone, 134, 313n14; wears cappo, 191

Bluegrass (grass), 47, 299n35

Bluegrass (region of Ky.), 29, 33, 40, 60, 91, 169, 182, 184, 187, 211, 221, 249, 279, 282, 349, 353

Blue Jacket (Shawnee chief), xxi, 198–99

Blue Licks, xix, 19, 36, 51, 108, 110, 126, 128, 172, 175, 255

Blue Licks, Battle of, xx, 54, 91, 95, 97, 101, 177–82, 190, 194, 321n37, 321n39, 349

Bodmer, Karl, 111

Boofman v. Hickman, 211, 301n36

Boone, Daniel: adoption by Shawnees, 134–38; ancestry, 3–11; appearance, 22, 173, 229–30, 293n8; attitude toward sex, 6, 25–26; biographers, xxi–xxii, 23, 25, 26, 31, 47, 93, 105, 134, 137, 234, 246, 265–68, 283, 288, 344–46, 355–56; birth and childhood, 3–11; and Boonesborough's founding and defense, 76–77, 81, 85–87, 90; and Boone's Station, 166–7; on Brushy Creek, 224; burial instructions, 247; as businessman, 167–68, 201, 203–15, 220–24; captured by Shawnees, 91, 126–29; captured by Tarleton's rangers, 173; character and principles, xv, 8, 168–69, 199, 236, 274–75; coffin, 2, 253–54, 259, 270, 336n9; commissary for militia, 221–22; commissioned as militia captain, 64–66, 117; court-martial, 136, 160–61; courtship, 22–23; creditors, 40, 44, 220–21, 231, 234, 251; in Culpeper County, 24; damns British for inciting Indian attack, 160; death and burial, 258–59; defends settlements during Dunmore's War, 61–66; depositions, 211, 238–39, 255, 299n45, 301n36, 303n18, 327n43, 337n17; at Detroit, 135–36; "elbow-room" need, 230–31, 277, 331n16; escape from Shawnees, 142–44; explorer, scout, and leader of immigrants, 51, 55–57, 162–63, 274; fame, 148, 216–19, 249, 260, 263; and farming, 10, 25, 40, 46, 55, 245–47, 277, 282; and John Filson, 216–19 (*see also* Filson, John); and Florida, 41–43; at Fort Osage, 248, 335n42; at French Lick (Nashville), 54; gauntlet run, 131; ginseng digger and trader, xx, 28, 201, 213–15, 220, 223, 232, 353; health, 27–28, 222–23, 236, 242, 246–48, 252, 254, 258; horse trader, 221; and Gilbert Imlay,

209–10, 217, 264, 327n35; land investor and jobber, 166–69, 201, 203–11, 215, 232, 245, 250–51; lawsuits and claims involving, xv, xx, 40, 206, 211, 215, 222, 228, 231, 233, 251, 328nn44–45, 327n41, 328n45, 353; legislator, 173–74, 221; on Levisa Fork of Big Sandy River, 223–24; at Limestone, 211–14, 353; literacy, education and spelling, xiii, 6–7, 42, 66–67, 181–82, 213, 221, 257, 275; and Little Sandy River, 228; at Marble Creek, 167, 319n94; marksmanship, 6, 10–11, 138; marriage and relationship with wife, 22–27, 166; militia leader, 117, 221, 239; moves to find game, 36, 44; Paint Creek raid, 147–49, 160; pelts taken from by Indians, 47–49, 52–53; in Pennsylvania, 3–8, 173, 214; petition to Congress for land grant, xxi–xxii, 246, 250–51, 336n50; petition to Kentucky legislature, 246; phrenological analysis, 271–72, 340n34; in Point Pleasant, xx, 214–15, 220–22; and Quakerism, 8, 138, 196, 199; reburies James Boone at Wallen's Creek, 58; reinterment in Kentucky, xvi, xix, xxii, 269–73, 340nn29–38; religious views, 3, 8, 199, 221, 255–57, 259, 275, 356; rescues daughter Jemima and Callaway girls, 106–12; and salt-boilers, 126–29, 160–61, 169; and Simon Kenton, 118–20, 247 (*see also* Kenton, Simon); singing, 51, 255; skull, xvi, 272–73; slaves owned or sold, 213, 221, 282–83, 328n54; spurious relics, 269–70, 274; as surveyor, xx, 167, 194, 204–08, 211, 224, 277, 348n15, 348n17–19, 353; as tavern-keeper, xx, 196, 198, 201, 206, 211–12; theft of money and land certificates from, 168, 319n97; trip to warn surveyors of Shawnee war threat, 61–63; wagoner with Braddock's army, 12, 18; and War of 1812, 248–49; warrant for arrest, xxi, 228, 231; and Wilderness Road, 44, 46–47, 55–56, 72–76, 224–25; wounds, xxi, 119–20, 155, 200, 316n39; and Yadkin Valley, 8–10, 24, 40, 161–62

—conflicting loyalties: to Americans, 99,

103, 236; to British, 99, 135–36, 153, 173, 281;
to Shawnees, 2, 137–40, 195–99, 244–45; to
Spanish, 236–37, 281

—hunting and trapping by, xiv, xvii–xviii,
xxii, 1–2, 6, 9–10, 22–23, 27, 28–36, 38–40,
43, 47–57, 75, 127, 138, 142–43, 167, 172,
195, 199, 200, 222–24, 231–32, 234, 237–38,
240–42, 245–48, 252–53, 277–78, 283, 347

—and Kentucky: blazes trail into, 72–77;
departs, 161, 228; explores, 51–52; first attempt to settle, 54–58; first hunting trip
in, 43; long hunt in, 46–53; whether he returned after 1799, 234, 254–55, 337n13. *See
also* Kentucky

—and Missouri: life in, 1–2, 238–40, 242,
245–59; loss of land grant in, 246, 335n33;
militia captain in St. Charles, 239; move
to, xxi, 225–37; in St. Louis, 229–30. *See
also* Femme Osage, Mo.; Missouri

—portrayed as: child of nature, 260–64;
slayer of Indians, 265–66; spearhead
of Manifest Destiny, 266–67, 338n2,
339nn22–23

—portrayed in: fiction, 112, 264; paintings,
1, 258, 267, 356, poetry, xxii, 2, 249–50,
260–63; sculpture, 266, 271; television,
xiii, 269. *See also* Bingham, George Caleb; Boone, Daniel: biographers; Cooper,
James Fenimore; Draper, Lyman Copeland; Filson, John; Flint, Timothy; Harding, Chester

—relations with Indians: adoption by Shawnees, 134–38; arranges prisoner exchanges,
196–98; childhood contacts with Indians, 4–5, 10–11, 137; contest over land,
195; friendships with Indians, 135, 137–38,
195–96, 244–45; how to deal with Indians, 195–96; killing of Indians, xiii, 2, 20,
52, 134, 179; possible taking of Shawnee
wife, 26, 139–40, 195. *See also* Indian-white
relations

Boone, Daniel Morgan (son): aids white-
Shawnee prisoner exchange, 197; and
Blue Jacket, 198; and Boone family move

to Missouri, xxi, 227–30, 232; at Boone's
Lick, 243, 276; Boone stays with in Missouri, 239, 246, 334n8; and Boone's trade
with hunters and trappers, 220; chainman
on Boone surveys, 204; collects debt due
Boone, 213; and Femme Osage, 227–28,
337n29; fortifies station, 249; horse trading by, 221; hunts deer with Boone in Missouri, 240; justice of the peace, 236; land
claim in Missouri confirmed, 246; and
land on Brushy Creek, 224; militia captain
in War of 1812, 248; slave of, 240; and surveys by Boone

Boone, Delinda (granddaughter). *See* Craig,
Delinda Boone

Boone, Edward (Ned) (brother): killed by
Indians, xx, 172, 183, 199, 320n9; marries
Rebecca Boone's sister, 43; moves family
up the Yadkin, 43; stories that he fathered
a child by Rebecca Boone, 25–26

Boone, George (brother), 166, 327n42

Boone, George, Sr. (grandfather), 4

Boone, Harriet (great-niece), 249

Boone, Isaiah (nephew), 148, 290n41,
309n22

Boone, Israel (brother), xvii, 7

Boone, Israel (son), xviii, xx, 25, 55, 166,
178–81

Boone, James (son), xviii–xx, 23, 40, 55–58,
74, 189, 191, 199

Boone, James (grandson), 252–53, 296n39

Boone, Jemima (daughter): birth, xviii,
25–26; capture and rescue of, xv, xix, 71,
106–12, 177; and Kentucky, 86; marriage,
110; at Moore's fort, 26; relationship with
Boone, 111; relations with Indians, 109–11.
See also Callaway, Jemima

Boone, Jesse Bryan (son), 55, 204, 220–21,
223, 330n22

Boone, Levina (Lavinia) (daughter). *See*
Scholl, Levina (Boone)

Boone, Mary (sister), 21–22

Boone, Moses (nephew), 148, 154, 156, 159,
315n4, 315n15, 316n39

Boone, Nathan (son): birth, xx, 167; at Boone's death, 259; 268; Boone stays with in Missouri, 240, 252–53, 259; captain, 248, 254; courtship and marriage, 24, 229; escapes Indians with father on Ohio River, 223; and Fort Osage, 244, 278; ginseng digging and trading, with Boone, 213–14; house on Femme Osage Creek in Missouri, 239–40; hunting and trapping by, 31, 222, 240; interviews with Lyman Draper, xxii, 6, 22, 42, 52, 58, 131–32, 136, 143–44, 168, 173, 181, 206–10, 234, 238, 247–48, 254–56, 258, 288, 344; land on Little Sandy, 228; in militia, 239; moves to Missouri, 228–29; and reinterment of Boone, 269; robbed of pelts by Indians, 243; salt-boiling at Boone's Lick, 243, 276; and surveys by Boone, 204–05, 326n20

Boone, Olive Van Bibber (daughter-in-law), 22–23, 181, 229, 243, 268, 344. See also Boone, Nathan

Boone, Rebecca Bryan (wife): ancestry, 21–22; assists Boone in hunting and trapping, 27, 223; and Boonesborough, 27; child-bearing, 23–24; courtship by Boone, 22–23; goes to and from Kentucky, 27, 55, 142, 162; illiteracy, 40; illness and death, 27, 252; life on the Kanawha, 227; loneliness, 26–27, 53; marriage, 23–24, 26–27; in Missouri, 240, 252; at Moore's Fort, 62–63; moves by, 43, 142; stories of her illegitimate child, 25–26

Boone, Samuel (brother), 7, 257

Boone, Samuel (nephew), 178

Boone, Sarah (sister), xvii, 4–6

Boone, Sarah Day (sister-in law), 7, 257

Boone, Sarah Morgan (mother), xvii, 4, 8

Boone, Squire (father): death, xviii, 41; deeds land to Boone, 294n22; justice of the peace, 10, 21, 23; marriage, 4; in Pennsylvania, 3–8; in North Carolina, xvii, 7–9; and Quakers, xvii, 3–7; and Saucy Jack, 11; tavern-keeper, 10

Boone, Squire (nephew), 178, 182, 257

Boone, Squire, Jr. (brother): and Boone's surprise, 294n27; buries James Boone and Henry Russell, 57; fights with Indians, 98, 174; goes to Florida with Boone, 41–42; goes to Kentucky, 55, 74; hunts with Boone in Kentucky, 46, 49–53, 223; land investments and litigation, 228, 246, 327n42; leads settlers to Kentucky, 85–86, 90; and Missouri, 228, 246; in North Carolina, 43; at siege of Boonesborough, 151–52, 155, 157; settlement attacked by Indians, xx, 174; at Transylvania convention, 79; ups and downs in his career, 228–29

Boone, Susannah (daughter), xvii, 6, 25–26, 62. See also Hays, Susannah Boone

Boone, William (son), 86

Boone, William Linville (nephew), 269–70

Boonesborough: appearance and condition of, 27, 76–77, 104–105, 140–41, 154, 164, 184, 308n6; attacks on, xix, 90, 104, 112, 118–20, 127–29, 145–61, 175; celebrates Declaration of Independence, 113–14; decline of, 279; food at, 81, 104–05, 126, 140, 164–65; founding of, xix, 76, 275, 347–48; population, 27, 78, 85, 105, 117, 120; siege of, 2, 34, 97–98, 143–61, 217, 316n35, 345; and Transylvania convention, 79–83. See also Boone, Jemima—capture and rescue of; Transylvania Company

Boone's Lick, 243–44, 276, 279, 282, 355

Boone's Station, xx, 166–67, 172, 176, 181, 234

Boone's Trace, 73, 303n18. See also Wilderness Road

Bowman, John, 120, 123, 126, 163

Brackenridge, Henry Marie, 264, 333n2

Braddock, Edward, xviii, 16–19

Braddock's Defeat, xviii, 12–30

Bradford, John, 316n27, 354

Breckenridge, Alexander, 187–88

Breckenridge, John, 201, 331n21, 332n28

Bridges, James, 247–48

British: encourage Indian attacks on American frontier settlements, 94–97, 116–17, 120–23, 127, 170–71; interests in Ohio

Valley, 12–13, 102–03, 114, 281, 349–50; number of settlers in North America, 15–16; objectives in Kentucky during Revolutionary War, 94–95, 114, 121; settlement of western Pennsylvania, 13–14, 41, 95. *See also* French; French and Indian War; Ohio Valley; Revolutionary War

Brown, Arabia, 194

Brown, John (son of Rev. John Brown): congressman, 186; discussions with Spanish over navigation rights on Mississippi, 332n28; and John Filson, 219; goes to Kentucky, 331n21; lawyer for Boone, xv, 327n42; and Liberty Hall, 280; and Kentucky statehood, 186; senator from Kentucky, xv

Brown, John Mason (1837–1890), xvi, 270, 298n24, 299n45, 340n34

Brown, John Mason (1900–1969), xvi

Brown, Margaretta, 280, 328n49, 341nn15–18

Brown, Mason (son of John Brown), xvi, 269–70

Brown, Rev. John, 84, 305n52

Bryan, Daniel Boone, 2, 249–50

Bryan, Morgan, 21–22

Bryan, Rebecca. *See* Boone, Rebecca Bryan

Bryan family: 40, 55; alleged British sympathies, 99, 135–36, 142, 162, 173, 307n29; and Bryan's Station, 175–76; graveyard in Missouri, 269, 272; and Kentucky, 55, 120, 162–63; landholdings, 21, 201; marriages with members of Boone family, 21–23; in North Carolina, 142, 160. *See also* Boone, Rebecca Bryan; Bryan, Daniel Boone; Bryan, Morgan

Buffalo: declining numbers of, 31, 36, 38, 222; east of the Mississippi, 31, 36; hard to kill, 33; hides of, 31–32; hunting by Indians, 38, 119, 279; hunting by whites, 30, 36, 54, 81, 127, 175, 297n61; in Kentucky, 19, 36, 40, 43, 49, 51, 62, 85, 105, 140, 166–67; meat and jerk, 32, 150, 175; other uses, 32, 104; roads (traces) made by, 51, 73, 109, 127, 279. *See also* Game, decline of

Bundrin, David, 157–58

Bush, William, 55, 119

Byrd, William, 60

Byron, George Gordon, Lord, 260, 264, 339n10. *See also* Don Juan

Caldwell, William, 175, 177

Calk, William, 76, 304n28, 348

Callaway, Elizabeth (Betsy), xix, 106–10, 113

Callaway, Flanders: and Baptist church, 257; at Boonesborough, 142, 152, 316n35; marries Jemima Boone, 110; in Missouri, xxii, 1, 112, 229, 246, 248, 258, 337n29; at rescue of Jemima, 107; returns to North Carolina, 161; with salt-boilers, 127; at surveys by Boone, 204

Callaway, Frances (Fanny), xix, 106–10. *See also* Holder, John

Callaway, Jemima: and Baptist church in Missouri, 257; at Boonesborough, 111, 119, 142, 144, 152, 156; at Boone's death, 259; at Boone's Station, 167; Boone stays at home of in Missouri, xxii, 1, 112, 246, 258; death, xxii; moves to Missouri, 229, 232; persuades Boone to sit for his portrait, 258; returns to North Carolina, 161. *See also* Boone, Jemima

Callaway, John Boone, 246

Callaway, Micajah (Cage), 194, 204, 324n42

Callaway, Richard: and blazing of trail into Kentucky, 73–74; at Boonesborough, 77, 86; commissioned to improve Wilderness Road, 161; and court-martial of Boone, 160; death and scalping, 161, 164, 187; ferry license, 161; relations with Boone, 142, 147, 150, 161, 166; rescue of Jemima Boone and Callaway girls, 107, 110–11; at siege of Boonesborough, 150, 152–53, 155, 177

Campbell, Arthur, 64–65, 90, 146–47, 300n12, 321n37

Caperton, Hugh, 222

Captain Johnny (Shawnee chief), 197–98, 200

Carleton, Sir Guy, 116, 121

Carondelet, François Luis Hector, 227, 331n3, 334n26

Castle's Wood, 55–57, 62, 64

Catawbas, 10, 37, 59, 192

Causici, Enrico, 266

Charette, Mo., 257, 259

Charles (slave of William Russell), 56–57

Charlottesville, Va., xx, 173

Cherokees: attack immigrants at Cumberland Gap, 106; attack Kentucky in 1782, 175; attack on Morgan's Station, xxi, 102; attacks on Yadkin, 24; beaver wars, 37; capture Jemima Boone and Callaway girls, 107, 112; Cherokee Billy's killing, 58–59; and Henry Hamilton, 117; incited to attack settlers by northern Indians, 106, 124; move west across Mississippi, 242, 277, 326n20; Overhill community, 353; raid northern Indians, 44; scalps taken by whites, 24; at siege of Boonesborough, 148, 153; Sycamore Shoals treaty and land sale, xix, 45, 68–72, 74–75, 78, 82–82, 84, 88; take pelts of white hunters, 28, 52, 295n3; at Wallen's Creek attack, 56, 58; wars with whites, xviii, 25, 115; white captives, 39. See also Attakullakulla; Chickamaugas; Dragging Canoe; Hanging Maw; Henderson, Richard; Oconostota; Treaties: Treaty of Sycamore Shoals

Chickamaugas, 115, 186

Chickasaws, 43, 242

Chillicothe, Old (near present Xenia, Ohio): appearance and location, 132, 135–37; base of Chlahgatha clan, 132; Boone at, 133–34, 136–40, 142–43, 244–45; burned by Americans, 163, 171, 182; staging point for attacks on Kentucky, 135, 143, 175. See also Chlahgatha clan

Chinn, George Morgan, 354–55

Chlahgatha (Chillicothe) clan, 132, 311n26

Choctaws, 35, 43, 242, 277

Christian, William: and Battle of Point Pleasant, 66; on Boone's parole, 173; death, 187–88; and Fincastle County militia, 63;

Kentucky land surveyed for, 60; money owed to Boone, 208–09; and Transylvania purchase, 79

Cincinnati, Ohio, 219–20, 230–31, 341n13

Clark, George Rogers: and armed boat to patrol Ohio River, 163; barbarity as only way to make war on Indians, 190; brings ammunition from Virginia to Kentucky, 115; captures Cahokia, 145–46; captures Vincennes, xx, 145–46, 163, 318n77; clothing, 192; delegate to Virginia Convention, 115; and Detroit, 163; estimates whites killed by Indians in Kentucky, 91; expeditions against Shawnees, xx, 171–72, 182–84, 187, 216, 276; and fort at Falls of the Ohio, 163; and Henry Hamilton, 96, 163, 170, 350–51; literacy and spelling, 7, 290n25; major in Kentucky County militia, 117; opposes Transylvania Company, 88; and release of Cage Callaway from Shawnees, 194; on vulnerability of Kentucky settlements, 105

Clark, Thomas D., 349, 354

Clay, Henry, 139, 328n44, 352

Coburn, Derry (slave of Daniel Morgan Boone), 240, 242, 247–48, 282

Coburn, Judge John, 246, 250, 266

Cole, Thomas, 264

Cooley, William, 46

Cooper, James Fenimore, 112, 264

Cornplanter (Seneca chief), 200

Cornstalk (Shawnee chief): heads Shawnee division, 104, 138, 140–41, 189, 352; killed by whites, xix, 124–27, 130, 132; leader at Battle of Point Pleasant, 66; seeks peace with whites, 104, 118, 124; and Treaty of Camp Charlotte, 66, 116

Cornwallis, Lord Charles, xx, 91–92, 101, 173–74, 183

Cottawamago. See Blackfish (Shawnee chief)

Crabtree, Isaac, 56–58, 152

Craig, Delinda Boone, 181, 257, 336n9

Craig, Emily, 272–73, 340n37

Crawford, William, 174–75, 187

Creeks, 37, 43

Cresswell, Nicholas, 140, 203, 287, 314n39, 348

Crittenden, John J., 269–71

Crittenden, Thomas L., 269

Crockett, Joseph, 224–25

Croghan, George, 315n42

Cumberland Gap, xvii–xviii, 7, 35, 39, 46, 50, 52, 55, 59, 73, 76, 105–06, 142, 163, 172, 216, 218, 220, 224–25, 267, 274, 277, 347, 356

Cutbirth, Benjamin, 28, 35, 54–55

Dandridge, Alexander Spottswood, 60, 300n19

Daniel Boone at His Cabin at Great Osage Lake (Cole), 264

Daniel Boone Escorting Settlers through the Cumberland Gap (Bingham), 267

Dartmouth, Lord, 56, 67, 100, 117, 121

Davis, James, 261

Declaration of Independence, xix, 97, 113–14, 117

Deer: clothing made from deerskin, 22–23, 31, 192, 243; declining numbers, 35–37, 166; deer's foot and Indian wedding, 140; dressing of deerskins, 30–31; hunting of, 6, 9–10, 19, 29–30, 33, 36, 37, 40, 85, 125, 175, 223, 240, 252, 255, 264, 319n54; importance of deerskin trade, 20, 30, 42, 47, 57; meat, 1, 105, 144, 167; tanning of hides, 31; transporting deerskins, 21, 31, 220, 369. *See also* Game, decline of

Deerslayer, The (Cooper), 264

Delassus, Don Charles Dehault, 230, 236, 246

Delawares: courted by British and by Americans during Revolutionary War, 96, 117, 122–23; in French and Indian War, 16–18, 24; Girty and, 142, 192; hear of coming Shawnee-white war, 60; hunting by, 37; and Iroquois, 45, 298n28; join 1782 attack on Kentucky, 175; land dealings with British and with Pennsylvania, 4–5, 289n6;

language and its kinship to Shawnee, 137, 314n28; move to Missouri, 227, 242, 244; objectives in Ohio Valley, 13, 16, 352; reaction to Gnadenhutten massacre, 174; relations with Quakers and others in Pennsylvania, 4–5, 8, 137, 140; and Treaty of Logstown, xvii, 16; at Wallen's Creek attack, 56

De Peyster, Arent Schuyler, 170–71, 176

Derry. *See* Coburn, Derry

Detroit, Mich.: attacked in Pontiac's War, 41; Boone at, 135–36; British delay leaving, after Revolutionary War, 102–03, 281; captured from French by British, 65; center of British encouragement of Indian attacks on American settlers, 95–96, 104–05, 116–17, 120, 121–24, 127, 146, 148, 170–71, 311n25; Clark's plans to take, 163; and Girty, 142; population of, 95. *See also* Hamilton, Henry

Discovery . . . of Kentucke, The (Filson), xx, 47, 50–53, 93–94, 135–38, 143, 153–55, 159–60, 162, 172, 179, 210, 212, 216–19, 233, 260, 287–88, 345, 356. *See also* Filson, John

Don Juan (Byron), 260–63

Dragging Canoe (Cherokee chief): accepts war belt for attack on American settlers, 106; and attack on Boone's axemen, 74–75; followers move to Chickamauga Creek region, 114; opposes Sycamore Shoals treaty, 71

Draper, Lyman Copeland: appearance, 267–68; biography of Boone, 268, 344; career, 267–70, 340n25; manuscript compiler, 268, 343–44; and State Historical Society of Wisconsin, 267, 343–44

Draper's Meadow killings, xviii, 16, 39, 56, 65, 74, 193. *See also* Ingles, Thomas; Patton, James

Dunmore, Lord John: becomes governor of Virginia, 55; denounces Richard Henderson, 71–72; interests in lands in Ohio Valley, 61, 67; letter to Lord Dartmouth, 67; orders Kentucky land sold to highest

Dunmore, Lord John *(continued)*
bidder, 93; on Pennsylvanians' encroachment on trade with Ohio Valley Indians,
100; requests capture of Cherokees, 58;
starts war with Shawnees, 61, 116. *See also*
Lord Dunmore's War
Dunn, Jack, 194

Elk, 36, 40, 85, 104–05, 279, 296n48
Emery, Will (Captain Will): adopts William
Hancock, 146; at capture of Boone and
salt-boilers, 128; Hancock escapes from,
146; takes pelts of Boone and fellow hunt-
ers, 47–49, 242; warns against returning to
Indians' hunting ground, 48
Eskippakithiki, xvii, 19, 44, 47
Estill, James, 175
Exeter, Pa., xvii, 4–8, 20, 214

Fallen Timbers, Battle of, xxi, 97, 102–03,
200, 308n37, 352
Falls of the Ohio: British planned attack on
settlements near, 171; commercial importance of location, 51–52; fort built near,
163; militia at, 182; routes to, 216; sickness
of settlers near, 164–65; surveys near, 20,
60, 89, 105, 353. *See also* Clark, George
Rogers; Louisville, Ky.
Faragher, John Mack, 210, 235, 287, 328n45,
346, 355–56
Fayette County, Ky.: Boone as deputy surveyor, 204, 208, 327n32; Boone as militia
officer, xx, 169, 230, 171, 182; Boone rep-
resents in Virginia Assembly, 173; court
issues warrant for Boone's arrest, 228; created, xx, 91, 169; militia at Battle of Blue
Licks, 176, 178; militia in Clark's expedition, 182–84
Femme Osage, Mo.: American settlers at,
278; Boone as syndic and commandant,
xxi, 230, 236, 238–39; Boones settle at, 230;
Daniel Morgan Boone explores, 227–28;
land grants at, xxi, 228, 246, 250; Nathan
Boone's house at, 239–40; Shawnees visit,

245; and trade with western Indians,
230, 232. *See also* Boone, Daniel Morgan;
Boone, Nathan
Filson, John: career, xx, 44, 217, 219, 329n10;
debt to John Brown, 219; disappearance,
219–20; land speculation by, 217–18, 329n5;
names site of Cincinnati "Losantiville,"
219; on navigation of the Mississippi while
Spain has New Orleans, 233; writing style,
50–51, 53, 133, 150, 183–84, 218, 329n8. See
also *Discovery . . . of Kentucke, The* (Filson)
Fincastle County, Va.: created, xviii, 59; Kentucky County carved out from, 89; militia,
66, 146, 188; and surveyors entering Kentucky, xix, 59–63, 70, 72, 79, 203, 353. *See
also* Floyd, John; Preston, William
Findley, John: disappears, 49; goes with
Boone to Kentucky, xviii, 46–47, 73;
leaves Kentucky after Indians take pelts,
48–49; Miamis attack trading party of,
315n42; tells Boone of Kentucky, 19–20,
39, 43–44; trading post with Indians, xvii,
47; with Braddock's army, xviii, 19. *See also*
Eskippakithiki
Fischer, David Hackett, 346–47
Fleming, William: at Battle of Point Pleasant, 66; on Harrodsburg's filth, 105; and
ivory-billed woodpecker, 299n53; journals, 348; as land commissioner, 208,
318n73, 353; letter to Shawnee chiefs and
warriors, 141; medical training of, 66; and
sickness in Kentucky, 164–66
Flinn, Chloe, 196–97
Flint, Timothy, 243, 256, 265–66, 279–80,
296n43, 331n13, 355. See also *Biographical
Memoir of Daniel Boone* (Flint)
Florida: access to sea transport, 298n13;
Boone's trip to, xiv, xviii, 42–43, 256, 274;
ceded by Spain to Britain, 41; deer trade
in, 37; proclamation offering land to Protestant settlers in West Florida, 41, 232;
Spanish governor of West Florida warns
about Boone, 236; Squire Boone lives in,
229

Floyd, John: appearance, 59; background, 59; Boone land records kept by, 210; captured by and escapes from British, 116; Catawba ancestry, 59, 192; and Clark's expedition against Shawnees, 182; grateful for Boone's warning trip, 63; and Hard Winter, 166; killed, xvi, 187–88; land investments, 201, 203, 208; leads party attacked by Indians, 174; letters to Preston, 63, 89, 93, 101, 112–13, 164, 166, 172, 174, 301n39, 309n32, 310n46, 318n82; literacy and spelling, 210; in Lord Dunmore's War, 66; premonition of death, 113, 187; as privateer, 116; rescue of Jemima Boone and Callaway girls, xv, xix, 107, 109–10, 201; return to Kentucky, 116; rifle of, xvi, 29, 295n5; at St. Asaph's (Logan's Station), 78, 83; scarlet coat, 187–88; as surveyor, xix, 59–61, 188, 203, 300n19, 353; and Transylvania Company, 78–79, 115–16; tutors Preston's children, 59. See also Fincastle County, Va.; Preston, William

Foley, William E., 354–55

Fort Boone. See Boonesborough

Fort Duquesne, xvii, xviii, 15–18, 24–25, 41, 46. See also Braddock's Defeat; Fort Pitt; Pittsburgh, Pa.

Fort Henry, 123

Fort Kittanning, 124, 191

Fort Leavenworth, 138, 248, 335n43

Fort Le Boeuf, 14

Fort Osage, xxii, 1, 244, 248

Fort Pitt: attacked during Pontiac's War, 41; building of, 18, 25; commander at, 123; deerskin trade at, 30, 35; during Revolutionary War, 142; and germ warfare against Indians, 191; meeting to seek neutrality of Indian tribes, 124–25; razing, 95. See also Pittsburgh, Pa.

Fort Stanwix, Treaty of. See under Treaties.

Fox, George, 5

Frankfort, Ky., xvi, xxii, 52, 60, 106, 269, 280, 328n49, 341nn15, 16

Franklin, Benjamin, 17, 54, 68, 116

French: encourage attack on Miamis at Pickawillany, 14; encourage Indian attacks on British settlers during French and Indian War, 16, 24, 90, 192, 350; and Louisiana, 226, 235; and Ohio Valley, 13,19, 293n42; population of, in North America, 16. See also French and Indian War; Ohio Valley

French and Indian War: and award of land warrants, 60, 70, 78, 92–93; begins, xvii, 4, 12; captives taken by Indians during, 116, 192–93, 324n35; causes of, 12–17; end, 40, 95; Indian raids on frontier settlements during, 18, 90. See also Braddock's Defeat; French; Treaties: Treaty of Paris (1763)

Friends, Society of. See Quakers

Frontier, in America: change in culture and economy, 277–81; movement of American center of population and of settlement line, 275–76; Turner and, 277. See also Manifest Destiny; Turner, Frederick Jackson

Fur trade: British try to control, in Northwest Territory, 102–03, 281; British vs. French efforts to control, 13–14, 19, 293n42; British vs. Spanish efforts to control, 226; Chouteau family and, 232, 244; commercial importance, 30; Virginian vs. Pennsylvanian efforts to control, 12, 100, 116, 281. See also Bear; Beaver; Boone, Daniel—hunting and trapping by; Buffalo; Deer; Elk; Game, decline of; Hunting; Long hunters; Missouri River; Ohio Valley; Osages; Otter; Shawnees; St. Louis, Mo.

Game, decline of: causes, 28, 35–38, 40, 44, 54, 85, 105, 186, 200, 231, 258, 277–78, 347; and Indians, 37–38, 186; and Transylvania Company, 80–81; and whites, 36, 186, 277–78. See also Boone, Daniel—hunting and trapping by; Hunting; and names of game animals

Gass, David, 57

Gass, John, 107, 150, 316n35

Germain, George, Lord, 121–22

Ginseng, 213–15, 328n55, 353. *See also under* Boone, Daniel

Girty, Simon: and Battle of Blue Licks; and Bryan's Station attack, 175–76; captured by Indians, 142; conflicting loyalties of, 99, 142; and Crawford's torture and death, 175; at Dunlap's Station attack, 190; Indian languages spoken by, 142, 192; leads attack on Squire Boone's settlement, 174; leaves Americans and joins British, 95, 142; as orator, 95, 175, 320n25

Gist, Christopher, 14

Gnaddenhutten, 174, 320n22

Goe, Philip, 247

Goe, Rebecca Boone, 247

Goodman, Ansel, 194, 312n51

Goodman, Daniel, 119

Grant, John, 231

Greathouse, Jacob (or Daniel), 58–59, 188–89, 300n14

Greenough, Horatio, 266

Grenier, John, 323n19, 323n32, 352

Gulliver's Travels (Swift), 2, 49

Gwynedd, Pa., 4

Hagerstown, Md., xx, 214, 220–21, 223

Haldimand, Frederick, 96

Half King, the (Wyandot chief), 123

Hamilton, Henry: background and culture of, 96; captive of the French, 116; captured by George Rogers Clark, xx, 163, 318n77, 350–51; commandant at Detroit, xx, 95, 116; encourages Indian attacks on American frontier settlers, 95–96, 120–23, 146, 148, 350; letters to Boonesborough, 149; meets Boone in Detroit, 135–36, 173; and payments to Indians for American scalps, 96; proclamation offering land to Americans, 121–23; treatment of as an American captive, 170

Hammon, Neal O., 72, 154, 180, 204–07, 285–86, 288, 303n18, 304n34, 318n74,
319n94, 319n97, 321n37, 321n39, 326n15, 326n21, 326n27, 327n41, 327n43, 328nn44–45, 344, 349, 353

Hancock, William, 138, 146–47, 149, 194. *See also* Salt-boiler captives

Hand, Edward, 123–24, 126, 191

Hanging Maw (Cherokee), 71, 75, 107, 109, 111, 152

"Hard Winter" (1779–80), 33, 166–67

Harding, Chester, 1, 258–59, 338n35

Harmar, Josiah, xxi, 102, 193–94, 198, 200

Harrison, Benjamin, 181–83

Harrod, James, xix, 55, 78, 83, 117–18, 216, 300n3, 349

Harrodsburg, Ky.: evacuation, 78; food, 114, 165; Indian attacks on, 61, 98, 118, 120, 137; population, 78, 86, 105, 117; resettlement, 78; sends men to help Boonesborough, 146; sends men to help Bryan's Station, 176; settlement, xix, 55, 78, 86; and Transylvania Company, 78–79, 83, 88–89, 92, 99, 115; unsanitary conditions at, 104, 165

Hart, Nathaniel: entrusts funds to Boone, 168; estimation of Boone, 168–69; killed by Indians, 175; raid on homestead, 110, 112

Hart, Nathaniel, Jr., 211

Hart, Thomas, 221, 280

Hays, Daniel Boone, 239

Hays, Susannah Boone: at Boonesborough, 105; at Boone's Station, 167, 330n22; character of, 26, 247; death, 239, 247; in Missouri, 229, 239; at Moore's Fort, 62; moves back to North Carolina, 142. *See also* Boone, Susannah; Hays, William

Hays, William: at Boonesborough, 105; character of, 239; killed by son-in-law, 239; leaves Boonesborough, 142, 161; at Marble Creek, 167; marries Susannah, 26; moves to Missouri with Boone, 229; teaches Boone, 7, 204, 210, 239

Hays, William, Jr. (grandson of Boone), 240, 242, 248, 335n42

Hemp, 279, 282

Hempstead, Stephen, 294n27, 335n42

Henderson, Richard: background, 69, 118; and Boonesborough's founding, 75–83, 302n1; journal, 304n30, 348; moves back to North Carolina, 86; praises Boone, 76; and Regulators, 69, 99; speech by, 79–80; and Transylvania Company, 68–90. *See also* Transylvania Company; Treaties: Treaty of Sycamore Shoals

Henderson, Samuel, 106–07, 109–10, 113

Hendricks, George, 216

Henry, Patrick: Boone requests more troops from, 212; brother-in-law of William Christian, 60, 188; land in Kentucky surveyed for, 61; recommends offensive against Indians, 123; and Transylvania Company, 79, 84–84, 86, 89

Hill, William, 43, 256

Hinderaker, Eric, 290n15, 350

Hinkston's Station, 112

Hite, Isaac, 88

Holder, John: ambushed by Indians, 175, 177; marries Frances Callaway, 110; and rescue of Jemima Boone and Callaway girls, 107; at siege of Boonesborough, 156, 158; swears, 156, 317n49

Holder, Joseph, 46

Holsteiner, George Michael. *See* Stoner, Michael

Houston, Peter, 8, 22, 254, 288, 293n83, 296n37, 337n10, 344

Hoy's Station, 175, 177

Hunting. *See* Game, decline of; *and names of game animals*

Hurons. *See* Wyandots

Imlay, Fanny, 264

Imlay, Gilbert, 208–10, 217, 264, 327n35

Indian-white relations: adoption of white captives by Indians, 134–34, 192–93; assimilation of adopted white captives, 192–95, 324n33, 351; fight for control of land, 13, 15–19, 24–25, 61, 74–75, 93–94, 200, 351–52; increase in mutual demonization, 192, 198–99, 323n32, 351; Indian adoption of white clothing, food, tools, etc., 191, 323n27, 351; Indian killings of settlers in Kentucky, 64, 98, 118, 170, 172, 179, 181, 185–90; Indian scalping of whites, 17–18, 64, 74, 98, 104, 107, 116, 118, 119, 125, 161, 170, 174, 179, 181, 188; indiscriminate hatred, 192; learning the other's languages, 195; marriage and sexual relations between, 139–40, 193–95, 314nn39–40; and relocation across the Mississippi, 257, 277; warfare and crop destruction, 92, 98–99, 102, 120, 126, 163, 175, 182–83, 352; white adoption of Indian clothing, food, tools, etc., 22, 118, 192; white bounties for Indian scalps or hands, 24, 90, 96; white germ warfare against Indians, 190–91, 323n23; white scalping of Indians, 24–25, 58, 64, 66, 147–49, 172, 176, 190. *See also* Boone, Daniel—conflicting loyalties; Boone, Daniel—relations with Indians; Boone, Nathan; Girty, Simon; Jackson, Joseph; Revolutionary War; Salt-boiler captives; *and names of Indians and of Indian tribes*

Ingles, Thomas, 193

Innes, Harry, 207–08, 331n21, 332n28

Iroquois: beaver wars, 37; cede claims to lands between Ohio and Tennessee rivers, xviii, 44–45, 54, 68, 88; concern over British and French encroachment, 15; defeat Shawnees and other tribes, 13, 15, 37; lose leverage when Americans win Revolutionary War, 353; and naming of Kentucky, 44, 298n24; support British in Revolutionary War, 120–21; trade with British rather than French, 14, 350; and Treaty of Logstown, xvii, 16. *See also* Mingos; Treaties: Treaty of Logstown, Treaty of Fort Stanwix

Jackson, Joseph: adopted by Shawnees, 194; captured by Shawnees, 130; conflicting loyalties, 194–95; kills self, 195; may have fought with Indians against whites, 194–95; meets Boone in Missouri, 195, 245; sees scalp of Richard Callaway, 161

Jay, John, 93, 233

Jefferson, Thomas: on Americans settling in Upper Louisiana, 234; on British encouragement of Indian attacks on the frontier, 97, 307n24; and chaining of Hamilton, 170; flees from Tarleton's rangers, 183; on importance of control of Mississippi River navigation, 234, 332n28; and Louisiana Purchase, 355; on Louisiana Territory as place for resettling eastern Indians, 235; on Osages, 241; on slavery and Missouri Compromise, 258; and Transylvania Company, 87–88. *See also* Louisiana Purchase

Jefferson County, Ky.: formed, xx, 169; Indian killings or captures of whites in, 184; militia, 171, 187

Johnson, Andrew (Pequolly), 137, 143–44, 147, 194

Johnson, Guy, 120

Johnson, Sir William, 56, 59, 120

Jones, Dr. John, 260

Jones, John Gabriel, 125

Judgment Tree, 238

Kamper, Ken, 285, 340n38

Kaskaskia, Ill., 95, 114, 145–46

Kenton, Simon: appearance of, 118; arrives in Kentucky, 118; assumes name of Simon Butler, 118–19; biography, 349; on Boone and salt-boilers, 161; as British prisoner, 159; finds Greathouse's body, 189; kills Big Jim, xx, 189; loss of land, 247; Paint Creek raid, 147; saves Boone's life, xix, 118–20; and Shitting Spring, 279; visits Boone in Missouri, 247, 335n41; at Washington, Ky., 278–79

Kentucky: cane, 31–32, 40, 48, 50, 106, 175; changing economy of, 184, 277–81, 354; changing leadership of after Revolutionary War, 231–32, 331n21; churchgoing in, 255–56, 337n21; conflicting land claims in, 92–93, 100–01, 210–11; counties, 169; as county of Virginia, 89, 115–16, 169; "forting up" to defend against Indian attack,

104–05; game in, 36, 39; immigration of settlers into, xiv, xvii, xviii, xx, 90, 163, 172; land speculation and investment in, 46, 84, 201, 210, 217, 220, 353; name of, 44, 114, 298n24; "settling out" as Indian threat recedes, 184; soil, 73; "Spanish conspiracy," 233, 355; statehood, xiv, xxi, 186, 222; tension between different groups during Revolutionary War, 92–93, 100–101, 302n4. *See also* Bluegrass; *and names of specific sites in Kentucky*

Kentucky Gazette, 185, 219, 225, 354

Kentucky River, 62, 72, 75–76, 106–07, 166

Kincheloe's Station, 184

Knox, James, 224–25

Land laws of Virginia: and commission to resolve conflicting land claims in Kentucky, 162, 210, 318n73; land grants under, 162, 318nn73–74; and pre-emption claims, 92; and settlement claims, 100; 1779 law, 162, 317n72; warrants under, 93, 162

La Salle, René-Robert, Sieur de, 13

Last of the Mohicans, The (Cooper), 112, 264. *See also* Boone, Jemima

Le Maigauis (Ottawa), 37

Lewis and Clark, 236–37, 241

Lexington, Ky., 279–80

Licks, 30, 43–44, 49, 51, 54, 76, 81, 164, 203, 252, 255

Life of Daniel Boone . . . (Peck), xxii, 134, 195, 244, 248, 253, 255, 257, 267, 283, 345

Limestone, Ky.: Boone goes to, 211; Boone leaves, 214; Boone's ventures in, 211–14; entry point into Kentucky, 211–12; and exchange of white and Indian captives, 196–98

Lincoln, Abraham (grandfather of president), 163

Lincoln County, Ky., xx, 169, 171, 176, 226

Little Carpenter. *See* Attakullakulla

Little Miami River, 132, 144, 163, 182

Little Turtle (Miami chief), xxi, 102, 193

Lofaro, Michael A., 343, 346

Logan (Mingo chief): character of, 63, 301n41; family killed at Yellow Creek, 58–59; raids on whites led by, 63–64, 66; speech, 66, 302n55

Logan, Benjamin: appoints Boone to arrange Indian-white captive exchange, 196; before and after Battle of Blue Licks, 176–79, 181–83; biography, 349; burns Lorimier's trading post, 182–83; captain of Kentucky County militia, 117; and Henry Hamilton's proclamation, 123; leads 1786 expedition against Shawnees, xx, 189; presides over captive exchange, 197–98

Logan's Station, 78, 117, 120, 123, 145–46, 159–60, 367

London (slave), 157

Long hunters, 28–36, 38, 50–51, 347. *See also* Boone, Daniel—hunting and trapping by; Game, decline of; Mansker, Caspar

Long Island, Holston River, 73, 315n14

Lord Dunmore's War, 61–67. *See also* Dunmore, Lord John; Point Pleasant, Battle of; Treaties: Treaty of Camp Charlotte

Lorimier, Louis: Americans burn his trading post in Ohio, 182–83; appearance, 105–06; at capture of salt-boilers, 127–28, 131–32, 135; goes to Detroit, 105; leads Shawnees and Delawares to Spanish land grant in Missouri, 244; as Spanish civil servant, 244, 334n26

Louisiana: American settlers in Upper Louisiana, xxi, 227, 230, 234–36; Board of Commissioners to resolve land claims in, 246; British threat to, 226; ceded by France to Spain (1763), xviii, 41; ceded back to France by Spain (1801), xxi, 235; land grants by Delassus, 246; territory of Louisiana, 239. *See also* Boone, Daniel—and Missouri; Louisiana Purchase; Missouri; Population growth: in Missouri; St. Louis; Treaties: Treaty of San Ildefonso

Louisiana Purchase: American administration of Louisiana Territory following, 236, 239; and American navigation rights on Mississippi, 233–34; background of, 235, 355; consummation of, xxi, 236; doubles size of United States, 235, 276; made more likely by American immigration into Louisiana Territory, 276, 281; provides space for relocating eastern Indians, 235, 278. *See also* Louisiana

Louisville, Ky.: appearance of, 229; founding, xv, 187; health conditions at, 166; Indian attacks near, 171, 174, 185, 188; land claims near, 20, 60, 89, 105, 202–03, 353; name, 91; site of, 51–52, 341n13; prisoner exchange at, 194; settlement of, 172. *See also* Clark, George Rogers; Falls of the Ohio; Floyd, John; Jefferson County, Ky.

Loutre Lick, 253, 260

Loyal Company, xvii, 39. *See also* Walker, Thomas

Lulbegrud Creek, 49

Lythe, Rev. John, 79, 81

McAfee family, 54, 331n21

McClelland's Station, 126

McClure, Rev. David, 140, 292n40, 301n41, 313n4, 324n33, 352

McGary, Hugh: at Battle of Blue Licks, 176–79, 321n37; character, 54, 176; death, 278; goes to Kentucky, 54; hatred of Indians, 192; hunts with Boone, 54; kills Indian outside Harrodsburg, 118; signs petition against Transylvania Company, 88; stepson killed by Indians, 118, 176; tomahawks Moluntha and Nohelema, xx, 189–91

McKee, Alexander, 59, 142, 175–76

Manifest Destiny, 266–67, 339n20. *See also* Frontier, in America

Mansker, Caspar, 28, 51, 317n3

Maquachake clan, 94. *See also* Cornstalk (Shawnee chief); Shawnees: clans

Martin, Josiah, 70–71

Martin's Station, 171

May, George, 188, 203, 208

May, John: killed by Indians, 187–88; land investments by, 172, 188, 206; Maysville

May, John *(continued)*
  named after, 188; moves to Kentucky, 172;
  notes Kentucky land value will depend on
  Mississippi navigation rights, 233
Maysville, Ky. *See* Limestone, Ky.
Mendinhall, John, 56–57
Mendinhall, Richard, 56–57
Methodists, 225, 270–71, 337n21
Miami River (or Great Miami River), 93,
  144, 182, 186, 190, 196
Miamis: attack John Findley's trading party,
  315n42; at Battle of Fallen Timbers, xxi;
  and Beaubien, 135; British encourage their
  attacks on American settlers, 94, 121; capture John Slover, 193; capture William
  Wells, 193; at Harmar's defeat, xxi, 102; and
  Louis Lorimier, 127, 135; and Ohio Valley,
  13; at Pickawillany, 14; receive an American scalp from Hamilton, 96; at St. Clair's
  defeat, xxi, 102
Michilimackinac, 37, 95
Miller, Henry, 8–9, 21
Millet, Jean-François, 111
Mingos: attacks on settlers, 61, 63–64, 66,
  106; and Blackfish's attack on Kentucky
  settlements, 136, 143; as Iroquois depen-
  dents, 45, 298n28; offer to help Braddock,
  17; and Ohio Valley, 13; Yellow Creek killings of, 58–59. *See also* Iroquois; Logan
  (Mingo chief)
Mississippi River: difficulty of going upstream on, 232; importance of navigation rights on, 232–34; and Jay's proposed
  treaty with Spain, 233; relocation of eastern Indian tribes across, 227, 242, 277–78;
  as route for taking of New Orleans, 226;
  Spanish barring American navigation on,
  233–34; and "Spanish conspiracy," 233,
  332n28. *See also* Jay, John; Louisiana; Louisiana Purchase; Missouri; Spanish
Missouri: America takes over administration of, 235–36; American settlers in,
  234–37, 243–44; Boone in, 1–2; 229–30;
  Boone's family move to, 225–29; control

sought by various countries, 226–27, 237;
  game in, 258; lead mines in, 235; removal
  of Indians from, 257–58; revivalism in,
  256–57; slavery in, 258, 271, 282, 330n1;
  Spanish administration of, 226–28, 234,
  333n35; statehood, 258. *See also* Boone,
  Daniel—Missouri; Louisiana; Population
  growth
Missouri River, 14, 25, 226, 249, 260, 335n42
Mocksville, N.C., xvii, 10
Mohawks. *See* Iroquois
Moluntha (Shawnee chief): and Boone,
  during Boone's captivity, 138; killed by
  McGary, xx, 189–91; son killed, 149; suc-
  ceeded by Captain Johnny, 197; with
  Boone at Boonesborough, 149, 151;
Mononghahela, Battle on the. *See* Brad-
  dock's Defeat
Mooney, James, 46
Moore, Arthur, 356, 338n2
Moravian Indians, 37, 174
Morgan, Robert, 288, 328n57, 338n35, 346
Morgan, Sarah. *See* Boone, Sarah Morgan
Morgan's Station, xxi, 102, 308n40
Morris, Robert, 213–14
Mountain Muse, The (Bryan), 2, 249–50,
  335n47

Neeley, Alexander, 49–50
New Madrid earthquakes, 256, 337n21
New Orleans, 30, 35, 41, 226, 232–34, 236,
  281. *See also* Louisiana
Nohelema, 190, 197
North Carolina. *See* Boone, Daniel: and
  Yadkin Valley; Henderson, Richard;
  Mocksville, N.C.; Salisbury, N.C.; Transyl-
  vania Company; Yadkin (river and valley)

Oconostota (Cherokee chief), 191
Ohio Company, 13–15, 54, 100, 313n9
Ohio Valley: British move troops from, 67;
  conflicting interests in, 5, 12–19, 92–95,
  102–03, 281; importance as trade route,
  100, 232; Indian efforts to keep control of,

15–16, 41, 46, 97, 102, 123, 174–83; as middle ground between whites and Indians, 349–51. *See also* British; French; French and Indian War; Indian-white relations; Mingos; Pontiac's War; Revolutionary War; Shawnees

Oley Township, Pa., xvii, 4. *See also* Exeter, Pa.

O'Malley, Nancy, 349

Osages: appearance, xii, 241; divisions among, 244; and fur trade, 240–42; incursions by other tribes into their lands, 242, 244; land cessions to United States, 244, 258, 277–78; power, population, and territory of, 240–42, 278, 334n14, 355; relocated out of Missouri, 244, 257–58, 278; take Boone's furs, xxi, 242; take furs from Nathan Boone, 243; use of white weapons, 191; views of Big Chief, 245; warfare as central to way of life, 241–42. *See also* Indian-white relations; Missouri

Ottawas: attack on Kentucky, 175; attack on Pickawillany, 14; ; incite Cherokees to attack Americans, 106; near Detroit, 117, 121; and Pontiac, 41. *See also* Le Maigauis; Pontiac; Pontiac's War

Otter, 10, 30, 33–34, 49, 220, 243

Paint Creek raid, 147–49, 160

Pathfinder, The (Cooper), 264

Patton, James: grant of large tract of western lands to, 16, 292n22; killed by Indians, xviii, 16, 56, 74, 187; at Logstown treaty, 16, 292n24; and William Preston, 65

Patton, William, 159

Peck, John Mason. See *Life of Daniel Boone . . .* (Peck)

Penn, William, 3–5, 289n6, 289n13, 290n15. *See also* Pennsylvania; Quakers

Pennsylvania: evacuations of western settlements during French and Indian War, 24–25; Quakers in, 3–8, 24, 307n19; relations with Indians in, 4–5, 24–25, 41, 63, 350; relinquishes claims to trans-

Allegheny lands, 25, 41; royal charter of, 5, 12; tensions with Virginia, 12, 14, 92, 100, 116, 281. *See also* Boone, Daniel: in Pennsylvania; French and Indian War; Gnadenhutten; Penn, William; Pontiac's War; Quakers; Treaties: Treaty of Easton

Pensacola, Fla., 41–43, 319n57

Philadelphia, Pa., 3–4, 9, 21, 86, 214, 216, 221, 295n2

Philips, Indian, 248

Pickawillany, 14. *See also* Miamis

Pittsburgh, Pa., xvii, 14, 30, 52, 58, 117, 140, 187, 211, 214, 216. *See also* Fort Pitt

Point Pleasant (now in W.Va.), xix, xx, 124, 188, 214–15, 220–22

Point Pleasant, Battle of, xix, 66, 68, 97, 101, 116, 118, 127, 176. *See also* Lord Dunmore's War

Pompey (black Shawnee translator), 128, 130–32, 149, 152, 158, 317n57

Pontiac, 41

Pontiac's War, 41, 94, 156, 192, 323n32, 350

Population decline of Indians: east of the Mississippi, 299–300; generally and in Ohio Valley, 15, 291n16; in Kentucky, 277; in Missouri, 257–58

Population growth: in British colonies and in United States, 275–76, 341n5; in Kentucky, xiv, 90, 184, 231, 257, 276, 331n18; in Missouri, 226, 257, 276, 330n1

Potawatomis, 14, 117, 121, 193

Powell's Valley, 52, 55, 73, 85–86, 189, 219, 329n10

Prairie, The (Cooper), 264

Preston, John, 65, 212

Preston, William: background, 65, 202; commissions Boone as militia captain, xv, 64–65, 136; and Cornstalk's killing, 125–26; death, 200; and Dunmore's proclamation on land sales to highest bidder, 93; and Lord Dunmore's War, 61–65; education, 65; expedition into Kentucky after Draper's Meadow killings, 16–17; and Fincastle County surveyors, 59–60, 78; and John

Preston, William *(continued)*
Floyd, 59–60, 78–79, 89, 93, 101, 112–13, 164, 166, 172, 187, 203; land investments by, 60, 79, 201–03, 208; letter to Shawnee chiefs and warriors, 141; opposes Transylvania Company, 70; and parole of Boone from British custody, 173; and James Patton, 16; sheriff and colonel of militia, 59, 64, 74–75; as surveyor, 70, 202, 208
Prock, Matthias, 156
Proclamation of 1763: difficulty in enforcing, 44, 46, 67, 95; reasons for, 41; trans-Appalachian land grants to officers, 93; and Transylvania Company, 68, 70–71, 87, 89; and Treaty of Easton, 41; Washington's views of, 60
Prophet, the (Shawnee), 37, 132–44, 191, 313n18

Quakers: ethical principles, 138, 290n30; inner light, 5, 8, 199; on marriages with non-Quakers, xvii, 5–7; persecution of, 3–4, 289n1; refuse to pay tithes or take oaths, 3; relations with Indians, 4–5, 8, 199; resign from Pennsylvania legislature in French and Indian War, 24. *See also* Boone, Daniel: and Quakerism; Penn, William
Quindre, Antoine Dagneaux de, 316n15

Ranck, George W., 288, 347–48
Raven, the (Cherokee chief), 72
Ray, William, 118
Regulators, 69
Reid, Nathan, 107–09, 201, 308n4
Revolutionary War: artillery's role in Kentucky, 97–98, 170–71; British support of Indian attacks on American frontier settlements, 94–97, 102–04; destruction of crops, 98–99; duration, 92, 101–103; in Kentucky (overview), 91–103; objectives of Americans, 92–93, 103; objectives of British, 94–95, 103; objectives of Indians, 93–94, 103; size of engagements in Kentucky, 97–98; surrender of Cornwallis, 92,
101; tensions between Whigs and Tories, 92, 99; tensions among other groups of settlers in Kentucky, 92–93, 99–100. *See also* British; Clark, George Rogers; Hamilton, Henry
Richmond, Va., 168, 173, 206, 208, 221
Rifles, flintlock (Kentucky or Pennsylvania), xvi, 10, 27, 29, 37–38, 48, 52, 97–98, 110, 128, 191, 264, 295nn4–5. *See also* Boone, Daniel—hunting and trapping by
Robertson, James, 64, 74
Rogers, Joseph, 115
Ruddle's Station, 171
Russell, Henry, 56–58, 74
Russell, William: attempt with Boone to settle Kentucky, 55–57; background, 55, 62, 300n4; and Castle's Wood, 55; engages Boone and Stoner to warn Fincastle County surveyors, 61–62; orders Boone to undertake defense of settlements on the Clinch, 63; and Wallen's Creek attack, 56–58. *See also* Castle's Wood

Salisbury, N.C., 11, 21
Salt-boiler captives: adoption by Shawnees, 133–35, 142; capture by Shawnees, xix, 91, 127–29, 140–41, 144; differing attitudes toward Indians, 138, 193–96; escapes by, 137, 139, 143–44, 146; sale of some to British, 134–35, 142; taken to Old Chillicothe, 130–32; vote on whether to kill, 130. *See also* Boone, Daniel: and salt-boilers; Boone, Daniel—relations with Indians; Hancock, William; Indian-white relations; Jackson, Joseph; Johnson, Andrew; Salt-boiling; *and names of other salt-boilers*
Salt-boiling, 127, 153, 243
Salt licks. *See* Licks
Sam (slave of William Twitty), 74
Sassanoon (Delaware chief) (alt.: Sassoonan), 4
Saucy Jack (Catawba), 10–11, 309n18
Sauks, 242
Scholl, Joseph, 204, 247

Scholl, Levina Boone (daughter), 247

Scioto River, 66, 136, 143–44, 147, 297n1, 323n27

Seminoles, 42

Seven Years' War, xvii, xviii, 12, 41, 156, 298n11, 323n32, 350. *See also* French and Indian War

Shane, John Dabney, 317n49, 344

Shawnees: adoption ceremony, 132–35; attack on Morgan's Station, xxi, 102, 308n40; attacks on Boonesborough, 118–20, 145–61; attacks on Harrodsburg, 61, 98, 118; attacks on whites in French and Indian War, 16–17, 24–25; at Battle of Point Pleasant, 66; capture of Boone, 127–29; capture of Jemima Boone and Callaway girls, 106–11; clans, 122, 132, 311n26; defeat by Iroquois, 45; dislike of Virginians, 116; ear-slitting, 131–32; ethics, 138–39; friends of Boone, 137–38, 195–96; gauntlet, 131; kill Ned Boone, 172; kill two whites near Harrodsburg, 61; move north after Clark's 1782 expedition, 183; move to Missouri, 163, 244–45, 278, 352; prisoner exchanges with whites, 196–98; raid settlers near Castle's Wood, 62; removal from Ohio, 244, 277; and siege of Boonesborough, 148–59; as spearhead of Indian resistance to white expansion into Ohio Valley, 46; torture and killing of captives, 132–33, 313n10; and Treaty of Camp Charlotte, 66–67; and Treaty of Fort Finney, 190; and Treaty of Greenville, 103, 353; at Wallen's Creek attack, 56; white expeditions against, 66, 182–83, 196. *See also* Boone, Daniel: adoption by Shawnees; Boone, Daniel—relations with Indians; Indian-white relations; Lord Dunmore's War; Treaties: Treaty of Camp Charlotte, Treaty of Greenville; *and names of individual Shawnees*

Shelby, Isaac, 204, 224, 232, 330n30

Sheltowee (Big Turtle; Boone's Shawnee adoptive name), 134–5, 149

Shingas (Delaware chief), 16–17, 219n28

Six Nations. *See* Iroquois

Slaughter (gambler who traveled with Boone to Florida), 42

Slaughter, Thomas, 79

Slaves and slavery: division of Methodist church over, 271; forbidden in Northwest Territory, 282; in Kentucky, 117, 271, 279, 282; in Missouri, 258, 282–83; slaves killed by Indians, 57, 74, 118, 157; slaves as percentage of population, 117, 279, 283, 330n1; slaves owned by Boone and his family, 213, 221, 229, 240, 248, 259, 272, 282, 328n54. *See also* Boone, Daniel: slaves owned or sold; *and names of slaves*

Slotkin, Richard, 329n8, 338n2, 339n17, 356

Slover, John, 193

Smith, Daniel, 64–65

Smith, William Bailey, 145, 150–52

Soelle, George, 26–27

Spanish: concern over threat posed by Americans, 227; concern over threat posed by British, 226–27; control navigation on the Mississippi, 233–34; encourage American settlement in Louisiana, xxi, 227–28, 230, 235; encourage settlement by eastern Indians, 227, 244, 306n12; land grants in Missouri, xxi, 227–28, 232, 244, 246; objectives in Louisiana, 226–27; and "Spanish conspiracy," 233, 281, 332n28. *See also* American national identity, during Boone's life; Louisiana; Mississippi River; Missouri; Wilkinson, James

St. Asaph's. *See* Logan's Station

St. Charles, Mo., 230, 236, 238–39, 243, 245, 331n13, 333n2, 335, 355

St. Clair, Arthur, xxi, 102, 194, 198, 200, 220,

St. Louis, Mo.: appearance, 229, 355; Boone's entrance into, 229–30; Boone's sale of furs at, 246, 248; Clark's arrival in, 192; founding, 229; and fur trade, 229; as Spanish headquarters, 229–30, 236. *See also* Stoddard, Amos

Stewart, John, 42, 43, 46–50, 298n14

Stoddard, Amos, 235–36

Stoner, Michael (George Michael Holsteiner): goes with Boone to Kentucky to warn Fincastle surveyors, xix, 61–63; as long hunter, 28; nearly gored by a buffalo, 62; visits Boone in Missouri, 247–48; with Boone's group on first attempt to settle Kentucky, 55; wounded at Boonesborough, 119

Sugaring, 252

Surveying: importance of, 202–08; Indians' feelings against surveyors, 59, 62, 187; in Ohio Valley after Treaty of Fort Stanwix, 54; profitability of, 203; techniques, 204–06. *See also* Boone, Daniel: as surveyor; Fincastle County, Va.; Floyd, John: as surveyor; Preston, William: as surveyor

Swift, Jonathan. See *Gulliver's Travels*

Swigert, Jacob, 269–70

Sycamore Shoals, treaty of. *See* Treaties: Treaty of Sycamore Shoals

Tahgajute. *See* Logan (Mingo chief)

Tanacharison (Iroquois chief), 15, 291n15

Tanner, John, 193

Tarleton, Banastre, 173, 200

Taylor, Richard, 355

Tecumseh (Shawnee chief), 132, 191

Tenskwatawa. *See* Prophet, the (Shawnee chief)

Thwaites, Reuben Gold, 268, 287–88, 310, 333, 340n25, 344, 346, 348

Todd, David, 254, 275

Todd, John, 117, 176–79, 182

Todd, Levi, 216, 321n37

Topographical Description of the Western Territory of North America, A (Imlay). *See* Imlay, Gilbert

Tories, 83, 92, 99, 101, 142, 147, 160, 162, 171, 173,

Trabue, Daniel: blockhouse description, 145; and buffalo killing, 33; and conditions at Boonesborough, 140; and court-martial of Boone, 160; and Hard Winter, 166; journal, 288, 345; siege of Boonesborough, 155

Transylvania, 72. *See also* Transylvania Company

Transylvania Company: compact of, 81–82; convention at Boonesborough, 78–83; land awards from Virginia and Tennessee to, 89–90; land claims attacked and rejected, 70–71, 86–89, 115; legislation, 80–81; livery of seisin to, 81–82; memorial to Continental Congress, 86–87; organization of, 69; promises acreage to Boone, 87, 90; promotes land sales, 69–70, 84–85; purchases land rights from Cherokees, xix, 69–72. *See also* Henderson, Richard; Treaties: Treaty of Sycamore Shoals

Treasury warrants, 93, 162

Treaties: Treaty of Camp Charlotte, xix, 66–67, 94; Treaty of Easton, xviii, 25, 41, 294n21; Treaty of Fort Finney, 190; Treaty of Fort Stanwix, xviii, 44–46, 54, 67–68, 88, 298n28, 353; Treaty of Greenville, xxi, 103, 193, 353; Treaty of Logstown, xvii, 16, 292n24; Treaty of Paris (1763), xvii, 41, 226, 298n9, 350; Treaty of Paris (1783), 213; Treaty of San Ildefonso, xxi, 246; Treaty of San Lorenzo, 233; Treaty of Sycamore Shoals, xix, 69, 71–73, 224

Trigg, Stephen, 176, 178–79, 182, 188

Trudeau, Zenon, xxi, 227–28, 230, 246

Turner, Frederick Jackson, 276–77

Twitty, William, xix, 73–74, 97

Twitty's Fort, 74

Upper Louisiana. *See* Louisiana; Missouri

Uskwaliguta. *See* Hanging Maw

Van Bibber, Isaac, 229

Van Bibber, John, 214

Van Bibber, Matthias (Tice), 243

Van Bibber, Olive. *See* Boone, Olive Van Bibber

Van Bibber family, 215, 221, 330n22

Vandalia, 54, 68. *See also* Ohio Company

Vincennes, xx, 114, 145–46, 163, 170, 351

Virginia (government/state): charter of, 12, 68; creates Fincastle County, xviii, 59; creates Kentucky County, 89, 93, 115–16; and evacuation of western settlements in French and Indian War, 24; land claims, 13, 16, 46, 67, 93, 202; tensions with Pennsylvania, 12, 92, 100, 281; Virginia Convention, 83–84, 87–88, 115. *See also* Dunmore, Lord John; Fincastle County, Va.; Land laws of Virginia; Patton, James; Transylvania Company; *and names of Virginians and locations in Virginia*

Wabash (Indian tribe), xxi, 102

Walker, Dr. Thomas, xvii, 39–40, 347

Walker, Felix, 73–77, 81, 83, 148, 347

"Walking Purchase," 5

Wallen's Creek, 56–59, 74

War of 1812, 193, 248–49, 260, 281, 352

Warrior's Path, 46–47, 49, 109, 118, 147

Washington, George: and Braddock's Defeat, 14–15, 17, 19; and Fort Necessity, xvii, 15; at French forts in Ohio Valley, 14–15; on Indian onslaught in 1756, 25; Kentucky towns named after, 91; and land claims in the west, 13, 60, 70, 92–93, 100, 201, 300n19; on land investment policy, 202; and Proclamation of 1763, 60; as surveyor, 202–03; wife's land ownership, 202

Washington, Ky., 278

Watauga, xix, 54, 58, 69, 72, 81, 107. *See also* Treaties: Treaty of Sycamore Shoals

Wayne, Gen. Anthony, xxi, 102–03, 132, 193–94, 198, 308n37

Weiser, Conrad, 291n15, 307n19, 324n52, 350–51

Wells, William, 193

Whigs, 92, 99, 101

White, Richard, 306n6, 349–51

Whitehouse, Richard, 236–37

Wilderness Road: blazing of, 72–73, 274; Boone seeks appointment to rebuild, 224–25; condition of, 172–73, 225; history, 348; rebuilding, 224–25; route for immigrants to Kentucky, 172, 220, 225. *See also* Boone's Trace

Wilkinson, James: appoints Boone captain in St. Charles militia, 239; is assigned large land tract belonging to Boone, 209; and Frankfort, 341n16; and Gilbert Imlay, 209; governor of Louisiana Territory, 239; obtains navigation rights on Mississippi, 233; Spanish secret agent while U.S. army officer, 233, 355; tells Spain to expel Boone's settlers from Missouri, 236

Williams, John, 87, 89–90, 304n36

Williamsburg, Va., 85, 116, 131, 148, 168, 170, 206, 319n97

Wimar, Carl, 111

Wolf, David, 272–73

Wollstonecraft, Mary, 264, 327n35, 339nn9–10

Wolves, 34, 56–58, 76, 247, 293n40

Wyandots: accompany Caldwell in attack on Kentucky, 175; ask Delawares to join against Americans, 123; Hendricks captured by, 194; and Henry Hamilton, 117; kill James Estill, 175; kill white captives who attempt escape, 315n48; at siege of Boonesborough, 148; at Logstown treaty, xvii, 16

Xenia, Ohio, 132

Yadkin (river and valley): Boone family members come (or come back) to, xvii, 8, 10–11, 21, 40, 43, 53, 55, 142, 162; Findley at, 44; game, 35, 40, 44; Indian raids in region, 24; and Kentucky, xviii, 46, 54, 86, 120, 162–63; land prices, 8; settlement of, 8, 10, 21, 40; weddings, 21–22

Yellow Creek, 58–59, 61, 63, 188–89. *See also* Greathouse, Jacob; Logan (Mingo chief); Mingos

Yellowstone, 1, 270, 335n42

Zeisberger, David, 37, 122–23